Never Invisible

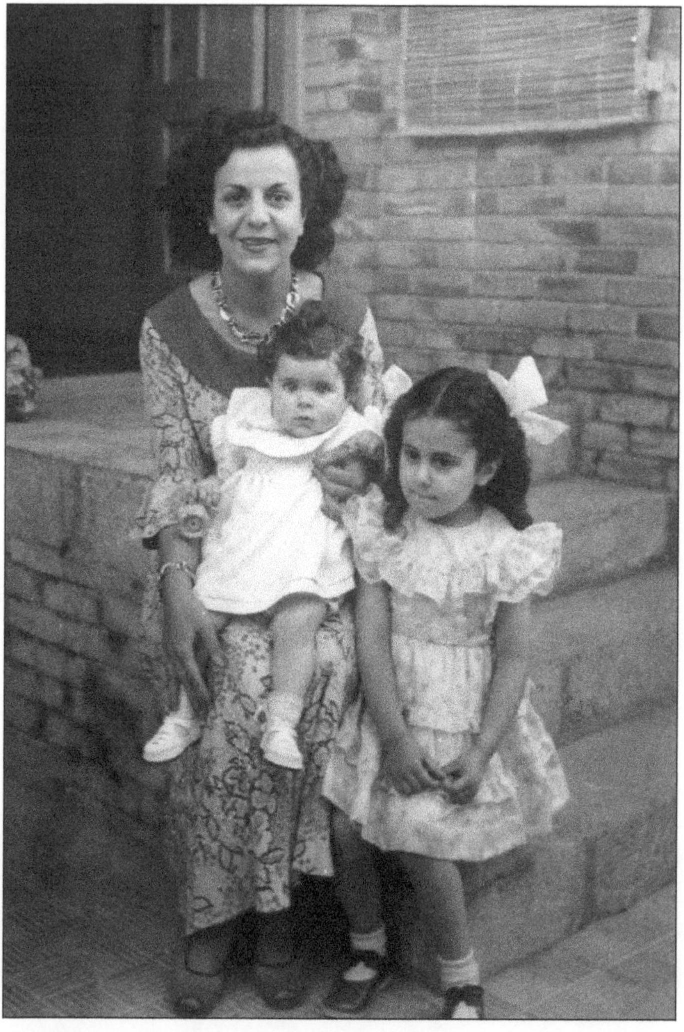

Houri in 1949 with her daughters Ladan, aged one and Mariam, aged five.

Never Invisible

An Iranian Woman's Life Across the Twentieth Century

Houri Mostofi Moghadam

MAGE PUBLISHERS

This book is part of a series of Iranian Studies publications made possible by the Hamid and Christina Moghadam Program in Iranian Studies at Stanford University.

Mage Publishers Inc.

www.mage.com

Library of Congress Cataloging-in-Publication Data

Available at the Library of Congress

ISBN: 978-1-949445-45-9 (hardcover); 978-1-949445-46-6 (ePDF)

Visit Mage online: www.mage.com

eMail: as@mage.com

یوسف گمگشته باز آید به کنعان غم مخور
کلبهٔ احزان شود روزی گلستان غم مخور

Lost Joseph will return to Canaan's land again–
do not despair

His grieving father's house will fill with flowers again–
do not despair

–Hafez/Davis

Contents

FOREWORD

Houri's Singular Journey

By

Abbas Milani

The arc of justice in Iranian women's relentless struggle for equality, always heroic in spirit, sometimes seemingly hopeless in trajectory, is today universally recognized in the name of Mahsa Amini, an Iranian Kurdish woman who, accused of wearing the hijab in an improper manner, died in suspicious circumstances in September 2022 after being taken into police custody in Tehran. The progressive nature of the movement is captured in the three words that have become its clarion call: "Woman, Life, Freedom." Like all apparent political "eruptions," this movement too has its roots in a struggle that has gone on for at least 150 years, and Houri Moghadam's memoir offers a reminder of the depth and endurance of this movement.

The Ardalans, on Houri's mother's side, were a prominent family from Kurdistan—the province whence Mahsa Amini hailed from. They held key positions of power not just in that province but in the central government of Iran. On her father's side, the Mostofis were an equally prominent family of trusted bureaucrats and diplomats, acclaimed writers and accomplished technocrats. Houri's father was both a respected government official and the acclaimed author of an important multi-volume memoir[1] that richly chronicles the history of Iran for much of the late-nineteenth and early-twentieth centuries. Houri's marriage to Mohsen Moghadam connected her to a family of innovating entrepreneurs whose commercial acumen and financial expertise—her brother-in-law, Reza Moghadam was the first Iranian to receive a PhD in economics from Stanford—made them pioneers of Iran's economic miracle in the 1960s and 1970s. If Houri's bitter estrangement from Mohsen Moghadam casts a long shadow over the latter part of her narrative, her account of her three children's accomplishments and challenges in exile makes the text also indispensable for its insight into the revolution of 1979, and the fate of Iranians of the ensuing diaspora. She enjoyed a particularly close relationship with her eldest daughter, Mariam. In many of our conversations she praised her daughter's brilliant mind and exemplary self-discipline, along with her humanity and humility. *Never Invisible* represents not only a labor of a daughter's love for her mother but also a confirmation of a mother's profound admiration for her daughter.

---

1. *Abdollah Mostofi,* Sharh-e zendegani-e man: tarikh-e ejtema'i va edari-e dowreh-ye Qajariyeh, *3 vols., Tehran, 1942, tr. Nayer Mostofi Glenn as* The Administrative and Social History of the Qajar Period, *3 vols., Costa Mesa, California, 1997.*

As Mariam was diagnosed with cancer, she fought against time, and hoped against hope that she would see this volume to print. Fortunately, she did see and proofread the entire manuscript before her death on 16 November 2022.

In a sense, Houri's memoir is like a *Bildungsroman*, covering the lives of three generations of Iranian women, from her mother, who emerges as the powerful but enlightened matriarch of the family, to Houri's aunts and sisters and her two daughters. The point of view of the narrator is that of a patriot, proud of her Persian heritage, a woman of unusual erudition and cosmopolitan sensibilities, unabashed about describing her own life of luxury and affluence and her pride in the many high-ranking members of her aristocratic family and no less candid, on the other hand, about her resentment, her righteous fury at those who facilitated the 1979 revolution. She blithely reminds us at one point that her mother and her aunts always called each other by their royal titles. Yet, while clearly enamored of these titles and the social hierarchy they represented, she was, even as a child, defiant of their incumbent rituals if they diminished her own sense of independence and dignity. She writes of how tears welled up in her eyes when, as one ritual demanded, she was expected to kiss her grandfather's princely hand, recoiling from that "wrinkled hand with its gnarled veins" despite the inducement of receiving a gold sovereign in return (p. 35). Reading the early parts of her memoir, and her descriptions of grand houses filled with antiques, of sumptuous meals in fancy hotels, of sun-soaked beaches on the Italian Riviera, one is reminded of the films of Luchino Visconti,[2] and his ardor for a dying European aristocracy, full of opulent beauty and faded grandeur. At the same time, her account of her battles with the mullahs of the revolutionary courts and their minions is at once Kafkaesque and comical, and her behavior consistently defiant. In short, she is "never invisible," leaving her mark in a classroom, a courtroom, a philanthropic organization—and, with her journals, on history.

Houri's attitude toward the *ancient régime* is similarly paradoxical. Though she and prominent members of her extended family worked with the Pahlavi regime, neither she, nor her father and brothers, uncles and husband were ever sycophantic supporters of the Shah, or his father. As *Never Invisible* clearly shows, she defended the regime when she thought it was right, and criticized, even defied it, when she thought it deserved it. She was, in short, sui generis.

I first met Houri Moghadam about twenty years ago. I had just arrived at Stanford, where her son, Hamid, and his wife Christina, had endowed the new Iranian Studies Program I still direct. She attended our events regularly, even regally. She was, as the memoir shows, always meticulous about her appearance, never shying away from wearing a mink stole if she wanted to. Sometimes, after these events, she would pass on her comments—whether

---

2. *An Italian filmmaker, stage director, and screenwriter, Luchino Visconti di Modrone, Count of Lonate Pozzolo (1906–76), was a major figure of Italian art and culture in the mid twentieth century. Regarded as one of the fathers of cinematic neorealism, Visconti later moved on to luxurious, sweeping epics dealing with themes of beauty, decadence, death, and European history, especially the decay of the nobility and the bourgeoisie.*

acerbic or complimentary, but always forthright—in the form of notes. Once, she wrote that watching a play written and directed by my colleague at Stanford, Bahram Beyzaei,[3] was like being present at a performance of a work by Ferdowsi. When the play ended, she led with her loud and repeated bravos. The views she expressed in those notes were usually well informed but she was also convinced of their righteous veracity—a quality also evident in many of the strongly held opinions she expresses in *Never Invisible.*

On one occasion, in one such note, she invited me to her apartment in San Francisco—"I will make you some *osh-e reshteh* (noodle soup) and we can discuss this matter in detail." Like every other conversation I had with her, she was keen on talking about culture and literature, and her family history, and offer advice on who to invite to the university as a speaker. All her life, she was as proud of her erudition and academic achievements as her culinary prowess not just in cooking but in training cooks—men and women—who then joined her extended household staff. Even in her account of their lives, we are given fascinating glimpses into a changing world. One member of staff, taught by Houri, goes on to become a government employee, another buys a taxi. Traditional housework, as practiced in traditional households, was giving place to the commodification of labor and the ethos of capitalism.

---

3. An Iranian playwright, theatre director, and filmmaker, Bahram Beyzaei (b. 1938) is often considered the greatest playwright of the Persian language, and "the Shakespeare of Persia." He was also a pioneer of the Iranian New Wave cinema, his Bashu, the Little Stranger *(1986) being regarded as one of the best Iranian films of all time.*

When I visited Houri, she was living in a two-bedroom, ninth floor apartment, in a fashionable neighborhood of the city, with a stunning view of the Golden Gate Bridge and the infamous Alcatraz. The rooms were handsomely decorated, full of antiques, some royal, all regal, and in the words of Shakespeare—a playwright she admired—"not expressed in fancy, rich, not gaudy." She, like her mother on whose modes and manners she clearly fashioned her own behavior, believed that the presentation of a room, or a house, "proclaims" the person and their social standing.[4] She was as punctilious about furnishings as about how she dressed, wearing what she thought befitted the occasion and someone of her stature.

As she showed me around the apartment, I noticed a notebook on her writing desk and when I inquired about it, she said it was her journal. On another visit, when I felt her rules of decorum about familiarity would allow it, I asked how long she had been keeping a journal—thinking maybe it was a pastime of forlorn days spent in exile. She told me she had been writing for decades, and even offered to read me some of her diaries. As she writes in her memoir, "Writing comes easily to me, but getting something published was never my interest." (p. 86). No sooner had I listened to her reading the few passages she had selected at random than I knew here was a rare treasure—the day-to-day life of a woman whose accomplishments

4. *See Shakespeare,* Hamlet, *Act 1, Scene 3.*

and attachments, her loves and losses, her daily habits as a pedagogue and philanthropist, her assertive feminism and her dedicated traditionalism, her secular demeanor and her firm faith in Islam, made her at once unique and emblematic of the struggle of Iranian women for equality, for a voice and presence that put them on a par, no more, no less, with men.

She was a member of the first class of Iranian women allowed to enter Tehran University, where, in her French lessons, she studied Molière and Beaumarchais, acquiring such proficiency in the language that a couple of years later she was busying herself at home "with a translation of Balzac's *Eugenie Grandet*" (p. 86). She taught at high school and university much of her adult life. Like many women today, she wanted to pursue a professional career while attending to her children, husband, and extended family. In 1960, she left Iran for six months as a Fulbright scholar to learn how to master the art and science of teaching. Everywhere she went—and all her life she was an inveterate traveler—she was keen to learn about the local customs, arts and culinary delights. From Kobe beef ("tender and delicious and, unsurprisingly, very expensive," p. 240) and kabuki theater (which she "didn't really understand or enjoy," p. 240) in Japan, to a ballet, or opera, a Shakespeare play or a high-class restaurant—all were of equal interest to her. At the same time, she eagerly describes her passion for shopping. In exile, she completed a doctoral degree at the Sorbonne and, instead of writing her dissertation about Iran, she took the road less traveled and wrote about a French writer, André Maurois, who reminded her of her father and whom she had met during her time as a Fulbright scholar in the U.S.

In contrast to this nonconformist life, Houri had an almost obsessive affinity for the rituals of marriage, the minutiae of which she sets out time and again in her account of various family weddings, and what she thought its vows entailed. She writes that she "was an idealist and sought perfection in a future partner" (p. 73). Of all the childish games she and her siblings and cousins played, she describes in some detail the game of marriage (p. 13). Idealized expectations of a traditional institution like marriage coupled with a determined desire to live an iconoclastic life are almost inevitably a recipe for disappointment. Houri was unhappy that, while away in the States on her Fulbright program, most of the letters she received from her husband "were critical and full of complaints about my absence" (p. 217). She was, she says, keen on giving her "husband an opportunity to realize that women are not like furniture in a house" (p. 218). She writes that even "though my husband never voiced his disagreement, in practice he was unwilling to share or go along with my interests" (p. 196). And when, as a result of the gradual grind of the tensions begot by these real or perceived differences, her marriage with Mohsen failed, her sense of injury is palpable, a thread of enduring anger that runs through her emotional odyssey as she relates it. Only future scholars can compare and contrast the narrative of *Never Invisible* with the raw descriptions found in her daily journals and decide whether and to what extent the bitter taste of separation from her husband and the agonies of exile have shaped or tainted her recollections of the past.

Exiles, they say, are custodians of dead treasures. Beneath the surface in Houri's account of her busy life, distilled from more than twenty volumes of journals, there pulsates the agonies of exile, of nostalgia for the days she "would be invited to three dinners" (p. 441) and had classes to teach and philanthropic activities to lead and organize. What resonates even more clearly in virtually every page is the unusual life of a singular woman whose personal struggles and significant achievements can be seen as part of a wider movement that is carrying Iranian society to a place where, at the time of writing, "Women, Life, Freedom" has become the *cri de coeur* of people marching to end misogyny and patriarchy and where women are free to lead the lives they wish.

In the Name of God

Day of Departure

24 November 1978
(3 Azar 1357)

Dawn on Friday morning. My daughter Mariam comes to take me to the airport in her small white car. Balancing a tray in one hand, Hajieh Khanum holds the Qur'an over my head with the other. As I step over the threshold, she empties onto the front doorstep behind me the contents of a turquoise bowl of water with a single floating green leaf. Ghasem is there too; he has made it in time from his far-away home in Gheytarieh in spite of the early hour. Witnessing all this with great interest is our new houseboy, Mohammad Ali, recently arrived from Bangladesh. My regulation 20-kilogram suitcase and large hold-all containing the overflow fit snuggly in the trunk of the car.

Turning to say goodbye to Ghasem, the most senior member of the household staff, I say, "Ghasem, our time is over. Now it could be your turn to help us out one day." Deep inside, I feel that a page has been turned. Even so, I could never have believed this would be my last time in the house we built on the land that I had bought so many years ago. My beautiful and elegant home that I was now leaving behind—forever.

I am leaving my house in Shemiran and going away for a month; my suitcase contains two dresses, two evening outfits, two pairs of trousers, two skirts, two jackets, two pairs of boots, and two sets of handbags and shoes—one black and one brown. Like Noah, I am taking two of everything with me. I am going away for one month for a medical check-up in the USA. I have bought $20,000 from Bank Melli at the official rate of exchange—$3,000 in cash on me and the balance to be sent to my sister in Houston. The currency officer in the bank assures me the money will be sent immediately. He recognizes my name; his wife had once been a student of mine. Sadly, I do not recollect the name of this honest man. It would be fourteen years before I return to my home country.

The French have a saying, "*Partir, c'est mourir un peu.*"[1] In Iran, we, like the English, put it differently: "Out of sight, out of mind." This is the story of one Iranian who left home for a short trip and stayed away for many, long years. Each one of us has an amazing tale to tell and this

---

1. This is a line from a poem, 'Rondel de l'adieu', by the French poet and novelist Edmond Haraucourt (1856–1941).

is mine. Hazrat-e Ali, Blessings be on His Name,[2] said the greatest act of courage is patience. I ask you, dear reader, for patience as I unfold my tale.

2. *Hazrat-e Ali (Ali ibn Abi Talib) was a cousin, son-in-law, and companion of the Prophet Mohammad. Much revered by Shia Muslims, his failing to succeed the Prophet caused the major rift between Shia and Sunni groups. According to some scholars, Ali did not want to involve himself in the game of political deception which deprived him of success in life, but, in the eyes of his admirers, he became an example of the piety of the primary un-corrupted Islam, as well as the chivalry of pre-Islamic Arabia.*

Part One

Childhood and The Family

(1919–1942 / 1298–1321)

My Entry to the World

Let us now turn the clock back to 18 August 1919.

Imagine Shemiran, just north of Tehran, in those days with its tree-lined streets, gardens, and green pools where tadpoles swam. The summer heat has peaked during August (Mordad) and is coming to an end. In the garden of Majd-ed-doleh in Dezashib, a baby girl is born. They name her Hourvash, after the family's second child, and first daughter, who died. Hourvash or Houri, as she is always called, is the fourth child; her older sister Mehrvash, or Mehri, who is only two years and four months old, is playing with the goldfish in a small tiled, indoor pool. The whole household is occupied with the mother and the newborn. The little girl falls into the small, shallow pool. The nurse arrives just in time and pulls her out of the water. What follows are the stories I heard about family life at the time and which I'll now share with you.

Shajan and Aghajan[1]

As well as my sister Mehri, I had two older brothers, Nasrollah and Bagher. My mother, whom we always called Shajan, had decided not to get a *dayeh* or wet-nurse for me. She was planning to breastfeed me herself. Apparently having three wet-nurses in the household and witnessing their conflicted emotions when each child was weaned seemed more trouble to Shajan than nursing me herself. The wet-nurses were chosen from respectable families known to ours, and had either lost their husbands or children. I recall that the husbands of my two brothers' wet-nurses worked in our house as *lallehs*[2] and had their own duties. So, I had neither wet-nurse nor *lalleh* and grew very attached to my mother.

Had Shajan, whose real name was Mariam Ardalan, been a man she would have become a prominent statesman. My cousin Abol used to say that she would have far surpassed her own brothers. She was intelligent, capable, and forward-thinking. At the same time, she was a devout Muslim and, encouraged by my father, she took charge of our upbringing.

---

1. Jan *in Persian means "life," but it is also used as a suffix to mean "dearest." Shajan is a shortened form of "dearest princess"* (shahzadeh jan). Agha *is used in Persian to mean "sir" or "mister." Both expressions were used in Iran as a loving way to call one's mother and father while honoring them.*

2. *A* lalleh *is a male dry-nurse, guardian, or tutor employed in the household of an elite family.*

My father, Abdollah Mostofi, who worked in the Iranian government as a high-ranking official, was a learned man, hard-working, honest, and God-fearing. He knew the Qur'an almost entirely by heart, but was also well educated in contemporary matters. He had been tutored in Persian and Arabic at home, in addition to studying grammar, logic, poetry and prose, and all subjects that were then deemed necessary for a proper education.

Later, when the Institute for Political Science was established by Hassan Pirnia, known as Moshir al-Dowleh,[3] my father enrolled there and mastered the French language perfectly. Years later, he translated into Persian a book on the French Revolution by François Mignet. The manuscript was kept by my brother Bagher and I sincerely hope that it at least escaped the wrath of the revolutionaries. More about my parents in due course.

Childhood Mishaps

I was barely a year old and could just stand. I took a sweet from the little box on my father's breakfast tray and put it in my mouth. I had swallowed several more of these 'sweets' without tasting the bitterness of the quinine before they found me unconscious under the table. Childhood curiosity coupled with my ability to open my father's pill box had

3. *Hassan Pirnia (1871–1935) was a prominent politician of twentieth-century Iran, serving four times as prime minister. He was also a historian, co-founding the Society for the National Heritage of Iran.*

Shajan photographed in mirrors, c. 1934

landed me in big trouble. Shajan was speechless. However, this piece of mischief served me well. Until the age of twenty-four I was spared the fever and shivers of malaria.

I was four years old when Shajan enrolled me in the Franco-Persian kindergarten. There, I learned the French alphabet and art, and how to draw and paint all this working with my left hand, which was frowned upon. Once the principal caught me using the offending limb and I was punished with a needle in that hand. The next day my mother went to school and confronted the principal. She said that there was no difference between the two hands and a child's nature should always be respected. But I never again used my left hand for writing, although to this day I use it for cutting and sewing, and for playing tennis and ping-pong. My right hand is the lady of leisure and the left hand does all the work. My granddaughter Sanam is also left-handed.

Life in My Father's Family Home

I have wonderful childhood memories of my father's family home in Mirza Mahmoud Vazir Alley, named for my uncle, who had died some years before, off Chahar Bagh Street. It was a paradise for children. My father, and our eldest uncle, Fatollah Mostofi, each lived with their families in their own quarters or *andarouni*,[4] comprising an internal courtyard and

4. *The* andarouni *is the private quarters of the house where women are free to walk around in without adhering to a dress code.*

the family accommodation. Connecting these two dwellings was a large garden that housed their joint *birouni*,[5] where the men received visitors and entertained.

All the cousins would usually congregate in this *birouni* without actually being permitted inside the house. Our leader was my cousin Ahmad Mostofi and his right-hand man my brother Nasrollah. The group included our other two cousins, Ali and Ghasem, my brother Bagher, the girls Derakhshandeh and Fakhretaj, my sister Mehri, and finally the youngest members—my cousin Mohsen and myself, who didn't really count!

One day we played a game called *arousi* (wedding). Ghasem, fair with blue eyes, and I darker with black hair were the bride and groom. The other kids scraped some plaster from the wall and used it as face powder on me; they used geranium petals as rouge. Then they sat the two of us on low stools and celebrated the marriage! Earlier that day, we had made some *albalu polow* (sour cherry rice) for the wedding feast under the direction of Ahmad using ingredients the older girls had cleverly borrowed from the two *andarounis*. The whole proceedings were over before lunchtime; they cleaned me up and sent me home. Shajan, who was very observant and impossible to deceive, saw the evidence on my cheeks and soon put an end to that game.

---

5. *The* birouni *represents the public quarters, used by the men, where business and ceremonies are conducted.*

Childhood Mischief

One day Ghasem decided to take a pair of scissors to my brother Bagher's curly hair. The two families were preparing to go on an outing that afternoon and it was impossible to hide the handiwork of the rookie barber. After that, I didn't forgive Ghasem for many years and kept avoiding him—which is not to say that I was an angel myself!

Another day, I spotted my cousin sitting by the large, round pool in her family's *andarouni* watching the goldfish. I pushed her into the pool and ran for my life into our own *andarouni*. The gate was open and the gardener was watering the plants. I believe it was only his presence, knowing that he would be on hand to intervene if needed, that gave me the audacity to do such a thing. Shajan immediately noticed my pallor and interrogated me. With tears streaming down my face, I confessed to the crime. They fished my cousin safely out of the pool. My brother's hair grew back and once again peace was restored.

More Childhood Misdemeanors

It was mid February. Shajan and her team were busy baking pastries and cookies (*shirini*) for Nowruz, the Persian New

Year.[6] The Mostofi family was renowned for its baking skills and that talent has luckily extended into the present generations. My mother, who was herself quite an expert, would admit that her in-laws were in a different league when it came to baking. The kitchen was situated on the floor below the living room and that is where everyone was busy working that day—all except me and my older sister Mehri, who had found a small rag and some matches under the honeysuckle bush on the veranda. Wanting to test her match-striking skills, she struck a match and lit the rag—leaving it under the dry bush. When the fire took and began to crackle, she became scared and ran away.

Far away from the activities of the household in our spacious playroom, I was busy eating the nuts and raisins that had been laid out for *Chaharshanbeh Souri.*[7] I cannot recall whether I had asked for permission to go in there or not but I was thoroughly enjoying this illicit feast of the gods and totally absorbed in what I was doing. I had no idea what was happening outside. The little fire had by now been put out with buckets of water but Shajan,

---

6. *The Persian New Year, or Nowruz (literally "New Day"), always falls on the first day of spring, the vernal equinox, 20, 21, or 22 March. However, the preparations for it begin at least a month earlier, with cleaning and redecorating the house, buying new clothes, germinating seeds, coloring eggs, and baking pastries.*

7. Shab-e Chaharshanbeh Souri *(the "Eve of Red Wednesday" or "Eve of Celebration") always falls on the evening of the last Wednesday of the old year. Bonfires are lit and people leap over them shouting,* "Sorkhi-e to az man, zardi-e man as to" *("Give me your beautiful red complexion and take back my sickly pallor"). With the help of fire and light, symbols of good, celebrants pass through this inauspicious night—the end of the old year. Seven different fruits and nuts are mixed together and served on this particular evening.*

who was worried by our absence, kept calling out to us. Of course, there was no reply from either of us two miscreants. She was about to become hysterical when we were discovered. My sister was reprimanded. In her defense, Mehri said that she had imagined it would be safer to leave the burning rag under the bush than throw it away. Childish reasoning!

I had my own fire-related episode. Our spacious playroom was empty except for a large carpet; it also had five French windows and two closets for our toys—one for the boys and one for us two girls. (Our youngest sister, Nayer, had not yet come into the world.) Each of us four kids 'owned' one of the French windows, each with a white-tiled window seat. We were free to do what we wanted within our own territory. I loved to light candles and watch the flickering flames. While I was never supervised, this was never usually a problem.

It was the month of Safar and an elaborate *rowzeh-khani*[8] was due to be held in the house of my maternal grandparents.

During the months of Moharram and Safar, and out of respect for the mourning period,[9] we girls used to dress in

---

8. Rowzeh-khani *(literally, "reading the rowzeh") is the Shia Iranian Muslim ritual of the Mourning of Moharram (see footnote 9). It is held every day of the year to commemorate the death of Hossein ibn Ali and his followers during the Battle of Karbala between the Umayyad Caliph Yazid and a small army led by Ali.*

9. *Moharram is the first month of the Islamic calendar (Safar is the second month). One of the four sacred months of the year when warfare is forbidden, it is held to be the second holiest month after Ramadan. The tenth day of Moharram is known as Ashura, on which Shi'i Muslims mourn the tragedy of Hossein ibn Ali's family, killed at the Battle of Karbala (see footnote 8), and Sunni Muslims practice fasting.*

navy or brown. Shajan had beautiful brown chiffon dresses made for us with four or five rows of ruffles all the way down, so we could attend the elegant mourning ceremonies. That afternoon I put on the dress for the first time to attend the *rowzeh-khani*. While waiting for everyone else to get ready to go to my grandparents' house I lit my candles in my window seat. As I turned my back to sit down, the top layer of ruffles must have brushed the flame.

At that moment, I heard my name being called. As I stood up, the flames enveloped the dress, causing me to scream at the top of my lungs. Shajan was the first to arrive on the scene and ripped the dress off me with her bare hands. Her fingers were all blistered and my beautiful brown chiffon dress was in shreds. I will never forget my mother's terrified face although she never rebuked me, being grateful that I had escaped injury. We arrived at the *rowzeh-khani* after some delay. Shazdeh Vali, my maternal grandmother, who had heard about the incident, gave me a reproving look as if to say, "You are the cause of the blisters on my daughter's hands." This is the only reproach I ever had from her; she adored her many grandchildren, and our greatest treat was to visit our grandparents' house.

At Nowruz, we used to receive presents that we had asked for as well as cash from our parents. One year, the boys asked for bicycles and Mehri and I each asked for a bouncing rubber ball. In those days they used to import balls in different colors and beautiful patterns. Mehri was given a white ball with a colored pattern and mine was red with a geometric design. We spent the holidays playing ball in the garden. I could count to a hundred while twirling around my bouncing ball. Our balls would then be safely stored in the playroom closets, although mine had a short life and was soon punctured. My sister continued to play ball with our older cousins while all I could do was look on in envy. At that young age, I remember thinking, "This is the way things will be so long as the white ball with the colorful pattern remains intact and since no one is buying me another ball." So, I took a chance when the playroom was deserted one day. I opened the closet and quickly punched a hole with a needle in my sister's ball.

The next day, a happy and expectant Mehri went to the closet to fetch her ball to play with the other kids. My eyes were glued to her face. I couldn't help a little smirk when she tried to bounce the ball without success, letting out a cry of disappointment. Fortunately, our misery didn't last long and two new balls were bought. To this day, I wonder if my ball had been the victim of a similar accident, or if it had just been defective from the outset.

An Important Life Lesson

We used to walk to school accompanied by a middle-aged manservant, the *lalleh* of one of my brother's. Male staff were employed in other functions too. Shajan had certain inflexible rules of etiquette, including that the door of the house had to be opened by a manservant. This went back to the days when a doorman would stand guard at the main door that opened on to the *hashti* or octagonal space in a traditional Iranian house. The rule continued to be followed by mother, although by then there was neither *hashti* nor doormen left. All the household shopping had to be done by a manservant; even delivering the hot lunches sent at midday to school was the responsibility of that person.

I was five years old when I started elementary school. Together with my older brothers and sister, I was given weekly pocket money and we would sometimes stop on the way back from school at the stationery shop to buy something, always accompanied by our faithful *lalleh*. One day I bought five postcards. On the way home, I noticed that the shopkeeper had given me six instead of five postcards. I knew that I should return the extra postcard or offer to pay for it, but ignored the guilty feeling and walked on.

Once home, I laid out my beautiful postcards on my own window seat, absorbed in admiring them. My brother Bagher, who was a year older than me, asked if he could have a look at the cards. I selfishly refused and quickly gathered them all up. His reaction was to grab them from me and rip them into little pieces, which he then threw to the ground. I was heartbroken and burst into tears; but my conscience was awakened. At that young age and on that fateful day, I understood that one wrong act can set in train a series of events that can destroy everything and I resolved never again to hold on to what wasn't rightfully mine. This was an important lesson for me.

A New Home

In his autobiography, my father, Abdollah Mostofi, relates how he came to lose the family home. Because of his strong opposition to the Anglo-Persian Agreement, negotiated by Vosouq al-Dowleh,[10] my father had no choice but to resign his prestigious position at the Ministry of Finance in order to be free to publish newspaper articles against the agreement. As a result of this, he was out of work for over two years. The income from the farmland that we owned was not sufficient to support our comfortable lifestyle, so the only solution was to sell the family home.

I remember our family moving to a large property at the end of Jaleh Street in Tehran. The neighboring garden with its imposing gate belonged to the Khaz'als;[11] years later this property became the Swiss embassy. One day out of childish ignorance, I took a cigarette from my father's cigarette box, lit it, and went out of our gate without permission to try and smoke it. As I hid behind one of the columns flanking the gate, I burst into such a coughing fit that I have never touched a cigarette since then. Since

---

10. One of the founding members of the Iranian parliament, or Majles, in 1906, Hasan Vosouq al-Dowleh played a leading role in negotiations that resulted in the 1919 Anglo-Persian Agreement, which led to allegations that he had been bribed by the British. Although Vosuq denied that he had enriched himself personally, and even offered to repay the money, his reputation was so damaged that he was forced to leave Iran.

11. In the early 1900s, Khaz'al Khan was the leader of an Arab tribe of the same name in the virtually autonomous Iranian province of Khuzestan. His power reached its zenith by 1919 after which Khaz'al's forces were defeated by Reza Shah in October 1924, and in early 1925 he was arrested and exiled to Tehran, where he died under house arrest.

A meeting at the Foreign Office in London in 1907/8. Standing on the left is Abdollah Mostofi. Moshir al-Dowleh (foreign minister of Iran at the time) is seated in the center and rear-admiral Slade (of British Naval Intelligence at the time) is seated on his left.

I wasn't able to mask the smell of the cigarette in spite of washing my mouth out with soap and water, my secret was discovered.

There was a large pool at the bottom of our garden and, because it was surrounded by trees, the water was always greenish and housed a large population of frogs who would make a huge racket as soon as it grew dark striking fear into our childish hearts. Our older brother Nasrollah was thirteen at the time and would always brag about his bravery, telling us he was not afraid to go to the end of the garden at night, pick a particular flower we had earmarked earlier and bring it to us. We looked up to him with admiration and, when he had duly carried out the dare, accepted him as a hero without question.

Idolizing Teachers and Fellow Students

Shajan was not someone who would send her children to just any school. After kindergarten and the first year at the Franco-Persian elementary school, my sister and I were entrusted to the care of the Varasteh sisters at their private school, Shams al-Madarres, in Tehran. There, we were taught French by the younger Varasteh sister, whom we called Younger Miss, while her elder sister was the principal. I finished the six years of primary school in four and obtained my primary-school diploma when I was barely ten years old. I had skipped the third and fifth grades to do this. My brother Bagher also managed to skip the same grades in his school. This practice used to be customary in those days but gradually lost its appeal.

Our teachers occupied an exalted position in our lives at that stage. One day during recess I fell down and cut my knee. There were two sisters in the upper school, Pourandokht and Tourandokht, who were my role models. Tall and slim with a gentle and kind manner, Tourandokht, the older girl, would sometimes act as a substitute teacher when our regular teacher was absent. I loved her and had great admiration for her. A few years older than me, Pourandokht, the younger sister, was my friend and protector.

That day when I grazed my knee, it was Tourandokht who took me to the teachers' room so they could attend to the wound. There I saw our regular teacher in the process of eating an apple. I was stunned beyond belief; was it possible that teachers also ate apples? I had placed teachers up there among angels and in my childish imagination I saw them as more than mere human beings.

On my return home, I related the story of my teacher eating an apple to my mother, who confirmed that of course teachers not only ate like the rest of us but they also slept, fell sick, and much more! I was really naïve.

Unfortunately, my friend Pourandokht, the younger of the two sisters at the school, died very young and I grieved deeply at her loss. Some years later, I came across *barouni-bazi*. High-school girls would become attracted to each other and everyone would know that so and so was the special friend of such and such a girl. As far as I can remember, I was never attracted to anyone in this way. By nature, I'm against idolizing anyone. I had many friends and acquaintances, but I don't believe anyone had an obsession about me, ever nor I about them.

My Father's Postings to the Provinces

My father had been posted to St. Petersburg as a diplomat before he was married. Other than that, his first postings outside Tehran once he was married were in the provinces of Fars and Sistan. We, the children of the family, had no choice but to continue our schooling wherever he went. First in Shiraz, then Isfahan, Kerman, and Tabriz. Shajan would never agree to our taking the sixth-, ninth-, or eleventh-grade exams in the provinces. She believed that since our father was a highly respected and prominent government official, our success would always be attributed to his position. So, my sixth- and eleventh-grade diplomas were issued in Tehran.

However, these frequent trips to and from Tehran interrupted our education. We had to attend the English schools in Isfahan and Shiraz, when our second language had always been French! We just had to work harder to keep up with all the changes. Luckily, Shams al-Madarres School always kept its doors open to us and understood our special circumstances.

I have a fond memory of the sixth-grade final exams. I had absolutely no problem with Persian, mathematics, science, history, or geography. But the sewing examina-

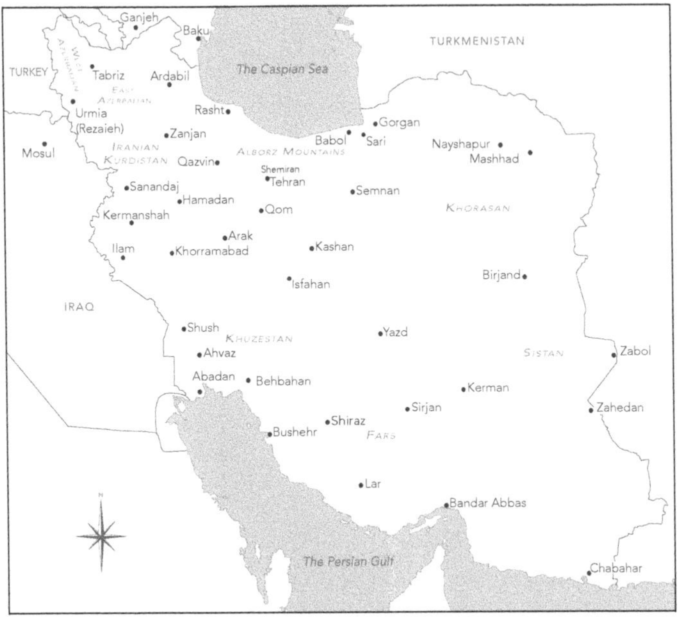

Map of Iran showing the locations to which Abdollah Mostofi was posted

tion, in which I had to cut out a dress and sew it during the exam, represented a real challenge and I scored only 10 out of 20. I remember how the much older girls who were taking the exam as external candidates were easily able to cut out the patterns and finish the dress during the allotted time while all I could do was to look on with envy. The score of 10 for sewing was the only low grade I received throughout my education, but the memory of this failure has stayed with me. My father used to give us cash as a reward for passing our exams. The going rate was 10 tomans (about $1.50) for passing the year, and 20 tomans for skipping a grade or for coming first in the class. And if we managed to come first and skip a grade, the reward was 30 tomans! The year I passed my elementary-school finals, my brother Bagher came first in seventh grade and my sister passed her year-end exams and, between the three of us, we were the lucky recipients of 50 tomans. After consulting Shajan, we decided to use the prize money to buy a gramophone and a few records. Listening to them became a favorite pastime.

Family Life in Kerman

Traveling from Tehran to Kerman involved traversing the Loot Desert and cars would often get stuck there. Once, we were impatiently expecting my eldest brother Nasrollah to arrive from Tehran, where he was studying. He was late and my mother, blessed with a sixth sense, became very agitated. My father tried to calm her down by reading from Hafez. This was the prophetic poem he read that day: "Lost Joseph will return to Canaan's land again—do not despair. / His grieving father's house will fill with flowers again—do not despair."[12]

Later that same evening, my brother finally turned up, accompanied by one of our relatives. Shajan's anxiety had not been without foundation for their car had actually broken down in the desert. Had it not been for another

---

12. Faces of Love: Hafez and the Poets of Shiraz, *translated by Dick Davis, bilingual edition, (Washington DC: Mage Publishers, 2019), pp. 57–9.*

car passing by and rescuing them, they might not have survived the night.

I learned to play bridge at the age of eleven in Kerman. My father was not interested in any form of gambling and never touched alcohol. The only alcohol to be found in our house was a small bottle used for medicinal purposes when an injection had to be given. He had worked as a diplomat for many years in Imperial Russia and had learned bridge there. In the evenings we would gather around the *korsi*[13] and my father would teach us this wonderful card game. Bridge in those days was very different from today—much less competitive and no money changed hands. Today it has become a science and players use intricate codes and signals in their bidding; maybe they will soon offer a university degree in the subject!

Another pastime was *mosha'ereh*, a game in which you had to recite a line of poetry starting with the letter at the end of the line recited by the person before you. My brothers used to beat me and my sister with the letter "L." While my sister and I stuck rigorously to the rules of the game and did our best to keep up, the boys were less scrupulous and would occasionally make up poems and persuade us that they were legitimate. Then my father would step in and act as referee so they couldn't cheat.

---

13. *Similar to the Japanese* kotatsu *or Spanish* brasero, *a* korsi *is a low table covered with a heavy blanket or quilted comforter and with a heat source under it. Charcoal is traditionally used as the heat source, though nowadays the table may also be electrically heated. During the winter months, families gather around the* korsi *to chat and get warm, and to celebrate special occasions.*

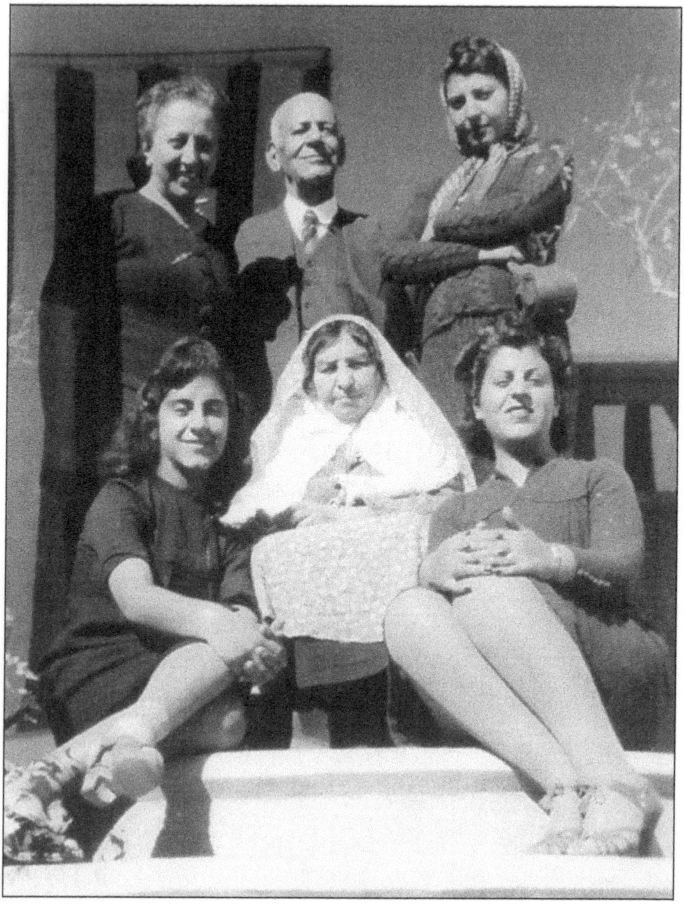

Standing from left: Shajan, Aghajan, and Houri's aunt Valieh Azam. Seated: Houri's sisters Nayer and Mehri to the left and right of their grandmother Shazdeh Valieh

When I compare the games we played as children with the sophisticated, hi-tech toys of today, I ask myself which is better for children. Today, my four-year-old grandson plays for hours by himself in his huge playroom; he chooses which videos to watch. I cannot claim to understand even a fraction of what he knows about the operation of tractors, fire trucks, cranes, trains, planes, and helicopters, but can there be any real substitute for the sharp wits and social skills honed through traditional games and pastimes.

My Mother's Family

Life away from the capital was not easy for my mother as she missed her family. Instead, she carried on an extensive correspondence with them. Our maternal grandmother, Shazdeh Valieh, would never write in her own hand, although she had beautiful handwriting. Her scribe was Dayeh Khan, the *dayeh* or wet-nurse of our two uncles. Grandmother would confirm the contents of the letters written on her behalf by signing them "Qorbanat,Valieh Khanum."[14]

Known by her many grandchildren as "Shajan Vali," her actual name was Abbasseh and she was the daughter of Abdolsamad Mirza Ezz al-Dowleh, the son of Mohammad Shah, who was only three years younger than Naser al Din Shah. Our maternal grandfather, Ezz al-Mamalek Ardalan, was the son of Reza-gholi Khan Ardalan, the Vali

14. Khanum *is an honorific used in Persian in a similar way to "lady" or "madam" in English.*

of Kurdestan, and Princess Touba Khanum, the daughter of Prince Abbas Mirza, Nayeb al-Saltaneh (the regent). Their son Abolhasan, known as Fakhr al-Molk, married his cousin Princess Abbasseh Khanum, the daughter of Ezz al-Dowleh.

This marriage produced five sons—Amanollah (Ezz al-Mamalek), Rezagholi, Nassergholi, Abbasgholi, and Aligholi Ardalan—and four daughters: Hamdam Saltaneh, Ezzat al-Moluk (Mrs. Salar Etezad), my mother Mariam, whose title was Fakhrol Saltaneh, and Derakhshandeh (or Valieh Azam, as we called her). I have no memory of Hamdam Saltaneh. Apparently, she was a beautiful girl, who had an unhappy marriage to the son of Nayeb Saltaneh, causing our grandfather to spend a fortune to release his daughter from this bad match. She later remarried, but unfortunately died giving birth—leaving no children.

I adored my other two aunts. Ezzat al-Moluk married the grandson of Prince Etezad al-Saltaneh, her mother's uncle, and had a special love for me. I will speak more about her later. Valieh Azam, my youngest aunt, is a whole other story!

My Aunt Valieh Azam

The youngest child of the family, Valieh Azam was an exceptionally beautiful young woman, tall and slim. Due to a *nazr*[15] made by her father, she was married at the tender age of ten to a distinguished gentleman old enough to be her father. On her wedding day, this lively girl who was the apple of everyone's eye took one look at her future husband in the mirror at the traditional wedding ceremony and promptly fainted. It wasn't because the poor man was ugly or in any way unpleasant; it was just that our aunt had always dreamed of marrying a handsome young man.

The tradition of marrying your offspring to a *seyyed* (descendant of the Prophet) was common in those days. It took years and much money to undo this system of forced, arranged marriage. When I first heard this story as a young girl, I was amazed. I confess I am still surprised, because my grandfather was a modern man and had traveled to Europe several times; he had even sent his sons to be educated in Europe. How could such a person have allowed his ten-year-old daughter to be given in marriage to a middle-aged gentleman who already had a wife and children?

Was it possible that his piety and regard for the Prophet's descendants had made him accept such an offer? Valieh Azam was as we used to call her, was so beloved by her

---

15. Nazr *is a vow or commitment to perform a particular deed, often of a religious or charitable nature.*

family that they affectionately called her *chokhi*, short for *cheh dokhtari*, meaning "What a girl!" Her first marriage was a formality and even her second marriage to her own cousin—a young man educated in Europe and the son of Nasir Dowleh, the minister for education, and the grandson of Assef Dowleh—was very unhappy. The marriage ended in divorce after the birth of a daughter.

Her third marriage was more to her liking but short-lived as her husband passed away. She took her only child, Assefeh, and moved to Geneva. Many years later, Assefeh married my brother Bagher and they had three children. My beloved aunt died at the age of eighty-five in Tehran after the revolution. She was an elegant and gracious lady with a passion for neatness and cleanliness. Life had dealt her an unhappy hand. Before her death, she donated all she had by way of material possessions to the Kahrizak Foundation (a charitable sanatorium founded in the early 1970s by Dr. Hakimzadeh for the elderly and the disabled). May her spirit be joyful.

Grandfathers and Grandmothers

I never knew my paternal grandfather. Haj Mirza Nasrollah Mostofi,[16] who had been a financial administrator in the Iranian government, died when my father was thirteen.

---

16. *Adding* Haj *or* Haji *(for a man) or Hajieh (for a woman) before someone's name indicated that they had made the pilgrimage, or Hajj (see footnote 33 on page TK) to the house of God (Kaaba) in Mecca.*

I have a distant memory of my paternal grandmother; Zibandeh khanum passed away while we were still living in our old house in Mirza Mahmoud Vazir Alley. My father writes about them both at length in his memoirs. However, I have fond memories of my maternal grandfather, Haj Fakhr al-Molk (Abolhasan Ardalan).

Once, we made a pilgrimage to the holy cities of Islam in the company of my grandfather, grandmother, mother, and servants in an eight-seater Dodge. After making the tour of the mosque at Najaf in Iraq, we visited the golden courtyard, where the Shia governors or Valis of Kurdistan were buried. We said a prayer over the tombs of our ancestors.

There was quite a ritual involved with the prayers for the dead, but I was more interested in the magnificence of this holy place. Shajan had told me that when I first saw the minarets of the mosque I could make any wish and my wish would come true. At the age of six, my needs were modest and I asked the Almighty for a dozen colored pencils and a few coloring books!

On our return, my grandfather (Shajan's father) became unwell and passed away after a short illness. I had grown especially close to him during our trip and his death deeply saddened me. In those days, mourning rituals were very extensive and the whole household was involved in the elaborate arrangements in the *andarounis* and *birounis*, the courtyards and the kitchen yard. I say *birounis* because my maternal uncles lived separately with their families, each with their own *andarouni* and *birouni*, although they shared a kitchen, which was organized like a hotel restaurant.

At mealtimes, large copper trays would be loaded on the heads of the servants in a procession from the kitchen to the *andarounis*. I even remember the name of the head cook, Usta Akbar. Many people took part in the mourning ceremonies; large tablecloths were spread on the carpets in the great halls both at midday and in the evening. Maids, in clean stockinged feet, would serve the female guests platters of food that had been placed in the middle of these tablecloths.

The men were entertained in my grandfather's *birouni*. My abiding memory of that place is a ferocious-looking stuffed tiger with open jaws that stood in the middle of the hallway and used to terrify me.

My Great-Grandfather

While our only grandfather was now gone, my mother's grandfather, Prince Ezz al-Dowleh, the father of Shajan Vali, was still with us. Every Nowruz, Shajan Baba,[17] as we called him, would receive his children and their spouses, his numerous grandchildren, and great-grandchildren. From a raised dais in the main hall of his residence situated at the end of the Shoemakers' Bazaar in Tehran he would hand out *eidi* (New Year gifts) to the whole family as each smaller

---

17. Baba *is an affectionate term in Persian for father and grandfather, hence "Shajan Baba" refers to Shajan's father.*

family unit would approach as part of a formal audience with him. Shajan Baba was a delicate man and suffered from gout, as did most of the Qajar royal family.

When it was the turn of our family, following my mother's careful instructions, we would enter the reception hall, bow, kiss his hand, and receive a gold Ashrafi sovereign. I remember very well that I had tears in my eyes; I didn't want to kiss Shajan Baba's hand nor did I want the sovereign. To this day, I will only kiss the hands of babies as I believe one shouldn't kiss their delicate faces. I was terrified of Shajan Baba's small, wrinkled hand with its gnarled veins, even though it was delicate and clean.

His wife, the daughter of Prince Etezad al-Saltaneh, had passed away long ago, leaving behind three sons and five daughters. The daughters had all married into prominent and distinguished families of the time and all the sons held important government posts, as did their children up until the Islamic Revolution.

Lunch on the day of Eid-e Nowruz was a huge gathering of the family, held in Shajan Baba's spacious residence with its interconnecting reception rooms. We would be dressed in our finest clothes; there was much competition between the various children and their parents to appear the best dressed or the most beautiful. After my great-grandfather's death, we never managed to get together again in such numbers. As the old houses were demolished to make way for modern buildings, so the old traditions and relationships began to break down.

My Grandmother

Shajan's mother, Princess Abbaseh Salour, our only surviving grandmother, lived to be eighty-four. She was a devout and peaceful lady who was respected by all. Until she passed away, in the summer of 1944 (1323), her residence was our gathering place. Later, my uncle Ezz al-Mamalek Ardalan took over this position and on holidays and fetes there was much coming and going in his spacious garden in Dezashib. Years later, my uncles and aunts and their children and families began a tradition of Ardalan family gatherings and, on one Sunday each month, fifty or more of us would meet in one of our houses for dinner and a chance to see each other. We welcomed these family gatherings wholeheartedly and participated enthusiastically until the revolution tore apart our lives.

My Sister Mehri's Wedding

The most important event in our young lives was the marriage of my sister Mehri at the age of fifteen, while she was still a student at the Behesht-e Ain High School in Isfahan. This was my father's third posting outside the capital and we lived in the most beautiful house. Designed by a German architect by the name of Scheunemann, it blended traditional Iranian architecture with the most modern innovations—exquisite and intricate tiling, a state-of-the-art kitchen with all the most up-to-date gadgetry, and a Junkers[18] bathroom, which was a rarity at the time.

The wedding, both the *aqd* and the *arousi*,[19] was held in the lovely garden of that house. Many guests came from Tehran, bringing with them the wedding dress, which had been made there. The groom was Gholamreza Safinia, a colleague of my father and the public prosecutor of the district of Isfahan. The bride and groom were to live in our house following the wedding as my sister was still attending school.

At the time, the garden was full of gladioli and tuberoses, planted by the gardeners at my father's request. Tuberose is *mariam* in Persian, my mother's favorite flower. She was named Mariam after the flower, though my father would often shorten it to Mari. The ladies and gentlemen were entertained in two separate areas; I have photographs of the men's area and some of the bride with her little bridesmaids. It was such a happy day.

Life in Isfahan

In Isfahan, we girls attended the British School, which had a boarding section, and we had private tutors for French. In the morning, we would assemble in the school audito-

---

18. Junkers and Co. was a German gas appliance manufacturer.

19. A traditional Iranian wedding is in two parts: the legal ceremony or aqd, *in which the marriage contract,* aqd nameh, *or* qabaleh, *is drawn up and signed; and the* arousi, *or reception, following the* aqd*—a splendid affair often held in the home of the groom.*

rium to hear the sermon. Apart from the Armenian girls, who were Christian, the rest of us were Muslim, Jewish, or Zoroastrian. The school principal had a small dog that would always hover around us and accompany our morning prayers with his barking. Whenever he approached one of the Muslim girls, he would receive a little kick.

Shajan had identical outfits made for my sister Mehri and me by a lady whose husband had an important position in the government and had traveled to Europe. The fabric was white silk with red polka dots and the outfits were a great success. One of my friends asked me to send her the dress so she could ask her own seamstress to copy it. With Shajan's permission, I wrapped the dress in some newspaper and secured it with pins. As I couldn't find enough pins, I unwisely took off my gold brooch— made by a famous goldsmith in Jolfa in the form of the letter "H"—and used it to secure the parcel, which I then handed to my friend's manservant. When the dress was returned, there was no sign of my pin. I related the incident to Shajan, who looked at me in amazement, saying, "Did you really use your gold pin instead of an ordinary pin to secure the package?" I replied that I had. Maintaining that no one would believe my story, my mother advised me to forget the incident.

The brooch was worth about 4 tomans (75 cents) in those days and had been bought from the jeweler Ghazarian. My mother then bought me another brooch to replace it and this one had "HOURI" written on it and cost 8 tomans! I did eventually tell my friend about the missing brooch, which she had never seen and the manservant also denied

From left: Nasrollah, Shajan, Mehri, Houri, Nayer, and Faramarz (Mehri's son)

knowledge of it. Unfortunately, the second brooch must have also caught someone's eye because, when we returned to Tehran, it too had disappeared.

Artistic Pursuits

Isfahan was a city of innovation and artistic activity. Great progress had been made in the theater and the heroic tales of Ferdowsi were acted out on stage in the form of opera. The tales of Rostam and Sohrab, Bijan and Manijeh, and many other stories from the *Shahnameh*[20] were performed in song. Watching these heroic and patriotic performances deepened our love of Iran; indeed, it's a pity that more is not made on stage of this rich, cultural heritage. My father would often accompany us to these shows to support the artists, even though he would never go to the cinema, as he found it tiring staring at the screen and it made his eyes water.

However, whenever we returned from seeing a movie, he would listen avidly as we recounted what we had seen. Shajan had bought me a violin and this kept me occupied for a while. On the whole, life was happy and busy. I remember Dr. Ali Amini[21] had recently married Batoul Khanum, the daughter of Vosough al-Dowleh, and they visited Isfahan for their honeymoon. They came to our house for a party. At the end of the party, my younger sister Nayer was to perform for them. She was wearing a ballet costume in the form of a butterfly and, as she began to dance, suddenly one of the butterfly wings broke. Years later, Mrs. Amini would refer to the butterfly with the broken wing, still remembering the event.

---

20. *Composed by the poet Ferdowsi in the late tenth and early eleventh century* CE, *the* Shahnameh *is the national epic of Iran. Its subject matter is the history of the country and its people from the creation of the world up to the Arab conquest, which brought the then new religion of Islam to Iran, in the seventh century* CE. *The stories mentioned above are all from the early parts of the* Shahnameh.

21. *An Iranian politician, Ali Amini was a member of parliament in the late 1940s and a member of the cabinet in the 1950s. He was prime minister of Iran from 1961 to 1962.*

Falling Ill

I caught scarlet fever while in Isfahan and, because it was contagious, I had to stay in my room at the top of the house by myself. My father, who was on his annual break, became responsible for taking care of me as all contact with the rest of the family was practically severed. My father would come into my room and read to me from *Robinson Crusoe* by Daniel Defoe, and I would try to imagine how someone could live for so many years on a small island. Dr. Shafter was the director of the British Hospital; his wife would refer to him as "Hakim Shaf" (Doctor Shaf) without realizing that *shiaf* is not so flattering in Persian (it means "enema"). I recovered thanks to the skill of this physician and my father's great care.

Of course, my mother who was busy taking care of the rest of the family and the house would peek through the door from time to time and enquire how I was getting on. We had an endless stream of visitors from Tehran and there was never a dull moment. My mother was kept constantly on her toes. Shajan was one of the founders of the Isfahan Red Cross with the help of other benevolent Isfahani ladies.

Tabriz

My parents, my sister Nayer, and I set off for Tabriz toward the end of autumn. The boys stayed in Tehran—that year my older brother Nasrollah was at Tehran University while

Bagher was in twelfth grade. My father's job involved reorganizing the courts and modernizing the justice system in Azerbaijan. The weather was so cold that we decided to stay for a while in a hotel. In those days, the best one in Tabriz was the Hotel Jahan-nama and there was a cinema of the same name next door. There was a young manservant who had come with us from Kerman and had worked in our house for two years in Isfahan. Trained by Shajan, he would serve us the food prepared in the hotel kitchen, as well as clean and take care of all our needs while we were there—our personal valet! Sometimes, accompanied by Reza Khak, which was his name, we would go to the cinema.

One night they were showing *Dracula*. I was so frightened by the film that I could not sleep in my own bed that night and Shajan had no choice but to let me join her and my father in their large double bed. There was a carpet hanging on the wall facing the bed and, in the dark, it looked to me just like Dracula's long, black cloak. As a result, I stayed awake the whole night.

School Years

I did my seventh and eighth grades in Kerman, ninth and tenth at the British School in Isfahan, and part of the eleventh grade in Tabriz. The students were of all ages. In the provinces, girls would start school at a later age and my classmates were all older and considerably more mature than me. My French was quite good since we had always had access to Shams al-Madarres School, where I had received a good grounding in French. There was great competition between the top students to get full marks for dictation. We would practice every night until I could do the dictations in the book *Cent dictées* almost faultlessly in class.

Our French teacher in Tabriz was happy that a good student had joined her class mid-year and very soon mutual respect and admiration grew between us. The teachers didn't have an easy ride otherwise, especially the weaker ones. Our Arabic teacher, for instance,' was the target of frequent pranks by the older students, but he suffered in silence and never complained.

One day one of these students, who had befriended me, brought a large pot of *osh-e reshteh* (noodle soup) from home and placed it in front of the Arabic teacher. Even though it was only eleven in the morning, she insisted that he should have some of this thick soup during class and dished out a bowlful. Apparently unable to resist, our teacher began to eat the *osh* with evident relish. Just then the door opened and the principal walked in, catching him red-handed. I will never forget the look of sheer terror on the poor man's face. I never found out whether this had been a coincidence, or someone had deliberately set up him.

In other instances, students would take advantage of the more lenient teachers by walking around in the middle of a class and even dancing in the classroom. I stayed in this school for only a few months before returning to the capital with my mother and Nayer, who attended the American School in Tehran. On our return to Tehran, I took my eleventh-grade exams at the age of fifteen and Nayer completed her sixth grade. I do not remember what we did with our cash prizes! During this time, I attended Madam Yelena's dance class with Nayer, my friend Arasteh, and her younger sisters. We learned Lezgi and Qafqazi (Caucasian) dances there—a bit of light relief from all the academic study.

God Willing, Misfortune Will Bring You Luck

Having successfully completed his twelfth-grade exams, my brother Bagher entered the Tehran Polytechnic, where he was one of the top students in his class. In the mid-term exams at university, it seems the professor had distributed the exam papers later than scheduled and then refused to give the students extra time. They protested, with Bagher standing up to put the students' case to the professor. His request was refused, causing a couple of students to leave the examination hall in protest.

The following day, all three of them saw their notice of expulsion on the notice board. This was hard to accept for my father; apparently mediation was to no avail. The minister of education at the time, who was a friend of my father's and had the task of adjudicating between the student and the teacher, chose the stronger party's side. He supported the stubborn and intransigent professor; as a lesson in coping with the unfairness life might throw at you, maybe he was right.

With only a few months left to the end of the academic year, Shajan decided to hire one of the teachers at the

American School to tutor my brother in English. Except for Nayer, the rest of us were proficient only in French. My brother had taken an intensive course in English and found it quite easy after studying French. He took the Concours exam for students wishing to go abroad and applied to universities in England to study petroleum engineering. He came out in the top seven.

Bagher was the youngest of this group, and, at the age of seventeen, he left Iran. We accompanied him as far as Karaj, where Shajan handed his passport, money, and other documents to one of the other students, Saifullah Moazami, who was older. A few years later, my brother graduated with honors from Birmingham University, majoring in petroleum engineering and geology. However, the advent of the Second World War prevented him from returning to Iran and he spent a year doing research in England. In 1940, he returned to Iran via the Cape of Good Hope and, as we will learn later, he gained great prominence and became a major figure in the progress of his country in helping to further the oil industry in Iran.[22]

---

22. Bagher Mostofi was selected by the Shah to be the managing director and founder in 1964 of the Iran Petrochemical Company, a subsidiary of the National Iranian Oil Company. He played an important role in the development of Iran's petrochemical industry until the revolution in 1979.

The Marriage that Was Not to Be

The year 1934 (1313) was an eventful one. My sister Mehri gave birth to a baby boy at the age of seventeen, making me an aunt at fifteen. My father was in Azerbaijan and we were in Tehran. My maternal aunt Ezzat al-Moluk, who was just a few years older than Shajan, was particularly fond of me. In those days, it was not customary for boys and girls to have close friendships, but we would often see our cousins, both male and female, in family gatherings. One of my male cousins, tall and handsome and six years older than me, came to stay with us for a few days. He was on the American School soccer team, and they were playing a match against the Isfahan home team. He may have had his eye on me from that time. I remember that we all attended the match and were upset that the Tehran team lost to Isfahan.

Later, when we returned to Tehran, my aunt Ezzat al-Moluk intimated to Shajan that I should become her daughter-in-law. My mother would have none of it. Having married off her eldest daughter early, she didn't want to lose me as well. That summer, having already passed my eleventh-grade exams, there wasn't much to do but eavesdrop. In the next room, Shajan was confiding in Khanumi, the daughter of one of my uncles' wet-nurses. She seemed upset that her older sister kept insisting on a match between her son and me.

"Agha [referring to my father] is in Azerbaijan, the girl is barely fifteen years old, and marriage between cousins is, in any case, not a good idea," I overhead her saying. "Maybe the two cousins have already had conversations that I don't know about. I saw my sister in the pastry shop yesterday and she said, 'Fakhr al-Saltaneh, I am buying all these cakes and sweets to send over to your house on Eid-e Ghadir[23] and will come over with Shajan Vali [my grandmother] to ask for Houri's hand in marriage to my son.'" My mother's title was Fakhr al-Saltaneh and it always used to amaze me that the three sisters never called each other by their first names but always used their formal titles instead.

Hearing this, I went into the room and said, "Shajan, I haven't made any plans with anyone; and so you won't be upset, I will call them right now." With that, I went straight to the telephone in the hall and dialed my grandmother, who was still living in the old house in Fakhr al-Molk Street. My younger aunt, Valieh Azam, who was experiencing problems in her own marriage, picked up the phone.

After the customary greetings and small talk, I plucked up courage and asked her to give a message to my grandmother. "Would you be kind enough to convey my respects to Shajan Vali and tell her I am too young to marry. She is most welcome to visit us on Eid-e Ghadir as long as there is to be no talk of marriage." Taken aback by this, my aunt asked, "Is it really you, Houri, who is saying this?" To which I replied, "It is indeed me and I ask you to please pass on my message and don't take it amiss."

---

23. Eid-e Ghadir is an Islamic commemorative holiday, considered to be among the significant holidays of Shi'ite Muslims. It is held on the date when the Prophet Mohammad was said to have appointed Ali ibn Abi Talib as his successor.

For me at fifteen, to give such a message to my grandmother, a figure revered by the whole family, was indeed revolutionary—a real coup de théâtre. The result was a rift between the two families. My aunt was quite rightly offended because her son was highly eligible; by contrast, Shajan acted as if nothing had happened! The only reason I had reacted in this way was to appease my headstrong mother.

My Cousin's Wedding in Khoramshahr

In those days, our eldest maternal uncle was the governor of Lorestan in western Iran and his second daughter, Forough Molouk, was about to be married. Shajan took charge of arranging for the wedding dress to be made in Tehran, as well as providing the special pastries and all that was needed for the wedding ceremony. Accompanied by my younger sister Nayer, we then set off for Khoramshahr, the seat of the governor, in a trip that lasted a month.

The ceremonies were conducted in a manner befitting the families of both the bride and groom. The latter turned out to be the son of a well-known and respectable family—neighbors of my grandfather and uncles in Dezashib; he had been posted to Khoramshahr, where he had met my cousin. Even though some time had elapsed since the incident between Shajan and her sister, the two remained cool toward each other at the wedding.

A little while after this, my father was recalled to Tehran to take up the post of the director of the Land Registry and the Bureau of Census, the second or third most important position in the Ministry of Justice, or Adlieh, as it was known in those days. It was during my father's time in this department that notary public offices were taken over mostly by the university-educated sons of the older generation who had occupied these positions before. My father remained in this post for many years, during which time he was able to oversee the modernization of all such institutions.

After this he was appointed governor first of West and subsequently East Azerbaijan. Up until the time of the Islamic Revolution, whenever I visited one of these notary public offices, as soon as they learned I was the daughter of the former governor, they would talk of him with great respect, even though he had passed away many years earlier. Interestingly, during his time in office he didn't buy so much as a meter of land or register any property in his own name.

A Trip to Khorasan

In the autumn of 1935 (1314), I left for Mashhad[24] in the company of my parents and my grandmother, stopping on

24. Mashhad was a major oasis along the ancient Silk Road. It is named after the shrine of Imam Reza, the eighth Shia Imam, who was buried in a village in Khorasan, which afterward became known as Mashhad, meaning "the place of martyrdom." Every year, millions of pilgrims visit the Imam Reza shrine.

the way at Semnan, Damghan, Shahrud, and Nishapur. Our driver, Suleiman, drove us in a 1934 green Dodge sedan. We would stay overnight in each place so my father could inspect the offices. We finally arrived in Mashhad, where we visited the shrine and enjoyed the hospitality of the holy place at lunchtime. That night they cleared the shrine and my father paid his respects by sweeping a small area around the sacred enclosure. At the same time, my mother made an offering of a large burgundy-colored tapestry embroidered with pearls that had her name, Mariam, sewn into one corner. This trip lasted several weeks before we returned to Tehran.

Youthful Pastimes

At the age of sixteen, I was one of the first girls to learn to drive—taught by my older brother, Nasrollah. We were living at the time in Jaleh Street a wide and quiet street. My brother would make me drive through all the narrow alleys; I was petrified especially if I saw another car approaching in the distance, but Nasrollah, sitting next to me, would always reassure me: "That car is going its own way and is not going to bother you." For years, I drove a car without a driving license; later when there were more women drivers, I took a driving test and in 1947 (1326) I got my driving license.

In the summer, we would go on short trips around Tehran in a large group. One such trip was to the shrine of Imam Davud in north Tehran by donkey. Among the friends who would accompany us on these trips was Fati; she and I were almost the same age. She was tall and beautiful, with black, shiny hair and a pale complexion; we had our photographs taken together in Ab-e Ali on the outskirts of Tehran. Destiny almost separated us from each other. My older brother, Nasrollah, had fallen in love with Fati but nothing came of it as her mother was against the marriage. Maybe because, some years before, I had turned down Fati's uncle's proposal of marriage! Fati later married at about the same time as me, and gave birth to a daughter; she subsequently divorced her husband and went to live in Europe.

Iranian Women Admitted to University

On 7 January 1935 (17 Dey 1313), Reza Shah decreed that women should no longer have to wear the black chador and, at the same time, young women were accepted into the university. Government ministries, military and civil organizations all gave tea parties at which men were invited with their wives, who were all dressed in long coats and wearing hats. The government had imported coats and hats especially for the occasion so that the women could make use of them. Among the Armenian ladies there were also milliners, who accepted orders for hats. This great change was difficult for some to accept, notably our grandmother Princess Hajieh Valieh, who became even more house-bound and hardly ever left home.

Seated on the grass are Houri (center) and Farrokhrou Parsa (to her right) in their class photo, c. 1939. (The Teachers' College and the Faculty of Letters, Philosophy and Education of the University of Tehran were administered jointly until 1942).

I was attending the Kamal al-Molk Art School[25] at the time, in my second year, and producing quite good water-colors, copying classical models and even making a few self-portraits as well as a charcoal sketch of the *Mona Lisa*. My parents called on me one day. Shajan started the conversation by saying I could always pursue art as it was more of a pastime that could be enjoyed at anytime and anywhere.

---

*25. Mohammad Ghaffari, known as Kamal al-Molk, was the royal painter (*naqqash bashi*) of the late-Naseri court (1880s). After the Constitutional Revolution of 1906, his school initiated a new style in Iranian art. The school's goal was to nurture new talents, giving them the best possible education. Kamal al-Molk also introduced other arts and crafts, such as carpet weaving, mosaic designing, and woodwork, in an attempt to revive these dying traditions.*

She went on to say my eleventh-grade diploma would not be worth very much in the future and that Mehri and I should get a university education as our brothers had done.

Our far-sighted mother spoke these words in the winter of 1935 (1314) and insisted that we should prepare to enroll immediately as registration had already started. My sister and I had no choice but to obey our parents and after a short time we entered the first year at Tehran University. This was a preparatory class replacing the twelfth grade, which we hadn't completed. Only a few young women, all older than us, who had previously been teachers or had studied abroad, were permitted to enroll in the first year.

My First Day in the French Class

On the first day, my sister and I joined the class almost an hour after it had started. The students were reading from *Paul et Virginie* by Bernardin de Saint-Pierre. Years later, when I became a French teacher myself, I discovered how annoying it is to have students arriving in the middle of a class. Our entrance disrupted the peace and discipline of the lesson; the professor in charge, Mrs. Amine Pakravan, invited us to sit down before continuing to speak to the student who was reading aloud and point out her mistakes. She then turned to me all of a sudden and asked me to continue reading. I had never read this text before. After I had read a few lines, she softened a little and asked me if I had attended the French school Jeanne d'Arc or studied the language abroad. "Neither," I replied. "I learned my French at the Shams al-Madarres School with Mrs. Varasteh." I was permitted to sit down again.

Life in Shemiran

At the time Mehri and I were starting at university, my father was busy building a house in Bagh-e Ferdows,[26] in Tajrish, Shemiran. The government was selling large pieces of land in this area to its senior employees, and we were able to take advantage of the opportunity. The design and the architecture of the building was copied from our beautiful house in Isfahan and we moved there in the autumn of 1936 (1315). Shajan had just recovered from a long and complicated illness that summer and was finally cured by the renowned Dr. Ghani, who used to visit her frequently. I will never forget this wonderful physician—may he rest in peace.

University Women

The young women who got through to the second year, after completing in the first year, were few in number. I will rely on my memory to recall their names. Shayesteh Sadegh, the daughter of the speaker of the parliament of

26. *In those days and for a long time until the massive expansion of Tehran today, Tajrish and its gardens, of which the Bagh-e Ferdows was among the most famous, were truly islands of peace and tranquility away from the hustle and bustle of the city, and indeed an earthly paradise, as its name suggests.*

Iran, had studied for many years in Turkey when her father was ambassador in Ankara. Highly intelligent, she was fluent in both French and English, in addition to her mother tongue, Persian. Shams al-Molouk Mosahhab later received a PhD in Persian language and literature, and Mehrangiz Manouchehrian became an attorney; these two ladies later became senators in the Iranian government. Mrs. Zahra Kia (Khanlari), who also obtained a PhD in Persian language and literature, went on to become the principal of Nourbakhsh High School for many years.

The girls who had completed the preparatory year and were entering the first year were numerous and chose many different fields. Some took Persian language and literature, others foreign languages, and a couple did history and geography. The following year some girls opted for natural sciences, physics, chemistry, and mathematics. The number of women attending university kept increasing.

The first-year language classes were very crowded because they were attended by students from other departments as well. We were taught by Professor Jean Hitie, a Frenchman, and studied *Les Femmes savantes* ("The Learned Ladies") by Molière and *Le Barbier de Séville* ("The Barber of Seville") by Beaumarchais. Although these two comedies were not very complicated, we spent many nights poring over the Larousse dictionary making sure we understood every sentence perfectly, as a different preposition here or there could completely change the meaning of a phrase. The professor would call on us in class and we we had to translate whatever passage we were reading on the spot.

There was a good reason we were called seekers of knowledge (*danesh-ju*, for university students) and not learners of knowledge (*danesh-amuz*, for schoolchildren).

After we finished these two plays, we were asked to perform *Les Femmes savantes* in class; the professor handed out the parts. My sister, who was only nineteen, married with a young son, was given the part of the mother, Philaminte. I was given the part of the youngest daughter, Henriette. My part included 250 lines of poetry, which I had to memorize and recite; this resulted in a great improvement in our spoken French. The class was divided into two groups with the stronger group having the first turn at reciting the play.

One day the professor asked me (I cannot remember in what context) whether it was possible to trust men. In my haste to answer, I replied *jamais* (never) instead of saying *pas toujours* (not always). My teacher fixed me with his blue eyes and said, "What makes a young girl of nineteen such a pessimist?" I remember feeling quite offended at the time because I was only seventeen years old! Now, as I write these pages, I ask myself what difference did being seventeen or nineteen really make? But I was young and proud of being the youngest in the class!

Lessons at University

I passed the first-year exams with flying colors. I remember the subject for the essay at the end of the first semester was

"*Tous les changements, même les plus souhaités, ont leur melancolie*" ("All change, even the most longed for, is inherently sad"). This is a quote from Anatole France, and while it appears quite straightforward, it is not an easy subject on which to write a dissertation. Our end-of-year essay, by contrast, was on Figaro, the Barber of Seville!

In the second year, there were fewer students in the class; some chose other subjects to major in and abandoned French literature. Professor Hitie's contract came to an end and he returned to France; he was then replaced by a young man from Corsica called Bonifacio, who was a graduate of the École Normale Supérieure. He was newly married and had a young son, born in Tehran. We studied French literature in the last two years and wrote our final thesis in his class. Later, when diplomatic relations between Iran and France broke down, they replaced the foreign instructors with Iranian teachers.

We studied the essays of Francis Bacon and Shakespeare's *Romeo and Juliet* under Professor Vahid al-Molk Sheibani, who had a very strong British accent. Later, several young men who had studied in England joined the department and taught us the poetry of Robert Browning and Thackeray's *The History of Henry Esmond.* The choice of four advanced texts for students learning English as a second foreign language didn't make it easy for us. Even though we were among the top students, we had to work very hard. Some of the students had learned English at the American College (or Alborz High School, as it was later called) and it was their first foreign language. Later Dr. Souratgar and his British wife became our professors.

The third year was much more engaging; we studied comparative literature with Dr. Fatemeh Sayyah. I was very interested in this subject because there was so much scope for discussion, and we would take notes since there was no textbook. Dr. Sayyah was very knowledgeable and knew four languages—French, German, English, and Russian—in addition to Persian, which she spoke with an accent and pronounced "kh" as "h" and vice versa. For example, when comparing Hafez to Goethe, she would say Hajeh Khafez Shirazi (instead of Khajeh Hafez Shirazi); we had to suppress our giggles. However, it was a most engaging class; we would compare the poetry of Ferdowsi in the *Shahnameh* with the poetry of Victor Hugo in *La Légende des siècles* and this gave us tremendous pride in our own poets, knowing that they were considered among the greatest in the world.

Our Persian classes were also very interesting; we had teachers such as the distinguished poet Malek al-Shoara Bahar (the king of poets) and the great scholar Badiozaman Forouzanfar. Our Arabic teachers were Seyyed Mohammad Tadayon and Ahmand Bahmanyar. One day Malek al-Shoara Bahar asked us to memorize 150 lines of poetry by Manouchehri.[27] The next day my sister and I and some of the other students who managed to recite them

---

27. Manouchehri Damghani (fl. 1031–40) was an eleventh-century Persian court poet.

perfectly received signed copies of our teacher's volume of poetry as a prize.

Humanities were also being offered at the university; Dr. Rezazadeh Shafagh taught philosophy and Dr. Aliakbar Siassi psychology. Dr. Shafagh's class started off being very interesting as he gave many examples and stories to bring the subject alive; Dr. Siassi, by contrast, was less engaging. His class was held in a large auditorium and was attended by students from many different faculties. Dr. Siasi spoke quietly and monotonously while we took endless notes. The boys, who were not really interested in the class, would lie down on the back benches and we girls, who didn't dare do such a thing, would sit in the front rows and shield them while they slept behind us!

Maybe this was one of the reasons we got so much out of the classes. We used to concentrate and would really listen as we took notes; we also didn't waste time. As a result, it wasn't necessary to review our notes too often at home. Years later, this was the advice I used to give my own students. I would warn them against too many absences and, worse still, inattentiveness while the teacher was speaking. These are the main obstacles to learning.

Later, we studied statistics; this was one of the mandatory courses that all students had to take. Putting his cards on the table in the first session, Dr. Afzalipour established absolute discipline in the class. Although he came across as overly strict and humorless, it was indeed the only way to deal with certain students. Dr. Hoshyar was one of the teachers whom no one respected; students would shuffle their shoes on the floor, making a terrible noise. The teacher had no choice but to interrupt what he was saying, and even when he implored the students to allow him to finish, no one would listen, and the class would come to an end.

The Gymnasium and the Auditorium

The gym was the place where the sporty students would congregate. I used to play tennis and was one of the stronger players among the girls; I also used to play ping-pong against the boys. The other students would gather around us to watch the game. Jahangir Amouzegar,[28] who was studying and working at Bank Melli at the same time, used to be one of my strongest opponents and would always win by a narrow margin. I recently had an opportunity to pick up a racket and have a go and I was not even able to hit one ball across the net. I was quite disappointed in myself. When it came to sport, the boys were altogether much stronger and made more use of the gym. In those days, girls were not really familiar with parallel bars or other gymnastic equipment.

Our large auditorium was the center for extracurricular activities. The head of the Daneshsara-ye Aali (Institute of Higher Education) which included the faculties of litera-

---

28. Jahangir Amouzegar (1920–2018) was an Iranian economist, academic, and politician. His younger brother, Jamshid Amouzegar, was prime minister of Iran during the Shah's reign.

ture and science, was Dr. Eesa Sadigh, who had studied in Europe and the USA and was very capable indeed. We would take part in lectures and debates; in fact, I learned public speaking in this great hall. Later, when Dr Sadigh took charge of the national radio he proposed that, following graduation, I should accept the responsibility for the French language program on the radio, including news broadcasting. It would have been an ideal job for me; however, it entailed full-time work and, after consulting my parents, I regrettably had to decline. I owe him a great debt for his part in my development. Again, I am getting ahead of myself; there is still a lot to relate about my university days.

Our class kept reducing in number as some of the girls got married. In 1939 (1318), a large number of girls and boys including my sister and I graduated. The first place went to a very deserving boy from Shiraz who was married as well; for the last three years he had sat with us girls in the front row. He was stronger than everyone else in all subjects especially in French, which he had taught in Shiraz. Years later, I heard that this wonderful and capable young man had died; we used to call him Monsieur Azimi and loved him like a brother. I took second place. At our graduation ceremonies I was one of the speakers and my talk was entitled "Our Motto." I was not yet twenty years old.

Rezaieh

We spent the summer of 1939 (1318) in Rezaieh (now called by its original name, Urmia). My father had been the governor of West Azerbaijan for some time and lived away from us. We set off for this province accompanied by a young friend called Puran P——, whom we called Puri for short. My father had built a very comfortable home in the garden of the governor's headquarters for the residence of the governor and his family. Exams were successfully behind us and we would spend our time with Puri, who was between me and Nayer in age, swimming in Lake Rezaieh. The water in this lake is so salty that there is no trace of fish or shellfish, nor is there any danger of drowning! We would float on the surface of the water like corks, but we had to take care not to get the water in our eyes or nose, which was most unpleasant. Large ships were anchored a little way from the shore and we would soon leave them behind. The problem was neither distance nor the depth of the lake; rather it was the saltiness we had to beware of.

Shajan, who complained of rheumatism, would take mud baths, which she found very helpful. My father never took part in these activities. His sport was walking and checking on the young trees that had been planted along the avenues leading to the governor's mansion. We had a driver called David who was Assyrian; he used to accompany us everywhere and spoke Persian and Turkish, in addition to Assyrian. As well as being a good driver, he was also an excellent interpreter.

Ahmad Agha, who was our old majordomo from Tehran and before that the *lalleh* of our eldest cousin, had accompanied my father from Tehran and ran the household. He spoke excellent Turkish, which was very useful. We used to play tennis in the afternoons; the best tennis players in town, girls from local families, used to play with us and then would be invited for tea by Shajan.

Puri, our friend, had become like a third daughter and participated in all these activities. I remember the first time she saw Lake Rezaieh she jumped into the water and was shocked by the saltiness that stung her eyes; we immediately put her under a cold shower to wash out the salt. She was sporty and, although she was Iranian and her father a prominent businessman, she had been brought up in Germany.

One evening, we were invited to the home of one of our new friends, who had a foreign spouse. After dinner, the hostess and her daughter entertained us by playing the piano; they played a four-handed *Danse macabre* by Saint-Saëns—a tone poem about a young girl who comes to life after she has been buried and tries unsuccessfully to save herself by attempting to break out of the grave, after which she really dies. The mother and daughter duo played very skillfully and brought to life the young girl's struggle to escape. Some time ago, when I heard another piece by Saint-Saens played by the San Francisco Philharmonic Orchestra, it all came back to me.

One of our other pastimes was horse-riding. The head of the military camp would let us ride their more docile horses. The only difficulty was that, on our return to the stables, the horses would break into a gallop and it was almost impossible to rein them in.

Three Weddings

We were living in Tehran when my father left for his post as governor of West Azerbaijan. One of the big events of that time was the engagement of the crown prince with Princess Fawzieh, the sister of King Farouk of Egypt in 1938. The bride-to-be, accompanied by her mother and sisters, traveled to Iran for the wedding and several receptions were given in honor of the young couple. On the day of the arrival of the wedding party, they were received at the Tehran Railroad Station in a magnificent ceremony. To celebrate this happy event, the government had authorized the importing of silk fabric as well as shoes and handbags from abroad.

Shajan attended the arrival ceremony and unfortunately lost her treasured emerald and diamond brooch—whether due to the weight of her brooch or the huge crowd pressing in around her. Each guest was given a memento of the occasion—a beautiful medallion with the image of the bride and groom in enamel work. I kept the medallion in a safe deposit box until the revolution; I don't know what became of it after that.

The Iranian Houses of Parliament also gave a large reception attended by the bride and groom and their families. We received an invitation to attend this event accompanied by Shajan, as her cousin Haj Mohtasham

The wedding of Fawzieh Fuad and Mohammad Reza Pahlavi was first held in Cairo in 1939 and then repeated in Tehran. Here, seated from left to right, are Gholamreza Pahlavi (the crown prince's younger brother), Fawzieh, Reza Shah, Fawzieh's mother Nazli, and the crown prince.

Saltaneh Esfandiary was the leader of parliament. Shajan asked our cousin to arrange transport for us to and from the Houses of Parliament for the party. This cousin always dressed in a black suit with a white shirt, and he wore a bow tie instead of a necktie. His car was also black and highly polished and, from a distance, it could be mistaken for the Shah's Rolls-Royce.

Shajan and I sat in the back of the car and our distinguished cousin in the driver's seat. As we passed Mokhber al-Dowleh Square, we suddenly became aware of the applause of the people who were lining the streets. They had mistaken me for Fawzieh and Shajan for Queen Nazli, her mother. Overcome with embarrassment, we didn't know how to respond to the cheers of the crowds. As we got out of the car outside the Houses of Parliament, the car carrying the real Princess Fawzieh and Queen Nazli pulled up behind us!

There were two other weddings, both family affairs, prior to the royal wedding; one took place in the famous park of Vosough al-Dowleh in Soleymanieh. Ghamar Vosough al-Dowleh was marrying Dr. Ashtiani. On the invitation envelope, alongside my parents' names, they had inscribed "Little Miss [*Banoocheh*]," in place of the more usual "Mademoiselle." I would never go anywhere without an invitation.

A most interesting religious ceremony was arranged for the marriage of our cousin Hasanali Mostofi with Galka Friedlippe, at the home of the bride. Galka and her sister Marina were the twin daughters of Mr. Friedlippe, who was responsible for the installation of cigarette factories and running the tobacco industry in Iran. They had a magnificent residence in Pahlavi Avenue and the wedding of the twin daughters and their husbands was to take place at the same time. The second groom, marrying Marina, was Jamshid Khabir. Two *aqd* tables had been set facing Mecca and decorated differently for each bride. The families of each groom sat behind the appropriate table and there was an aisle in the middle for people to pass.

The Qur'an, mirror, candelabras, and the rest of the paraphernalia for the *aqd*[29] were arranged on each table by the grooms' families. The band started playing "Here Comes the Bride." The brides' father, with his goatee, entered with a daughter on each arm and started to descend the great staircase into the hall. They then walked up the aisle between the two rows of chairs and each bride took her special place, while the respective grooms stood behind their chairs and waited for the marriage ceremony. At the end of the formalities, lunch was served. This event was considered a great novelty.

Reza Shah's Birthday

The 15 March (24 Esfand) was Reza Shah's fifty-first birthday. In Rezaieh, the arrangements for the reception and dinner were being carried out under Shajan's supervision; and everything had been prepared in Tehran for the event in Rezaieh. We were traveling by car to Rezaieh in very cold weather and accompanied by a capable cook. I was still at

29. *For the* aqd *(wedding ceremony), a* sofreh-ye aqd, *a fine hand-sewn wedding cloth glittering with gold and silver threads, is spread out before the mirror. Food and objects traditionally associated with marriage are arranged on the* sofreh, *including: a tray of* atel-o-batel *(multicolored herbs and spices to guard against witchcraft and to drive evil spirits away); an assortment of sweets and pastries; two large loaves of sugar,* kallehqand, *to be used in the ceremony; fresh flowers, such as roses, tuberoses, gardenia, and jasmine, to symbolize the beauty that it is hoped will adorn the couple's life together; an open flask of rose water to perfume and purify the air; a needle and seven strands of different-colored threads to sew up the mother-in-law's mouth—only figuratively, of course; a small brazier burning wild rue, the fumes of which are said to drive away evil spirits; and an open copy of the Qur'an or* Divan *of Hafez.*

university at the time and Nayer in high school. The invitations and menus were all designed after consultation with my father, who had been a diplomat in Imperial Russia and was familiar with all the rules of etiquette. To begin with, there was a seated dinner for a select group of people, followed by a buffet dinner for a much larger number.

All the dignitaries and heads of various government offices, high-ranking army officers, the British and French consuls, important businessmen and their wives were invited to the seated dinner. The buffet dinner and gala were attended by a younger crowd, and it is from this time that I became interested in the art of hospitality. Shajan played a very important role in the proceedings and did much to improve the standard of these receptions. In later years, we would entertain up to 120 guests at a seated dinner and up to 300 people at a buffet. All the materials and the cooks would be sourced locally.

Rezaieh–Tabriz

Toward the end of the summer of 1939 (1318), my father was appointed by Reza Shah as governor of East Azerbaijan; we were in Rezaieh in West Azerbaijan, spending the summer vacation with him. We immediately packed up everything and set off for Tabriz. Naturally, Puri also accompanied us. This was not the first time we had visited Tabriz. Alighapou, the governor's residence, had served as the home of the Qajar crown princes for many years, which they left only

Aghajan in his formal governor's attire in Rezaieh

when they traveled to Tehran to take over the monarchy. The main building was on two floors and situated in the middle of the large garden; we occupied only the upper level. There were huge reception halls and a wide veranda that wrapped around the building. The most impressive parts of the building and a reminder of its former glory were the main entrance, staircase, and hallways.

The property was not in good repair and had been neglected for some years. The swimming pool and tennis courts had also not been used. The pool area was surrounded by tall plane trees that served as a roosting place for hundreds of crows; they created so much noise and polluted the swimming pool to such an extent that occasionally guns would have to be fired to scare them away. This only worked for a short period, however, and the crows were soon back. We gave up on the swimming pool and, with my father's permission, set about cleaning up the tennis courts.

The governor's office, where my father worked, was situated at one end of the garden. My father had an open-door policy and people of all levels of society were welcome to enter his office. He was a man of great knowledge—from astronomy to agriculture and everything in between—and he used this to advise people when they came to him with their problems. In Tabriz we had a driver called Akbar Agha. Our old majordomo, Ahmad Agha, returned to Tehran and left the running of the house to three menservants: Bagher Khan, Taymour, and Fereydoun. The cook and his assistant worked in the basement area; and we had brought a young housemaid with us from Tehran called Fatemeh, who was quite a character.

Discipline and cleanliness ruled in our household and Shajan would spend the first few days after our arrival arranging for this old building to be cleaned and put in order before she was satisfied. On Mondays, she had an open house, which started with tea served from 4 p.m. and then eventually followed by dinner. Some visitors would come for tea and then leave, and some others would stay for dinner; we tried to rotate the friends who would dine with us. The younger crowd, and some who were not so young, came to play tennis and were served tea in the garden; Shajan would always join us after the game was over.

Life in Tabriz

Tabriz was a city with considerably more going on than Rezaieh. Our official guests were housed in a wing of the governor's residence and many dinner parties and recreational programs were held in their honor. My brother Bagher was studying in England and my sister Mehri came to stay with us for a short time with her young son. My father invited the young official Mahmoud Hedayat to work with him and take up the post of deputy governor of Tabriz. Until such time as a suitable house could be found for them, he and his wife stayed with us as our guests.

I used to paint in my spare time and Mr. Hedayat, who was a talented artist, would help me with my watercolors. Witty and yet very serious, he was a great admirer of my father, with whom he would spend many hours in conversation in spite of their age difference. They would share their experiences and stories and would laugh aloud, so you could hear them from anywhere in the house. Not only was Mahmoud Hedayat a highly capable politician, he was also well versed in poetry, music, art and literature; his brother was the author Sadegh Hedayat.[30]

During Nowruz 1319 (1940), all my various friends competed with each other to invite me to see them first. I used to ask my father's advice about this so as not to cause

---

30. An Iranian writer and translator, Sadegh Hedayat was born in 1907 and died in 1951. Best known for his novel The Blind Owl, *one of the earliest in Iran to adopt literary modernism.*

offence. Later, all these friends moved to Tehran. Another friend of mine, Saideh, had just returned from Beirut; she was a little younger than me and we would correspond in French. I still see her in Paris and we sometimes communicate by phone when we're in the USA.

The academic year had started and about a month had already passed. I was invited by Shahdokht High School in Tehran to teach French in place of a teacher who had left. I would go to school every day and teach French to classes of 30–40 students from seventh to eleventh grade. I'd then return home with a whole pile of exercise books full of dictations, essays, and translations, all carried by our driver, Akbar Agha. The next day I would return them, corrected, to the students. I was the first graduate teacher and quite popular. Some of the eleventh-grade students were the same age as me, some were younger and a few were older.

Marriage Prospects

I should take a moment to discuss the situation of girls who were of marriageable age. We had hardly any contact with boys and, as you will have gathered, marriages were arranged by families, sometimes even in childhood. Our friends were all girls of our own age. I found it difficult to pursue these relationships because in Tabriz the girls were not particularly sporty. Aziz A—— was soon engaged to be married; her future husband had recently returned from Europe and was a good tennis player. Some girls developed friendships with boys at the university and this led to marriage.

I had a less pragmatic view of marriage; I was an idealist and sought perfection in a future partner, both physically and mentally. I had read many romantic novels by French writers and watched many romantic black and white movies in which the heroes were all handsome and noble. I never regarded marriage as an escape from my parents' home and I was therefore hard to please.

Shajan made a trip to Tehran and I accompanied her. My cousin had just returned after many years in Germany and we met again at a family party. The following day, we returned to Tabriz. I am not sure whether this trip was strategically arranged or whether Shajan wished to mend the rift that had developed some years before. Nothing came of this trip and my aunt Ezzat al-Moluk soon found a beautiful and accomplished bride for her son. We all attended the marriage of what must have been the most handsome bride and groom of that year.

Man of Principle

My father had many interests over and above his official duties. He was a man of God and never neglected the care of the less privileged members of society. He would often visit the leper colony outside Tabriz, for instance, coming into close contact with the patients. Such visits obliged those responsible to pay more attention to those enduring a life sentence of disease. Naturally, he took great care not to become infected himself. Even so, he was often advised of the dangers of this activity and his answer was, "What about the doctors and nurses who care for the lepers? They don't become infected. My blood is not a different color than theirs. Census day took place on a particularly cold winter day. Early in the morning, he set off for a low-income neighborhood with an armband, like the other census officials, and worked until late in the evening. Years later when he was recalled to Tehran, his opponents, who could not fault his capability, professionalism, and honesty, started a rumor that my father had referred to the census not as *sar-shomari* ("a counting of heads"—the literal translation of the Persian word for census) but as *khar-shomari* ("a counting of donkeys"—a Persian word that rhymes with "heads"!).

A man who would knock on the doors of people in the poorest part of the city on a frozen winter day to carry out a census instead of staying in his warm and comfortable residence would never speak in this way. Later, in his autobiography, he denied this allegation, saying, "I would never speak in this way about the noble Azeris; what can I do if others insist on saying otherwise?" My father was very outspoken and feared no one.

On the day of sacrifice, Eid-e Ghorban,[31] my father would personally buy five sheep in the name of his five children and would send the slaughtered meat in the care of his trusted staff to the Tabriz leper colony so the patients would eat better on that day. I remember returning to Tabriz from Tehran with our driver and his wife while Shajan stayed behind in Tehran. The car got stuck on the heights of Ghaflankouh Mountains and we arrived really late.

When we entered the compound, all the lights were on in the main residence; my father was pacing up and down on the veranda. When I approached to embrace him, he patted me on the back and said, "My child, I was worried about you and, while I waited, I prayed for your safety as well as your companions'."

Our relationship with our father, who was a model of piety, honesty, integrity, wisdom, and love, cannot be adequately conveyed in just a few paragraphs. I never heard him speak a word in anger although he sometimes used to complain about the boys and would jokingly say, "The older they get, the more trouble they are."

---

31. Eid-e Ghorban (Feast of Sacrifice) is the second and the bigger of the two main holidays celebrated in Islam (the other being Eid-e Fitr). It honors the willingness of Abraham to sacrifice his son Ishmael as an act of obedience to Allah's command. Before Abraham could sacrifice his son, however, and in recognition of his great act of faith, Allah provided him with a lamb that he was supposed to kill in his son's place. In commemoration of this intervention, animals are ritually sacrificed. Part of their meat is consumed by the family that offers the animals, while the rest of it is distributed to the poor and the needy. Sweets and gifts are also given, and members of the extended family are typically visited and welcomed.

At home, my father was always peaceful and gentle. Outside the house and especially in the course of his work, he could be tough and authoritative. He had no patience for flattery or standing upon ceremony. His faith was unshakeable and hence he was fearless. When I was very young, Reza Shah made a trip to Fars province, where my father was chief justice at the time. The governor presented him to Reza Shah and spoke of his capability and merit.

Reza Shah then remarked, "I hope he doesn't use these qualities to appeal against my decision if he were to be recalled to Tehran." Apparently, my father then approached the monarch with great respect and said, "Sir, that is not my style; I would never appeal to another out of self-interest." It was at the beginning of Reza Shah's reign and all those present feared the consequences of my father's outspokenness. In fact, nothing happened and my father enjoyed the king's patronage throughout his reign.

Years later, in Rezaieh, a difference of opinion arose between my father and the commander of the army, who happened to be an old friend of Reza Shah. My father formally objected to the overbearing language used by this person in correspondence with him, employing words that only a monarch should use. Seven years later, that powerful commander was recalled to Tehran and my father was promoted to governor of East Azerbaijan and transferred from Rezaieh to Tabriz. The commander was later sent to Khuzestan, a demotion—proof that Reza Shah appreciated honesty and competence in those around him as long as they remained modest and didn't abuse their position.

During the time we were in Tabriz, a crisis developed. In Tehran, there was a shortage of wheat, while we had no such problems in Azerbaijan. The head of the relevant department of the Ministry of Agriculture traveled to Tabriz to supplement the grain in short supply at his end from the stores in Tabriz. My father could not allow this, arguing that he could not risk depleting the food reserves of the people of that province to feed others, not even as a temporary loan. After much negotiation and persuasion by the Interior Ministry in Tehran, the Tabriz reserves were emptied. My father found this hard to accept and repeatedly reminded ministers in correspondence that they had an obligation to return the wheat to Azerbaijan before there was a famine in that part of the country.

A short while later, there was a bread shortage in town and it seemed as if all the promises made by Tehran had been no more than empty words. Autumn arrived and landowners who had private reserves of grain would hide them and hoard their supplies. The people were forced to eat bread made from barley. My father personally inspected the bakeries and bought the same barley bread for us. He was eventually obliged to imprison the hoarders, who could not be persuaded to sell their wheat, even at a higher price.

The bricked-up silos were forced open and the mayor of Tabriz was able to solve the bread problem by buying the grain. Shajan had never trusted the representative who had come to take our grain and even accepted our hospitality. She had always said that he was only interested in solving his own problem and had no intention of honoring his promises. Neither my father nor the mayor had any choice but to obey the orders coming from Tehran. My mother's hunch turned out to be correct.

My Father's Personal Assistant

My father had a personal assistant who was university-educated and very interested in photography. He used to follow us around outside office hours and take pictures that he would then have printed and present to us. His father was a well-known physician and would entertain us at his house a couple of times a year. On those days, they would borrow our head waiter, Bagher Khan, to help out. First there would be an elaborate tea and, after that, dinner would be served; they also had a small Qafqazi (Caucasian) band to entertain us. Holding aloft their small *tars* (long-necked lutes), they would sing Turkish songs in a melodious voice. Alcohol was never served at these gatherings, even though my father did not forbid it; others would respect his wishes on the subject.

Some time ago, this young man called me in Paris from Texas and introduced himself. He had continued to serve during the governorship of my uncle, who succeeded my father; he later moved to Tehran and served in many important positions. Having obtained my telephone number from my sister, Nayer, who lived in Houston, he wanted to acknowledge the gratitude and respect he had felt for the statesman he had worked for in Tabriz. If, after sixty years, my father's assistant could remember his employer's character and personality with such fondness, I am sure he couldn't have been exaggerating.

Getting Bagher Back to Iran

The war in Europe had now broken out. Neville Chamberlain, the British prime minister, was unable to stop Hitler's advance and the people in Tehran would sing this rhyme: "Chamberlain, Chamberlain, is this how you captured Berlin? You dilly-dallied for so long that Warsaw turned into copper" (in Persian, Warsaw also means "tin"). Shajan was concerned about my brother Bagher, who was studying in England, and finally, with the persistence that only she was capable of, succeeded in getting him to Tehran and eventually to Tabriz by way of the Cape of Good Hope. Having developed into an attractive and refined young man, he soon became the apple of the eye of all the ladies who had daughters of marriageable age. Shajan was now happy and at peace. Bagher brought each of us a suitable present; mine was a navy-blue suede handbag with matching gloves, as well as a beautiful scarf.

The Pleasure Gardens of Tabriz and Our Last Visit

The Yam caravanserai and Shah Goli park were among the sights of Tabriz, as well as the private gardens of important landowners and other prominent inhabitants. It was said that over seventy varieties of grapes grew in these gardens. In winter, the temperature would fall so low that people had to cover their ears, hands, and necks with thick woolen scarves and gloves or eyebrows and men's moustaches and beards would freeze. One evening, we were invited to a birthday party at the home of a landowner whose daughter had been my student and later became a friend. I attended the party, accompanied by my parents, Bagher, and Nayer.

My friend, a beautiful young girl, and her mother, a renowned hostess, looked after us splendidly and we had a delightful evening. On our return home, my father paused in the hallway on his way to his bedroom and announced in French, "*Conseil de famille*"—I still remember this phrase after so many years. We all gathered in the small sitting room. My father took out a telegram from his pocket and read it out to us. He had been recalled to Tehran and my uncle, Shajan's brother Haj Ezz al-Mamalek Ardalan, was to replace him as governor of Tabriz. Even Shajan had no prior knowledge of the telegram. My father hadn't wanted to spoil the party we had just attended. He turned to Shajan and asked if she could be ready to leave the following afternoon.

Shajan said that it shouldn't be a problem as we only had to pack our suitcases and that wouldn't take long. We all retired to our rooms and started packing. The following day the local dignitaries who had heard the news gathered in the Alighapou residence to bid us farewell. Akbar Agha was driving the governor's car; my brother and father sat in front and Shajan, Nayer, and I sat in the back—we were on

Houri wears a dress made out of popcorn to a fancy dress party, 1939.

our way to Tehran. The same car brought my uncle, who had now replaced my father, back to Tabriz.

I remembered my father's conversation with Reza Shah all those years ago, about whether he would appeal against the Shah's decision to recall him to Tehran. My father had moved himself and his family from their home and his place of work in the space of twenty-four hours. After tipping all the staff and doormen, when we were in the car, he put his hand in his pocket and counted the money in his wallet. He told us that after years of service, and after having to sell his properties in Hosseinabad and Digizak for a low price, he only had 140 tomans left in cash. Since then the properties increased tenfold in value due to the war.

Bagh-e Ferdows, Shemiran

On arrival in Tehran, we went directly to our house in Bagh-e Ferdows, Shemiran. It was autumn and the people who only summered in Shemiran had already returned to the city. The neighborhood was quiet and peaceful; we knew all our neighbors and were quite friendly with most of them. The grown-ups had a regular gathering every two weeks and my sister and I would occasionally join them. These neighbors were mostly civil servants or people of a similar social and professional background.

Among them was a younger man who had recently returned from France and whose presence was pivotal in making these evenings more stimulating. A pharmacist by

The two sisters (Houri in front, Mehri on the right) and their aunt Valieh Azam, with Aghajan at the Bagh-e Ferdows house.

profession, he and was married with a child, but he had been away from them while pursuing his studies in France. He was intelligent and very capable and years later became the mayor of Tehran. He had a beautiful garden full of flowers that he tended personally. A witty raconteur, he used to entertain everyone with his stories; he would even act out various little scenes for us in French.

I had lived in this house from the age of sixteen when I started at the university. In those days, houses were built with lower ceilings and wall-to-wall windows, but our house was different. It had high ceilings with plaster moldings and tall, narrow windows. There were ancient plane trees on three sides of the garden, which was on a corner site, and we just had one neighbor with whom we shared a wall. Across the street from our garden was the home of a close friend whose daughter Eshrat would accompany us to school each morning.

She was younger than me and maybe a little older than Nayer; her father and stepmother were members of this small group of friends. Mr. Mohammad Mosaddegh[32] had a

---

32. A beloved Iranian politician, author, and lawyer, Mohammad Mosaddegh (1882–1967) served as the thirty-fifth prime minister of Iran from 1951 to 1953. He was a member of the Iranian parliament from 1923, and served through a contentious 1952 election into the seventeenth Iranian Majlies, until his government was overthrown in the 1953 Iranian coup d'état orchestrated by the intelligence agencies of the United Kingdom (MI6) and the United States (CIA). Before its removal from power, his administration introduced a range of social and political measures, such as social security, land reforms, and higher taxes, including the introduction of taxation on the rent of land. His government's most significant policy was the nationalization of the Iranian oil industry. In the aftermath of the overthrow, Mohammad Reza Pahlavi returned to power, and negotiated the Consortium Agreement of 1954 with the British, which gave split ownership of Iranian oil production between Iran and Western companies until

summer residence just below ours on the right-hand side of the steep street where we lived. My father had cordial relations with him and Shajan would occasionally visit his wife. The minister of state of the time also had a large property on the same street where he lived with his Qafqazi wife.

There was a very beautiful building in Bagh-e Ferdows, where interesting lectures would be given from time to time, attended by a large audience. The father of Puri P——, our friend who used to stay with us in Rezaieh and Tabriz, had a lovely garden at the bottom of Bagh-e Ferdows and lived in a modern house.

We were delighted to be living so close to Puri and I have many memories of her and her family. She and her older sister were the children of their father's first marriage. Her father had then married a German lady and had three daughters with her. The second of these three daughters, whom we called Iri (for Iran), was an attractive, slightly chubby girl who loved to chase the many geese they had in their garden. Once her mother told her that, since the geese didn't know her well, they might peck her if she got too close to them. One day Iri got very close to them, extended her hand and said, "My name is Iri P—— and I am very pleased to meet you." We all laughed at her innocence. Both Iri and her older sister Touri were among my bridesmaids. More about this later!

1979. Mosaddegh was imprisoned for three years, then put under house arrest (in his farm) until his death and was buried in his own home so as to prevent a political furor. In 2013, the U.S. government formally acknowledged its role in the coup, as a part of its foreign policy initiatives, including paying protesters and bribing officials.

We spent our student years in this garden and in springtime we prepared for our exams in this same leafy street, often resting under a tree, enjoying the babbling brook that flowed along the street. I always used to long for a spring when we no longer had anxiety about exams. But our life always revolved around exams of one kind or another, and that is still the case, even now.

The winter of 1940 (1319) came to an end. My father was offered several good positions that didn't materialize, including the post of Iranian ambassador to Baghdad in Iraq. My brother Bagher moved to Abadan for his job in the oil industry and I busied myself at home with a translation of Balzac's *Eugenie Grandet*, as well as some short stories that I sent to magazines in the hope that they would be published. My father would often help me with this work. The manuscript of my translation of *Eugenie Grandet* was left behind in my small library in Elahieh, Tehran, never to be seen again. Writing comes easily to me but getting something published was never my main interest. One of the reasons I chose teaching as a career was my dislike of office work.

Shajan's Pilgrimage to Mecca

In the winter of 1940 (1319) Shajan wished to make a pilgrimage to the holy city of Mecca. My father told her that going to Mecca was not obligatory for him because he only had one house in which we lived.[33] Since the age of thirteen, my father had owned several large properties in Savojbolagh (a county in the Alborz province), which he had sold one by one to support and educate his family and to subsidize his government salary. But Shajan had inherited something from her father and the exemption from this sacred duty did not apply to her.

Her journey lasted three months and, while she was away, I, twenty-two years old at the time, ran the house and instructed the cook about our meals. When Shajan returned from Mecca, she had lost several kilos in weight. In those days, this journey was very arduous. My daughter Ladan recently visited both Mecca and Medina in a return trip from San Francisco that lasted only ten days. Nowadays there are luxurious hotels in Medina with first-class service; the images in the postcards Ladan sent might have been palaces from *One Thousand and One Nights.*

Superficial luxury had replaced the simplicity of the past; there was a gap of almost sixty years between these two journeys. A pilgrimage taken by my grandfather, Haj Fakhr al-Molk Ardalan, had lasted nine months and was

---

33. The fifth and final Pillar of Islam is the Hajj, or pilgrimage. During their lifetime, a Muslim is required to make the pilgrimage to Mecca (at least once or more) in the twelfth month of the lunar calendar. Inability to make the Hajj, on physical, economic, or other grounds, excuse the duty of Hajj. The Qur'an specifically says that only those capable of making the pilgrimage are required to do so. The pilgrim, or haji, *is honored in the Muslim community. Islamic teachers say that the Hajj should be an expression of devotion to God, not a means to gain social standing. The believer should be self-aware and examine their intentions in performing the pilgrimage, which should lead to constant striving for self-improvement. A pilgrimage made at any time other than during the Hajj season is called an Umrah.*

quite another story. My father was delighted to welcome back his capable and cheerful wife. One day we had *ghormeh sabzi* (herbs and lamb shank braise) for lunch; my father jokingly told my mother, "Khanum, it is only since your return that our eyes have lit upon *ghormeh sabzi*." I suddenly remembered that, since I didn't like this particular dish, I had organized the menu according to my own likes and dislikes, but my father had never mentioned a word about it!

Another Cousin Asks for My Hand

Shajan had only been back a short while when Shazdeh Valieh, my grandmother, summoned me. As we were taking a gentle stroll in her garden and talking about this and that, she mentioned that my eldest cousin, Malek M——, had asked for my hand. She also added that she was just the messenger. After a long silence, such was my lack of interest, I eventually said politely, "Shajan Vali, years ago relations between us and my dear aunt were soured over a suggestion of marriage. Why start it all over again? Malek is very dear to me, but but, as you know yourself, we don't have much in common." At the time, my cousin had an important position in the Anglo-Iranian Oil Company, which was run by the British, but that did nothing to sway me, and nothing further came of the marriage proposal. Some years later he married a very tall and beautiful young woman and we attended their wedding.

My Father's Posting to the Southern Ports

In the spring of 1941 (1320), Reza Shah appointed my father to a very important post. My father was to represent His Majesty in the southern ports and carry out a thorough inspection of all the far-flung and forgotten areas, then prepare a comprehensive report and proposal for their improvement. Shajan accompanied my father in a new royal-blue Buick, driven by our Assyrian driver David, to this remote posting. David had been our driver in Rezaieh; he was very intelligent and an accomplished long-distance driver and the perfect person to have on hand.

The trip lasted three months during which much was uncovered about Bandar Abbas, Minab, and other ports; a complete report was prepared. My parents had many stories to tell about these far-away places. Life was basic and the climate very hot. Dates were a staple foodstuff. According to David, the local people would climb straight up the date palms and pick the fruit for their daily meal. They would then jump into the water to cool off.

They were completely cut off from what was happening in other parts of the country. The day my father arrived in Port Tiab (near Minab), accompanied by his entourage, the locals gathered around his car with amazement, having never seen one before. My father would ask them many questions and the answers he received pointed to the total isolation of these parts from the rest of Iran. On one occasion someone said to my father, "Please convey our regards to Naser al-Din Shah." This reference to the former shah, who had died in 1896 (1275), was not a joke; that is the absolute truth.

Radio broadcasts had recently started but the network was still very restricted. These far-flung ports on the Persian Gulf were in a complete time warp and implementation of my father's recommendations, together with Reza Shah's foresight, went a long way to remedy the situation. The fierce heat of these areas caused my father to fall ill on his return, in spite of Shajan's tender care; it was the first time I had seen my father take to his bed in a long time.

Reza Shah's Departure

The events of August–September 1941 (Shahrivar 1320) were sudden and catastrophic for us. The Russians, or more accurately the Soviets, attacked from the north while the British advanced from the south, sinking the few warships owned by Iran. These unwelcome and uninvited guests also brought with them the Americans, who had begun to provide assistance to the Allied forces.and didn't want to be left out of the plans for Iran. The following is a true story related by my friend and Parisian neighbor Hamideh A——, the daughter of the late Foroughi;[34] she told me this story in a café in Paris.

---

34. *A writer, teacher, diplomat, and politician, Mohammad Ali Foroughi (1877–1942), also known by his title Zoka al-Molk (Sun of the Realm), served three terms as Prime Minister of Iran. His three-volume* Evolution of Philosophy in Europe *covers the works of European philosophers, from the Seven Sages of Greece in the seventh century* BCE *through to Henri Bergson in the twentieth century.*

"I was not yet married and living in my father's house in Sepah Avenue. My father was the head of a large family and, although a high-ranking government official, he was not very rich because he had to support an extended family of twenty-seven people! One day there was a knock at the door, and it so happened that I was the one who went to open the door. I noticed Reza Shah's black Rolls-Royce in front of the house and our visitor was none other than the Shah himself. His Majesty asked about my father; I invited him into the house and my father soon presented himself. Reza Shah said to him, 'I am leaving the country; this is what has been decided. But I leave the crown prince and Iran in your capable hands; take good care of both.'"

The Young King

With Reza Shah's forced departure, the country he had worked so hard to improve collapsed and his previously defeated opponents gained in strength. The rivals started attacking each other and, almost immediately, Russian and British forces appeared in Tehran and the border towns and practically took over the government. Food and other supplies that had been scarce now became practically non-existent. Hoarders, who were always looking for an opportunity, began to stockpile sugar and wheat, the staple foodstuffs of the poor. Long lines began to form outside bakeries.

The crown prince succeeded his father on the shaky Iranian throne and was to be sworn into office at the Houses of Parliament. My father, as a former governor, was among those in attendance; it was still warm but everyone was obliged to wear full formal attire, including embroidered jackets. Our RCA radio was working but the reception was quite weak because of the distance from Shemiran to the capital, so we all accompanied my father to town.

Shajan's aunt, Princess Afkham al-Molk—the daughter of Prince Fakhr al-Dowleh and the granddaughter of Mohammad Shah—lived adjacent to the Houses of Parliament in the Loghanteh Gardens with her two sons. She read all the newspapers and was very knowledgeable about politics. After my father had been dropped off at the Houses of Parliament, we went to Shajan's aunt's house without a prior invitation to listen to the Shah's speech on her radio. I was about the same age as the young king and had recently graduated from the university; I listened with great attention to the speech, which had been drafted by Foroughi.

This was the first time I heard the expression "social justice," and it reminded me of the writings of Jean-Jacques Rousseau. The twenty-two-year-old king spoke in a trembling voice: the son of Reza Shah could never be a dictator, he said. After taking the oath and swearing on the Qur'an, the new shah departed, and we accompanied my father to Shemiran. Pahlavi Avenue (or Vali-e Asr Avenue, as it is known today) had very little traffic then. When we reached what is today Vanak Square, two young Russian soldiers who were armed with guns and riding a tank blocked our passage and made it clear that we could not pass beyond that point.

My father, having spent five years in St. Petersburg, tried to speak to them in Russian and explained that we lived in Shemiran, but to no avail. The soldiers made it clear that we could instead reach home via Gholhak. My brother Nasrollah was driving; he tried to get us home via the Old Shemiran Road, but we were stopped by British soldiers. At least it was possible to have a conversation with them, though we were forced to go to the British embassy for permission to pass. My brother drove us back to town yet again; this time we went to my grandmother's house while Nasrollah went to the embassy to get a pass. The weather was still warm and my father, who was suffering in his starched collar and thick embroidered jacket, asked his mother-in-law's permission to remove his jacket and collar.

My brother finally returned with the pass and we got back to Bagh-e Ferdows via the Old Shemiran Road. The reason I relate this incident in such detail is that I have told the story many times and remember it well. The young king had just spoken of freedom of expression and speech; very soon there were tens of new political parties and newspapers representing them. The opposing sides started a smear campaign against each other and their opponents, including my parents.

The occupying armies stayed for many years in Iran. Thanks to them, five thousand sick Polish men and women were sent to our country and typhus was the gift we received in return. Many Iranian physicians died of typhoid fever while tending to these patients. Many Polish women also married our young men. My father's report on the southern ports, and his practical suggestions for improving the lives of their inhabitants, were completely forgotten.

He had no more work. The presence of foreign armies in Iran and the chaotic political situation due to successive changes of government deeply upset my patriotic father. It was at this point that he decided to write his memoirs. He stayed home and poured out his heart in his book. No one could entice him away from this work and he was his own boss. The first volume of his autobiography was completed in Aban 1321 (November 1942); in those days, autobiography represented a new literary style in Persian letters.

The Effects of the War upon Iran

We were not directly affected by the war but its consequences could be seen everywhere. Our railroad system deteriorated under the occupying Allied forces. This railroad network had been constructed by Reza Shah with his authoritarian powers and paid for by a tax levied on sugar and widows' pensions. When the foreign troops left after many years, they left behind a worn-out rail system and very few cars, all past their useful life. Second-hand American clothing found their way to middle-class shops and, while my family never looked at mass-produced clothes, there was no doubt that they were very popular. The "new rich" replaced the "new poor." Now, as I write these lines, history is repeating itself. We each have a turn and the drama of the creation continues.

Our Life in the War Years

We entertained on Fridays with an open house for all our friends and relatives. In winter, few families lived in Shemiran and, for our visitors from the city, an open fire-place, hot tea, and cakes were very attractive. Whenever my father grew tired of writing, he would go for a walk, sometimes as far as Vanak. He would visit his brother who lived in the city and with whom he had a very close relationship, and we would then have an opportunity to see our cousins. My sister Mehri had given birth to her second son the previous spring; Khosrow was seven years younger than his brother Faramarz. My brother Bagher returned to Tehran after working in Abadan for a while and started work at the Water Company.

The holy month of Ramadan was almost upon us. My parents and us girls observed our prayers and fasted, but the boys didn't. My father would gently tell them, "Pray and fast even though we will not be buried in the same grave and I don't like to insist." During this month, the routine of lunch and dinner would change to *Sahari* and *Iftar* (a meal before sunrise and one after sunset). My father was responsible for waking the cook to prepare *Sahari*, since he would stay awake all night and then go to sleep after his morning *namaz* (prayers).

My brothers would attend *Sahari* out of respect for our parents. On the *Ahya* nights (during which special prayer ceremonies are performed and it is believed that sins are forgiven and supplications accepted), we would be woken before *Sahari* to read the Qur'an. We would all gather and repeat the prayers after my father. I remember this ritual from childhood, especially when the boys were noisy and disrupted the peace. My father would be reading the prayers and then in a louder voice would say, "Silence!" Being the youngest at that time, I imagined the word "silence" to be part of the prayer and I would repeat it too. This repetition of "Silence!" would make everyone laugh, including my father. Ah, the world of childhood!

The fact that we fasted did not stop us from playing tennis during Ramadan. In fact, we seemed to play even better, having lost a little weight. In winter, we would ski. The best woman skier in those days was Khadija, who came first in all the competitions; I came second. Another pastime was movie-going, and I would often relate the entire plot of a film for my father, an exceptionally attentive listener, unlike Shajan, who was always in motion and couldn't be relied upon to listen carefully unless we really needed her advice on something.

Shajan and our aunts were obsessively neat and clean. From the time she woke up for morning prayers until she retired to bed, she would be supervising the servants and inspecting the house. The two garden gates, one large and one small, and the entire garden had to be swept and tidied twice a day—once in the morning and again in the afternoon, except in winter. Autumn doubled the work because of the falling leaves. My father would jokingly say about the zealous housework, "Khanum, these carpets will curse us for sweeping them so often." Actually, this came to pass—but that is a story for later.

There were many arguments in our house. The older, devoted servants who had always been in the family had died or were doing so well that they were living independently and had their own businesses. The old *lalleh*s and wet-nurses had been replaced by new people, who did not have the same ties to our family.

A Teacher's Work is so Little Respected

When I started teaching at Nourbakhsh High School in 1942 (1321), being a teacher was well respected. University graduates who had majored or minored in education or psychology would be employed on *Rotbeh-ye Dabiri* (government pay scale) 2 at the Ministry of Education, and those who wanted to enter the Civil Service would start on *Rotbeh* 3. During the time of Reza Shah, it was preferable to teach rather than have a desk job. Our salary was 25 percent higher and we had three months' summer vacation as well as the Nowruz holidays. High-school teachers, especially in twelfth grade, taught only twelve to fourteen hours per week since they had additional work at home marking papers and preparing for lessons. Unfortunately, these privileges were later cut and fewer people wanted to enter the profession. As a result, the standard of teaching deteriorated.

In our high school there were some remarkable teachers; one of them was my friend Shayesteh Sadigh. She later obtained a PhD and went to live in Paris with her daughter and never returned to Iran. We had highly respected teachers in math, physics, chemistry, Persian, and Arabic. Later, the profession was so downgraded that very few university graduates chose it as a career. Years later, when I was teaching at the National University of Iran, I would ask my students how many of them planned to enter the teaching profession. Not one person would raise their hand; they were all aiming for better-paying professions. What a pity that those who could not get any other job would turn to teaching as a last resort—we saw the results in due course. A teacher who cannot make ends meet and has to find other means to support their family cannot be the best inspiration for young people.

The Foundations of the House Are Crumbling and Khajeh[35] is Concerned about the State of the Veranda

I am going to finish what I have to say about the how education is regarded today, and not wait for the right point in the chronology of my story. Our youth start their education with their mothers and then their schoolteachers. Whatever profession young people choose to follow in the future, whether it is the army, the civil service, business, or another career, they have no choice but to pass through the educational filter of a teacher. How can an unhappy teacher who has no faith in their own work be entrusted with the education of our children? These days, the real teacher is TV, video games, and electronic gadgets. Maybe this subject is taking me too far away from the topic in hand, but I find it hard to remain silent when I witnessed the decline of education in my country with my own eyes.

Students with postgraduate degrees in languages were incapable of writing a few lines without errors. The salary of a high-school teacher is lower than a secretary starting work at the entry level. They changed the employment laws and if you attained *Rotbeh* 11, your salary was only 4,000 tomans; this for someone who needed to be an Einstein in math, a Malek al-Shoara Bahar in literature, and with published research in physics or chemistry. At

35. Khajeh *is an honorific used across the Middle East, particularly for Sufi teachers. In Persian, it can be translated as "lord" or "master."*

Detail from a Tehran University student association photo in 1939. Seated in the front row, Mehri Mostofi is fourth from the left and Houri is on the far right.

the same time, a young girl, recently employed, would be found sitting behind a beautiful desk in a plush office just to make appointments for her boss, who himself was not much to speak of.

When I was teaching at Nourbakhsh, the classrooms and desks were of a much higher quality than at the university, where there were metal chairs and cold, soulless classrooms, rarely cleaned. I saw how the garbage would pile up outside the rooms and I once saw the wife of a janitor at the university spread her baby's diapers out to dry on the handrail of the staircase. The dean did not even care. He was just concerned about his own position. Toward the end, this negligence and carelessness had grown to such an extent that I once entered the dean's office and addressed him angrily, saying, "Why don't you take a walk outside this office and see what is going on?" In response, he invited me to have a cup of tea; I left his room in tears. Was all this really the Shah's fault?

Part Two

Marriage, Children, Travels, and Work

(1942–1978 / 1321–1357)

Houri and Mohsen Moghadam's wedding photo, 1943

Something unexpected happened in the winter of 1942 (1321). My classes usually started a little later on Wednesdays and I was taking my time to get ready. Shajan was on her way to the city but she suddenly returned home after only fifteen minutes, accompanied by a few others. I didn't see who they were but I could hear their voices. As usual, the maid went to the living room with a tray of tea and Shajan asked me in a loud voice to bring cakes and cookies for the guests.

As I entered the room, I saw a young man sitting on the sofa; he was handsome with big blue eyes. There were several older men on the other side of the room talking to Shajan as well as one of my mother's distant relatives. Introductions were made and I acknowledged each one of these gentlemen with a nod and, after placing the cakes and chocolates on the table, I left the room. As I was about to leave for school, I saw that Shajan and the guests had moved to the garden. I waved goodbye to them from the veranda and forgot about the incident.

Two days later, on a Friday, I had a movie date with Bagher and Nayer. We were just getting ready to leave when two Chrysler cars, one pale green and the other cream, drew up to the house. As I looked out of my bedroom window, I heard the doorbell ring. The occupants of the two cars, all men, entered the house and went straight to the living room. My father was busy writing in his own room; he had just started the second volume of his memoirs.

It seemed as if Shajan was taken by surprise, even though we had an open house on Fridays. The men were again accompanied by Shajan's relative. I was a little annoyed that these unexpected guests were about to upset our plans, so we left Shajan with them and prepared to take our leave. I went into the living room and, quickly nodding to the guests, I whispered in Shajan's ear that we were about to go to the movies. Shajan didn't react and so we headed off to the city without further delay.

On our return home, I noticed that Shajan was visibly upset and reprimanded us for leaving her alone with a group of men. In the same breath, she volunteered the reason for the visits. She told us that this was a merchant family with two grown-up sons and they were looking to purchase a house in Shemiran. Our relative had been their guide and had accidentally run into Shajan; hence the first invitation to come in and have a cup of tea.

I was thinking, "OK, the first time was an accidental meeting; what about the second visit?" Shajan confessed that the young man with the blue eyes had taken a fancy to me and had asked for my hand. Caught unawares, it dawned on me that this was becoming serious. I told Shajan that I was not interested and it would have been better to politely refuse the gentlemen. Shajan kept insisting that I should consider the proposal and I kept resisting.

Soon after that, I was told to expect a visit from the women in that family. I begged Shajan: "You receive guests regularly on Fridays; this is just one of those Fridays. I am neither accepting a ring nor am I prepared to promise anything. I will participate in the gathering simply because I am a member of this family and I live here."

Shajan wanted to present a splendid spread for tea and needed to buy baguettes for the sandwiches. These were almost impossible to find because of the war and the presence of the occupying forces. So instead she made various sandwiches with *lavash* flatbread. The tea table and the sandwiches really caught the eye of the father of the family, who was very complimentary about them. All the guests were accompanied by their wives, but I stayed away from the living room. My father was present this time.

After a while, Bagher and I entered the living room. I shook hands with everyone and took a seat next to the young daughter of the family called Ezzat. Beautiful with thick black hair and fair skin, she had just finished eleventh grade and was between Nayer and me in age. The mother was taller than her husband and was wearing a black chador; the grandmother was also present. Shajan had at first mistaken the grandmother for the wife of the head of the family. The young man with the blue eyes was accompanied by one of his cousins, who was apparently a business partner of his father's. There was no mention of a ring or an engagement at this introductory meeting. It appeared that Shajan had made them aware of my reaction. The day ended uneventfully.

Mohsen Moghadam, 1943

The following day, a Saturday, my future husband, Mohsen Moghadam, accompanied by his grandfather, who was the head of the family, turned up at our house early on a cold winter morning. I behaved like a detached observer, listening to everything as if they were talking about someone else.

They invited us to their home in the city; they lived at the end of Dargahi Street, off Sepah Avenue. I didn't plan to attend this visit and stayed home. They were apparently surprised at my absence and sent my young suitor to invite me to join them. By the time Mohsen drove all the way up to Shemiran, I could not very well refuse. I was received very warmly and, once again, I sat with the young daughter of the family. Fate had already decided my future.

The Day of the Wedding Ceremony

On 7 January 1943 (17 Dey 1321), I sat at the *aqd* table facing a copy of the Qur'an, the *aqd* mirror and candelabras, and the union of two recently acquainted young people was consecrated Shajan had bought the fabric for my wedding dress from Mecca. My veil was provided courtesy of my uncle Aligholi Ardalan, who was the Iranian chargé d'affaires in Paris. The veil was purchased by his wife, Mehri Khanum, who had then asked Dr. Iran Alam to bring it to Tehran. Made from a delicate fabric, it was eight meters long and five meters wide. The dressmaker Ounanian, famous for being the dressmaker to Queen Fawzieh, made the dress. The witnesses to our marriage were Haj Mohtasham Saltaneh, the leader of the House of Representatives, and Mr. Saheb Ekhtiar, a prior governor of Fars and minister of war. Looking back, it feels as if I just went along with all the arrangements that had been made. This is the absolute truth.

My mother's side of our family were in mourning because my aunt Valieh Azam's husband had recently passed away after a serious illness. So on my mother's side only the younger generation attended, together with Mehri Khanum, my uncle's wife, and my uncle, who had been recalled to Tehran from France. Many dignitaries attended our *aqd*, including the prime minister of the time, Ahmad Qavam, and some of the cabinet ministers.

My mother was very innovative and didn't like to copy what others did. The *aqd* cloth was spread on a table that was placed in my now empty bedroom; she believed that, if the cloth were to be on the floor, then the Qur'an would be at the feet of the bride and groom and this she didn't want this. There were two comfortable chairs for us and the guests were seated behind us, in rows and without crowding us. The room was out of bounds until the start of the ceremony, and everything proceeded in an orderly manner.

The *aqd* mirror, which was round and with a silver frame, later served as my dressing-table mirror; the candelabra were of a modern Danish design—made of crystal with five branches and in the art deco style. Made by the jeweler Reuben, my wedding ring was platinum with diamonds all around and was considered very original at the time. All this was chosen by Shajan and paid for by the groom in a tradition that still holds. We had invited friends and many guests from my father's side of the family.

The tea table was set up in the large dining room and the service was elaborate. We were getting married oblivious to the war that was escalating in Europe. There was a small hitch at the signing of the *aqd* agreement, of which I was unaware at the time. I did notice, however, that Shajan was not quite herself and behaving a little more coolly than at the beginning of the day. The reason was a secret that had just been revealed. She had discovered that the father of the groom had two wives!

In those days, bigamy was not illegal, but the practice was frowned upon on both sides of my family. Shajan was a modern and forward-thinking woman and was very sensitive to certain issues. Mohsen said in his father's defense that this should have no bearing on our future life, to which Shajan replied, "The apple doesn't fall far from the tree." I sensed that she regretted the speed at which events had taken place, but she managed to keep quiet about her concerns.

There was an interval of eight months between the *aqd* and our wedding reception. This was supposed to be an opportunity for the young couple to get to know each other. We continued to live in our separate homes but we were free to see each other. Mohsen knew that I was keen on sports and enjoyed riding, skiing, swimming, and tennis; he had even shown my photograph albums to his parents. He bought himself ski equipment and decided to accompany my brothers, my sister Nayer, and me to the slopes. On one of these occasions, he twisted his ankle and, as a result, spent a few days in bed. I went to visit him; this was the second time I had visited their home and it was an opportunity to get to know his younger sister Ezzat.

Nowruz 1322 (1943) was upon us. Many gifts arrived from the groom, the most beautiful being a four-piece set of jewelry in gold and miniature pearls. A famous Armenian jeweler had first made a set for Queen Fawzieh, including a large brooch in the shape of a four-leaf clover, a wide bracelet, and a pair of four-leaf-clover earrings. He later left Iran and settled in the U.S.; many tried to copy his work but never achieved the same level of excellence.

Mohsen was young and industrious—that was his capital. There was a big age gap between my father and Shajan, who believed that when a man and woman were the same age, they would grow together as a couple. She sometimes complained that my father had had his fun and seen the world before they married, whereas she hadn't.

From left: Pouri Pirayesh, Mohsen, Houri, and Nasrollah at the Lashkarak ski resort in northwest Tehran, 1943

Trying Times

One evening Mohsen was driving north from Lalehzar-e Now (New Tulip Field) Avenue and I was in the passenger seat. A drunken British soldier threw himself at our car, which was moving quite slowly owing to a blockage in the road, while another soldier opened the door on my side. The car in front of us had stopped, waiting for the road to clear. I was wearing a white fur coat; maybe the sight of a well-dressed young woman had attracted their attention. Mohsen, in one move, struck the second soldier such a blow that he fell to the ground. Stepping on the accelerator, he

Front row from left: Mehri, Shajan, Aghajan, and Nayer. Back row: Gholamreza Safinia, Houri, Bagher, Luigi Formenton, Chloe Formenton, and Nasrollah, 1944

moved off sharply, saving us from that situation. I have since learned to always lock the car from the inside.

Another time at Ferdowsi crossroads, an American soldier wanted to attack us but, since the doors were locked, he was unsuccessful.

Mohsen was a sensitive and moody young man; whenever he was upset about something, he would sulk and remain silent. He confessed that he had a habit of sulking, even as a child, when he would hide in his aunt's attic. Sulking is a form of protest and I was twice the victim of this silent treatment in those eight months. It doesn't matter who was at fault. When two young people from different backgrounds want to start a life together, there will inevitably be some friction.

One day we went to visit my aunt Valieh Azam. Now on her own after losing her husband, she lived in a beautiful house with a daughter from her first marriage. Mohsen came to collect me. On the way back, I was a little subdued—maybe reflecting on my hasty decision to get married—and I suddenly burst into tears. Mohsen stopped the car and said, "It is clear you are not so happy about this union. If you are truly unhappy, I am due to go to India on business and we can quietly separate before I go." I was shocked at his frankness and said nothing. He dropped me at our house and left. Two days passed in deafening silence. The matter was eventually resolved through the intervention and diplomacy of our respective mothers.

My future husband started to think about providing us with a home. His family built a two-story house on a piece of land in Dargahi Street, opposite the home of my in-laws. I was able to shape the building to my own taste with the help of Mr. Edward Aftandelian, the architect who had designed my sister Mehri's house. He introduced us to his cousin, Eugene Aftandelian, who had recently graduated from the École des Beaux-Arts in Paris and who contributed to the design of the house. He performed a near miracle simply by eliminating a few doors, changing the fireplaces, and introducing a design in the art deco style. Our house soon became the talk of the town!

He designed the furniture for the bedroom, living room, dining and family rooms, and commissioned Deghat Furniture Makers to make them. After more than half a century, art deco is back in fashion again. This furniture

From left: Nasrollah, Houri, Shajan, Nayer, and Mohsen, 1945

was priceless, although we didn't appreciate it at the time. I was busy with the interior of the house and Mohsen was responsible for supervising the building work. I chose all the colors and fabrics; we collaborated really well and the result was that this new house became a beautiful home.

The Wedding Reception and the Start of Our Married Life

It was 15 August (24 Mordad); the invitations to the gala dinner had gone out some time before. Two separate rooms, one for the men and one for the women, had been prepared for the groom's family and our grandmother Princess Hajieh Valieh, who was meeting the groom's family for the first time. But the younger generation and my family, who were no longer in mourning for my aunt's husband, moved freely between the two rooms. The party went on until the early hours of the morning. The orchestra was a band called "Jolly Boys," who played on the large veranda overlooking the garden.

Finally, after midnight Mohsen and I were driven to our newly decorated house in the city. The following day there was an afternoon reception at Mohsen's family home across the street from us. Afterwards everyone came over to our house for the grand tour and all they could talk about was the beautiful furniture and decor. We had a cook called Ibrahim and a maid by the name of Soltan, who was Kurdish. Occasionally, Shajan's wet-nurse, Ahujan, who was also Kurdish, would stand in when Soltan had a day off so I wouldn't be left alone with with the cook, Ibrahim.

Witness to a Secret Meeting

One morning, Mohsen dropped me off, as usual, across the street from the high school where I taught, opposite the Russian embassy. As I waited for the traffic to slow down before crossing Hafez Avenue, I noticed a black Rolls-Royce with Churchill, Stalin, and Roosevelt in the back pulling up to the Russian embassy. I was astonished because there had been no mention on the radio or in the newspapers of the arrival of the heads of three such important countries. When I returned home for lunch that day, I related the incident to Mohsen. Disbelieving, he asked, "Are you sure you weren't dreaming?" The following day, after the three leaders had left Tehran, the newspapers wrote about the Tehran Conference. Sometime later, a film was produced about this historic and secret meeting, the beginning of which I had personally witnessed.

The New Bride

One day, Mohsen asked me if I knew his friend Abolhassan E——, who had been a student at the university at the same time as me. I said that we had not been in the same faculty but I knew of him as he had been in charge of the faculty yearbook. Mohsen said they had been classmates in high school and had run into each other the previous day. Apparently when his friend noticed Mohsen's wedding ring, he had congratulated him and asked whom he had married. "My wife is Houri Mostofi," was Mohsen's response. "Oh yeah? And I suppose I am engaged to the Shah's daughter!" said his friend. These are my husband's exact words, expressing pride in the reaction of his friend to our union.

My father-in-law always paid me compliments and would often say, "You are in a different class from other women; you are an educated lady." I was pleased to be loved and respected by my in-laws and I loved my two sisters-in-law as my own sisters. I was not the Shah's daughter but possibly, at that time, I was like a princess to them. While there was not much socializing between the two families because their world was so different from ours, there was always mutual respect.

Our First Child

At midnight on 12 May 1944 (21 Ordibehesht 1323), God gave us a daughter, born in Bank Melli Hospital, whom we named Mariam. We had prepared a beautiful room for the baby on the second floor of our house. Soltan was in charge of her care but we were so obsessed with this first child of ours that she never left our sight. Everyone loved this newcomer. She was a beautiful girl with large brown eyes and lots of curly brown hair. In the same year, the Allies defeated Hitler's Germany, Mussolini's Italy, and faraway Japan. Mariam's first birthday coincided with the end of the Second World War and we took this as a good omen.

About this time, Mariam's Uncle Reza, Mohsen's brother, left for America; he was the first member of this family to go to the U.S. for his university education, accompanied by two second cousins. Mohsen was instrumental in sending Reza to America; some years before, their eldest cousin had gone to Germany, returning to Iran with an engineering degree and a German wife. Mohsen had to persuade his father to cover the expenses involved for Reza; the two brothers were very close. Reza was away for eleven years and visited Iran only once during this time. In those days, it was not customary for students to return home each summer.

Our Son, Iraj

Mariam was almost two years old when God gave us a son we named Iraj. Sadly, this child only lived for one month; he had a hole in his heart that hadn't closed at the time of his birth and the best doctors were not able to save him. Mariam would pray every morning at breakfast for her little brother to recover, but even the prayers of this young child had no effect. Losing Iraj was a terrible blow for me. On the first night, my husband reminded me in a harsh tone that Iraj had gone and would never come back; we had to go on living and look to the future. From that point, I learned to control my feelings.

The next day, my father-in-law came to visit as I was saying my evening prayers. In order to console me, he related a story from the Prophet Mohammad. Apparently, the Prophet had asked God to give him a child and then take it away, since the loss of a child was so very painful that enduring it carried great spiritual merit. Shajan and my brother Bagher were away in London, while my sister Nayer was studying in Edinburgh. My father and sister Mehri were a great support during this time, but the shock was such that it turned part of my hair gray overnight—at the tender age of twenty-six.

I have to confess that I wasn't too happy to have had two pregnancies so early in my marriage, but when Iraj was born, in Najmieh Hospital, I was so overjoyed that I couldn't sleep a wink that night. I said to myself that we now had a daughter and a son and it would suit me fine not to become pregnant again. Maybe I was being punished for this negative thinking. We never truly appreciate the blessings of our life. When I see what an effort it is for some women to conceive, it makes me realize that we are not the decision makers in our lives. These days science has advanced in this area, providing fertility treatment for couples who can't conceive, but not without its own problems. In French, there is an expression that roughly translates as "Everything has its pros as well as its cons."

Mariam

Mariam was three years old when I left her in the care of Miss Mary, after visiting all the kindergartens in Tehran and on the advice of my friend Puri. Mariam was the first Iranian student to register at this small nursery school. The three- and four-year-olds were looked after in two separate rooms in the basement of Miss Mary's house in Sefarat-e Faranseh (French Embassy) Street. The other children were mostly from diplomatic families. Miss Tamara and another lady whose name I have forgotten were in charge of these two classes.

Mohsen would take Mariam to school in the mornings and bring her home at lunchtime; we still only had one car in those days. He was often late picking her up and Miss Mary and her husband, who didn't have children themselves, would take Mariam to their home on the upper floor of the school. Mr. Yervand Pezeshkian, Miss Mary's husband, would often joke with Mariam and say, "Your father's car is no good and has broken down." But Mariam would defend her father, saying, to everyone's amusement, "It's your car that's broken; my father drives the best car!"

That same summer, Mariam woke up one morning with crossed eyes. There was an eye specialist in Shemiran who prescribed glasses, and since there were no unbreakable spectacles in those days in Iran, we mailed the prescription to her uncle Reza in the U.S. and he sent her the proper glasses. The day I had to accept this reality was a difficult one for me. That year we were spending the summer at my parents' house in Bagh-e Ferdows. All day I held back my tears, thinking that no one would want to marry a girl who wore glasses. At lunchtime, my nephew Faramarz, who was about thirteen at the time, came to console me, saying,

"Houri *Joon*, don't worry. I promise you that I will marry Mariam myself." I couldn't help bursting out laughing. Destiny helped these two, however, and fifteen years later, his promise became a reality.

Ladan

Mariam was four years old when God gave us another daughter, whom we named Ladan. She was a beautiful child with large blue eyes. As it happened, we were again staying at my parents' that summer and the baby was born on 11 July 1948 (20 Tir 1327) at Najmieh Hospital. Mohsen left after three weeks for his second trip to Europe. Shajan, who had just returned from a trip abroad took charge of looking after the baby. Once when she was bathing the newborn, she noticed what looked like a small pimple. Dr. Sheibani, whom Shajan knew and trusted, had recently returned from London and we made an appointment to take Ladan to her. The doctor diagnosed this small pimple as a fistula and told us that dealing with it surgically was a simple matter. However, as Tehran did not have a a clean enough water supply, she was concerned about the aftercare.

Ladan was three months old when we left for Geneva, planning to go from there to Hamburg to have the operation. My husband had naturally approved of this trip and had sent me the necessary invitation. However, his family were not too happy about it. When I handed my father-in-law the letter from Mohsen, he said, "Houri Khanum, you have made up your mind to leave and there is nothing we can do to stop you." In reply I said that, while traveling with two small children to foreign lands was not ideal, the baby needed the operation and we had no choice.

Tehran–Rome–Geneva

We flew with Scandinavian Airlines, or SAS; the Swedish air hostesses were lovely and caring. Ladan was brought into the plane in her beautiful bassinette, which I had decorated myself with lacework. Unaware that there was an economy class, I had bought us expensive first-class tickets; as a result, we were very well looked after. Our destination was Geneva, but we had to spend the night in Rome and continue to Geneva the next day on a different plane. One of the passengers, Mr. Ghashghaie, who was traveling with his family, recognized me and expressed his warm regards for my father and my eldest uncle, saying in his inimitable way and with great humility, "I am the servant of your father and uncle." I thanked him; in return I said I would be happy to help him fill in the necessary landing documents as he could only speak Persian.

At this moment, one of his daughters, who was unusually thin and pale, fainted. The hostess reclined her seat and put an oxygen mask over her face to ease her breathing, saving her from a difficult situation. Mr. Ghashghaie was very grateful and asked me in Persian how he could express his gratitude to the two air hostesses on the plane. Glancing at his two daughters, I noticed that they each had several bangles on their wrists. I suggested giving each of the air hostesses one of these gold and pearl bangles, for which they would be very grateful. So, each young girl removed one of her bangles and gave it to one of the hostesses.

That night we stayed at the Hotel Quirinale in Rome and arrived in Geneva the next day. Many people had come to meet the Ghashghaies; Mohsen was also at the airport. On arrival, the customs officers wanted to charge me a tax on Ladan's small blanket because it appeared new to them. I explained that, as the baby was only three months old, her blanket hasn't had a chance to look worn yet. Finally, they charged me 20 francs for the silver box I had with me. Mr. Ghashghaie offered to take us to the city in his car and to stay at the Richmond Hotel as his guest. I expressed my gratitude for such generosity and introduced Mohsen to him, who said that he was actually staying at the same hotel and already had a car ready for us.

The Richmond Hotel

We all headed toward the city. It was the beginning of autumn; the leaves on the trees were just turning gold and a cold wind was blowing. Mohsen had a suite at the hotel with two interconnecting rooms. After the first night, I decided that I didn't want to leave the two children alone in a separate room and it was, in any case, more economical to have only one room. Ladan had her Moses basket and the hotel staff brought a cot for Mariam into our room. Now, I am not sure if it is a good thing to be always saving money for your husband!

Of course, it was with Mohsen's approval, and we were, in any case, not staying in the hotel for long. In those days, service in in European hotels was always superb. There was a woman attendant on each floor at night and, when we left the room for dinner, whether in the hotel or in a restaurant elsewhere, she would take care of Ladan. Naturally, we would tip her well. In the evenings we would go with friends to restaurants and night clubs and enjoy music, dance, or comedy acts. Mohsen left for Hamburg on business after a week and, as I would be staying on in Geneva with the girls, we moved to a boarding house.

La Caille

Our friends had suggested I leave Ladan in a daycare nursery. So, we visited a few places with Mohsen. But I found it hard to leave my beautiful daughter with strangers just so I could enjoy myself. In addition, I was her mobile restaurant and she needed her mother! So, we moved from the hotel to La Caille—a boarding house in a very good neighborhood. This establishment was managed by a Swiss lady who had two members of staff—an Italian couple. The wife looked after the cooking and cleaning and the husband would serve the food at mealtimes in his white jacket. Not only was there no equity between their respective workloads, but the husband often used to raise his voice to his wife.

During this time, Mariam was very good and would help with the baby, whom she loved dearly. She may have experienced some jealousy at the beginning, but she now knew that we were a family and was a real help.

One day I wanted to buy a new coat as it was getting quite cold. I had made a new Iranian friend, who was a very experienced with children. I left Mariam and Ladan with her for a short while to go shopping. In my absence, Ladan had woken up and created quite a fuss. My friend had managed to calm her down. On my return, she told me that my older daughter had acted in a way that was truly responsible and mature, since all the time her little sister had been crying, she had tried to calm her down and kept apologizing to my friend.

At the time, Mariam was only four and a half years old, and not many children would have been so well behaved at that age. This quality of consideration and helping others is part of Mariam's nature. After one month in this boarding house, our visas were ready and we were able to join Mohsen in Hamburg.

Hamburg

It was toward the end of 1948 (1327); Germany was going through a very difficult post-war period. Food was expensive and scarce. As visitors, we had privileges that were not available to Germans, no matter who they were.

Our German nanny, Sister Hannelore, was a trained children's nurse and I cannot praise her enough for the responsibility and care she showed toward both children. She stayed with them in a very large room with an attached bathroom and we had our own room. We also had a private dining room where we would eat our meals. In those days, an American dollar was equivalent to 25 German marks, and overnight we were considered millionaires in this city that had been practically destroyed by the Allies' bombs.

In Hamburg we met many Iranians who had suffered in the war—previously successful businessmen who would turn up for meals at our table every day, uninvited. After I arrived with the children, this practice gradually came to an end. Hannelore would eat at the table with us and was very happy to do so. In the evenings, she would repair her white shoes and darn her white stockings. She would do all the laundry and ironing for us and the children. In those days, there were no washing machines; whenever we told her that she didn't have to wash our clothes and that there were people in the hotel who would do this, she would reply, "The most important thing is that you have soap; otherwise washing is a simple matter."

My fur coat, which I had lost en route, found its way to Hamburg after having traveled through northern Europe, and we had to go to the airport to collect it. I had sewn some dollars into the pockets of the coat and sealed them; the money was untouched when I got the coat back. I was almost happier to have recovered the dollars than be reunited with the coat itself. When the dollar fell in later months, the exchange rate was 20 marks. We bought Ladan a pram and the nanny would take the girls out every day for a walk. We made friends with the Vladi family, who knew Mohsen. Mrs. Vladi was German and spoke Persian fluently but with a Turkish accent. During the week, she would take me around Hamburg where the reconstruction work was noticeable from one day to the next.

We visited a hospital just outside Hamburg to attend to Ladan's problem. On the first visit, as the taxi drove through the city, I saw the destruction on the streets. The specialist we consulted was called Dr. Jung and the operation was successful. The doctor spoke a little English and explained how the wound had to heal without stitches. Our nanny would stay with Ladan at the hospital during this time while Mariam and I returned to the city. Soon I learned how to make the long journey by train and to recognize all the stations along the way. The food they used to serve Hannelore in the hospital was a mixture of potatoes, cabbage, and carrots; the sweetener was also artificial. It was superior to the food we were served at the boarding house.

On Saturday nights, when the hotel chef had a night off, we were served a cold dinner. As I was breastfeeding a five-month-old baby, I was always hungry and not able to eat the cold food. So, one evening Mohsen and I went instead to the famous Alsterpavillon restaurant, where we were greeted by a maître d' in tails, who presented us with

Houri with Mariam, Ladan in pram, and Sister Hannelore

the menu. Mohsen asked him to bring us the best dish on the menu and the maître d' recommended the steak tartare. Little did we know that this "best dish" consisted of raw, lean ground beef.

He then stood over us to hear our compliments about this exceptional dish. We toyed with the accompanying toast, butter, and egg yolk, but our Persian reserve did not allow us to return the food, which was inedible. We had escaped a cold meal for this! We should have trusted our own judgment and ordered our usual dishes, or at least we should have asked what exactly he was proposing for us. We returned home that night practically starving and satisfied our hunger with apples, bananas, and some chocolate.

A Trip to the Theater

Christmas was near. There was a performance of Humperdinck's *Hansel and Gretel* for children at the Garrison Theater in Hamburg; I took Mariam to see the show. I also bought some chocolates and a bag of oranges on the way. The hall was full of children accompanied by their parents. In the interval I had started to peel an orange for Mariam when I noticed that the children sitting around us were attracted by the smell. I peeled all the oranges and divided them and the chocolates between the children. A lady sitting next to me confessed that, because of the war, these children had never tasted oranges and didn't know what they were.

Houri and Mohsen with Ladan and Mariam in Hamburg, 1948

New Year 1949 (1327)

I took Mariam to the ophthalmologist one day and he prescribed eye drops for her. These produced brown spots on the skin around the eyes that wouldn't go away. Our nanny, Sister Hannelore, assured us that these spots would disappear with a solution she would get from the ophthalmologist. And she was right.

We were due to go to Zurich for the New Year 1949 (1327). We had brought some small presents of chocolates, cookies, cigarettes, bananas, and oranges for our Iranian and German friends as well as the staff of the small hotel where we were staying. We distributed them for the New Year, along with bouquets of flowers, all of which were very well received. Food was the most welcome present in Germany at that time. We were able to shop at the American stores using our dollars, while the residents of Hamburg did not have this privilege.

One of our German friends invited us to spend the day on his houseboat. His wife had prepared a delicious dinner using great ingenuity despite the food shortages. The shortage of soap and shampoo forced the ladies to wash their hair only once a month at the hairdresser. This surprised me since Germans were well known for their cleanliness. In due course, the shortages disappeared and life started to get back to normal. In Iran we never suffered from shortages, which were all because of the war. I often wondered what German people on a lower income must have had to cope with if this was the state of affairs among our wealthy business associates.

Another German friend invited us to dinner at the Rathaus (City Hall) restaurant in an old and beautiful building. Forty-three years later, in the spring of 1992, I went to Hamburg to attend a wedding. It seemed to me that, in the intervening years, Hamburg and the City Hall had somehow lost their integrity. There was a hamburger and hot dog stand catering to tourists in front of that beautiful building—in sharp contrast to my earlier memories of the city, in spite of the damage it had suffered during the war.

Back to Work at Nourbakhsh High School and a Clash with the New Principal

I had sought permission from the Ministry of Education to be absent for four months; this counted as sick leave. It was the only time in thirty-nine years of teaching that I took such a long leave of absence as my children were conveniently born during vacations. I had also asked my sister Mehri to stand in for me during this time.The day I returned to school after four months away, an incident occurred that is worth relating.

The principal had changed and Dr. Shams al-Molouk Mossahab had replaced Dr. Zahra Khanlari. That day I had the use of our car as Mohsen was unwell and staying at home. As I arrived at Nourbakhsh, I briefly sounded the horn to alert the doorman to open the gates. The doorman had also changed; he peered through the gates and said, "Khanum has forbidden me to open the gates." I asked, "Who is Khanum?"

When I realized he was referring to the new principal by the title "Khanum," I said, "All the ladies here are referred to as 'Khanum' and this enormous gate is for the entry of cars. Please open the gate; I take full responsibility." I entered the spacious school yard and went straight to the new principal's office. We knew each other from Parvin Ehtessami High School, where she had been the principal. We were never close, although I had great respect for this very educated lady who was older than me.

I greeted her and asked, "Did you instruct the doorman not to open the gate?" She replied, "Bringing the car into the school compound is a distraction for the students." I explained that the compound was so spacious and the building so solid that even a truck entering would not cause a distracting noise for the students. Moreover, most of our students were dropped off at school by the latest-model cars and mine would not be a novelty for them.

I then left her office and went to my class. The next day, I didn't have a car and Mohsen dropped me off at school. I saw the principal in the main hall. As I was going up the stairs, "Khanum" called me and said, "Mrs. Mostofi, I don't see your name on the staff list." I politely replied, "I have been a French teacher at the school since 1942 [1321] and just returned from a medical leave to take my infant daughter to Europe for treatment. My older sister, Mrs.

Mehrvash Safinia, has been standing in for me, taking my classes. I have now returned to my post."

The students and staff at the school had been very happy with Dr. Zahra Khanlari and her removal in the middle of the school year was quite disruptive, but I had been absent and unaware of all this. Another time, the new principal created a problem for my younger sister, Nayer, who had just returned from England and was teaching English to the seniors. She was a graduate of the American School and the faculty of literature at Tehran University, having obtained her postgraduate degree at Edinburgh University.

The new principal accused her of having leftist political leanings. My father was so upset by this slander that he made an appointment to see the education minister, Dr. Zanganeh, who had been our professor in law school. The young minister had telephoned our house, saying he would personally go to visit my father on Friday.

Friday arrived. I had gone to Bagh-e Ferdows to visit my parents, accompanied by Mohsen and the children. We saw the driver and the official ministry car with its tricolor flag parked outside the house. Dr. Zanganeh and my father were talking in the living room. Later I discovered that my father had related the incident in detail to the minister and had remarked that "no member of my family could ever be a communist. This new principal is probably very capable, but she is a difficult person and not very diplomatic in her dealings with people. My highly educated daughters work at this school and should be free from such accusations."

Dr. Zanganeh left, expressing his regrets and no more was said on the matter.

The Faculty of Law and Its Teachers

My sister Mehri was one of the first women to enter the law faculty. I joined her the following year, taking advantage of this opportunity given to women. At that time, the Faculty of Law consisted of only three departments and it took three years to complete the course. In the first two years we all took courses in politics, economics, and law and were not separated into our specialties until the third year. Mehri and I had both chosen politics and my sister was graduating that year—I was in the second year. Our regular presence in the class was not compulsory, so long as we completed the course work and passed the exams. This fitted in well with me as it enabled me to continue teaching at Nourbakhsh. We had superb teachers including Dr. Shayegan, Mr. Meshkat, Dr. Zanganeh, Dr. Matin-Daftari, Dr. Mesbah-Zadeh, and Professor Varasteh, our language teacher.

It was in the winter of 1327 (1949) when the Shah was shot during a visit to the university. Luckily, he survived the assassination attempt, but the whole country was in turmoil. Going to the university and teaching at Nourbakhsh was not without danger. The brightest students were recruited by the Tudeh party.[1] There were no text-

---

1. *Formed in 1941, Tudeh (masses) was an Iranian communist party with considerable*

books for the courses and we had to rely on notes dictated by our teachers. These notes were often confusing and the examples—possibly translations from foreign books—were unduly complex, yet there was no reason that they couldn't have been fluent and clear. Notes are like the individuals who write them: some are straightforward, able to convey exactly what they mean, while others digress to the extent that the facts are lost in a morass of detail.

There is an anecdote I would like to relate that was told to me by the university chancellor, Dr. Jahanshah Saleh, about Mr. Meshkat, our divinity teacher, who dressed in an *abba* (a long loose robe) and wore a turban. We all loved and respected him and I never missed any of his classes because I learned a lot from him.

"It was decided that some of the older teachers should gracefully retire," Dr. Saleh told me. "We were planning to hold a reception in their honor, presenting them silver vases and with plaques inscribed with words of gratitude. One day Mr. Meshkat entered my office. He was one of the few teachers who simply came in for his classes and was not usually to be seen in my office. He was not one to waste time in the staffroom or sit around drinking tea and gossiping, and he never asked me for anything.

"I was genuinely pleased to see him in my office; I got up to greet him and noticed that he had a bulky object under his *abba*. In his inimitable way, he said, 'Sir, I have

---

influence in its early years. The crackdown that followed the 1953 coup against Mosaddegh is said to have "destroyed" the party, although a remnant persisted.

heard that you are about to pension off some of the older teachers, and will be giving them each an inscribed plaque and a silver vase. I have brought my own vase to save you the trouble.'"

My Sister-in-Law Gets Married

It seemed that my arrival as a daughter-in-law in my husband's family was propitious. My young sister-in-law had not yet met the groom-to-be chosen by her parents but had agreed to this marriage out of respect for them. A simple marriage ceremony took place in our very large bedroom, which was as big as the living and dining rooms upstairs, in which the men were entertained while the ladies were received on another floor of the house, with its own separate sitting room. Later, a much bigger reception was held in the bride's parents' home, with many more guests.

Traditionally, there would be quite a gap between the religious ceremony and the wedding, as there had been for me and Mohsen, with a period of eight months between the *aqd* and the reception, to allow the young couple to get to know each other more intimately. My in-laws were preparing the trousseau for their daughter. The groom had bought a lovely house in Kakh Avenue and moved from his large parental home on the other side of town to the new house. On the wedding night, at the insistence of the groom's parents, who had strong religious beliefs, the bride

Mariam and Reza Moghadam's wedding. From left: Ladan, Mariam, Reza, Agha Borzorg Moghadam (peeking), Houri, Mehri, and Bagher's wife Assefeh, 1960

was expected to attend the reception at the groom's parents' house wearing a black chador over her wedding gown.

She was very upset by this. Mohsen asked for my help in persuading his sister to agree to this so there would be no disagreements between husband and wife from the outset. I was against the black chador myself, but it didn't seem reasonable to break up a marriage over this issue. I empathized with her and told her that I was on her side since I had entered their family wearing neither headscarf nor chador.

I told her that fanaticism had different degrees and even I, who still prayed five times a day, might appear fanatical and extreme to certain people. I pointed out to her that if she agreed to wear the chador at the reception, she could revert to wearing the headscarf when she lived in her own house. This was something to discuss later with her young husband and not with his family.

Little did I know that, many years later, all Iranian women would become the prisoners of chadors and manteaux (a long coat). Today, women in Iran live as if in the Middle Ages while the younger generation secretly indulges in even the most shameless excesses of the West. In our country, there is no happy medium. In spite of the differences, the marriage between my sister-in-law and her husband has worked out well; their four children are all well-educated and capable citizens and live happily with their families in Iran, Europe, and the U.S.

Ibrahim's Antics

Our cook, Ibrahim, was present at the formal marriage ceremony of my sister-in-law, dressed in an elegant suit and tie. He greeted the guests at the door and guided them into the house. Ibrahim was so excited about this important function that he would tell exaggerated anecdotes about it for a long time afterward. He would say that his right hand was now priceless since it had shaken the hands of so many important people.This young cook of ours was quite a character. He had a day off every two weeks when he would blow his entire month's wages, which was 35 tomans. He would dress up in a suit in order to go to the cinema to watch *Arabian Nights.* Lord only knows how many times he had seen this film. He would then go for to a *chelow-kababi* (traditional rice and kabab restaurant) for lunch and would criticize the waiter if the rice or the kabab was less than perfect or if his after-lunch tea was not freshly brewed.

We had a friendly relationship at home with the staff. I would sometimes ask Ibrahim how he had spent his day off. He would tell me what he did. Then I would ask him why he blew his entire month's wages in his two days off. He would reply: "Khanum, I take orders from you for a whole month; I love to be the one giving the orders on those two days." I realized that he knew the Epicurean philosophy better than I did. Even though I was the one who had studied it, he was the one who actually lived it. I always forgave his mistakes since I knew him so well. He would sometimes draw in charcoal on the walls outside the house—what we would today call "graffiti"—and then I needed to be strict with him.

He had many run-ins with Soltan, the maid my mother had sent with me when I got married. A woman from Kurdistan in her fifties, she had been raised in my maternal grandfather's house; she was practically a member of the family. Ibrahim would make a mask out of watermelon skin and place it on a pole outside her window on the second floor to frighten her. Knowing that Soltan enjoyed sucking the marrow from cooked lamb bones, he would remove the marrow, mix it with large amounts of salt and pepper and then replace it in her bowl of *abgousht* (lamb and chickpea stew) to burn her tongue and throat.

Whenever I returned home, Soltan was always complaining about Ibrahim's antics. When things got really bad, my husband would step in and bring an end to these practical jokes by rebuking him. Soltan didn't live long, however; Ibrahim took great care of her during her final days and would often apologize for his past behavior. Later he got a job at Tehran University and would visit us from time to time. The passage of time and having a family had turned him into a more mature person.

The Death of My Father

My father remained without a post after his return from the southern ports in the time of Reza Shah; as we have seen, he spent his time instead writing his memoirs—the history of the Qajar period. He had an assistant, Mr. Adili, who was one of his devotees and, although employed in the Ministry of Education, was always keen to visit my father and spend time in his company. As the distance between Shemiran and the city was considerable, he would take my father's manuscripts to the publishers and help correct the proofs of the printed version. One day, Mr. Adili came to see my father accompanied by an Egyptian historian. I happened to be visiting with two-year-old Ladan; we have a group photograph taken that day on the steps facing the garden.

On the day of this visit, my father was in perfect health. The following day he attended the big march to celebrate 12 December 1950 (21 Azar 1329) in Tupkhaneh Square,

Two days before Aghajan's death. Aghajan standing with Mr. Adili, Houri, and two-year-old Ladan

dressed in a top hat and tails, and I accompanied him instead of my mother. That is why I remember that day so well. At the end of the month of Safar (9 December 1950) according to tradition, the *nazri* (charitable religious vow) for us five children amounting to 30 kilos of rice and the same amount of *ghormeh sabzi* was being prepared. The martyrdom of Imam Hasan was on 27 Safar; the following day was the anniversary of the death of the Prophet Mohammad and a large amount of *sholeh-zard* (saffron rice pudding) would be prepared for dessert. Shajan had invited many of their friends and family to this ceremony while my father received his guests in the adjoining room.

The next day, the Faculty of Law had invited my father as a speaker on a historical subject about the Qajar period; a large audience had gathered for the occasion. My father began to feel unwell after lunch and we had no choice but to call the law faculty and tell them he had to cancel the engagement. My sister Nayer had left to study in the U.S. some months before, but Mehri and I and our two brothers quickly arrived at my father's bedside. Shajan had called four of the most prominent physicians of the time. My father complained of chest pains and was moaning quietly. We spent the night there with my father pacing the corridor and saying, "It feels as if my heart is being pierced by a dagger."

At dawn, he said his morning prayers. My brother and I drove off to collect two of the physicians, Dr. Azizi and Dr. Ameli, waking them from their Friday morning lie-in. When we walked into my father's bedroom, he was sitting up with perspiration pouring down his face despite the cold weather on that winter's day. One of the doctors listened to his heart and seemed happy; the second doctor took my father's blood pressure. My father started to say, "I have no complaints from my heart, but right now . . ." Suddenly his blood pressure dropped like a stone, from twelve to zero, and he left this world before our terrified eyes. I will never forget that moment.

Very soon the house filled with visitors; family and friends who had heard the news were coming to pay their respects. It was the first death I had witnessed and the greatest blow in my young life. At that tender age, the emotions are very strong. My nervous system had not yet calcified like an old kettle—life toughens you and makes you less sensitive. Our world had collapsed and the pillar of strength for all of us was there no longer. Friday morning, 15 December (24 Azar), we lost our biggest support, though to my amazement, the world continued as if nothing had happened.

After twenty-four hours, the ceremony of the washing of the body took place in our garden, with a special dispensation. The funeral procession went from Sepah-Salar Mosque to the family mausoleum in the courtyard of Shabdolazim,[2] accompanied by large crowds of mourners from all walks of life. The following day, his obituary read: "Abdollah Mostofi died while giving a lecture at the Faculty of Law."

Newspapers and newspaper reporters have a way of making the sweet sweeter and the bitter more bitter so they can attract more readers. And maybe that is not a problem. But my father died in bed early one morning after only fifteen hours of illness. On the day of the memorial service for him, so many people attended the ceremony that there was a traffic jam, according to Mohsen, even though my father did not hold a government post at the time of his death.

Our family mausoleum, where my paternal grandfather and uncles rest, had a small kitchen attached to it that overlooked the Bagh-e Tuti (Parrot Courtyard). It was midday, the muezzin was chanting the noon prayer from the minaret; my father was a man of God and had lived a pure life. His faith was unshakeable and his surrender to the

---

2. *A shrine and Shi'ia pilgrimage site located in the town of Ray (now part of greater Tehran), Shabdolazim contains the tomb of Shah Abdol-Azim, who was buried there in the ninth century. Naser al-Din Shah, Reza Shah, and many other notable Iranians are buried there.*

Almighty was complete. My mother worked very hard to build his burial site, which had pride of place in the mausoleum. She chose a beautiful headstone in a lemon and black two-tone marble on which was inscribed the dates of his birth and death.

Thirty-odd years later, under the Islamic Republic, they dug up the tombs of our ancestors, of my grandfather, Haj Mirza Nasrollah Mostofi, his children, my mother, and my brother, Nasrollah and leveled it with the surrounding courtyard. The beautiful French windows with their lovely stained glass and the ancient headstones were destroyed and I suppose we have to thank them at least for noting my parents' names on a small headstone. The headstones of my grandfather and my uncle Mirza Mahmoud Vazir had the Ya-Sin verse[3] etched on them by a famous calligrapher 150 years ago; all these people were devout Muslims and had led pious lives!

I wish they had saved these artifacts in the museums since the art of calligraphy is dying nowadays. The walls of the mausoleum were decorated with spiritual and religious poetry in beautiful, framed calligraphy in the *nastaliq* style.[4] There were many other mausoleums with even finer works of art that fell victim to the aggression of these so-called

---

3. *With great eloquence, the Ya-Sin surah presents some of the essential themes of the Qur'an—the sovereignty of God; the unlimited power of God as exemplified by His creations; Paradise; and the right path.*

4. *Probably developed from* naskh *(a rounded script in Islamic calligraphy) by scribes from Shiraz or Tabriz between the tenth and sixteenth centuries,* nastaliq *was particularly suited to Persian poetry, and remains widely used in Iran, as well as in India, Pakistan, and Afghanistan, both for written poetry and as an art form.*

men of God and ignorant Muslims! But I am getting emotional again and ahead of myself. The month of Azar was a turning point in our lives; my father had come into the world on the third of Azar and departed on the 24th; at the age of seventy-four.

The Marriage of My Sister Nayer in America

My younger sister Nayer had gone to America in 1950 (1329) to pursue her studies. Shajan received a letter from her one day asking permission to marry a young man from the American South whom she had met at university. Pandemonium broke out. Shajan waved this incriminating evidence of Nayer's betrayal in my face; to which I remarked that the sons of our family had married European and American girls. This was the same thing in reverse.

We were still in mourning for my father and wearing black, as only six months had passed since his death. The young man in question, called Kirk, had been of great support to Nayer at the time of the loss of our father, and naturally they had grown close. Shajan kept repeating that Gorg (very similar spelling in Persian to "Kirk" and meaning "wolf") had stolen her daughter! I wrote a letter to Nayer, consoling her and sent her $200 from my savings. My sister and I had a great correspondence over the years about which you will hear more later.

The Garden of the Tarjomanians

We had moved to Shemiran for the summer in the year 1951 (1330) and had rented a villa in the garden of our friends the Tarjomanians, in which my sister-in-law Ezzat and her husband Kazem had also rented a larger villa. Mrs. Tarjomanian and her husband occupied the third, smaller villa in that compound. They were very kind and loved our children; we celebrated Ladan's third birthday in that lovely garden. I prepared the cakes and sandwiches with the help of this kind lady, who didn't have children herself. The garden was truly beautiful and the gardener, under the supervision of the Tarjomanians, grew varieties of flowers that I had never seen before, such as the delphinium. Kazem would leave for the city in the mornings with Mohsen, who would usually return home for lunch.

Our neighbors were Forough and Jafar Akhavan. They had a daughter named Fataneh, who was slightly older than our two. There was a very large pool and a smaller children's pool in their garden and the three girls, who became very good friends, would play and swim together all summer. We grown-ups, who had known each other for many years, became closer friends as a result of living next to each other in Shemiran. We continued spending the summers in the Tarjomanians' enchanted garden until we moved permanently to Shemiran.

Houri had the outfit of a doll Shajan had brought from Europe copied and made into dresses for Mariam and Ladan, 1951.

A Riding Accident

I turned thirty-two on 19 August (27 Mordad); on that same day, Ezzat gave birth to a little girl called Niloufar and we celebrated with a big garden party to which all our friends and relatives were invited. We had many pastimes in those days. The Kazemis, who lived near us, had a tennis court in their garden and I often used to play tennis with their children. The Akhavans owned a piece of land next to their garden in which they kept horses, and used to go riding early in the morning. I had previously ridden in Rezaieh. Shajan, who had Kurdish blood in her veins, was an excellent rider. My father also used to ride on his farms and, many years earlier, my parents used to get around on horseback, even in the city.

One early morning when I was out riding with Forough's husband, we were galloping across a field near Gheytarieh,[5] when my horse went down and threw me into the harvested wheat. I heard my right arm breaking. Jafar dismounted and when I told him that I had broken my arm, he had no choice but to leave me there while he rode back home and returned by car to rescue me. I could hardly breathe, the pain was so bad.

A doctor was called, as well as an old-fashioned bone-setter from the bazaar, who would reset the broken bone. In those days, some of these simple remedies had truly miraculous results. In this case, however, I had to have a cast on my arm extending from the wrist to my elbow. Luckily, I was mostly left-handed since childhood and only used my right hand to write, therefore I was not too incapacitated and remained fairly independent.

Mohsen could not hide his displeasure, even though I only went riding with his blessing. Accidents will happen; one can break an arm just coming downstairs. One day, he told me, "Houri, once you were a young girl with no responsibilities and you used to go horse-riding; now you are the mother of two children who need you. This kind of sport will inevitably lead to accidents." Not at all interested in sports himself, he perhaps did not understand my

---

5. Originally on the outskirts of northern Shemiran, Gheytarieh is now an affluent and built-up part of Tehran.

need for it. After forty days, the cast was removed from my arm but it was a good six months before I was able to lift anything heavy with that arm and the file was thus closed on my future horse-riding.

The Shah Came to Visit but We Were Out!

Back in Tehran, it was a Thursday and I had just left home to collect the girls from school. On my return, I heard that the Shah had visited my in-laws, who lived across the street from us. The story went as follows. The Moghadam family had ordered a very grand golden door to be made by artisans in Isfahan and transported to Najaf, in central Iraq, as a gift for the mausoleum of Hazrat-e Ali, peace be on his name. One of the Shah's adjutants had already seen this magnificent door, which had been placed on the carpet in a large room at my in-laws' house. The Shah, who had deep religious beliefs, chose that day to pay an unexpected visit to see the golden door... He drove himself, accompanied by the adjutant, parked the car at the top of Dargahi Street and then walked the rest of the way to the house, knocking at my mother-in-law's door.

The old family servant, Masht Abbas,[6] opens the door and pays his respects to the adjutant and, as he later related to us, doesn't pay too much attention to the young man in uniform accompanying him. Then, seeing how the adjutant

---

6. Used as a prefix to a first name, Masht or Mashti, is an honorific used to refer to a man who comes from the eastern Iranian pilgrimage town of Mashhad.

behaved toward his companion, Masht Abbas supposes him to be one of the Shah's brothers. In those days, there was no TV and Masht Abbas did not read, so it took him a little while to realize that this was indeed the king.

His Majesty goes upstairs to the room where the door was displayed; he removes his shoes. He closely observes the fine gold work on the door and admires the calligraphy and poems inscribed in the enamelwork. He then bends down and kisses the door.

While the Shah is putting his shoes back on, Masht Abbas runs to alert the lady of the house of the identity of their unexpected visitor. As the Shah is leaving, Masht Abbas approaches His Majesty and says, "Sire, please stay awhile; tea is ready". Having politely declined the offer, The Shah comes down the stairs, smiling, and leaves the house.

Dargahi Street was almost a private road, since Mohsen's older brother Taghi also lived there. My sister-in-law comes out of her house and pays her respects. There was some graffiti on the outside wall of their house and in large black letters were the words "Death to the Shah, Long Live Mosaddegh." His Majesty addresses Tayebeh Khanum and gently says, "Khanum, why don't you have this cleaned?" My sister-in-law politely replies, "Sire, as you can see, these walls have recently been repainted. This is the work of ignorant children and I hope you will forgive them." The Shah shakes his head and says, "Never mind." The two men then walk along the street while a few of the neighbors come out of their houses to pay their respects.

Then His Majesty gets into his car and drives to the palace, which was quite close by.

During lunch that Thursday, we all spoke about the Shah's visit and how we felt cheated that we were not home on that day and at that hour. I later saw this golden door in Najaf on a visit there; it was one of several magnificent doors in gold and silver and *minakari* (enamelwork), mostly made in Isfahan, which had been donated to this holy shrine.

How Mehri Became a Widow at a Young Age

My sister's husband had been suffering from diabetes for many years—and how he loved sweets! Gholamreza Safinia followed a strict diet; I remember he could only eat bread that was toasted. A so-called healer made him far worse through his unorthodox treatments and then he developed liver cancer. Mehri was pregnant with their third child when she accompanied her husband to England for further treatment. In their absence, I looked after Faramarz and Khosrow since they still had two months to go to the end of the school year. I prepared the spare room upstairs for them; they would go to school in the mornings and return home in the afternoon. Each day they would take a packed lunch to school with them. Khosrow would often lose his cutlery and when I asked him what had happened, he would reply, "Houri *joon*, I put them under the lunch box!" and he would indicate exactly how. Years later, this became a family joke since it was abundantly clear how the cutlery must have gone missing. He is now a renowned orthodontist, and we still laugh together whenever we remember this incident.

We spent that summer at the Tarjomanians' place but Faramarz stayed with Shajan in Bagh-e Ferdows. He was preparing to continue his education in England, and was just seventeen when he left Iran. Khosrow remained with us and became our family's eldest child, since he was three years older than Mariam. I remember many stories from this period. He was naturally a little moody because of the absence of his parents and the departure of his older brother. At the age of ten, he wanted to get into bed with us most nights because he thought he could hear mice in his bedroom. To be fair, the mice may have been real since the house was in a large garden.

We all loved him and both my nephews have fond memories of Mohsen, who was very kind to them. However, Khosrow would sometimes complain in the letters he wrote to his parents. "Is it my fault if Mariam and Ladan don't like cutlet?" he would say, for instance. Apparently, he had a wish for cutlet (a kind of hamburger) and this was his way of expressing this desire.

My sister Mehri stayed in England for seven months and her third son, Dariush, was born in London. They returned to Tehran that autumn while her husband's condition deteriorated. Once, when my sister was out of the house on an errand, I stayed with him. The postman brought a letter, which I handed to the patient, who was in bed. His stomach was very swollen and every now and then they had to extract the liquid. The potions and medications of that fraudulent healer had given him cirrhosis of the liver, although he had never touched a drop of alcohol in his life.

He opened the letter. The Ministry of Justice had terminated his employment at the age of fifty-one by the order of Prime Minister Mosaddegh. The news was the last straw for this honorable and hard-working man. I had never seen his tears until that time; he moaned aloud, striking his forehead, and said, "This is the thanks I get for a lifetime of honest service." It was true that this high-ranking member of the Ministry of Justice was too ill to carry on working, but was such treatment fair and considerate? He had not received any financial help with his illness and now he was being laid off. Gholamreza Safinia died a short while after this, and left my sister to look after three sons aged seventeen, ten, and eighteen months, all on her own.

She inherited a building in Shemiran and a house in the city, together with a huge debt. Gholamreza's burial, funeral, and memorial services were held with all due decorum, after which my sister settled down to raise her children with God's help. Her education came to her assistance. She sold their house in town and paid off the smaller debts she had incurred to pay for the trips to England and the medical expenses. With the balance, she founded a kindergarten and primary school, calling it Safinia School after her husband.

Years later she established a high school in the adjoining property, which she named Abdollah Mostofi after our father. Thousands of young people were educated at this excellent establishment and went on to serve our society. After the revolution, the school had to be renamed and was run by the Ministry of Education of the Islamic Republic.

This renaming is a disease; my father and brother-in-law had both been honest and devout men of great learning. This property was the only inheritance of Gholamreza's three sons, who all went on to become upstanding citizens. My sister devoted her youth and her energy to this work; she was imprisoned in 1979, as were so many other prominent individuals, and her children's rights disregarded. Such was our revolution, carried out in the name of Islam. Shajan was in Europe at the time but she wore black for a whole year after the death of her son-in-law.

A Break-in and Its Aftermath

On the night of 27 October (4 Aban), Shajan had taken a sleeping pill to get a few hours' rest. The household staff were fast asleep, including Reza Khak, the young man from Kerman who worked for us and was now living with his family in the staff quarters on the property. Thieves entered the garden by climbing up some trees and jumping over the large gate at the bottom of the garden. They then entered the living room through the terrace and, with a minimum of noise, took whatever they could of the carpets, silver, and anything of value they could find. These they then loaded onto their truck, which was parked right outside. They must have had ample time because they even helped themselves to the chocolate cake that was in the fridge!

In the morning, when Shajan got up for her morning prayers, she discovered that the living area of the house had been emptied of carpets and ornaments. My father had been a great admirer of Iranian carpets and had commissioned fine and beautifully designed pieces from Kerman and Tabriz for our house in Shemiran. The silverware taken included cutlery, large samovars, braziers, and *ghalamkar* (engraved) trays from Isfahan. Despite wasting many days with the police and detectives, Shajan was unsuccessful in tracking down any of these lost heirlooms.

Ramadan approached and she would often spend the day in the city while she was fasting, returning home after evening prayers disappointed, frustrated, hungry, and exhausted. One evening, after she broke her fast very late, she began to feel unwell and, at the age of sixty-one, she suffered a stroke. The left side of her body was paralyzed. She spent nearly three months at Najmieh Hospital and only came home when she could move independently. But she was no longer the active Mariam Mostofi of yore; she would drag her left leg, and her left arm was practically useless.

The doctors had saved her life and we had to be content with that. Two years passed. The following summer she invited Nayer, her husband Kirk, and their newborn son Jamie (Keyvan in Persian) to Iran. We also moved with the two girls to her house in Bagh-e Ferdows to help with the visitors. All the responsibility rested on my shoulders;

I was on my feet from early in the morning until late at night, even though we had capable staff to help. Mohsen's brother Reza and his ever-expanding family lived separately nearby. We hired a temporary maid for Nayer and her family. Shajan was very fussy even though she spent most of her time in bed. A hairdresser used to come once a week to style her hair and do her nails, and we had to entertain the hairdresser and her daughter, who accompanied her. An endless stream of friends and family came to visit Shajan and later my sister and her family.

The arrival of my sister Nayer was a big event. She had a magnificent wardrobe with matching shoes, bags, and accessories; I used to amuse myself by trying everything on. Kirk was a man of great taste and he still advises on my sister's choice of clothing, although we are all much older now and no longer have the same enthusiasm for such things. Our talented seamstress, Khanum Siran, who had moved to Tehran, copied one of my sister's dresses in a different color for me. The copy ended up being almost better than the original! I have fond memories of this hardworking and talented lady, who supported her only son through her sewing and lived an independent life. She would make the most beautiful coats, dresses, suits, and evening gowns for me and we really appreciated her. A pity that you can no longer find this kind of seamstress.

Shajan's mood improved considerably after the arrival of her youngest child and family. We gave a wonderful dinner party in their honor with an orchestra and all the trimmings. Nayer and I both worked hard for this event, which resembled a wedding. All her friends were invited; we have a beautiful photograph commemorating that night.

Mariam's Eyes

From the age of three onwards, Mariam had worn glasses. A friend of Kazem and Ezzat who was studying to become an ophthalmologist spoke highly of one of his professors, Dr. Z——, and promised that he would be able to correct Mariam's lazy eye with an operation in Tehran. After Mohsen and I had discussed the matter, we decided to trust this young doctor and prepared Mariam for the procedure. It was summertime and we were staying at Shajan's. We went to the city with Mariam, who was now ten years old. She walked fearlessly into the operating theater while Mohsen and I stayed nervously outside.

Suddenly, I heard my daughter scream; apparently the operation was being carried out without general anesthesia. They had inserted a needle into her eye and she had called out in fear and pain. After a while, they transferred her from the operating room to a private ward. My brave Mariam had turned into a hysterical patient who would faint at the sound of the doctor's footsteps in the hallway, perspiration dripping from her fingers. She spent the next few days with one eye bandaged and we invited Reza Khak's daughter Aqdas to spend time with Mariam, reading her books and her favorite stories. Mariam had always been an avid reader.

Aqdas was older than Mariam—a very attractive girl with beautiful long hair. We loved her like an older daughter.

The day arrived for the stitches to come out, and we drove to Dr. Z——'s office in Naderi Avenue, parked the car, and went upstairs to his office. Mohsen stayed with Mariam while her stitches were being removed. Mariam was being brave and remained quiet; I led her down the stairs and we were just about to cross the street when I heard someone saying, "Khanum, the gentleman has passed out." I turned around. Mohsen was lying unconscious on the sidewalk. I abandoned Mariam and went to his side. Fortunately, there was no serious damage; he came to and, with the help of a passersby, I managed to get Mariam and Mohsen to the car.

We drove to my parent-in-laws' house and there Mohsen rested and recovered before we returned to Shemiran. Apparently, he had fainted after witnessing the removal of Mariam's stitches. At the recommendation of the doctor, we made regular visits to Miss Ghahremani, an ophthalmologist, for Mariam's eye exercises. Unfortunately, all our efforts were in vain, and Mariam continued to wear glasses. The school year was about to begin and, with it, all my responsibilities toward our children and my students.

A Visit to England in the Summer of 1955

My closest friend, Noori Ram, was two years older than me and we had married at about the same time. We also each had our first child at the same time; she had a daughter named Shahla whose nickname was Shushu, followed two years later by a son called Shahryar. Noori was a remarkable young woman—peaceful and beautiful both on the inside and outside. One day, her husband, Ahmad A——, mentioned an Englishman called Tufnell who had come to Iran looking for a company with which he could establish a joint venture for a new prefabricated building system. Tufnell visited our house and spoke about the building system at a dinner party attended by Noori and her husband. Ahmad was not interested in this sort of project. With an excellent position at the oil consortium, and a good salary, he was content and preferred an easy life.

Mohsen was excited by the proposal, however, and arranged to visit England to learn more about the project. The conversation turned to Mariam's eyes; I expressed our dissatisfaction with the operation. Tufnell said that he knew and respected Sir Stewart Duke-Elder, an ophthalmologist to Queen Elizabeth; he promised he would speak to him and get an appointment for us. School was over and we set off for Europe for the second time, as a family of four, staying in London at the Cumberland Hotel. In spite of painful memories of her eye operation in Tehran, Mariam didn't mind seeing another doctor about her eyes.

This doctor had consulting rooms in Harley Street and appeared quite old to us. The day we took Mariam to the London Clinic, a private hospital, we had to pretend that we were all going there for a check-up, first the children and then the parents, to make Mariam less anxious. On the day of surgery, the nurse gave Mariam a capsule mixed in a spoonful of honey and they took her into the operating room asleep. There she was given a general anesthetic. When she was brought into her private room, both her eyes were bandaged and she was not yet fully conscious. It was almost evening; I suggested to Mohsen that he and Ladan should go back to the hotel for dinner and rest while I remained at the hospital, sitting in an armchair in the dark.

Mariam was gradually waking up. She asked where she was and I explained that we were in a hospital. She asked what had happened and whether she was about to go in for another operation. I told her that the operation was over; she couldn't believe it and, smiling, asked me, "Mummy, are you telling the truth? I never felt anything and I have no pain." I reassured her that I would stay by her side all night, and she went back to sleep. It was late and I hadn't eaten anything since leaving the hotel in the morning. I knew that I was not allowed to stay the night and so I didn't dare order any food. The night nurse came in, saw me sitting in the armchair and didn't say anything. She asked whether I had eaten and explained that the kitchen was closed but she could bring me some tea and biscuits. I spent that night in the armchair; Mariam woke up several times in the night and would say a word or two before going to sleep again.

In the morning, they served a good breakfast for both of us; Mariam was feeling better. The doctor came to visit her, and I left the room. Mohsen and Ladan had also returned from the hotel. I was concerned about the changing of the bandages, the trauma of the operation the previous year still fresh in my mind. I could hear the doctor and Mariam talking; the door opened and the tall, thin figure of the silver-haired physician appeared like an angel. Taking my arm, he said, "Everything is fine." I mentioned that Mariam's voice had seemed very loud—was she upset? He smiled and said, "You must be joking; Mariam and I are good friends—we were just laughing together." Mariam's recovery was miraculous.

While we were spending those few days in the hospital, we thought about having Ladan's tonsils removed since she was always suffering from tonsillitis. The specialist assured us that she could also have a general anesthetic. The nurse brought the capsule in the honey again and the tonsillectomy was carried out painlessly. We were given a larger room so the two sisters could be together. The staff looked after them well; Ladan, who was almost seven, would read to her sister. We spent a total of ten days in this renowned hospital and I managed to find a few hours of freedom during this time. Mariam loved sharing the ice cream that Ladan was offered while she was recovering.

We returned to the hotel and stayed in London until both girls were well. Meanwhile, Mohsen was totally absorbed in his work with Reema Construction, as the company was called, and he invited Iranian government officials to visit and see samples of the proposed building system, which consisted of entire prefabricated walls made from reinforced concrete with the doors and windows already in place. He wanted to persuade them to adopt this system instead of the traditional brick construction.

Mr. Tufnell who lived just outside London, used to visit us on Sundays. Once he invited us to the countryside for with his wife and daughter and her boyfriend. I was surprised to see how Mrs. Tufnell kept ordering her husband around. The following week we toured Oxford University, of which he was a former student; with great pride he showed us his father's name carved in the list of alumni.

The weather had suddenly become very warm. One day, Mr. Tufnell invited me to Green Park to play tennis. Because of the heat, he was wearing his white shirt outside his trousers. When his wife arrived, she scolded him and told him to "tuck his tail in"! It seemed useless to protest, and he had no choice but to obey. Once the girls and I were invited to their house for tea; a taxi came to collect us. Tea was served in antique china cups that she assured me were 150 years old and had been passed down from her great-grandmother. We were warned by her to be very careful, just in case . . .

Reema Construction in the UK

One day we left London to meet the managing director of the company. The name Reema was a composite of Reed and Malik, its two founders. Mr. Reed was the senior partner; he lived with his wife outside London in the grounds of an old castle. According to him, the building, originally used as stabling for horses, had since been renovated and converted into a comfortable home. They were very proud to be living in such a historic property and showed us around the house. To us, then in our early thirties, they seemed quite elderly though they were probably not much past middle age. They were both extremely courteous and kind and Mrs. Reed treated me like a daughter. I was much more impressed with this gentle couple than I had been our hostess of the previous day, who did not have the same level of refinement even though she was also outwardly very polite and hospitable.

As the weather had turned cooler, I was wearing a blue gabardine suit, tailored by Khanum Siran, and had also brought my beautiful mink stole with me. Full of admiration for my outfit, Mrs. Reed asked if she could try on the stole. We were in her bedroom, Mohsen and Mr. Reed were discussing business in the living room, and the girls were playing. I offered her my stole; she put it over her shoulders and, looking at herself in the mirror, said with great sincerity, "I wish I had something like this." I explained that the stole had come from the U.S. and had been bought by my sister at my request. To myself I was thinking, how come the wife of a successful businessman such as Mr. Reed does not allow herself the luxury of such a garment?[7]

7. *Food rationing in the UK continued up until 1954 and clothing rationing—when buying a coat might have used up a whole year's clothing coupons—lasted until 1949. A parsimonious attitude may have still prevailed, lasting for many years.*

We spent a wonderful day with this delightful and educated couple, during which the girls spoke English. Mr. Reed never came to Iran but his younger partner, Mr. Malik, came for a visit in 1960 (1339) and we gave a dinner in his honor. Our stay in London and Mohsen's business meetings came to an end, and Reema was assured that they were dealing with a capable and responsible young family man.

London–Hamburg

From London, we went to Hamburg in our second visit to this city, scarcely recognizable from how it had been seven years earlier. With no visible signs of the earlier ruins, the German mark was no longer traded on the black market and the exchange rate was now 5 marks to a dollar instead of 25. While Mohsen was busy working, the girls and I visited the city. In the evenings, our friends and acquaintances would invite us to the St. Pauli district with its many cabarets and restaurants. The girls would have dinner in the hotel and go to bed; I no longer worried about them. In those days, there was greater security, a fact that we took for granted.

At the cabarets, Mohsen and I saw transvestites for the first time—men on stage who dressed in women's clothes and were so natural-looking that it was impossible to tell that they were in fact men. Now that I am writing this in San Francisco, it is no longer a big deal. A few days ago, there was an LGBTQ Halloween parade in Castro Street. As I review this material after five years (summer of 2015), men are lining up to marry each other; everything changes with the passage of time. It would be interesting to see what the conservative Mrs. Tufnell would have thought of all this; after our visit to the UK, we lost touch with each other.

The French and Italian Riviera

In the summer of 1955 (1334), we paid our first visit to our Nice for a holiday; the weather was hot, our hotel full of tourists, and the beaches filled to capacity. I wasn't too excited about swimming since the beaches were pebbly, but I had to keep an eye on the girls. Mohsen was napping under the umbrella; little did he know that his legs were gently roasting in the blazing sun. Every now and then he would go in for a dip and then return to his place under the umbrella, which provided only partial shade. In the evening, as he was dressing for dinner, we noticed huge blisters on his knees and had no choice but to go to the pharmacy and get a special ointment for sunburn, which was administered with great care. We returned to the hotel. Mohsen was feverish with sunstroke and had to go to bed.

What a night! A short distance from the hotel, the famous *Bataille de Fleurs* was taking place on the Promenade des Anglais, which had been closed to traffic. Mohsen was resting. I jokingly said, "This is what happens to people who sit under an umbrella and ogle the bathing beauties!" The participants in this spectacular parade were all dressed in white; the girls and I came out to watch. Lovely young women rode in flower-filled floats and the audience showed their appreciation for all this beauty with their applause. Despite spending many summers in Nice subsequently, I have seen the *Bataille de Fleurs* only once since then, when I took my grandchildren to watch the event.

The following day, Mohsen was feeling much better and we decided to do some sightseeing. In the elevator, we met a young girl wearing a black T-shirt and pink shorts; it was the eighteen-year-old Brigitte Bardot, who was just beginning to make a name for herself in the film world!

We had airline tickets for Milan but, not knowing planes would get booked up, we had not reserved a flight and the earliest availability was in fifteen days. As a result, we decided to take the train instead. There was no TGV or Eurostar in those days. It was hot, and when the train went through a tunnel, we had to close the windows or endure an influx of soot and smoke. It was not a pleasurable journey and we arrived late in Milan. We had reserved rooms at the Grand Hotel, which in those days was a four-star establishment. We all took a bath to wash away the dirt of the journey, and as we hadn't eaten a proper lunch on the way, dinner at the hotel that night was most welcome.

The next morning, Mohsen and the girls were ready for breakfast while I frantically searched for my platinum and diamond wedding ring, unable to find it. I asked them to go down without me and leave me to look for it in peace. I wasn't sure if I had left it in Nice or maybe lost it on the train. Upset and losing hope, I bent down to look under the bed, where I found the ring twinkling; I was ecstatic.

A half century later, I ask myself why the loss of a ring could upset me so much; little did I know that the day would come when I would lose everything I had and, more importantly, my country, language, and culture.

Our Italian Friends

We arrived in Milan, the hometown of our Italian friends the Formentons. Mohsen had previously visited Italy on two occasions, whereas I had only spent one night there, in Rome. I knew the Formentons through my husband. Luigi Formenton was an Italian nobleman. Born before the First World War, he had spent many years in Iran and Afghanistan and was an expert on antique carpets. His wife, Chloe, was younger than him and came from Venice; they had two sons, Mario and Fabio. The older boy had been born in Tehran and both spoke Persian. They had lived in Iran for some years, building themselves a beautiful home in an Italian/Iranian style which they had to vacate during the Second World War, since Italy and Germany were fighting the Allies and Reza Shah wanted Iran to remain neutral and stay out of the war, though in the end this was not to be.

Years ago, when Mohsen had first traveled to Europe, he paid them a visit and sent me some presents through them as the Formentons had once again resumed trading with Iran. This is when I first met Chloe, and we became good friends. Ten years older than me, she spoke good French and also a little Persian; her husband had a better command of our language since he had learned it in order to be able to trade in the bazaar. She was a very pleasant, optimistic woman who loved her life and always accompanied her husband in his travels.

Their older son, Mario, married Pucci, daughter of the famous Italian publisher Arnoldo Mondadori. Mario and his wife visited his parents in Iran and stayed at the Park Hotel. We would often invite them to dinner and spent weekends with them in the countryside. Mario and Pucci were a modern and active young couple and we became good friends. A few years later, the younger son, Fabio, who studied at the Razi School in New York, married a Frenchwoman. The Formentons returned to Iran and this time they rented a beautiful villa in Gholhak district of Tehran. Mario, meanwhile, had entered the world of publishing, and eventually took over many of the responsibilities of his famous and wealthy father-in-law after he passed away. One of his ideas was to publish highly illustrated coffee-table books about different countries, including *Persia: Bridge of Turquoise.* Years later, Fabio sent me a copy of this book—but I am getting ahead of myself again.

After arriving in Milan, we traveled to a villa in Cernobbio, close to Lake Como, where we were entertained by Fabio. Mohsen returned to London after a couple of days to greet and receive the Iranian officials who were coming to visit the Reema factories. The girls and I stayed in the villa; Luigi and Chloe also joined us on their return from Iran. In those days, the Venice Film Festival established in 1932, was already famous and I really wanted to visit this unique city. Leaving the girls with Chloe for forty-eight hours, I took a train to Venice and stayed in the Lido.

I remember there were no tickets for sale for the premiere of *Rhapsody*, starring Elizabeth Taylor, and I didn't have an invitation. Fortunately, I overheard someone saying that journalists could enter. I am not sure whether it was the blue gabardine suit again or the French that I spoke without an accent which gave me access. The film was very moving and Venice was unforgettable. I visited the Doge's Palace and St. Mark's Square and fell in love with the beauty and art of this extraordinary city.

On my return, Chloe had found a guesthouse for us in Rapallo. Included in our room rate were a table and chairs on the beach where the girls could play and swim. I watched them from under the parasol, spending my time sewing or reading. In the evenings, the three of us would go sightseeing after dinner; all the shops were open and we admired the window displays. One day Mario and Pucci, who were spending their vacation in the beautiful Mondadori villa in Portofino, invited us over. Mario came to take us in his car and drove at breakneck speed, much to the delight of the girls but to my great consternation.

The whole family was gathered at the villa overlooking the sea built on top of a cliff; the sea and sky were the same azure blue. Pucci was water-skiing and I was watching her from the cliff top when Mario suddenly pushed me into the sea. It was a dangerous prank and he was reprimanded by his wife and mother. Luckily, I was a good enough swimmer to be able to swim back to the beach. After two weeks in northern Italy, we went on to Rome.

Ups and Downs of Life

We were returning to Tehran after nearly three months in Europe. Mohsen was really happy to see us. Apparently, the three-week separation from us when he had been in London hadn't been easy for him; I had never seen him so happy and excited. School was about to start again and life was getting back to normal. It took a long time for the construction project to be approved by the authorities; empty promises and unfulfilled expectations are a part of our Middle Eastern bureaucratic culture. In the end, Mohsen's perseverance and hard work paid off—but that story has to wait until later.

While I was in London, I visited a gynecologist who had been recommended by Mariam's ophthalmologist. I was in good health but had had an unexplained miscarriage two years previously. Mohsen believed that my fall while horse-riding could have contributed to it, although there was quite a time lapse between these two events. The doctor gave me some practical and easy-to-follow instructions that were very useful, including advice to be careful when climbing the stairs. I needed to rest for a few days each month and Nourbakhsh High School kindly arranged to move my French classes from the second to the first floor.

The year 1955 (1334) was coming to an end and Mohsen was working hard to enter into a formal contract with the government. He had invested a lot of money in the Reema project, to which the officials were oblivious, and they continued to make exploratory trips at our expense, often entailing visits to foreign countries that they took just for pleasure.

It was Nowruz 1335 (1956). My brother Bagher and his family were traveling to Europe and my sister Mehri was also away with her two younger sons. I was four months pregnant. The phone rang and I was told that Shajan, who was all by herself with only her staff for company, had fallen in the living room and had been taken to the hospital by my older brother, Nasrollah. You can imagine my state of mind. Because of the New Year holiday the hospitals were poorly manned and I was naturally worried about the level of care Shajan would receive.

On the one hand were my duties as a wife and mother, and on the other my responsibility to my mother, which put me in a tricky position. Should I abandon my sick mother? The girls were not so much the problem as the expectation by Mohsen that I should attend all the ceremonies of Nowruz, including visiting and receiving all the relatives. It was a very difficult time.

Shajan spent four months at the Najmieh Hospital; she was operated on twice within a space of twelve days and had a pin inserted into her useless hip bone—all to no avail. We only found out later that inserting a pin into a softened bone was a waste of time; there were no artificial hips in those days—certainly not in Iran. The site of the operation became infected and things went from bad to worse. My brother and sister had by now returned from their travels, but they were powerless to change events. My cousin Dr. Abol-Ghasem Mostofi, who was a pediatrician, came to visit my mother in the hospital. After examining her and seeing the extent of the infection, he recommended that we should take her home—strange that we had to hear this from his lips and not from the professionals responsible for my mother's care.

Shajan came home and spent the next seven years suffering and bedridden. She lost her independence, and while she never complained, her tears never stopped. Sometime later, Shajan was operated on again in England, in a third surgical procedure. Dr. Fari Safinia transferred his grandmother from London to Newcastle, where the examining physician had apparently asked, "What butcher operated on this lady?" Putting a pin into soft bone had been a disastrous mistake, and to have attempted to do this twice within such a short time! Shajan had lost the use of her left leg, though the doctor managed to get the infection under control—after which Shajan felt a little better.

The Nowruz holidays somehow passed, though I felt as though I had let down both my mother and my husband. I had worked hard to safeguard the baby I was carrying while attending to my demanding husband, who was so easily upset, supervising the schoolwork of my two daughters, and looking after my mother, who lived in Shemiran while we lived in the city. In the meantime, life went on.

The Birth of Hamid Reza

We celebrated Ladan and Dariush's birthdays that summer at my mother's house and returned to the city at the end of the summer. Two days later, on 26 August 1956 (4 Shahrivar 1335), we were blessed with the birth of a son at Dr. Sheibani's hospital—we named him Hamid Reza. Just then, Mohsen was in the process of signing a contract with the Rahni Bank for the construction of a series of prefabricated houses. My sister Mehri and sisters-in-law were waiting outside the delivery room and anxious because the baby was not crying. Dr. Sheibani solved the problem with a gentle slap—we all breathed a sigh of relief.

A few weeks before the birth of the baby, whose gender was not yet known, I went back to bed at dawn after my morning prayers—it was the birthday of the Eighth Imam, Hazrate Reza. I had a dream in which an old man with a shining face and a flowing white beard was telling me that I would give birth to a son. I woke up immediately and remembered my dream. We often dream during the night and forget those dreams in the morning; that is why early-morning dreams are more easily remembered, giving rise to the superstition that such dreams will come true.

In those days, a baby's gender could not be known before birth. I told Mohsen about the dream and suggested that, if the baby was indeed a boy, we should name him Reza in honor of the saint whose birthday it was. Mohsen's younger brother was called Gholamreza and known simply as Reza. To add to this, Mohsen was told about the baby's birth

Hamid's first brithday. From left: Ladan, Mariam, Houri, and Hamid, 1957

by telephone while he was in the office of the Minister of Labor, Agha Khan Bakhtiar (whose first name was Hamid), in the process of signing the contract. We took the event to be auspicious, and therefore decided to include Hamid, which is another name for the Creator, and called the baby Hamid Reza. I was in the hospital for a few more days and then returned home.

I salute women who give birth to many children; these angels devote their youth to pregnancy, giving birth, breastfeeding, and caring for the future generations—it is not an easy task. Men sometimes say that they give birth every day at work; thank God, women now do both—go out to work and give birth.

We employed an experienced nanny for Hamid. She had raised several children in the family of one of our relatives; her husband was also employed at the new Reema factory in Tehran. At this time, Tehran was blessed with a piped water supply and our worries about contaminated water were over. We enjoyed the advantage of this blessing ahead of many others since we lived in Sepah Avenue, close to many of the original royal palaces. Hamid entered a home with two adoring older sisters and enough of an age difference for them not to feel any jealousy toward their baby brother.

The Inexperienced Thief and the Clever Thief-Catcher

A few weeks later, the whole family went off to the countryside for the day. Mohsen decided to join the party, accompanied by the girls, and I chose to stay home with the baby. They returned home quite late after spending the whole day out. Hamid was asleep in his cot in the sitting area of our bedroom; I was breastfeeding him, as I had done with the two girls. The staff were sleeping 'al fresco' in the yard, having locked up the house first. They would unlock the front door early in the morning when they arose. Mohsen had just fallen asleep when he was woken by the sound of a thud has if someone had just jumped into the yard. Looking out of the window, he saw a man crouching under our bedroom window.

He went upstairs quietly and telephoned his parents' house, opposite ours,' asking Masht Abbas and the rest of the family, who had luckily not yet gone to bed, for their help. Within a couple of minutes, they were outside the front door, but someone needed to unlock it to let them in. Mohsen called out to wake up Hakimeh, who had been our cook for a long time, and asked her to unlock the door. She was terrified because she had to pass the burglar to do this. Finally, the door was opened and the hapless thief became the victim of a severe beating at the hands of Masht Abbas.

In the meantime, fearful that someone would take the baby, I pushed his cot into a corner and stood shielding him. Later, I laughed at my own naïveté. Why would a simple cat burglar be interested in a baby? I thanked God that Mohsen and the girls had returned home in time and I had not had to witness this event on my own. Best of all, the thief was an amateur and Mohsen had cleverly trapped him in the yard thanks to the locked door.

The Start of a New School Year

Schools reopened that fall and we signed up Mariam at the Jeanne d'Arc High School. At this bilingual institution, they offered Persian classes in the morning and French classes in the afternoon, a language Mariam did not know. I came to an arrangement with the principal and the French nuns to keep Mariam home in the afternoons for half the school year. I could then prepare her with intensive French tuition so she could join girls of her own age in the French section. Mariam was eleven and knew English; she was somewhat familiar with a few French words through her ballet and piano lessons, but absolutely did not enjoy being in a class with children much younger than herself. I had been teaching French for many years to both juniors and seniors in high school and was familiar with the great literature of France.

I started my daughter off with *Le Livre rouge*, which, in my opinion, is one of the best teaching books for an intensive French class. After four months working with her at home, the nuns tested her in the middle of the academic

Cousins, 1956. From left (facing the camera): Nazi, Pouran, Parvaneh, Nayer, Houri, and Mehri

year. Soeur Claire, who was known to be extremely strict, had no choice but to accept her into the 4A class. In the usual way, children have to complete four years of French at a high level before they enter this class—since each grade was divided into an A and a B stream. Soeur Claire wasn't very happy about upsetting this tradition. Mariam managed to skip the fifth grade and was able to join the sixth grade after completing 4A. She obtained her sixth-grade French certificate from Jeanne d'Arc after only two years!

Mariam and Soeur Claire

Soeur Claire was a favorite with the students, but I felt she resented the fact that Mariam had completed six grades in only two years. In my opinion, flattery never serves the person who is being flattered; worse still, it keeps them unaware of what is going on. This was the situation with Soeur Claire; she was a victim of flattery. One day she called me to her office; this was the first time that I was being summoned for an apparent transgression by my daughter. I turned up at the appointed hour and was told that Mariam was a trouble maker in class with more control over the students than the teachers and school staff.

I asked her if there were any problems regarding Mariam's schoolwork. She replied, "No. Mariam is an intelligent girl but her behavior is disruptive and incites the others to misbehave." I told her that I was a teacher too and I had learned how to manage bright, energetic students. I suggested that they give Mariam some responsibilities in the classroom, saying how I would bring my good students to the blackboard and ask them to write up the lesson on the board or correct the other students' dictation. I supervised what they did, of course, so they didn't abuse their special privileges.

Soeur Claire seemed to calm down at this. I knew that they had a charity drive to help the underprivileged in the winter. I proposed that she should use Mariam's influence over the other students and make her responsible for collecting donations in class. She seemed to like this suggestion; that year the collection from Mariam's class was several times greater than that of the other classes. I was never called to Soeur Claire's office again!

Many of the teachers from Nourbakhsh High School also taught at Jeanne d'Arc. The Persian-language teacher was Mrs. Ehteshami, who was an expert in her field; she was a very good teacher but had a sharp tongue—the students were in awe of her. One day Mariam came home and told me that they had been asked to write a composition entitled "A Comparison of City and Country Life" and that she didn't know where to start. I had never done my children's homework for them although I often steered them in the right direction.

An experienced teacher can always tell the difference between the work of a student and the work of an adult. I made the following suggestion: "Imagine a wonderful goodbye party being given to celebrate someone leaving to go to college in Europe. At the same time, the cook's brother is spending a couple of days in that house, having come from the village to visit his brother for his birthday, laden with gifts for him. Put yourself in the shoes of the villager and describe what you see in the big city from his point of view."

In this way, I started Mariam off and set her imagination racing in an interesting direction; it seems that she wrote an excellent composition and Mrs. Ehteshami praised her for it in class, judging hers to be the best composition that day! The girls would study French and Persian literature under my supervision; their father would help them with their math and religious studies. We had no TV in those days and obviously no computers or internet, so there were few competing distractions at the time.

Inauguration of the Reema Factory in Iran

Mohsen was hard at work getting the new business off the ground; this involved setting up a construction company and a prefabricated-housing factory in Iran. It was the summer of 1957 (1336) and we were spending the summer months in the larger of the three units in the Tarjomanian garden in Shemiran. We also celebrated Hamid's first birthday in this magnificent garden. Mr. and Mrs. Parks from Reema in the UK were our guests, although they were staying in a hotel; I arranged a sumptuous party in their honor.

Mariam was just finishing middle school and we were considering whether we should send her abroad for her high school or keep her in Iran. Mr. Parks accepted the responsibility of being Mariam's guardian in England. We made a trip to the UK to visit a few boarding schools and finally decided that, after she had completed ninth grade, we would send Mariam to a school in Dorset.

My husband had purchased a large piece of land close to Mehrabad airport for the proposed factory and several British engineers had come over to get the prefabricated-housing project off the ground. They put up three model homes in one part of the factory—a five-room, a three-room, and a two-room house were built out of reinforced concreted using this new method. I had the responsibility of furnishing these three units as show homes. Mrs. Tarjomanian assisted me in the sewing of the curtains and, all in all, we spent a very busy summer there.

Toward the end of fall, the factory was to be inaugurated with a visit by His Majesty the Shah and Queen Soraya—a date had been set. The night before the visit, we were invited to a magnificent wedding at the Officers' Club and I wore a beautiful dress made by Khanum Siran. I was ready and waiting for Mohsen to come home and get changed for the party. Mohsen came home, found me dressed and made up, and calmly said, "Houri, tomorrow is a big day for me; I am tired and I want to rest." Naneh, Hamid's nanny was in the room; without a word I turned around so that my back was facing her and asked her to unzip my dress. I understood that he was tired but it wasn't fair to cancel at the very last minute. I don't know why the memory of that night is still so clear in my mind.

The following day, the Reema factory was inaugurated; the girls—aged thirteen and nine at the time—and I were responsible for looking after our royal guests. Everything was ready, the rooms were furnished, the curtains hung. I had spent many days working on this project in addition to teaching school and looking after the home and family. Several security personnel, including Colonel Nassiri,[8]

---

8. Born in 1910, Nematollah Nassiri, a member of the Imperial Guard and the security forces, became the director of SAVAK, the Iranian intelligence agency, in 1965. He was one of the 438 individuals who were arrested and executed in 1979 following the Iranian Revolution.

turned up and dismissed many of the factory employees, leaving only the crane operators and the workers responsible for erecting the walls, plus the British engineers.

Mohsen and his brother Reza, who had recently returned from the U.S., together with the girls and myself, welcomed the guests, including members of the cabinet, the prime minister Dr. Eqbal, General Yazdanpanah, Mr. Agha Khan Bakhtiar, and Mr. Taleghani. The Shah and Queen Soraya arrived in a green convertible Chrysler, unaccompanied by any security personnel or other cars. They inspected the facility; the reinforced-concrete walls with the windows already in place were lifted by the giant cranes and placed on a foundation that had already been poured. The Shah observed this new method of construction with great attention and asked many questions about the details.

There was one amusing episode. Just as the crane was about to lift the concrete wall, the Shah enquired, "How will the wall be installed?" Reza replied, "You will soon see." Standing next to Reza, I gave him a gentle nudge to remind him that one didn't address His Majesty as "you." The correct form of address was either "Your Majesty" or "Sire" and it was customary to refer to him in the third person. We made fun of our Westernized brother-in-law for a long time about this faux pas.

Soon it was time for Their Majesties to visit the show homes; Queen Soraya remarked that they reminded her of Swiss chalets. She was very beautiful and wore a copper-colored suit with a delicate pillbox hat and matching gloves, shoes, and handbag—she had amazing green eyes like bottomless pools. The waiter offered tea and the girls served cookies; they had already presented Her Majesty with a bouquet of flowers. She inspected every detail of the units and asked me many questions.

Time passed very quickly in their presence and the queen suddenly glanced at her watch. The Shah was speaking with the prime minister, other cabinet members, and his entourage were in conversation with Mohsen. Queen Soraya managed to attract her husband's attention and they both prepared to leave. They shook hands with everyone present, and the girls curtsied; at least all the ballet classes had paid off in this instance. The royal couple got into the green car, parked nearby, their only protection a Colt revolver that lay on the seat between them. The Shah was very popular at that time. Three months later, Queen Soraya had left Iran forever.[9]

---

9. Born in 1932 in a British missionary hospital in Isfahan, Soraya Esfandiary-Bakhtiary's father, Khalil, was a nobleman from the Bakhtiary tribe and her mother, Eva Karl, a Russian-born German. Soraya became queen of Iran as the second wife of the Shah, whom she married in 1951. Their marriage suffered many pressures, particularly when it became clear that she was infertile. She rejected the Shah's suggestion that he might take a second wife in order to produce an heir, as he rejected her suggestion that he might abdicate in favor of his half-brother. In March 1958, their divorce was announced. After a brief career as an actress, Soraya lived alone in Paris until her death in 2001.

Preparations for Sending Mariam Abroad

We spent the summer of 1958 (1337) once again in the Tarjomanian compound. That summer my sister Nayer was visiting us from Venezuela, accompanied by her two sons, Jamie and Jan (or Keyvan and Kayhan, to use their Persian names). She had come to visit our ailing and bedridden mother. My other sister, Mehri, had started the kindergarten. Her first students were my nephew Abdi, Nayer's sons Jamie and Jan, and Hamid—the eldest was five and the youngest nearly two years old. The person responsible for running this class at the time was Mariam—truly a family business!

Mariam left for boarding school in England at the end of that summer. Her cousin Khosrow was also leaving, to go to college, and the two cousins flew out of Tehran together. Not having Mariam around was very difficult for me; I was particularly depressed on Friday afternoons and would often cry. I needed time to adjust. Ladan had always done her homework under Mariam's supervision. With Mariam no longer there, the responsibility fell to me.

Mariam would write regularly; her letters were full of humorous observations. She spent her first Christmas and New Year in the home of Mr. and Mrs. Parks. "We have been eating turkey for a whole week thanks to our Christmas Eve meal," she said in one letter. "We started with turkey breast, then we had a pie made up of the bits and pieces; the rest went into sandwiches, and now we are enjoying the poor bird's bones in a soup!" It was all said in jest, for she was clearly happy, and not by way of complaint or criticism.

The Construction of Our New Prefabricated Home in Elahieh

We decided to build a prefabricated house on a piece of land I had purchased from my sister-in-law at Elahieh in Shemiran. My aunt Valieh Azam had donated a 2,000-square-meter piece of land between Fereshteh and Nasser (later called Shirin) streets to her daughter Assefeh as part of her dowry when she married my brother Bagher. He and Assefeh also wanted to build a house; their architect had recommended that they dispose of a part of this rather thin, long piece of land. They kept the piece on Fereshteh Street, a site measuring 1,100 square meters, for themselves and sold the rest to me. Mohsen and the architect Edward Aftandelian designed a home to suit our family; all the walls and ceilings were cast in the Reema factory and the skeleton of the house went up in forty-eight hours on the previously poured concrete foundation.

A Visit to Isfahan

For Nowruz 1338 (1959), I made a trip to Isfahan with Ladan and Hamid, now aged two and a half. We were accompanied by Mehri and Dariush, the only one of one of my sister's sons still living with her in Tehran. Mohsen was on a business trip to England for meetings with his British colleagues regarding high-rise buildings. I had not been to Isfahan for many years, and revisiting a city in which I had spent much of my youth was a nostalgic experience. Among the places we visited, I went to our old house near the British Hospital; sadly the garden was no longer filled with the gladioli and fragrant tuberoses planted by my father.

I bought some items for our new house from the shops in Chahar Bagh and revisited the workshop of an Armenian artist called Sombat. Now middle-aged, he didn't recognize us as we had also changed and were no longer schoolgirls. I bought two original watercolors from him.

He had a habit of experimenting with colors on a piece of newspaper when he was in the process of doing one of his paintings. When the main work was completed, he would make another painting from the newspaper with all the colors on it—his work was quite innovative. I have one of those paintings in Paris; a portrait of a mullah wearing a turban, it is one of a kind. When we returned from Isfahan, Mohsen was also back from Europe and life fell back into its usual routine.

Moving to Our New House

That summer, we moved to our new home in Elahieh and left our little house in Dargahi Street after sixteen years. I had started buying furniture for the new house in the spring of that year. Our old furniture was in the art deco style and fashioned out of the best wood but it all looked rather dated now. So many pieces, good and bad, had been made in that style that it had lost its originality. This time, I commissioned the new furniture from the Youhas and Azimi workshops in Tehran and, guided by my experienced friend Chloe Formenton, I decided to furnish the house in a classic yet contemporary style. She was of the opinion that this would be less affected by subsequent changes in fashion.

Some of the fabrics were sent over from England by Mariam and a huge difference of opinion arose between my husband and me over these issues. He wanted us to furnish the house in an ultra-modern style and to order from a catalogue given to him by one of his friends—who was in fact a dealer of furniture imported from Europe. But I did it my way. We had the curtains made with the help of a seamstress who came and worked for us at home. Once the house was furnished, Mohsen was delighted with the result and many friends copied the ideas used in the decoration.

Mariam was home from boarding school; the pool was ready for use and, little by little, the house was becoming a home. At the end of that summer we organized a large dinner party—at that point we were among the first residents of Elahieh. We had constructed a metal staircase between our house and my brother Bagher's house. He had two sons, Abdi and Ali—the first was three years older and the second six months younger than Hamid. The boys would get together during the summer holidays and swim at our house—our pool had a fence around it, although the boys could all swim well.

Fereshteh Street was quiet in those days with two-way traffic. Our uncle Aligholi Ardalan had built a beautiful home on a spacious plot of land nearby. At that time, it was rented to the Spanish embassy since my uncle was the Iranian ambassador to the U.S. and lived in Washington DC with his family. Living in Shemiran had its pros and its cons. There was no municipal water supply and we didn't have a telephone for a long time; we made use of my brother's phone when necessary. The new house was beautifully decorated and had a well-equipped modern kitchen, with central heating, which made housekeeping much easier.

I still taught at Nourbakhsh High School and, since we had two cars, commuting was not a problem. Shajan was gradually coming to terms with her disability; to help her pass the time, she had a black and white TV set that she would watch, albeit reluctantly. I would visit my ailing mother for an hour every day; I was always concerned about her. I was finally able to persuade her to pay a visit to our new home—I can't remember how she came to accept this invitation and leave her bed and her house for a few hours. Our house was single story and I gave her a tour while she sat in her wheelchair. On her return she sent us her own dining room chandelier as a housewarming present. She replaced the chandelier with a simpler light fitting, although she never set foot in her own living or dining room again. This was her first and last visit to our house; she never left her own house after that date.

Houri, sitting with Hamid, Ladan (left) and Mariam standing

Preparations for My Trip to the U.S.

At sixteen, Mariam had obtained her O and A levels (British high-school graduation exams) within two years and was about to start at university. The plan was for her to enroll at Wilson College, a girls' college in Chambersburg, Pennsylvania, in the U.S. Change was afoot in other ways. As the French language was gradually losing popularity and being replaced with English, our senior French classes in high school were disbanded since the Razi School in Tehran was able to absorb those who were truly interested in studying French. My classes had dwindled to only four or five students, and this wasn't very stimulating for me.

After seventeen years of marriage and successive pregnancies, the responsibilities of life and my career as a teacher had so engaged me that there was no time left for myself—I had gradually forgotten my favorite pastimes of reading, sports, and skiing. I still played tennis with my young friend Shirin K—— until she had a car accident and became severely handicapped. At that point, I stopped playing tennis. In those days, high-school teachers were able to take advantage of a Fulbright scholarship and visit the U.S. for an intensive six-month course of study in their chosen field. It occurred to me that an intensive course of study in the States would make me a better teacher of the English language. I wanted my second foreign language to be at the same level as my French and I needed further education to achieve this. Mariam's departure to the U.S., along with my unfamiliarity with the American education system and my decision to become a teacher of English, led me to take part in the Fulbright examinations.

Mrs. Farrokhrou Parsa, the principal of Nourbakhsh High School at the time, sat next to me in the exam as she also wanted to apply for the scholarship. I completed the test and handed my paper in. A short time later, I found myself accepted among the first ten of 500 applicants. We also had an oral exam, which took the form of an interview in English. I was asked whether I had relatives or friends in the U.S. I replied that I did. When asked for a name, I mentioned my uncle. When asked what he was doing there, I modestly replied that he was the Iranian ambassador in Washington. There was silence followed by a smile on the face of the interviewer. A short while later, I received a letter from them informing me that I had been accepted.

At the time, Mohsen was deeply involved with Reema. They were building several hundred single-story units in the Kan district of Tehran for the Rahni Bank. I informed him about the scholarship; he made no objection—maybe he agreed that I also needed some time off. That summer, we spent many happy times together as a family under the pergola by the pool.

To help with the work in the garden, a young man was sent from the Reema factory who had worked on the construction of our house from the start and had been responsible for the storage of all the building materials. In later years, I brought him into the house to help with cleaning. He was bright and dutiful, and I gradually taught him to cook and bake cakes. Years later, he learned to drive while he was doing his military service. I taught him, and he was a very attentive student. Gradually, I taught him to read and write and would use the quiet hours after supper to work with him. He was able to pass the fourth-grade exam. He was loyal and hard-working; he later married his cousin. I will talk about him again—his name was Ghasem.

Our life looked very good on the surface, but in fact Mohsen's intense involvement with work was gradually creating a distance between us. The return of Mohsen's brother Reza gave fresh support to my husband. Soon, I began to feel like the third party in a marriage and I felt uncomfortable about this sense of estrangement. I was happy that my husband's family was growing in number owing to many suitable marriages and I considered them as my own brothers and sisters. In fact, because my husband was happier being with his own family, we used to spend much more time with them.

It was not easy for me to leave the home and family that I had worked so hard to build, even for six months. It was hard to be away from Ladan and Hamid, who was only four years old at the time. So, this trip was not planned on a whim. There were many causes which led me to go to the U.S. to study.

I had been feeling unfulfilled for several years after the birth of Hamid. If it hadn't been my love for my children and the family circle, it would have been difficult to continue living with a spouse who paid little attention to his partner. I don't want to point a finger at my husband; I am sure he would have had much to say on his own account as well. Our biggest problem was the deafening silence between us. What had originally attracted Mohsen to me now lay at the root of his dissatisfaction.

The sporty young woman of earlier years had now left all her activities behind. Even though my husband never voiced his disagreement, in practice he was unwilling to share or go along with my interests. I had promised myself at the start that I would let my husband rule the house in order to avoid argument and discord. And that is what I did, but silence and a reluctance to discuss our problems or find solutions gradually developed into a tumor whose malignancy threatened the health of our marriage. Mohsen expected more than I was able to give; maybe he took advantage of my fears. When I observe marriages in America today, I am amazed at the strong position of women.

Queen Farah Pays a Visit to Our School

It was around this time that, following the divorce from his second wife, Soraya, the Shah married a young girl, Farah Diba, from a prominent Iranian family. My sister Mehri was invited to the wedding. Iran was filled with joy at his event. One day, we were told that the young queen would be paying a visit to the Reza Shah Kabir School, which we still affectionately called by its old name, Nourbakhsh. Our twelfth-grade French classes were still being held; I had a small classroom on the top floor with around fifteen students. I hadn't been given any special duties in relation to the queen's visit; that day we were studying one ofVictor Hugo's poems, "Après la bataille." One of my best students had written out the poem on the blackboard; just then the queen and her entourage passed by my classroom.

Queen Farah visits Houri's French class at Reza Shah Kabir High School (Nourbakhsh) with principal Mrs. Farrokhrou Parsa

One of her ladies-in-waiting, Banoo Diba, recognized me and nodded a greeting. The queen entered our classroom, followed by Mrs. Parsa, while the rest of the group stayed outside the glazed doors. We spoke for a while and she asked the students some questions. This was the first time I had seen Her Majesty up close and I was touched by her youth and simplicity. I was surprised at my own colleagues and especially the principal, whom I considered a friend, not to have included the only French class in the royal itinerary. I have a beautiful photo of that day that I keep as a souvenir. In life, things often happen unexpectedly.

A Trip to Abadan

At Nowruz 1339 (1960), Mohsen was away in England; my brother Bagher was also abroad on business. I joined Assefeh and my nephews, together with Hamid and Ladan, on a trip to Abadan and we stayed in the guest house of the Oil Company. We visited Kharg Island accompanied by Jamshid Amouzegar, minister of agriculture at the time, and his wife Ulrike. In the afternoons, we swam and snorkeled—the water was so clear and clean that we could easily see the coral reef and the fish.

One day, Ulrike came out of the sea with her leg bleeding badly; she had been attacked by jellyfish without realizing. She was hospitalized and had to have stitches in her ankle—she spent the night in the hospital. We returned to Abadan by plane and she joined us the following day. Jamshid Amouzegar had no children and was very drawn to Hamid, who was four at the time.

An Audience with His Majesty at Sa'dabad Palace

One morning, I was informed by the Ministry of Education that I would be presented to the Shah that same afternoon along with other Fulbright scholars. The presentation of top students from the universities and high schools had long been planned but Dr. Mahmoud Mehran, the minister of education at the time, had decided at the last minute to

His Majesty and Houri at the gathering of Fulbright scholars, 1960

include Fulbright scholars in this gathering. That same afternoon, we were presented to the king at Sa'dabad Palace in Semiran. I stood among my own group on one side of the hall, but the main event, speeches and, formalities took place at some distance from us. The photographers were busy. His Majesty started walking toward us after the speeches were over. Dr. Mehran followed the Shah, giving explanations and introducing each of us. The Shah shook hands with us and expressed his satisfaction.

The next day I went to Naderi Street to have my watch repaired. The two daily newspapers, *Kayhan* and *Etelaat*, were on the jeweler's counter—he kept glancing from one of the newspapers to me and back again. I couldn't understand his curiosity and the reason why he was looking at me so intently. Showing me the front page of the newspaper, he asked if that was indeed me in the picture. I glanced quickly at the paper and, sure enough, there was a picture of me shaking hands with the king, with Dr. Mehran standing next to him, while another lady stood by me, waiting her turn. I replied that, yes, it was me, but that I had no special role in the ceremony. Later, I sent a clipping of this newspaper to my sister Nayer in Venezuela; she luckily saved all the letters and newspaper clippings I had sent over the years and returned them all to me after the revolution.

My Trip to the U.S.

At the beginning of September 1960 (Shahrivar 1339), I was ready to leave; Mariam was also leaving the following week to begin her studies at Wilson College. Thirty Fulbright scholars were traveling together to the U.S. I will never forget Hamid's beautiful face pressed to the glass at Mehrabad airport; he was more interested in the planes than he was in my leaving. But it broke my heart and I couldn't help the tears as they spilled down beneath my sunglasses. Most of the young people in our group were flying for the very first time and it was an important and exciting experience for them.

We had a short stop in Paris and arrived in New York late at night, where we stayed at the New Yorker Hotel. I hardly slept that night and the following day, after breakfast, I called one of our relatives who lived in New York. He and his wife invited me to spend the weekend with them. That afternoon I accompanied them to Tenafly, New Jersey. In the interim period, I had toured Manhattan and was most impressed by its grand scale. I visited the shops on Fifth Avenue and decided that I would not accompany the group but would join them on the first day of orientation and the start of the program.

The University of Michigan, Ann Arbor

The participants in the Fulbright program were from all five continents. Numbering in excess of 600, we were all being sent to different states. I was sent to the University of Michigan in Ann Arbor in the company of two young Iranians, together with a group of thirty students from Japan, Chile, Brazil, Austria, Ecuador, Turkey, and Argentina. Traveling in a large and well-equipped bus, we started our tour with a visit to Niagara Falls and all the cities and states on route to our destination, where we were put up temporarily in a hotel while accommodation was being arranged for us.

My hosts were a family whose son was away at college in another state; I was given his room. They were a very kind couple and invited me out to dinner on the first evening—which is when I had my first taste of the famous American hamburger. I had already tried frankfurters when I was in Germany; here they were called hot dogs.

These two dishes carry the names of the cities where they originated—Hamburg and Frankfurt. American cuisine is made up from the food of all five continents; every nationality that emigrates here brings their favorite dishes with them. After a period of ten days, I decided to find myself a room in the graduate women's dormitory and left my hosts with many apologies. I did, however, keep in contact with them and we corresponded for many years.

Mary Markley Hall

This was a state-of-the-art building situated on campus, close to all my classes. Graduate students occupied this dormitory and we took all our meals in the enormous cafeteria. As a result, I didn't have to waste any time shopping or preparing food. My room was at the end of a long corridor. Since term had already started, the other rooms were already filled. My roommate was a young girl by the name of Marion Blizzard. The daughter of a successful physician in Philadelphia, Marion was the only child of a well-to-do family and had attended private schools since childhood, where she had always worn a uniform.

It was surprising that, coming from such a conservative family, this rebellious young girl was determined to go in the opposite direction to her parents. I came to realize that the reason she had no roommates was her difficult behavior. Our room was not large but well equipped, with desks, bookcases, and closets, in addition to the beds;

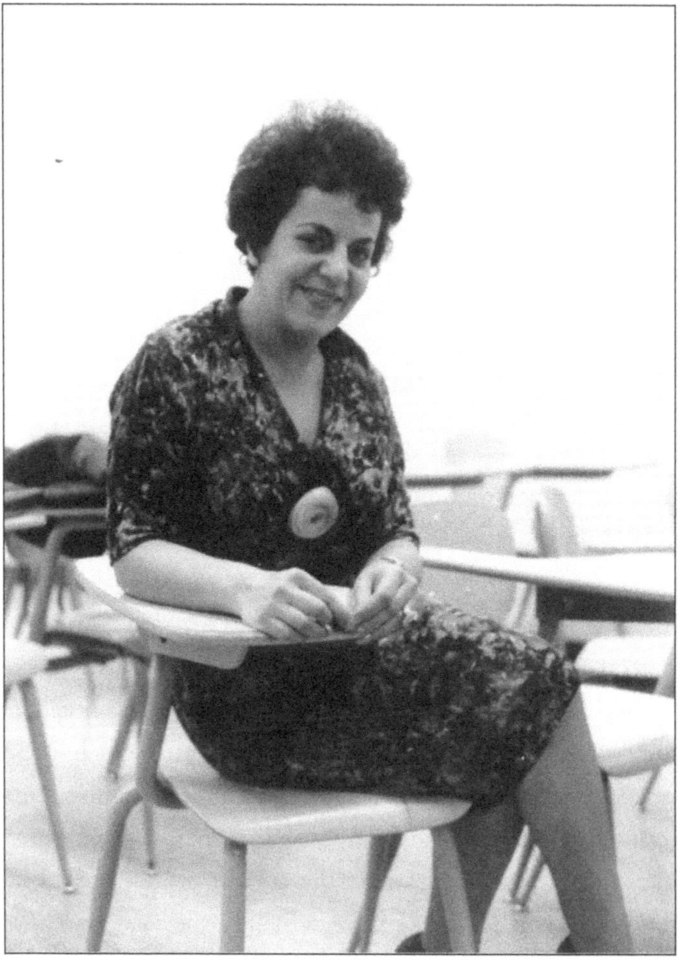

Houri as a student at the University of Michigan in Ann Arbor, 1960

cleaners would clean the room once a week and change the bed linen. Marion always returned late in the evenings; the hall monitor was on the lookout to make sure the girls were back in time. The curfew was 11:30 p.m. on week nights and midnight on weekends. The penalty for every five minutes a student was late was being grounded one evening—these were the rules and they were strictly enforced. Boys were not allowed in the girls' dorms except for holidays, when there was an open house.

Marion and the Girls in the Dorm

All our meals were self-service except for dinner on Saturday night and lunch on Sunday, when we were served. Food was always abundant, even wastefully so; the girls would throw out more than they ate. My arrival was a novelty for the students; they were not aware that I was married and had a sixteen-year-old daughter at college.

My first friends were two girls who were both called Judy! They were very curious about Iran, which they would pronounce "I–ran"! They would often come to my room and actually take notes on my replies to their many questions. I first taught them the correct pronunciation of the name; I believe they were writing papers on Iran and my presence was a help to them. They were conscientious students and didn't waste their time like Marion did. In their spare time, they would play bridge sitting on the floor.

My roommate Marion didn't have any friends and everyone kept their distance from her. One day I asked them why my two new friends were not friendlier toward Marion; they kept avoiding my question until I finally discovered that Marion's crime was that she had a black boyfriend. In those days in Iran, it was not customary for girls to have boyfriends; at least in my family, it was considered wrong. In America, at the time, the issue was less to do with having a boyfriend than having one who was black. Marion had a guitar that she would play from time to time and would sing sad songs. When she got back late on the days we were given clean sheets, she would often go to sleep on the bare mattress without making up the bed. On those days when our meals were served, the other girls would often invite me to sit at their table. I used the same tactics and asked Marion to sit with me—this she accepted happily. On those occasions, she would attend to her dress and makeup so she would look less like a hippie!

I was not unhappy about living in a dorm with girls much younger than myself. It was a short walk from there to the English Language Institute where I had most of my classes. It was autumn and the trees were glorious in their copper tones; the squirrels with their bushy tails fascinated me and I would lose myself and the sense of time watching them scamper about. Sometimes these beautiful creatures would stand on their hind legs and look around with their large eyes—listening intently.

The best student in our class was a Japanese man. There was also a girl from Chile called Silvia who was the best among the girls, the most attentive and hard-working. The participants on the course were of all ages and social levels; there were some who were older than me and many who were younger. The language labs were new to us all; I was the only person in the group who knew French. The rest were mostly from Latin American countries and spoke Spanish. Then there were some from Turkey, Japan, Iran, and Austria, all of whom were fairly fluent in English and were teachers of English in their native lands. Our instructors were all kind and responsible, including a younger man called Daniel Glucksberg, who was in charge of our group and acted as coordinator.

Extracurricular Activities

One of the first things I did upon arrival at the University of Michigan, which had over 40,000 students at the time, was to buy tickets to concerts, plays, and shows. These tickets usually sold out quickly. One day we had a sit-down lunch and a beautiful young girl was serving us. That same evening, I was due to attend a performance by Marcel Marceau, the world-famous French mime artist, and was waiting for a taxi to take me there. I noticed the same young girl, all dressed up, who offered to share her cab with me and pay half the fare. Of course, like all people from the Middle East, I asked her to be my guest. This young girl worked as a waitress during the day for extra pocket money; she was a full-time student but had bought a more expensive seat than mine for the show!

I saw Handel's *Messiah* just before the New Year, performed by the Boston Philharmonic Orchestra with more than a hundred male and female singers—this was most inspiring. At the end, the entire audience got to its feet and accompanied and applauded the orchestra and singers. In those days, there was much courtesy; this was 1960 (1339), eight years before the women's movement was in full swing. Everyone would dress up for such occasions; women's clothes were elegant and no one would have dreamed of attending such an event dressed in jeans. Every night, when I returned to the dorm, the inevitable embracing couples were all around me and their parting before the curfew was always difficult.

A Gathering in Chicago

At the end of October there was a large gathering of teachers in Chicago; thirty of us, including myself, took part. Many of the attendees had to speak about the method of English instruction in their own country. The more developed countries mentioned language labs. Although I taught at the most advanced high school in Iran, I had never used any teaching tools other than a blackboard, chalk, and books. I decided to come clean; I explained that Iran was in a difficult economic situation and, in the provinces, the classes were overcrowded and the facilities non-existent.

At the start of my talk, there were not many in the audience but, within a short time, the hall had filled up. I had not intended to belittle my country; I simply wanted to illustrate the different circumstances we faced and to emphasize that we Iranians were intelligent and capable of learning foreign languages with simple facilities. In my opinion, gadgets are not the deciding factor; with determination and hard work, a blackboard and chalk should suffice for teaching any subject. The standing-room-only crowd applauded the presentation—I told the truth then and still believe in what I said.

Educational tools are very important but they can lead to complacency in the student. Nowadays with all the electronic gadgets at the disposal of children, mental arithmetic has long been forgotten—we have acquired Alzheimer's disease instead! What I see as a problem in the American educational system is that it has become too easy for the students; and now—forty-four years after this story—Americans are still lagging in their ability to learn foreign languages.

Later, I heard from Daniel Glucksberg that people had been standing in the hallway to hear my speech; this had aroused his curiosity and he too had come closer in order to hear me better. I didn't have a prepared speech; often when there is a written speech, the audience becomes bored unless the topic is an important political message or a life-or-death matter.

The Three "Cs"

The Fulbright program required each of us to give a talk about our particular country; once again I was chosen to speak. The two young men who had come with me from Iran bowed to my seniority in age as well as years of teaching. In those days, Iran was a little-known country and did not enjoy the notoriety of today. Some had heard the name Mosaddegh. I began my talk with the three "Cs." There was a large map of Iran that resembled a cat—this helped with the first C, "cat," followed by "carpet" and "caviar." I told them that our carpets, our caviar, and our cats were famous.

Then I started to talk about ancient Iran, which traced its history back 3,000 years; I spoke of Ferdowsi, Hafez, Sa`adi, Attar, Rumi, Ibn Sina, Razi, and absolutely did not touch on religion or politics. It was Susan's turn next, the young girl from Turkey. She started her speech by referring to the writers and poets from her country and mentioned Molana Jalal Adin Rumi.

When I raised my hand and objected, the moderator asked, "Do you have an objection, Mrs. Mostofi?" I said that Rumi was Iranian; he traveled to Konya with his father as a young man. However, his poetry was in Persian; while it was true that he died and was buried in Konya, which was in Turkey, but that didn't make him Turkish. For example, if I were to die and be buried in the U.S., that would not make me American. My objection was sustained. One of two young men who had come with me fancied this young girl and there will be more about her later.

Short Trips

In Iran, the Shahbanu[10] gave birth to a son in 1960 (1339), which brought great joy to the Shah and the whole population. My brother Bagher also welcomed a daughter into his family—they named her Niloofar. On 8 November (17 Aban), general elections were held in the U.S., with John Kennedy and Richard Nixon battling it out for the presidency. President Eisenhower was on his way out and Nixon was having a hard time against the Democrats. I made a trip with friends to Detroit during this time; President Eisenhower was driving to Cobo Hall in an open-topped car. He was visiting an automobile show and we were able to visit the same show soon after. We saw fabulous cars in metallic colors on turntable stands, with beautiful young women sitting in them.

We subsequently visited the Ford factory and watched a car being assembled from start to finish. It was amazing to watch pieces of the car body, including the doors and the roof, painted in different colors, move along a conveyor belt above the cars, and to wonder how these different-colored parts would be matched up with the rest of the car body. But the whole thing was so carefully designed that all the pieces miraculously came together.

---

10. The title Shahbanu (literally, "Lady Shah") was given to Farah Pahlavi when she was crowned queen in 1967. This was the first time it had been used since the Sasanian period in 630 BCE.

I have always believed in universal order, and just as the conveyor belt deposits the right part in the correct sequence, so I have faith that, in the end, everything will turn out exactly as it should, even if, in the short term, there is the appearance of chaos. This belief has enabled me to remain positive in life and always hopeful for a better future.

These were day trips; Detroit is quite close to Ann Arbor and an easy bus ride. We took advantage of its proximity and spent several Saturdays in this industrial city—the birthplace of the motor car. My friends and I also saw performances of Shakespeare plays, including *A Winter's Tale*. One afternoon, we went to an ice-skating show where Olympic gold medal winners now turned professional were performing. My daughters, who were in Tehran, had recently learned to ice skate.

Another new area for me was American football, which in my humble opinion should have been called handball—the only part of the players' anatomy that has nothing to do with the ball is their feet! We were first given a complete explanation of this national game by a professional player—then we were taken to see a game between the University of Michigan and the University of Minnesota. I couldn't make head or tail of the game; I still can't, though my young grandson is an expert.

Visiting Mariam at Wilson College

The presidential elections were in full swing. John Kennedy came to the University of Michigan to give a speech and collect supporters; there was a long weekend ahead. Mariam had been studying at Wilson College for a while and I was in touch with her by phone. I decided to use the few days' vacation and visit her in Chambersburg, Pennsylvania. I couldn't fly there as I would have had to change planes three times. It was simpler and faster to go by Greyhound bus. I took a small suitcase with me and set off to see her, spending one night en route.

There was a long stop in Cleveland; it was close to midnight. I used the two hours to walk without fear around this unfamiliar city, looking at shop windows. Suddenly I noticed a police car following me; the car stopped and one of the policemen said, "You are taking a risk but we are watching out for you." With that, I turned around and went back to the bus depot. These days I hardly dare walk by myself, even in the main streets of the city where I live.

Mariam was waiting for me at the bus terminal in Chambersburg and we went to the college by taxi from there. Mariam's roommate was away for the weekend, visiting her family, and so I had no need to go to a hotel. Wilson College was celebrating its ninetieth anniversary and had invited André Maurois, the renowned French author, as their guest speaker. He spoke English well but with a charming French accent. I was familiar with his work and biographies; his two books *Ariel*, Shelley's biography, and *Lelia*, on the life of George Sand, had just been published and were on sale there.

After his presentation, which took place in the main auditorium of the college, I approached and asked him, in French, to sign the books for me. He smiled and said, "Madam, please put your card inside the books so I don't make a mistake spelling your name." This I did and the two signed books were returned to me the following day. That same day, a large outdoor lunch had been arranged in the magnificent college grounds for all the students, their families, and the faculty, as well as the guest speaker. The dormitories were open to visitors and a team of students was responsible for looking after them. I was most impressed with the discipline and manners of these young women.

At Wilson, there was no self-service and all the meals were served on beautiful china and elaborate silver platters. The following day—a Sunday—Mariam and I, both dressed in simple pants and T-shirts, spent the day on campus. One of the girls asked which of us was the younger sister; I laughed and said, "I am Mariam's mother and I am here to visit her." Mariam, then aged sixteen, stayed at the college for a year; the following year she transferred to Carnegie Institute of Technology—now called the Carnegie Mellon University. She wanted to study architecture and Wilson College, which was a girl's school, felt too small and restrictive for her.

A Visit by Mr. and Mrs. Richard Nixon

On my return to Michigan, I heard from my colleagues and fellow students that John Kennedy had been very well received, since most students tended to be Democrats. By contrast, the same students, once they enter working life and start to earn money, tend to join the Republicans. After a short while, Richard Nixon arrived in Michigan accompanied by his wife and traveling by train. Their visit was very short, just a whistle stop. Nixon did not meet the crowd or the students; he just made a short speech in the train station.

Mrs. Nixon was wearing a camel-colored coat, like her husband, and walked among us; she shook hands with those closer to her. Having missed Kennedy's visit and speech, I joined the students to meet the Nixons. Every person who got to shake hands with Mrs. Nixon would state their home town. When it was my turn, I said that I came from Tehran, Iran.

She was carrying a large bouquet of Baccara roses that had been presented to her; she pulled out one rose and gave it to me saying, "This is for the lady from Iran." My fellow students later joked that, if Nixon won the election, this rose would become very valuable. I put it in among the pages of one of my textbooks and kept it for a long time, even after my return to Iran.

Our Curricular and Extracurricular Activities

Thanksgiving came and I was invited to the home of one of our women teachers where I tasted Mexican-style paella for the first time. The program director wanted each of the thirty visiting teachers coming from different countries to teach the rest of the group a song from their own country so they could make a commemorative record. My two male compatriots left the responsibility up to me; one of them confessed on the day of the first rehearsal that he had a date and wanted to cook for his girlfriend, the aforementioned Turkish young lady.

I don't have a good singing voice and was not looking forward to this. I decided on the song "*Gol-e gandom*" ("Wheat Flower") because I knew the words and could hum the tune. I wrote out the lyrics in transliteration, had it photocopied, handed it to the whole group, and acted as conductor while the group of thirty practiced singing it. The others proceeded in the same way and we all learned each other's national songs. We had several rehearsals, resulting in quite a good performance. I asked my two fellow countrymen to be present on the day of the recording; they cooperated, and didn't abandon me, and we all came away with a copy of the record.

The U.S. Presidential Elections

At the university, the American students participated actively in the elections and we all stayed up on the night of the elections. We also visited different polling stations to familiarize ourselves with the system of elections in the U.S. Kennedy beat Nixon with a small majority; I will never forget the look on the face of the vice-president, Richard Nixon. Looking as if his world had come to an end, he seemed to age ten years overnight. Most people had predicted his loss and Kennedy's win; the Democrats were overjoyed and the whole campus lit up with excitement.

A Short Trip to Canada

I made a short trip to Canada, accompanied by two Argentinian colleagues who were slightly older than me. We stayed in Toronto, a part of Canada that felt like an extension of the U.S. except for the fact that the streets bore the name of kings, queens, or princes instead of numbers. In those days, the Canadian dollar was worth five cents more than the U.S. dollar. The governor of Canada, the representative of Queen Elizabeth II, was inaugurating a winter agricultural show where huge turkeys were on display, an astonishing sight for someone like me. In a different section, young men and women raced each other in pony-drawn carriages and the winner was awarded a medal by the governor, himself quite a sight in his tight white jodhpurs and red jacket.

Reflections on Life

The Christmas holidays were approaching; I was in regular touch with Mariam. A trip I'd planned with a group of fellow students to visit the West of the U.S. would involve practically circling this vast country. It had started from New York to Washington, Chicago, Michigan, and Detroit, and would continue from there. I had hoped that Mariam could accompany me on this leg of the journey, but then I thought maybe this young girl might be bored by the company of so many older people. I figured that if she spent the vacation with Nasrollah and, she would feel less homesick—that she would prefer spending time with them.

Later, I regretted not having invited her to join me. I was in regular correspondence with Tehran; most of the letters I received from Mohsen were critical and full of complaints about my absence. His brother Reza was visiting the U.S. on business and called me, urging me to return as soon as possible. I replied that I had come for a six-month program, that the house and the children were in good hands, supervised by their father. A trustworthy nanny, cook, and a trained houseboy were at their service. I didn't think I was being missed.

Every time I received a letter, I hardly dared open it; there was not one encouraging word in there. I had left my comfortable home and was spending time studying in a corner of a small dormitory, occasionally visiting places of interest. There were many other married teachers on the program; they also had husbands and children. I wish I had been appreciated while performing my duties at home! I wanted to give my husband an opportunity to realize that women are not like furniture in a house; that we have our own ideas and thoughts. Men can leave whenever they wish and go on trips, and the excuse is that they work and are the breadwinners. As if women are idle, even those with no responsibilities outside the home.

Pregnancies, rearing children, educating them, and managing the home are as important as any job, although they come with no time off, benefits, or pay—not to forget women who also have outside jobs with additional responsibilities. Of course, we were told that we had so much help at home, as if men didn't have help in their offices and places of work! The training of domestic help is an important job; entertaining and managing a family are no less time-consuming than running a company or an office.

As a woman, one is responsible even for the smallest error; if the children are well brought up, that is to be expected. But God forbid if they stray from the expected path—it is the mother's fault. If there is a problem with the house or with meals, again the finger is pointed at the wife. Do men ever truly appreciate their wives, who are always at the service of the family? The surprising thing is that the less capable the wife and the more demanding she is, the dearer she seems to be to her husband. We Iranian women don't quite know which tune to dance to. But enough complaining!

I sent the children gifts from time to time. I loved my life; this temporary separation was quite painful for me too.

What middle-aged married woman do you know who would leave her comfortable life if there wasn't a serious reason? I tried to warn my husband about this; I was a forty-year-old woman with a university-age daughter, even though I didn't look my age. People never believe me when I tell them how old I am; even today, at the age of eighty, they ask me for evidence! Even if they are just asking out of politeness, they are always surprised when I tell them how old I am.

Men should also occasionally take a good look in the mirror—the mirror never lies. I had taken beautiful photographs with me of my home and my family and I would show them to young men who would approach me so they would see I had a family and was participating in this program for my education and for the experience.

By contrast, men often remove their wedding rings when they travel to show that they are a free agent. But do they realize what is at stake? Human beings never appreciate what they have; sunshine, blue skies, gentle rain, fresh air—it is so easy to take such things for granted. We only really value them when the bad weather comes and we suffer storms, tornadoes, and earthquakes!

I replied to all the letters; I described the museums, sporting or cultural events, and all the experiences I had had. Hamid was in the Safinia kindergarten and my sister kept an eye on him; Ladan was twelve and busy with school and homework. For Hamid, I was third in importance. He adored his nanny; next came his father and finally myself. Mariam was in her own world, studying and developing her remarkable talents. I was proud of all three of my children and they never had any complaints about me. But I am certain that my absence had disturbed my husband's peace and comfort to some extent. He had temporarily lost his rock—his stable base.

A Christmas Road Trip

Our group of thirty set off on our road trip and for twenty days we visited different states, always traveling westward. We visited Chicago, Denver, Colorado, and Salt Lake City, followed by San Francisco, Los Angeles, Las Vegas, Arizona, Kansas City in Missouri, and New Mexico, plus all the points in between. Packing and unpacking, being ready to leave on time, and getting along with others were among the things we learned during the tour.

Salt Lake City was cold but sunny; there had previously been a heavy snowfall. It reminded me of Shemiran. We learned a little about the Mormons and their lifestyle. Our city guide, who had a full-time job running the town dealership for Chrysler cars, volunteered a half-day each week to be a guide for tourists. He showed us the Mormon Tabernacle and pointed out the famous organ there. Most of us had no prior knowledge of the Mormon faith and found it very interesting. As a young girl, I had read a book called *At the Crossroads of Life* that described the Mormon way of life, including plural marriage, which later became illegal. Mormons don't drink alcohol, tea or coffee, and lead a conservative and apparently purer lifestyle.

I spent Christmas Eve in San Francisco. One of my cousins, Fereydoun Shahin-Nouri, lived in Richmond with his wife and children and invited me to their home for dinner that night. After dinner and the exchange of gifts, he accompanied me to the train station where I took a train to Los Angeles and rejoined the group. It was an overnight journey and I dozed in my seat, arriving in L.A. on Christmas morning. I had spent the few days in San Francisco and had not only looked around the city and the surrounding sights, but I had also taken a bus to Palo Alto and visited Stanford University—an elite private institution.

The student dormitories were constructed in the Spanish style; I visited the classrooms, the public halls, and the Hoover Tower. As it was near Christmas, they were decorating the chapel with beautiful flowers. Over the entrance to the chapel there is a carving of the only son of the founder of Stanford University, who died at a young age. Several years after his death, his parents were also buried near him, their graves covered in flowers too.

I returned to San Francisco wondering how anyone could concentrate on their studies in such a romantic and beautiful spot. Reza, my brother-in-law, had obtained his PhD at Stanford. What I didn't know then was that, some years later, my son Hamid, followed by my granddaughters Firouzeh and Sanam and many of the younger members of our family, would be educated in this famous university. In the year 2006 (1385), Hamid and his wife Christina founded the Program in Iranian Studies at Stanford and Hamid joined the board of this renowned university—who would have imagined this back in 1961 (1340)?

Los Angeles was very different; it felt like a massive freeway loosely connecting several smaller cities. We were invited on Christmas Day to the home of a lady who was a yoga teacher and a vegetarian. She had prepared a delicious meal for us of fresh vegetables and pulses; these occasions had been pre-planned and our hosts were most gracious everywhere we went. We visited the film studios and the Chinese Theater in Hollywood and its famous cemetery.

In Arizona, we visited the amazing Grand Canyon; I took some excellent photographs with a camera given to me by Shajan many years before. Las Vegas was not on our agenda, and although I never gamble, I was curious to visit this city and made a short trip there. I discussed this with my Iranian colleague Rostam and the two of us, accompanied by our friend Susan, the Turkish girl, obtained permission to leave the group for twenty-four hours to spend a day in Las Vegas.

We visited the famous hotels and casinos; I spent $5 in the slot machines. It was a marvel that such a city could be created in the middle of the arid desert, that they could import shows such as Lido and Folies Bergère and make a fortune out of it! Recently, after nearly thirty-nine years, I went to Las Vegas again, accompanied by a young friend, and revisited the even more amazing city it had become.

Maybe I will have something to say about this second visit at a later time.

The story of our return from Las Vegas is interesting. We had planned to hire a car to take us as far as the Arizona border and then take a train from there to Albuquerque in New Mexico. Susan had bought some fruit to eat on the train. The driver of the car charged us a lot of money, which we had no choice but to pay since there was no other way of getting there. On the way, he told us about his home and his swimming pool and implied that he was no ordinary driver and was doing this just as a favor to us. As we passed the great Hoover Dam, our driver told us the story of its construction and stopped the car for a few minutes so we could see the dam up close. It was a truly amazing structure.

As we got back in the car, the driver told Susan that she should eat any fresh fruit she had as we would be inspected at the border and he couldn't lie about it. If he hadn't seen the fruit, Susan might have gotten away with it; as it was, he had no choice but to tell the truth if the inspector asked him the question. Susan started to eat the fruit, all the while swearing in Turkish under her breath. She offered us some of the fruit but we had all just eaten dinner and couldn't help her out.

Finally, she had no choice but to throw the fruit out of the car into the desert—piece by piece. When we reached the border, the driver was asked if there was any fruit, vegetables, or alcohol in the car and he replied that there wasn't. The car passed the checkpoint without an inspection. Susan asked the driver why he had forced her to throw out her fruit and the driver reiterated that he could not tell a lie, as the possibility of a physical inspection was always there.

We reached our destination, paid off the driver and boarded our train, rejoining the group after a short while in Albuquerque, New Mexico. The town really looked more like a town in Mexico than in the U.S. I enjoyed a wonderful lunch at a restaurant that had been recommended to me and was not part of the tour—this was my first taste of Mexican food. The head waiter gave me a beautiful menu to keep; I had never tasted tortillas or spicy food until then and it was a new experience for me.

From Albuquerque we went to Kansas City in Missouri where each of us spent New Year's Eve 1961 (11 Dey 1339) as the guest of a different American family; I have a pleasant memory of that evening. My hosts had a beautiful home that was very well decorated and furnished and reminded me of my own newly built house in Elahieh. We finally returned to Ann Arbor at the end of the first week of January; it had been an interesting and instructive trip and I had really enjoyed myself.

More about Marion Blizzard

I returned to my dorm room after an absence of twenty days. As I entered the building, the other girls congratulated me saying, "Marion had a wash!" As I walked into the room we shared, Marion welcomed me with clean and shiny hair and a neat appearance. She helped me with my suitcase and unpacked my clothes. Then she opened her closet with great excitement and showed me the neat piles of sweaters she had washed. I embraced her and wished her a happy New Year; this young girl had learned a lesson without me having to utter a word. Sometimes, when dealing with young people, acceptance works better than criticism, which often has the reverse effect. I tolerated her behavior and never chastised her or tried to give her a lesson in manners; I simply ignored her shortcomings.

Opening up to me, she said, "My mother is the chief volunteer of our town's biggest church. I have been under pressure since childhood to attend a private school and wear a uniform. I love art, painting, and music and I became a bit of a rebel. But I learned discipline and tidiness from you."

The contraceptive pill was not yet widely used and I sometimes hinted to her that girls could not be as free as boys in their relationships and have multiple partners. If girls get pregnant, they can ruin their lives from a young age. When I finally left the university, she helped me pack; in return, I invited her to choose whatever she liked from my clothes or shoes for herself. She picked a dress that suited her and a matching pair of shoes. She also gave me a modern painting she had done, which I later gave to Mariam. She accompanied me to the bus that took me to my train but I later lost touch with her.

An Intensive Academic Program Comes to an End

Like many of my friends and relatives, I was not in the habit of carrying my own heavy suitcases and, as a result, I began to suffer severe back pain and had to spend several days in bed soon after my arrival at Ann Arbor. The girls used to give me back massages, which were soothing but not particularly effective; and I eventually had to visit a specialist. He told me that there was a problem with my lower back and I would have to learn to live with it.

Now, our final exams were approaching, and I had no choice but to stay up late at night to revise and study. Thus, I completed the course, and my second university career came to an end. Our group had produced a newsletter in which each of us had to write an article on a subject of interest to us. I wrote an article on life in an American women's college dorm in which I described my experiences in a tongue-in-cheek manner.

I also remember writing an essay right at the beginning of the course entitled "The most unforgettable person I know," in which I wrote about my father, his life and personality—in particular during the period when he was writing his autobiography. I received a mark of 93 percent for this work. I believe writing is fairly simple as long as one stays close to the truth. Just as an artist paints on a blank canvas, so a writer writes on a blank sheet and describes what he or she sees and understands on the page.

A farewell dinner was arranged for the group; our representative and speaker was the young Japanese man, who truly deserved first place among us. He had become a friend and had given me a beautiful picture of himself and his Japanese bride dressed in a traditional wedding outfit. Speaking with great humility, he said, "Ladies and gentlemen—in my country we are taught not to speak in front of our parents or our elders and so I have not learned to be a good orator." His words came from the heart and were a testament to his intelligence and powers of observation while, at the same time, they were quite witty—laughter broke out among the audience many times during his speech.

All our teachers, male and female. were gathered at this farewell dinner and we received our diplomas, which counted as a master's degree when added to my years of experience. It remained for me to write a short thesis that I had to hand in to the university to receive the MA after having spent some time at the high schools chosen for us in order to experience at first hand their method of instruction. I had kept many notes of my travels and experiences that I later included in that thesis.

Community Assignments

We were each sent to a different city and a different state; I was sent to the city of Montpelier, Vermont. The weather was very cold and the city streets covered in ice and snow. We took part in the state assembly and learned how issues were presented and handled. Senator Carriere later volunteered to drive me to Bennington, and we had a good conversation on the way. I told him that I was familiar with his name as our central-heating furnace in Tehran was a Carriere; he replied that the name belonged to a different branch of the same family.

He drove with great care over the icy roads and on the way jokingly said that Bennington College was a girls' school and different from other girls' colleges. "Why are they sending you there?" We reached the university town in the afternoon where I was to meet my host family. A young couple, dressed in jeans and heavy sweaters, awaited us; they introduced themselves, we shook hands, and I introduced the senator. He took one look at my hosts and left with a smile on his face. His parting words as he shook my hand were spoken quietly: "I wish you luck and an enjoyable time!"

Bennington and Its Surroundings

A big old car awaited us; my suitcase was placed in the trunk and we set off under the astonished gaze of the senator. My hosts lived quite a distance outside town; everywhere was covered in thick snow. From a distance, a two-story structure appeared in the middle of a field of snow. I later found out that the house, which was in a state of great neglect and disrepair, was over a hundred years old. My hosts were an educated couple; Philip had an MA and his wife had been a classmate of Jacqueline Kennedy.

They lived with their two sons, one daughter, and a cat called Gorbeh in this old house in the middle of nowhere. Theirs was a simple and almost primitive lifestyle. I told them that *gorbeh* in Persian means "cat" and asked them how they had come across this name. They explained that one of their relatives had lived in Mashhad many years before and had suggested it. This distant connection with Iran had been the reason they had volunteered to be my hosts!

There was an old stove in this two-story house that was the sole source of heating; the little second-floor room allocated to me was freezing cold. It did seem as if I was destined to be paired up with hippie types, although at heart they were good people. At times, the lady of the house would earn a little extra money posing as an artist's model. There was a room on the ground floor that received absolutely no heat and was used as a natural fridge or even freezer! Legs of lamb and all sorts of foodstuffs would typically freeze there.

I went to bed that first night dressed in thick trousers and a sweater. The following day was a holiday and we were planning to go skiing. As I didn't have my ski clothes with me, they lent me some of their own; I put on a thick woolen hat and hardly recognized my own reflection in the mirror! We drove to the slopes and skied a few times down the easy runs. The children were also busy playing when, all of a sudden, their son Timothy twisted and broke his leg. Help was immediately on hand and he was taken on a stretcher into the car. We all set off to the hospital, the child quiet in the back, where the specialist put his leg in a cast and we returned home. The following day was Sunday and my hosts had invited several of their school colleagues to meet me. Their living room, which was extremely untidy, was cleared up and the party got under way without anyone rushing or getting stressed.

The school principal was a distinguished lady and introduced me to all the teachers; our hosts looked after everyone and had prepared a delicious dinner. The principal invited me to spend a few days with her before leaving town so I could familiarize myself with their style of city living—this was part of the program! The following day, my hosts drove me to town and to the school, where I spent some time in the eleventh and twelfth grades, meeting the staff and talking to the students. I moved to the principal's house the same day, having obtained the permission of my hosts, and spent the next few days going to and from school with her.

One day, one of the twelfth-grade boys asked me what role the United Nations had played in the liberation of Azerbaijan and the quashing of communism. I described the efforts of my country in cooperation with the United Nations and stressed the importance of the resistance of my fellow countrymen in stopping this movement. I spent my spare time having my notes typed up by volunteer students so that my final thesis was ready to be handed in to the authorities before my departure from Washington DC.

Most of my fellow students sent in their theses after their return to their various countries.

It is worthy of note that in those days there was no ministry of education in Washington DC, the capital of the U.S. The Department of Health, Education, and Welfare was the responsible body in each of the fifty states. The reason for this is that the different states are totally autonomous when it comes to education at all levels, including universities—both public and private.

This was a little difficult for me to understand when I was used to seeing all the government departments concentrated in the capital city and exerting authority over the whole nation. The U.S. is not to be considered a country; it is in fact a continent. I was shown around Bennington College, where 100 percent attendance in class was not mandatory; many students had jobs off campus. However, they were responsible for preparing for the exams. It reminded me of the time I used to attend the law faculty irregularly and yet still managed to pass the exams.

A Short Trip to Boston

I spent the weekend in Boston in the company of my host the school principal, staying at the Sheraton Hotel. She was participating in a seminar and I wanted to explore this traditional East Coast city. I managed to buy two tickets for *The Sound of Music*, a musical new to the stage, and invited my host to see it with me. It was a truly wonderful performance.

The little children reminded me of my own family back in Iran and I wondered if we would ever have a chance to see this show together. We fell victim to a huge snowstorm during our short stay in Boston and for twenty-four hours we were unable to leave the hotel. The streets were full of snow; shops were closed and it was impossible to get around.

We returned to Bennington as soon as we could, my host driving. I had bought some presents for my original hosts and I donated my Zeiss camera to the couple. They told me that the entire contents of their home had been donated to them; they had never paid for anything, including the piano, the sewing machine, and even the car they drove!

Vermont–Washington DC

My closest friend in the program was a middle-aged lady called Dr. Tronik from Klagenfurt in Austria. She had been assigned to stay with a wealthy family who had live-in staff while I, by contrast, had ended up with this hippie couple in their remote house! Either a mistake had been made in matching me up with a host family or it was a deliberate attempt to introduce me to a very different lifestyle from my own. My friend was entertained and housed in a grand manner, while I had been the guest of a family living in the freezing climate of the East Coast with only the most rudimentary means of heating!

When we returned to Washington, my cousin Parinaz and her husband would not allow me to go to a hotel and insisted that I stay with them. I was invited to lunch by His Excellency Ardeshir Zahedi; Dr. Khosrovani the consul and another cousin of mine, Ahmad Ardalan, were also present at this reception. The ambassador was most gracious and perhaps wanted to compensate for the fact that he had been given a position that should have gone to a career diplomat. He asked me what I intended to do after the end of the Fulbright program.

I told him that I was on my way to Venezuela to see my sister and then I was returning home via Guatemala, Hawaii, Tokyo, and Hong Kong. With great self-deprecation and wit, he asked, "Don't you need anyone to carry your suitcases, Khanum? I would love to make such a trip." At the time, he was not only the Iranian ambassador to the U.S. but he was also the Shah's son-in-law. I was very touched by his charming and easy manner; and we had a delicious halva made by the chef for dessert!

A Meeting with President John Kennedy

Our six-month program was over; the Fulbright scholars had gathered together from the four corners of the country in the main hall of the Department of Health, Education, and Welfare. John Kennedy, the U.S. president, went up to the podium bearing the seal of the president. He spoke about the importance of sports in all aspects of education and he welcomed us, guests from all over the world. Behind him sat the vice-president, Lyndon Johnson, the attorney general,

Robert Kennedy, and the secretary of state responsible for sport. At the end of his speech, the president left the hall through the back of the stage. I left the hall accompanied by my Austrian friend only to spot Lyndon Johnson and Robert Kennedy, who were talking in the hallway.

We made our way to them and introduced ourselves, mentioning where we each came from, since that is the only piece of information that can make an impression. They shook hands with us and asked, "Would you also like to meet the president?" In one voice, we said, "Yes, but he has already left." Robert Kennedy, a handsome man with delightful hair, replied, "He has just returned to the hall to meet the participants. You should take advantage of this opportunity." We thanked him and went back to the hall. Secret-service agents in their khaki raincoats surrounded the president and kept urging the crowd to stay calm: "Easy; easy."

We were lucky to get close to the president; my Austrian friend introduced herself and said, "I come from Klagenfurt, Austria." Kennedy replied, "We spent part of our summer vacation there this year." Now, it was my turn to shake his hand. I said, "Mr. President, we do hope that you will visit us in Iran too." He smiled and said, "For sure." I bade farewell to Washington, all the friends and Fulbright colleagues. Mariam traveled from Wilson College to spend the weekend with me. We said goodbye and she returned to school. It was the end of February.

Miami, Florida

I left for New York and from there went to Miami, Florida. Although it was still winter, the weather there was sunny and warm. I packed my coat in my suitcase and bought myself a summer outfit. I spent two nights in a hotel and saw some of the sights. I then flew to Maracaibo, which is the petroleum center of Venezuela and resembled Abadan. I also had a stopover in Jamaica. On my arrival in Maracaibo, there was no one at the airport to meet me and, for the first time in six months, I became aware of men eyeing women. This was not done in the U.S. It suddenly occurred to me that I was in a Latin American country where this kind of behavior was acceptable.

I took a cab to my sister Nayer's house. I believe a mistake had been made in my arrival date. She was overjoyed to see me. Her two sons, Jamie and Jan, were now six and five respectively; I was so pleased to see them and, as I hugged them, I felt I was embracing Hamid, whom I hadn't seen for six months. A young girl worked in my sister's house but the cooking was up to Nayer. She had arranged a wonderful party for me and invited many of her American and Venezuelan friends.

They, in turn, responded by inviting us to dinner, lunch, and even breakfast either at their homes or club. Kirk, Nayer's husband, was a quiet young man, very precise and softly spoken; he smiled appreciatively all the time and we had a cordial relationship. With Kirk's blessing, Nayer and I left for Caracas for a few days and Kirk promised to take care of the two boys, aided by their nanny.

Caracas–Los Angeles

We reached Caracas by plane and stayed in the famous Tamanaco Hotel. Located on a high hill, it was considered the best place to stay at the time. My sister and her husband had lived in Caracas for a while and they had many friends there; we were therefore very well received. The orchid is the national flower of Venezuela and you find it everywhere in different colors and sizes, sometimes cascading down the walls of houses.

We went to watch a bullfight or *corrida*; it was the first time that I had witnessed this traditional and cruel sport, which I later saw again in Barcelona and Madrid. It seemed unimaginable to me to torture an animal in this way and I sincerely hope that the practice will end one day soon! It was a short but enjoyable trip; we also saw the tallest building of those days—the Humboldt—and then returned to Maracaibo.

It was time to leave. Kirk and Nayer accompanied me to the steps of the airplane and we bade each other farewell. Nayer promised to come and visit us in Tehran so our children could get to know each other. I arrived late in the evening in Los Angeles. I had not realized that I only had a one-time visa and, since I had exited the U.S. by going to Venezuela and was now returning, I no longer had a valid visa. I stayed in a motel that was part of the airport; it was my first ever stay in a motel and I spent an anxious night there.

Having recently seen the movie *Psycho*, I had vivid memories of the horrible events that could take place in a motel and how a young woman could be brutally murdered! My room, the curtains, and the bathroom bore an uncanny resemblance to those in the film. I was so scared that I didn't even take a shower that night and postponed it to the next day when I left Los Angeles for Honolulu.

Honolulu–Hawaii

The plane reached Honolulu around noon; I had two huge suitcases full of presents for my family—including four suits for Mohsen, clothes, shoes, and toys for Ladan and Hamid, and other presents for our staff. I had sent my books and diaries ahead by freight so that my luggage would not be too heavy. It was a beautiful day. At passport control, the officer took one look at my passport and told me that I had to leave on the midnight flight to Tokyo. I said that I wanted to stay a few days in their beautiful city and see the sights. He replied politely that my visa was for one visit only and that, by leaving the U.S. for Venezuela, my visa was no longer valid. However, there was a little time to see some of the sights.

I asked him, "What if I don't show up?" He looked at me in great surprise and said, "Can you wait here for me?

I will be right back." He returned with a young woman who was to be my guide; she was going to take me around in her car and I was to be their guest for both lunch and dinner. She was responsible for returning me to the airport in time for the midnight flight. I was delighted at this offer, since I was by myself and didn't know my way around.

I left my big suitcases at the airport and, taking only my hand luggage, I joined the young lady in her red convertible as we set off for the town center. I thought to myself that it never hurts to speak the truth. The officer saw that I was being truthful by openly announcing my intention to stay and he came to my assistance while making sure he was also doing his duty. These days, such an outcome would be unlikely; the sheer volume of tourists and all the dangers involved have made air travel and negotiating airports a big headache—especially in the United States.

We first went to a hotel so I could freshen up and had lunch there, then we toured the city and Waikiki Beach. At my request, my guide drove outside the city center and we briefly visited the University of Hawaii. I even went shopping and bought a swimsuit, a large straw hat, and matching handbag decorated with the local handicraft. We stopped at a delightful café and had afternoon tea.

In the evening, we were joined by my guide's boyfriend and had dinner at a famous open-air night club where we watched local dancers. Amid the tall trees, in the beautiful night air, lovely young girls danced with garlands of flowers around their necks. It was 10:30 p.m.; my two escorts took me to the steps of the plane. Most of the passengers were from Japan; a tall young man put a garland of flowers around my neck and I mounted the steps into the plane.

Honolulu–Tokyo

The plane took off at midnight, it was early March (Esfand) by then. After a long day sightseeing, I really needed my sleep. I reached Tokyo two days later, having lost a day en route. A colleague of my husband's cousin had booked me a room in a traditional hotel. He drove me around this remarkable city, then in the process of being transformed and rebuilt after the Second World War. It was Sunday, and the beautiful Japanese gardens were at their most glorious. Many weddings took place in these gardens, and brides in their traditional wedding costumes, makeup, and hair, accompanied by their young grooms, were being photographed here. The young men often wore Western-style clothes, by contrast, and it was rare to see them in traditional outfits.

At one of the big hotels, another wedding was in progress. We stopped for a short while to satisfy my curiosity and watch the guests, the men all dressed in tuxedo-like black suits. As each guest arrived, the host would bow all the way down to his knees. The guest would respond in kind, and this would be repeated several times, the host being obliged to continue bowing until the guest straightened up; if the guest decided to bow again, the host also had to do the same.

The thought crossed my mind that the host would very likely be suffering major neck pain the following day.

We had lunch at a restaurant situated in a famous park and I tasted the traditional Japanese tempura—morsels of fish, fowl, and seafood were first dipped in a very light batter and then deep-fried in front of us. We were served these delicacies piece by piece as they were prepared. One night, accompanied by the daughter of this gentleman, we visited a very fancy restaurant, and I tried sukiyaki for the first time. Kobe beef is world famous, the cattle for the beef and veal being raised in a special way. Their bodies are massaged and the animals do not exert themselves so that their flesh is particularly tender and delicious and, unsurprisingly, very expensive.

The following day we visited temples, the royal palace, and many other sights, including the very long Ginza Street, known as the Champs-Elysées of Tokyo. Still recovering from the after-effects of the war, Japan was very different from the country that I visited on more than one occasion many years later. I attended a performance of traditional kabuki theater, though I have to confess I didn't really understand or enjoy it! The world I experienced in Japan was very different from Europe, the United States, or indeed our own country. I watched a traditional tea ceremony and learned about the life of the geishas and the men who, on their way home, visit these young women, who were highly trained in the art of entertainment.

I was surprised by the face masks worn by people to prevent the spread of cold and flu viruses; the underground trains that swallowed and then disgorged streams of men and women were a novelty and my mind was filled with these wondrous sights in the four days I spent in Tokyo. I left my host and his daughter after thanking them profusely for looking after me so well and took off for Hong Kong.

Hong Kong

I had booked a room at the Miramar Hotel in Hong Kong. This busy, international commercial hub was not yet so filled with high rises at the time as to make it almost unlivable. It still carried traces of pre-communist China and I had forty-eight hours to explore the sights. I bought two lengths of silk—one black and one straw-colored—together with all the trimmings, and had two beautiful suits, which I designed myself, made by a tailor recommended through the hotel. I wore and enjoyed these two outfits for many years; they were miraculously produced without me even setting foot in the tailor's shop! I also bought two black bamboo armchairs that I added to my luggage at the last minute. Hong Kong is a city of contrasts. Great wealth and opulence on the one hand and poverty on the other, with poor Chinese squatting and hurriedly eating sticky rice out of small bowls. I don't think poverty and wealth sit so closely side by side anywhere else in the world. Finally, on 16 March 1961 (25 Esfand 1339), I flew home to Tehran.

Back Home Again

My Japanese host had promised to send a telegram to let my husband know the exact details of my arrival. On reaching the airport in Tehran, there was no sign of anyone and I discovered that my suitcases had gone to Jakarta by mistake. I was left with only my hand luggage. I called home from the airport and Mohsen drove to meet me after a short while; it seemed he had not received the telegram. I walked into my house with great joy. Everyone was awake even though it was very late; Hamid, now four and a half, ran around the room with huge excitement and kept visiting the bathroom. I asked his nanny why he kept doing this. Mohsen replied that he wanted to show off that he could go to the bathroom by himself and didn't need help anymore.

Ladan seemed a little more mature than when I'd left. I was upset to return home empty-handed even though the boxes containing presents for the family that I had sent by freight had already arrived and the missing suitcases mostly contained my personal belongings. Mohsen was also happy that the bird which had flown away was back in its nest and would soon be taking over the running of the house and the family. All seemed to be back on an even keel.

Nowruz 1340 (1961)

There were only a few days to go to our Persian New Year. I looked out of the window the next morning and saw a strange black car parked in the driveway; this was Mohsen's gift to me. In recent years, the American car industry had been producing more compact cars to reduce the number of large cars clogging the cities and my new car was one of these—a Valiant, or baby Chrysler. My suitcases also arrived the same day, together with the two bamboo armchairs; the only thing missing was a set of lace place mats—someone had obviously admired them and taken them home.

The house was in excellent shape, the children were both well, and Nowruz was around the corner. What could be better? I was delighted to see members of my family and my friends. Shajan, who was bedridden, had a sad smile on her face—maybe my absence for six and a half months had affected her more than anyone else but she didn't reprimand me and pretended that all was well. She had visited Europe twice herself and in her trip to the United States she had been to New York and Washington and I could share my impressions with her. Her health was still the same; she was confined to her bed and needed constant care and assistance. My friends and family would come to visit me and would stay for lunch or dinner; the house was busy.

The International Women's Club of Iran

I had been a member of the International Women's Club of Iran for many years, having joined when Mrs. Farangis Shadman was president. I was not actively involved with the club as I had no spare time and was content simply to attend the monthly meetings and I started going again after my trip to the U.S., soon becoming more involved. The organization had been founded in Tehran in 1951 (1330) by a group of Iranian women and the wives of foreign diplomats and businessmen. In the past, the wife of the minister of foreign affairs would generally become the club president and the three vice-presidents would be chosen from among the wives of foreign ambassadors. There was also an Iranian club secretary and a non-Iranian treasurer.

I was a friend of Farangis Shadman, whom I regarded as a mentor. She was admired and respected by all, not because her husband was minister of foreign affairs at the time but for her own character—her fine upbringing and pleasant manner. Fluent in English, she had translated two of Shakespeare's tragedies into Persian, copies of which she gave me, and was awarded a richly deserved, honorary doctorate from the University of Tehran. During her presidency, the club's meetings were conducted in both English and Persian. These meetings were sometimes held in ambassadors' residences and sometimes in the homes of the Iranian members. Tea and cookies were served—the main purpose of the meetings being the introduction of our foreign members to Iranian culture and traditions.

One of the most interesting programs during Mrs. Shadman's presidency was an exhibition of the national costumes of all the club members, held at the Golestan Palace. At that time, my involvement was limited to selling a few tickets for this event, the proceeds being dedicated to the foundation of a children's convalescence home.

The Marriage of Mariam and Faramarz

That summer, our elder daughter, Mariam, returned for the holidays. She was eighteen, and about to start her third year at university. Her presence lit up our family. Now qualified as a dental surgeon, her cousin Faramarz had returned home from England for the summer vacation at the same time. Having not seen each other in years, these two young people fell in love during family gatherings. Seeing this, and wanting to pre-empt the possibility of a future British daughter-in-law, my sister Mehri encouraged Faramarz to ask Mariam to marry him. Our daughter shared her secret with me. When I asked her whether she loved him, she replied that she did.

I asked her if she was ready to get married at such a young age and, again, she said yes. I advised her to ask Faramarz to make an appointment to see Mohsen at his office, which in those days was located opposite Tehran University, and discuss the matter before the news was leaked to him. I reminded her not to let her father know that I was already in the picture because I knew he would feel slighted. I was also going to feign ignorance if Mohsen told me the news.

On Saturday morning, Faramarz went to the Reema office and formally asked for Mariam's hand. Mohsen reflected for a few minutes and then said, "Mariam is very young but you are a commendable and outstanding young man and, if Mariam is happy, I have no objection." Mariam was at home, waiting for a telephone call. Faramarz didn't wait to get home and called her from a public telephone in Shah Reza Avenue to let her know that her father had agreed to the match.

When he came home for lunch, Mohsen shared the news of Faramarz's request with me at the table. I agreed that he was a suitable candidate, but I also said that, in my opinion, there were two problems with this marriage: first that Mariam was just eighteen and, secondly, that they were cousins and marriage between such close relatives was not ideal.

My objections were overridden, however, and the engagement and marriage took place in the limited time available before Mariam had to return to the States. The religious ceremony, the *aqd*, took place in our home and the wedding dress and bridegroom's outfit were also made in Tehran. The Qur'an, mirror, candelabras, and sweets for the *aqd* table were supplied by my sister and the dinner that night was held in the Safinia home. The young couple were not keen on a big wedding, but Mohsen believed that, since Faramarz's father had passed away, he had to act as the father of the groom and arrange a big wedding and this was to take place the following day in our house and garden. The invitations were sent out.

In the run-up to the wedding, I visited Mr. Fatollah Amir Alai, the manager of Hotel Darband, to see about hiring their band and floor show. He pointed out to me that holding such a large party at our house was not a good idea and suggested that we hold the whole event at Hotel Darband with its extensive grounds and delightful open-air

The wedding of Mariam and Faramarz Safinia at the Hotel Darband in Shemiran, 1962

facilities. He promised that he would put all their resources at our disposal and mentioned that, since a new rival hotel had recently opened in Vanak, he wanted to make sure that our daughter's wedding would be such a success as to lure back many of their old customers.

I asked him to give me time to consult Mohsen and then respond to his suggestion. Fortunately, Mohsen had no objection but made it clear that the budget would remain the same; I assured him that I would make up any shortfall and we would not have any financial disagreements.

That wedding at Hotel Darband was one of the outstanding social events of the year. The bridesmaids, all cousins and close relatives ranging in age from eleven to fifteen, wore identical turquoise chiffon dresses and all had their hair up. The bride's bouquet was a most original gift from our friend Homa Fattollah-Zadeh. Looking back and remembering how I calmly sat by our pool earlier in the day, knowing that the wedding would be handled perfectly at Hotel Darband without any worry or stress on my part, I can honestly say that it was one of the best days of my life.

My sister had invited several of her colleagues at the Safinia School and one of them had my sister's permission to bring along a friend recently returned from Europe. This gentleman, who was apparently unmarried, had taken a fancy to me that evening—it seemed there was a suitor for me too! My sister had replied good-humoredly that the young woman in question was in fact the mother of the bride. We have an expression in Iran: the neighbor's hen appears to be a goose—or the grass is always greener on the other side!

Shajan did not participate in the marriage of her two grandchildren and decided to stay at home in bed, although the bride and groom, who passed under the Qur'an at the end of the *aqd*, paid their grandmother a visit. Shajan gave them a wonderful camera, chosen by the groom, and wished them a long and happy life together.

Shajan's Parting Gifts

Nowruz 1342 (1963) was upon us. Shajan had asked me to send her antique handwritten Qur'an to Nayer. This copy of the Qur'an was the handiwork of the great calligrapher Bader and the names of all the children and grandchildren in the family had been inscribed in it, first in my father's handwriting and later by Shajan.

I entrusted this treasured item to William Clements, a prominent Texan oilman who was in Iran at the time. I stressed that he should keep it on his lap during the long journey back to the U.S. and he promised me that he would do so. I don't know why I had a feeling that Shajan wouldn't be with us for very long and that, by sending this copy of the Qur'an, she was saying farewell to her estranged and faraway daughter. In later years, Mr. Bill Clements became the governor of Texas; he kept his promise to me, in the meantime, and delivered the Qur'an safely to my sister, whose husband had now been posted to Texas.

On another occasion, Shajan instructed me to open my father's antique bookcase that was in their bedroom and take out an even larger copy of the Qur'an. Commissioned by my paternal grandfather, Haj Mirza Nasrollah Mostofi, it had been handwritten on parchment in a beautiful *nastaliq* calligraphy with unique designs. This was the Qur'an my father had always used and read; Shajan entrusted it to me with the words "Take good care of this; I know you will appreciate it."

I knew then that my mother was at the end of her journey. She also gave me two beautiful prayer books, handwritten on parchment and exquisitely decorated, saying, "Houri, I entrust these books to you." Luckily, all three books were not seized by those who took everything else from us, although the two prayer books have not yet been returned to me. Nayer wrote telling me that she also knew that Shajan was bidding her farewell when she received her copy of the Qur'an.

Shajan asked me to open an account in my name and keep some of her money in it; I asked her why she didn't leave the money in her own account, for which I was a signatory. With irritation, she replied, "Why don't you understand?" I suddenly understood what she meant. I replied that I would open a separate account for this purpose at the Melli Bank. Shajan stressed that she didn't want anyone to spend any money out of their account for the necessary final expenses and charged me with making sure her wishes were carried out. I write all these details because my mother was very proud and hated owing anyone anything. At the time, she was still completely coherent yet somehow knew that she wouldn't be around much longer.

The Death of Shajan

Early one morning in April (Ordibehesht), the telephone rang in our house. The sun had not yet risen. Always afraid of an ill-timed telephone call, I woke up immediately and picked up the receiver. The call was from Shajan's house, letting me know that she wasn't at all well. I hurriedly got into the car and drove to Shemiran. I arrived at her bedside, where she seemed to be resting. Her face looked radiant and youthful, her hair covering part of her forehead; her body was warm. I took her pulse—there was no beat; I listened to her heart—there was no beat. After nine years of illness, Shajan had quietly left us. She was seventy years old.

I alerted my sister and brothers. Dr. Hashemian, her friend and physician since the time she was in London, arrived and confirmed that my mother's heart had stopped just before dawn that morning. In his great novel *Les Misérables*, Victor Hugo describes death as a sinking into the sand and uses these words, to describe the slow death of a traveler engulfed in quicksand, as the "*Sinistre effacement d'un homme.*" Adapting Hugo's words, I would say, "What a sad ending for a brave and active woman, what a sinister, drawn-out death that took so many years to engulf her."

Following her death, my brother spoke on the phone to Kirk in Tyler, Texas. Kirk immediately left his office at the Exxon campus to join Nayer. Later, my sister wrote to me that for a whole week her neighbors and close friends brought over meals for her and her husband. They didn't let my grieving sister do any work; they even took

Shajan bedridden at home after her fall. From left: Ladan, Hamid, Shajan, Mariam, Houri, and Shajan's devoted caregiver Khadijeh

the unwashed dishes back with them or brought food in disposable containers.

This is an American custom and a world of difference from ours. In our culture, we have to be ready from the moment someone passes away to serve our visitors and those who come to express their sympathy with endless meals. At the same time, one is expected not to move from one's seat. Death gives no warning; and it is not possible to make preparations for such hospitality in advance!

My mother rests next to my father in the family burial ground. We ordered her gravestone from the same mason who had created my father's gravestone according to her design. My mother didn't have a good quality of life after my father passed away. The support, encouragement, and patience of Aghajan with Shajan were exemplary. Shajan was a strong woman, courageous and liberal; she was able to use these gifts with my father's backing. She was at the same time devout, disciplined, and very modern in her outlook—at least a half a century ahead of her time. May she rest in peace. Let us now turn our attention to what was happening in the outside world.

The Participation of Women in Political Life

In 1963 (1342), an important aspect of what was known as White Revolution,[11] between the Shah and his people, resulting in a series of far-reaching reforms bore fruit. For the first time, women were allowed to vote in the elections

---

11. Launched by the Shah on 26 January 1963, the White Revolution was intended to bring about a great redistribution of wealth to Iran's working class. Socially, the platform granted women more rights and poured money into education, especially in the rural areas. A Literacy Corps was established, which allowed young men to fulfill their compulsory military service by working as village literacy teachers. Land reform, which was the focus of the White Revolution, did what it was intended to do—weaken the nobles and landlords. In their place, however, emerged a new group of commercial farmers, and many previously large landowning families, including the Pahlavi family, managed to reinvent themselves as commercial farmers. Moreover, the Shah's reforms gave inefficient bloated industries precedence over agriculture, leading to a sense of neglect among the farmers. Mismanagement and corruption resulted in a huge waste of funding earmarked for agricultural development.

and were able to be elected to parliament. My sister Mehri became a candidate for the Majles (House of Representatives), though, in the words of the sage Bouzarjomehr, there were those who rose earlier and got there first.

Six women entered parliament, including Farrokhrou Parsa, the principal of Nourbakhsh High School. Along with my sister, I announced my candidacy for the Senate; the law required prospective senators to have previously held posts as ministers or deputy ministers, or lawyers to have been members of parliament on three occasions, or to have been paying at least 30,000 tomans in tax per annum.

As I was on the board of Reema, I could have claimed that I paid sufficient tax—indeed, Reema paid considerably more than this figure—but I didn't make much progress on this front and nor did I make much effort to promote myself either. At the time, these elections were largely a formality and candidates had to have the support of His Majesty or the backing of high-ranking members of the government.

It became clear that my sister and I didn't have the connections it took to get elected to these posts. Others were more successful. Mrs. Shams al-Molouk Mossahab received a posting for a few hours as a deputy minister of education, which qualified her to become a senator. Mrs. Mehrangiz Manouchehrian was a qualified lawyer and therefore eligible. Mrs. Parsa did not stay in parliament long before she was appointed deputy minister of education and then minister of education.

The Iran Novin Party

The leading members of Kanun-e Moteraghi (Liberal Association) constituted the core of the newly formed government of Javad Mansour, including Amir Abbas Hoveyda, who became minister of finance. The Iran Novin (New Iran) Party replaced the Liberal Association—or to put it another way, there was a change of name, and many new branches were formed. My friends Farideh Mansour, Leila Emami, and Victoria Khajeh-Noori joined the ninth district committee, whose president was Hoveyda. One day, Leila suggested that I should join their branch; up until that time I had never belonged to any political party as my family and teaching responsibilities didn't afford me the time.

I have no choice but to get ahead of myself at this point. Ladan had left home at sixteen to continue her education in the U.S. at Wilson College; Hamid had grown up too and was busy at school. At the same time, I had two members of household staff, both trained by me and perfectly capable of running the house. I asked Leila why she hadn't also asked my sister. She replied, "Mrs. Safinia is very active in the Shemiran branch, in addition to running her school; you have no such commitments at the moment. We are three women in the ninth district with little knowledge of the legal and social status of women; you would be a great asset to us. We have been charged with researching the areas of change in women's rights and believe you would be the best person for this."

At her invitation, I visited the ninth district committee, where Amir Abbas Hoveyda introduced me to the other members. I had prepared a preliminary but comprehensive report, using many legal references, highlighting the shortcomings of the law regarding women's rights. Hoveyda was impressed with my informal presentation and paid me many compliments about my family background. I knew him from afar but this was the first time I had met him in person.

I later found out that district nine was a desirable committee and that many wished to join it. Following the assassination in 1965 (1344) of Javad Mansour, after which Mr. Hoveyda took over as prime minister, the committee meetings were often held at the prime minister's office; we would all gather around the cabinet table and I would often sit in the place usually occupied by the minister of state. Our meetings would take place on Sunday afternoons when there were no cabinet meetings and Mr. Hoveyda would make every attempt to be there.

There was a brief conversation about the current political situation in the country before dealing with the agenda for each meeting when our comments were invited. One day, I mentioned the bureaucracy surrounding the entry and exit visas of students studying abroad who came home for the summer vacation, giving instances of young people I knew in the family. Mr. Hoveyda made a promise to look into this and there was a noticeable change after that—much appreciated by the students. The government even organized sightseeing visits for them in the provinces.

Mehri Safinia being sworn in as a member of parliament, 1972

One day the principal of Azarm School was removed from her post very close to the end of the academic year, due to an unfortunate incident. On a Thursday afternoon, a group of students from this school were on a field trip outside the city. On their way back, one of the twelfth-grade girls decided to ride in her boyfriend's jeep instead of the group bus. The jeep was subsequently involved in an accident, killing both the young people. The girl's parents descended on the prime minister's office and Hoveyda instructed the minister of education to sack the school principal and appoint someone else to the post. The students, who were very happy with their principal, protested about the change and started a riot.

In one of our committee meetings at the prime minister's office, I also objected to the removal of the principal, particularly since it was right at the end of the academic year and had resulted in so much agitation. Hoveyda interrupted me and said defensively that he had taken this initiative to calm the young woman's parents. I pointed out that the person immediately responsible was the group leader; the principal had not even been present on this trip.

I went on, if this reasoning was used, then the minister of education should also resign! A young woman of eighteen, in her last year of high school, had made a bad decision and an unfortunate accident had happened. The same accident could have befallen the school bus. The correct response would have been a written reprimand to the group leader and the removal of the principal could have taken place during the summer holiday.

Hoveyda was a man of great intelligence coupled with humility; nevertheless, he didn't like to be criticized—particularly since the dismissal of this lady had occurred at a time when the deputy minister of education was also a woman.

The Story of Pars Hospital

Mohsen had undergone a simple surgical procedure at Pars Hospital to remove a fatty cyst on his elbow. A few days after this, he visited the surgeon, who was the deputy health minister at that time. I left him there for a half hour to collect Hamid from school, but Mohsen decided he didn't need to wait for me to pick him up and said he would make his own way home. When I got home and realized he was not there, I became worried and immediately returned to the doctor's office in France Avenue opposite Pars Hospital, where I found Mohsen in a sorry state.

It turned out that he had been sitting on the examination bed while the stitches were being removed one by one. Watching the procedure, Mohsen had succumbed to the familiar fainting fit and fallen to the ground, hitting his nose which bled profusely. The doctor had immediately attended to him and bandaged his nose. We left Mohsen's car there and I drove him home in my car; the bleeding continued all night and he had a difficult time. When the doctor's bill arrived, there was a hefty charge for the treatment of the damaged nose!

This happened on a Sunday and I was not able to attend Hoveyda's committee meeting; at the meeting the following week my colleagues asked about my absence before the start of the previous meeting. The prime minister was also present and I related a brief account of the events. A couple of days later, my husband's doctor, the deputy health minister, was appointed minister of health.

My colleagues jokingly requested that I should complain about them so they could also be promoted!

Later, when I became the president of the International Women's Club, I stopped attending these meetings even though many envied my position in this branch since the prime minister headed it. Mr. Hoveyda remained prime minister for thirteen years; he was of great help to the International Women's Club on several occasions.

Around this time, my father-in-law passed away and was buried in the holy city of Najaf. I made an appointment to see Mr. Hoveyda to get special permission for the body and the attendants to travel to Iraq. He looked at me and said, "These Iraqis treat Iranian residents badly and this is the reason our relations are strained with our neighbor. However, I cannot say no to you." He then wrote a note, signed it, and gave it to me. A few days later the body and the attendants left for Iraq.

Treasurer of the International Women's Club of Iran (1963/1342)

Every two years in the month of November (Aban), elections took place at the club. The president and secretary, who had to be Iranian, were elected, and the three vice-presidents and the treasurer would also be appointed. Farangis Shadman's term was over and one of her colleagues, Fatemeh Pirzadeh, took her place, having received the highest number of votes; I was appointed treasurer. These were truly democratic elections and the members were very active in promoting their candidacy. Over 150, and later 200, invitations would be sent out each month to the members; this was done by my husband's secretary at his office under my supervision to ensure no name was missed out. We prepared the addressed envelopes in advance, and when the invitation had been typed and photocopied, we would fill the envelopes and mail them.

I organized the list of members as well as the list of those who had applied for membership, together with their contact details and the date of their application. Mrs. Pirzadeh was a wonderful president and accepted all my suggestions without any objection; she knew I had the best interests of the club at heart. My husband used to call Mrs. Pirzadeh 'Mrs. Half Hour' as most of our conversations were on the phone. The list of applicants for membership was long and we couldn't accept everyone as the gatherings were held in people's homes and occasionally ambassadors' residences.

None of the long-time Iranian members ever left the club; they belonged to the older and more prominent families. As a result, we almost had no members from the community of industrialists and businessmen, who could have been very useful to us. Other women's groups were constantly in search of new members while we had no space to accommodate the ladies who wanted to join our club! The month of Esfand (March) was upon us and we were busy arranging the gathering for the Persian New Year.

Nowruz Gathering of the Club in 1343 (1964)

Mrs. Pirzadeh agreed that I should contact old friends of mine, Alireza Amir-Soleimani and his wife Safoura, who generously agreed to hold our Nowruz meeting at their sumptuous and historic home. It was a magnificent reception; the decoration of the dining table and the table for the *haft seen* (ceremonial New Year spread) was outstanding. I was responsible for the event, with the exception of the food. We had borrowed original costumes from the club members. Hamid, who was seven, wore a long, embroidered coat of white gabardine from the time of Ahmad Shah,[12] together with a matching hat. Ladan, who was fifteen, wore a jacket and wrap-around skirt of hand-woven Termeh fabric with a gold-embroidered headscarf. Lily and her brother Ali, Mohsen's niece and nephew, wore outfits from the Naser al-Din Shah era.[13]

Wearing traditional outfits that had belonged to their family, the host and hostess presided over the *haft seen* table.

---

12. The seventh and last ruler of the Qajar dynasty, Ahmad Shah (1909–1925), was declared shah of Iran on 16 July 1909, the same day his father, Mohammad-Ali Shah (1906–1909), was deposed for opposing and seeking to overthrow the constitutional order.

13. The fourth Shah of Qajar Iran, Naser al-Din Shah reigned from 5 September 1848 to 1 May 1896. He was the first modern Persian monarch to formally visit Europe, and wrote of his travels in his memoirs. A modernist, he allowed the newspapers to be established in Iran and made use of modern forms of technology such as telegraphy and photography and also and authorized the construction of railways and irrigation works. Despite his modernizing of education, his tax reforms were abused by those in power, and the government was viewed as corrupt and unable to protect commoners from abuse by the upper class which led to increasing anti-government sentiment. He was assassinated while visiting a shrine.

Large *morghi* bowls and antique porcelain dishes were filled with delicious sweets. An antique Qur'an, a mirror, and a pair of candelabras graced the table, together with bowls of hyacinths, rue incense, and the other items of the seven "Ss"[14]—all this for the pleasure of our guests.

Mrs. Farideh Diba, the mother of the Shahbanu and our guest of honor, stood admiring all the beauty on display. Hamid, who was the youngest member of the presentation, was especially popular and Mrs. Diba invited him to attend a Nowruz party being given by the crown prince. I thanked her and mentioned that, as we would be on our way to Shiraz the following day, Hamid regrettably could not accept the invitation. I added jokingly that he would like to take a rain check! That opportunity never arose, however. Four years younger than Hamid, the crown prince was only three years old at the time and with no control over his social calendar.

Our foreign guests were captivated by all they saw; I can safely say this was the most outstanding event arranged by the club that had taken place in a private home. To express our gratitude, we accepted Mrs. Safoura Amir-Soleimani as a member.

---

14. The haft seen *is a collection of seven objects, each beginning with the letter "S" in Persian that symbolize good luck and good health, as well as rebirth and renewal, in the New Year.*

My Responsibilities at the Club

The club activities took a two-month break in the summer when our members all dispersed on their vacations. At the start of my second year as treasurer, we experienced an unfortunate event. Mrs. Pirzadeh, to whom I had grown very close, had to travel to England to accompany her son who was receiving treatment for cancer. Since she was away, her responsibilities naturally fell to me and I took over the management of the club with the help of a new treasurer and the board of directors. Our regular meetings took place in the homes of our members and I would conduct the gatherings in the name of our absent president, who was away for seven months.

Unfortunately, the cancer treatment in England did not succeed and the young man passed away. The grieving mother returned to Tehran with the body of her son. We held a dignified ceremony for him; all our members, including the board of directors and our foreign members, took part in the memorial service. Later, in the last session of the club before the summer holidays, Mrs. Pirzadeh formally thanked me for covering for her during her absence.

Ladan Leaves for the U.S.

Ladan was a few months shy of her sixteenth birthday. Uncle Reza and his wife Mariam were returning to Washington after their visit home. Reza had a good job at the International Bank and they had moved to Washington. At my suggestion, Ladan accompanied them and enrolled at Wilson College. Mohsen never begrudged spending for the children's education; nevertheless, I temporarily accepted the financial responsibility for Ladan's education.

To earn the extra money, I agreed to teach English at the Safinia School in the afternoons while still teaching at Nourbakhsh High School. I had to carry this extra responsibility for only one academic year as business gradually improved and we came out of the financial difficulties we had been experiencing. I missed my two daughters but I knew that it was best for them to study abroad. Mariam was now studying in Newcastle, England, and Ladan in Chambersburg, USA—preparing for their future life, of which we shall speak later.

Broadcasting for the Club (1965/1344)

The summer holidays were an opportunity to enjoy a well-deserved rest. Schools were closed and the work of the club (referred to for short as the IWC) had also slowed down. The IWC was in the process of compiling a booklet of women's social services in Iran together with a "Who's Who" of prominent women in the field of social services and administrative work. I was principally responsible for this last part, assisted by several club members to ensure that no one was left out. We only had a short time to do this and were successful in completing the work and publishing the booklet. When this was done, the board of the IWC had an audience with the young Shahbanu.

This booklet was the first of its kind and there had not been research done in the past with respect to women. We were very happy to be meeting the young queen and to be able to speak to her informally. She had learned English and later made so much progress in this language that she was as fluent in English as she was in French; a most impressive achievement.

On the occasion of the publication of the *Guide to Women's Social Services in Iran*, we were invited by the Television Network for an interview. Mrs. Pirzadeh was in mourning and did not wish to appear in front of the camera; I therefore took her place. This was the first time I had appeared on television, although I had often spoken on the radio in the past.

A Trip to Europe

Iran Air had recently begun its operation and they were offering discounted rates to educators for foreign travel. My sister Mehri, Hamid, and I took advantage of this opportunity and planned a month's tour of Europe. The flight first took us to Frankfurt, then Madrid, where we were joined by Nayer, her husband Kirk, and their two sons. We visited the Prado Museum and its incomparable treasures. Kirk, who is a great aficionado of good local restaurants, invited us to a traditional Madrid establishment where large slabs of different meats were grilled in a wood-burning oven. In the evenings, we would watch flamenco dancing and in the daytime bull fighting (a brutal sport I had first seen in Venezuela).

From Madrid, we traveled to Barcelona and spent a few days there. We visited the Picasso Museum and saw his very first paintings, which were done in the classical style and different from his later Cubist works. At this point, Nayer and her family separated from us as they were planning to tour Granada and the Alhambra and later Toledo, while we were going on to Paris. They were to join us later in Newcastle. In Paris, my cousin was the Iranian ambassador, but we preferred not to inconvenience him and arrived without letting him know.

The Russell Hotel

From Paris, we continued to London. The Iranian ambassador in London at the time was Ardeshir Zahedi while Houshang Safinya was the consul general. The latter had booked us into the Russell Hotel. As soon as we arrived at this grand and traditional establishment, we booked tickets for three shows, unaware that our movements were being watched. We were given a large room with three separate beds for my sister Mehri, Hamid, and myself. The first evening, we went to a show after dinner; Hamid, at nearly nine years of age, was able to go by himself from the TV room to our room to sleep. In those days, not every the room in a hotel had a TV; we even tried to rent one, though unsuccessfully. On the second night, our routine was the same, but on our return to the hotel, I noticed that the bag containing my makeup and jewelry, which had been locked, was open.

Hurriedly, I inspected it and discovered that an emerald and diamond ring that had been a gift from my husband was missing, together with all the cash I had with me. My sister went to look through her beauty case and discovered that her diamond ring, along with an antique agate ring from the Sasanid period and a large pearl ring were missing. We called the hotel manager at midnight; Hamid had also woken up. He was questioned and couldn't remember anyone entering the room. Soon the police and detectives from Scotland Yard arrived—in short, none of us got any sleep that night.

We spent the next day in the hotel, depressed and suffering from a lack of sleep. Hamid and I had appointments with the hairdresser to have our hair cut at the hotel. I took Hamid first to the barber. There I saw a man who was having a haircut; I remember only his burgundy-colored trousers since he had a big towel over his chest. I was going to leave Hamid there and go next door to have my own hair done but Hamid refused to be separated from me. The man who was having his hair cut smiled and said, "A big boy like you shouldn't be afraid to stay alone." To defend Hamid, I replied, "Last night someone entered our hotel room and took our jewels and money; my son no longer trusts this hotel and he is right." The man asked me to describe what had happened in more detail.

My sister had spent the morning with an English friend. By the afternoon, I realized that we were suffocating at the hotel. I suggested that we should take Hamid with us to the show for which we already had tickets and buy another ticket for him at the box office. She refused and said she would prefer to stay in the hotel. Hamid and I went to the theater, though the play was totally unsuitable for him—I think it was *Richard III.* It went by in a blur, and I remember almost nothing from that evening.

We returned to the hotel in a taxi. The doorman in his splendid uniform recognized us and said, "Your thief has been found and your sister is waiting for you in the office of the hotel manager." That is where we headed. I saw Mehri sitting surrounded by our suitcases and personal effects with an accusing look on her face as if to say, "You went to the theater and I found the thief." I kissed her and asked, "So, why are you upset?" The story she related could be the basis for a movie called "To Catch a Thief"!

To Catch a Thief

After Hamid and I left, my sister didn't want to stay in our room, which gave onto a balcony overlooking Russell Square, so she called the police station and asked for help. Two detectives turned up from Scotland Yard and, at the insistence of Mrs. Safinia, went through the hotel guest list once again. At the same time, the hotel bartender, who was the man in the burgundy-colored trousers I'd seen at the barber's, noticed a suspicious-looking person who was drinking at the bar and about to leave for the casino to gamble. Since he knew the story of the theft and his suspicion was already aroused, he offered to call a taxi for this free-spending customer and left him briefly to report the man to the police.

At this point, the man smelled a rat and started to run toward the main staircase. The Scotland Yard detectives, who were at that very moment coming downstairs at the insistence of my sister, immediately chased after him. My terrified sister, hiding in a corner, witnessed a scuffle between the man and the police. The thief tried to leave the hotel when one of the policemen overpowered and arrested him. It seems the man and his collaborators were part of a band of jewel thieves who specialized in the theft of high-value but easy-to-carry jewels. They had stored our stolen jewels in the safe of another hotel and had already spent some of my money.

They took advantage of our absence during dinner or, possibly when Hamid was downstairs in the TV room, to enter our room. I was interested to discover how such people could easily move about in these large hotels without arousing suspicion. The way they operated seemed to be as follows: they would enter the hotel wearing a khaki raincoat and a hat, like many hotel guests, while underneath they would be dressed as waiters in tails, which they would pin up to avoid detection. They probably chose their victims at the airport and followed them from there.

They must have noticed that my sister, Hamid, and I were well dressed and had probably seen us buying theater tickets. Once they saw us leave the hotel, they knew we would not be back for several hours. Having taken the elevator to our floor, they removed their raincoats and hats and hid them behind the thick curtains in the corridor. Having unpinned their tails, they could move about as if they were waiters and they used their master key to enter the room. If they were spotted, they would simply nod and say good evening. While one of them entered the room, the second one would be in the corridor as a look-out for him.

That night my sister refused to sleep in the room and we were finally transferred to another room. The following day, we settled our bill, never once thinking that we should ask the hotel for compensation for the lost cash—maybe we were too proud. We were escorted by the police to Holborn Police Station, where we identified our jewels from all the recovered jewelry. A third of our money had been spent; the rest was returned to us. The Iranian ambassador and consul, who had heard about the incident, were informed that the stolen goods had been recovered.

A newspaper wanted to interview us and report the event; we refused as we didn't want to provide our names and pictures for future would-be thieves. For the past year, there had been several large jewelry thefts from important hotels and Scotland Yard had been unable to catch the thieves although they had learned everything about the way they operated. When we finally reached the airport, we had missed our flight and had to take a train to Newcastle, arriving there late in the afternoon. Mariam, her husband Faramarz, and his brother Khosrow were waiting for us. Mariam was still studying, Khosrow was now a dental student, and Faramarz was practicing as a dental surgeon.

For years after this incident, my sister would say, "Houri left me alone and went to the theater." And I would reply with a smile, "If I hadn't spoken to the bartender that morning and if I hadn't left you alone, you wouldn't have contacted Scotland Yard again. Accept the fact that we were both instrumental in helping the police catch this thief." When Mohsen heard about these events, he wrote sardonically in a letter: "Why did you ladies travel with so much jewelry anyway; did Her Majesty the Queen invite you to dine?"

Student Life in Newcastle, England

Nayer also joined us in Newcastle, with Jamie and Jan, her husband Kirk having returned to the U.S. Faramarz (or "Fari," as we always called him) and Mariam were living in a neat, small house that they had decorated themselves. Sometime later, Mariam told me that, when they had almost finished painting the kitchen, she knocked over the bottle of turpentine, streaking the newly painted kitchen cabinets, which then had to be repainted! We all traveled in two cars to Edinburgh in Scotland, driving through the magnificent Princes Street to Holyrood Castle—once the home of Mary,

Queen of Scots, famously condemned to death by Queen Elizabeth I. We toured Edinburgh University, where Nayer had studied, before driving to the beautiful Lake District.

Fari took us to his dental practice, where he gave both Nayer and me a check-up. I encouraged him to return to Iran, where he could continue practicing as a dentist. One of his elderly patients invited us all to dinner at her home. My sister Nayer then took her leave from us to return to the U.S.; it had been a wonderful opportunity for us to get together as a family. My daughter was also expecting a baby in a few months. Mehri, Hamid, and I flew to Cologne, then the capital of the Federal Republic of Germany and where my uncle Dr. Aligholi Ardalan was the Iranian ambassador. We stayed as guests at his home for a few days. Hamid's birthday fell on 26 August (4 Shahrivar) and Mehri Ardalan, my aunt, arranged a splendid party, with a cake, for his ninth birthday. We then flew to Frankfurt and returned to Iran from there.

French Examinations

It was the start of the academic year. Hamid was attending Safinia School in Bagh-e Ferdows. Every day he would go down the metal staircase that connected our house to my brother Bagher's and would accompany his two cousins in their car to school—he would also return from school with them. I taught twelfth-grade English at Reza Shah Kabir High School. Demand for French was on the decline; I had only a few students at twelfth grade who were still studying French and with whom I would read and discuss great works of literature and poetry.

For several years, I was responsible for setting the nationwide French examination questions, which I would prepare toward the end of spring and make as many copies as there were centers where French examinations took place. The copies would be placed in sealed envelopes that I kept in my safe at home, delivering them just before the exams to the Ministry of Education.

On the morning of the exams, I would go by car to the city; people who were responsible for setting exams and didn't have cars would be driven to the centers by government jeeps. Typists were ready in the copy room and we would spend all day in this confined space. The written French exams included dictation, composition, and translation. The typists would type up my handwritten questions and adequate copies would be made for every examination center.

Years later, in Paris, Bernard Pivot, the famous TV presenter, would test volunteers on their knowledge of the French language while reading out a dictation on TV in a program watched by some 6 million people. These were particularly difficult dictations; I also participated as a volunteer on several occasions and wrote out the dictation, though I never managed to do it without making a mistake.

During the French examinations in Iran, on one occasion, when we were locked in the examination room, where lunch was also provided for us, a problem arose. A young blind student was among the candidates and obviously could not take a written exam. I was asked to test him orally; I would read out the dictation to him and he would spell out each word. It reminded me of the spelling bees held in the U.S. I also invited him to deliver the composition orally, which I then wrote down for him. The young man was able to answer the questions relatively well, but I have to confess to some leniency when it came to him.

Elected President of the International Women's Club

It was October 1965 (Mehr 1344). Mrs. Farangis Shadman and Fatemeh Pirzadeh contacted me, and since I was effectively running the IWC at the time, they suggested that I announce my candidacy for president, to which I agreed. Two other members of the club were in competition with me. They were married to very influential men—the husband of one was a government minister and the other was married to a famous ophthalmologist who was also the head of the Iranian American Association.

I was not very good at campaigning for myself. I knew that running the IWC required hard work and experience and it was not just a fancy title. The non-Iranian club members included women of all different nationalities—from American, Canadian, British, French, and German, to Argentinian, Indian, Turkish, and Norwegian—in addition to which, the wives of ambassadors were honorary members. I was elected president with a majority vote, while a younger member, Guity Fallah, was elected club secretary. The outgoing president handed over all the documents she had and the treasurer handed over the balance of the account, a sum of 150,000 tomans, to the new treasurer, Mrs. Harlan, the wife of the American economic adviser.

The following day, I spent some time at home going over the past activities of the club and came to the conclusion that Mrs. Farangis Shadman was not an easy act to follow and that I had taken on a huge responsibility. Naturally, it was not a question of competition or imitation; I needed to be patient and not underestimate myself. My first task was to choose the vice-presidents, with two existing vice-presidents happy to stay in their posts: Mrs. Aars, the wife of the Norwegian ambassador, and Mrs. Sevim Kent, the wife of the Turkish ambassador—representing Europe and Asia respectively.

I also asked Mrs. Silvia Warder, the wife of the head of the oil consortium, if she would accept the post of vice-president. As Mrs. Aars was due to leave soon, I also had to think about a replacement for her. To say farewell to this colleague, I invited many of the club members to my home for tea. We presented Mrs. Aars with a silver platter engraved with the club logo. The following day many of the French and English newspapers carried pictures of this event without us having to spend a cent in advertising.

I requested an audience with the Shahbanu through Mr. Nabil, her chief of staff. This was a tradition established by the club from the time of Queen Soraya and I wanted to use the opportunity to introduce the third vice-president. Mrs. Shadman advised me that it was best if I did not approach anyone directly myself and to ask one of the other vice-presidents to do so on my behalf, so that if the response was negative, it would not compromise my position as the president.

Mr. Armin Meyer was the new American ambassador to Iran; his wife, a former journalist, regularly attended our meetings and showed a great interest in the club. On the day of the elections for club president, Mrs. Meyer had made sure that fifteen of the American members, along with Mrs. Beenie Thatcher, the wife of the American consul, attended and voted. I asked Silvia Warder, whom I knew well, to contact Alice Meyer. On the eve of our audience with the Shahbanu, Mrs. Meyer accepted the post of vice-president, in place of Mrs. Aars, and the following day at 11 a.m., she accompanied us to the office of Her Majesty.

We had previously submitted the list of attendees to Her Majesty's office, which did not include Mrs. Meyer. It was necessary to make sure that her name would be included and I managed to contact Mr. Nabil and resolve the situation. We all gathered at the Turkish embassy in Ferdowsi Avenue prior to going to the palace to plan the presentation to the Shahbanu. The reason I am describing all these events in such detail is to explain what happened afterward, which was important.

At the same time, I had appointed an English-speaking secretary to record the proceedings of the board meetings of the IWC. Our seven-member committee included the president, three vice-presidents, and a treasurer, plus two elected Iranian secretaries and one appointed British secretary. Novin Afrouz, a young concert pianist, who was due to perform in a recital for the IWC, was also accompanying us; she had recently returned to Iran from Milan and had composed a poem in praise of the Shahbanu.

An Audience with Her Majesty the Shahbanu

On such occasions, it was customary to wait and see what language Her Majesty had decided to use when addressing the group; later it is possible to switch to another language. Naturally, the Shahbanu addressed me in Persian; I had recently met her regarding the booklet on women's social services in Iran and she therefore knew me already. I introduced the board members and our conversation gradually turned from Persian to English. When the Shahbanu asked about the activities of the club, I responded that Mrs. Warder had a suggestion that I had found interesting, and Her Majesty asked me to invite Mrs. Warder to speak about the project.

I then asked Silvia to describe her idea, which was to establish a children's convalescence home to care for those who could no longer stay in hospital, nor could be cared for at home. Her Majesty, who was fluent in French,

An audience for members of the IWC with the Shahbanu (far right) at the Niavaran Palace

began to speak in English and I realized how much her command of the English language had improved. She was very supportive of this idea and, as we were leaving, she mentioned that she might be able to help us with the project and would be in touch later.

Club Meetings

The first monthly meeting of the IWC, which is hosted by the new president, was held at the home of Ezzat Khosrowshahi, my sister-in-law. She lived in Farmanieh in a large and beautiful home with a splendid garden. We had invited my

Prime Minister Hoveyda addressing an IWC meeting, 1973. From left: Mrs. Silvia Warder, Houri, Hoveyda, Lady Frances Ramsbotham, Vanna Fillipedes, and Guity Fallah

old friend Mrs. Monir Vakili to honor and entertain us with her magnificent singing voice. I had also invited Madame Osario, my own piano teacher, to accompany Monir on the piano.

On 14 February (25 Bahman), Valentine's Day, the meeting was held at the home of Mrs. Alice Meyer. Intelligent, strong, and very capable, Alice could perform miracles with her handiwork. She had prepared heart-shaped red invitation cards and the whole house was decorated in the Valentine's Day theme, while the tables were a showcase for the sandwiches and pastries prepared by her chef.

Our Nowruz meeting was held at the home of one of the club members, Marina Khabir. Jamshid and Marina were extraordinary hosts and had invited all the ambassadors on that day. There was a performance of scenes from a play about the story of Amir Arsalan and Farrokh Lagha[15] that had been arranged through the auspices of the Ministry of Arts and Culture and with the participation of well-known actors such as Entezami and Nassirian. The beautiful performance described the story of Amir Arsalan both in English and Persian. The Japanese ambassador, camera in hand, recorded the whole proceedings like a professional filmmaker. It was a truly memorable occasion as the play had been a hit in Tehran, featuring performances by the country's leading actors, who offered their time to the club on a purely voluntary basis.

A Joyful Letter

Summer arrived and our monthly meetings came to a halt. A letter came by special delivery from the Shahbanu's office. It stated: "Mrs. Houri Moghadam, at the request of Her Majesty from His Majesty the Shahanshah,[16] a plot of land measuring 5,000 square meters situated behind the Gendarmerie Hospital in Pahlavi Avenue is being put at your disposal to construct a children's convalescence home within a period of three years . . ."

---

15. A popular epic tale, the adventures of Amir Arsalan and his love for Farrokh Lagha in Turkey were originally related in the evenings by the royal storyteller to help Naser al-Din Shah fall asleep.

16. Shah, and Shahanshah (King of Kings) are royal titles that go back to at least the sixth-century BCE in Iran.

I don't remember the exact words as I no longer have the letter, but this was the essence of the communication. I was so elated at receiving this news that I felt I had to share it with my colleagues. The following day, accompanied by Mrs. Warder, Mrs. Meyer, and our treasurer, we went to inspect the piece of land. The rest of the board were away and we decided to arrange for a complete survey of the plot of land and to request the architects of the Ministry of Development and Housing to prepare the architectural plans.

This plot of land had previously been earmarked for the construction of a club for the Gendarmerie and plans had already been drawn up by a private firm of architects. It was only though the efforts of Her Majesty that it had been given to our club for the convalescence home. I spent the next eight months getting this donation formalized and notarized through the ministries of agriculture, state, the Gendarmerie and the Tehran mayor's office—all of whom had their eye on this piece of land and were not keen to cooperate, even though I had Her Majesty's handwritten letter. Finally, the matter was approved by the office of the prime minister.

Everyone was on vacation, leaving only Lois Harlan, our treasurer, in Tehran. On the instructions of Alice Meyer, she asked a group of young American Peace Corps volunteers, who were working in Iran, for help in drawing up plans for the convalescence home. Two architects from the group who were working in the provinces were invited to visit the plot of land in Tehran. They drew up comprehensive plans but advised that the building should be constructed under the supervision of Iranian architects. Theirs weren't the only plans, the Ministry of Development and Housing had also come up with some plans as well as the brother of one of our oldest members!

However, none of these met our requirements, which was to have six dormitories each with the capacity for ten beds, a full-sized kitchen, bathrooms, and a large hall that would be able to accommodate the meetings of the IWC and also serve as a covered, multipurpose room for the children who were still convalescing. At the time, our budget was only half a million tomans raised through the concert, an art exhibition at the Turkish embassy, and a gala dinner at the Hilton Hotel.

I didn't want to use the club's past reserves for this project; every project needs its own dedicated budget. The American design had been estimated at 2 million tomans; the other designs were also each estimated at more than one million tomans as they covered an unnecessarily large area. More importantly, none of the designs had incorporated our requirement of a large hall and therefore didn't meet our needs. Alice Meyer believed the American plan should be implemented, even though she was not too happy with their design.

Mariam and her husband Fari had returned to Iran in 1966 (1345). A bright and capable young woman, Mariam was now an architect and had also made me a grandmother with the birth of a little girl called Leila. I discussed our problem with Mariam, showing her the list of require-

The good old days. From left: Mohsen, Ladan, Houri, Mariam, and Fari, 1966

ments that had been voted on by an extraordinary meeting of the board. We knew exactly what we needed. Mariam promised to see if she could help. Using Reema's facilities, she drew up a simple and comprehensive plan in just two days that covered only 1,200 square meters.

The plan met our requirements; it had six large dormitories each with ten beds, bathrooms, and a kitchen, as well as staff rooms and a large multipurpose room over 200 square meters in size for the use of the club and the children. The staff accommodation was in the basement and care had been given to provide adequate ventilation to take into account Tehran's hot summers and cold winters.

We added this fourth plan to the three previous ones and, in a meeting of the board held at the American embassy, a vote was taken on the designs. Since Mariam's design was one of the four, I didn't attend the meeting in order to leave everyone free to decide.

Rotary Meetings and the Sudden Death of My Brother Nasrollah

The Tehran Rotary Club had invited me to speak about the activities of the IWC and the plans for the construction of the convalescence home. The president and vice-president were Dr. Radji and Mr. Radji. As the keynote speaker, I was seated between the two brothers. One of the rules of Rotary is that the retiring president stays on for another cycle as vice-president to preserve some continuity. Mr. Radji, who was our neighbor in Elahieh, jokingly said, "Mrs. Moghadam, today you are a Radji sandwich." I replied, "You're wrong, this is a Moghadam sandwich. The bread is never mentioned when speaking of sandwiches!"

North Tehran had another Rotary Club, headed by Dr. Farhad, the famous radiologist. He invited me the day before our meeting at the U.S. embassy to be their speaker; I knew many of the prominent members of the Rotary Club. Dr. Farhad opened the meeting by introducing me and mentioned my father, Abdollah Mostofi, as a learned man who had long served the country. When my turn came, I explained our plans for the foundation of the convalescence home and requested the help of the industrialists present with food and sanitary products, TVs and radios. I also announced that a donation of 10,000 tomans would pay for one bed with a mention of the donor's name. My suggestions were warmly welcomed and I received several verbal commitments.

Nasrollah Mostofi in formal attire

At the end of the meeting, I was told that there was a phone call for me. I was surprised that someone had found me at the Rotary meeting. The call was to inform me that my brother, Nasrollah Mostofi, had passed away suddenly. He was only fifty-two years old. I immediately set off for Shemiran. His burial, the memorial services, which were held at the Majd Mosque, and the remembrance service a week later, occupied me to such an extent that I forgot all about my responsibilities at the IWC.

The Choice of Design for the Children's Convalescence Home

The selection of the architect and plans for the children's convalescence home took place at the American embassy in my absence. The following morning, Silvia Warder, my friend and the British vice-president, called me to say that Mariam's design had been chosen. The plans had been produced by Mariam free of charge. When I called Mariam, whose daughter Leila was just a few months old, to tell her the news, she seemed unsurprised, calmly responding that she had expected the design to win since she had not sacrificed the main requirements of the plan and had met all our needs. The building was efficiently designed and would have been the logical choice. I suspected that Alice Meyer would not have been too happy that the plans drawn up by the Peace Corps were not chosen.

The Beginning of Our Differences

There were other difficulties afoot. All the women's organizations in Iran had come under the umbrella of the Women's Organization, headed by Princess Ashraf Pahlavi, the twin sister of the Shah. We were under pressure to join them too. Half of our members were non-Iranians and spoke no Persian; they were also occasionally at odds with our political systems—we had members, for instance, from the USSR and Eastern Europe. The reason the IWC attracted so much attention was that it was considered to be among the top organizations for women in Iran and offered eye-catching and important programs. We were the first to establish and run a free children's daycare center, for example, and we were about to build the first convalescence home for children.

The past presidents of the club and I objected to becoming part of a government-affiliated women's organization. When the suggestion was made to me through one of our own active members, I politely refused. Unfortunately, the representative of the Women's Organization contacted one of our vice-presidents, Alice Meyer, and told her that Princess Ashraf was keen for us to join. In turn, during a board meeting, which was usually held at our house, Alice Meyer then brought up the subject of joining the Women's Organization.

I explained that, according to our constitution, we had half non-Iranian membership and therefore could operate only in the field of culture and charitable works—never anything political. Everyone, with the exception of Mrs. Meyer, accepted this reasonable argument. Alice was a smart lady and knew that my argument was correct. However, she wanted to do a favor for Princess Ashraf and get closer to her, and also to score a point with this issue.

In response to my explanation, she said, "Houri, don't you see that I am in a difficult position as I have been approached today by the representative of the princess and asked to bring her proposition to the board?" I asked her whether the person who had approached her was a certain young lady, giving her name. Surprised, Alice said, "Yes—

how did you know who it was?" I replied, "I know this young lady. I am sure the original suggestion had come from her and, since the princess is very busy, she must have left her to get on with it.

"Let us make a deal. You can take care of the American problems in the club and I will take care of the Iranian problems. I will also write to the Women's Organization and set out the issues preventing IWC from joining them. And I will make sure that Silvia Warder sends you a translation of my letter." Everyone was happy with my suggestion, although Alice Meyer still looked unhappy.

A few days later, I composed a long letter, citing our constitution and presenting a strong case for our inability to join the Women's Organization. I sent the letter in two copies, one to the headquarters of the Women's Organization, and the second copy to the home of Mrs. Diba, the vice-chair of the group. A couple of days after this, I was in class when the school doorman brought me a note from the then principal and also a friend, Forough Kia (later Moadel). I had been summoned to the Women's Organization by Princess Ashraf. It was close to noon and the class was coming to an end; I went to the offices of the organization in Ghavamsaltaneh Street, where I was kept waiting for quite some time.

I was finally called in. Holding my letter in her hand, the princess asked me, "What do you have to say?" I said, "I have put everything down in this letter. However, I will briefly explain our problem." She listened to me carefully and then asked Mrs. Yousefi, the head of the organization at the time, "Why don't you leave them alone? They have a valid point; let them get on with their own work." I requested that the IWC should be informed of this decision in writing. We were about to start work on the building of the children's convalescence home and I didn't want us to be distracted every now and then by such matters.

The same afternoon, the monthly meeting of the club was being held at the residence of one of the club members, Mrs. Taheri, with a fashion show by the designer and couturier Mrs. Iran Farhoudi. I happened to be sitting next to Alice Meyer during the show and I was able to inform her that the problem had been resolved and we would be receiving a letter to this effect. She didn't react except to smile. Wouldn't it be wonderful if one could pre-empt incidents at the international and national level by saying a firm "no" without fear of reprisals? All the other women's organizations merged into the Women's Organization.

Going on a Holy Pilgrimage (1966/1345)

I decided to make the Hajj or pilgrimage to Mecca at the end of that year. At the suggestion of a friend who accompanied me, I went to visit Ayatollah Jazayeri, who lived in a humble house at the end of the bazaar in Tehran. There was a small paved yard and a few rooms; his wife offered us tea in simple glasses and served it herself on a metal tray. The ayatollah was sitting on a simple mat covered with a blanket; a young disciple stood at attention behind me.

After the preliminary niceties and tea, I opened the conversation by saying that I wished to go on a pilgrimage to Mecca and wanted to make an offering. I had 100,000 tomans saved from my years of teaching, I owned my family home, and I had some jewelry that I used every day. I suggested that I wished to donate part of the 20,000 tomans *khoms*[17] that were due toward the establishment of a bed at the children's convalescence home and offer the rest of the money to him.

The elderly holy man smiled and said, "Khanum, I didn't ask you for anything and don't want anything from you." I replied, "It is I who requests your permission to make a donation of 10,000 to the convalescence home and offer the balance to you to be used for charitable purposes under your direction." The young attendant said, "Khanum, there is approximately 2 million tomans in checks and donations under this mat, offered by people for the construction of a mosque in Hamburg."

It was agreed that I should write two checks, each for 10,000 tomans, and give them both to the ayatollah. He would then return one check to me; in this way, I had made the donation to him and he had returned part of it for the children's convalescence home. I was most impressed by this meeting. In those days, holy men lived simple and humble lives and their homes were always open to people—

17. *In Islam,* khoms *(literally, "one-fifth") refers to the required religious obligation of any Muslim to pay one-fifth of their acquired wealth from certain sources toward specified causes.*

they did not engage in politics. Later, my husband donated funds for three beds in the names of our three children for the convalescence home. Many of the other club members joined us in this charitable effort.

A Pilgrimage to the House of God

On both sides of my family, participating in modern life did not conflict with profound religious beliefs. My father, when working in St. Petersburg and still single, never forgot his religious duties and said his prayers and fasted without fail. He never touched alcohol even though he was considered forward-thinking and very up to date! In those days, he wore dinner jackets and tails made by Henri, the tsar's tailor. He knew the whole of the Qur'an practically by heart and would quote from it in daily life. He was in touch with many of the religious teachers of his day while, at the same time, translating Mignet's account of the French Revolution, the manuscript of which was with my brother, Bagher. It was never published, the reason for this being given in my father's autobiography.

Respect for both the old and the new runs in our family. My mother, Shajan, had made her pilgrimage to Mecca many years before and it was the turn of my sister Mehri and me to make the trip. We first flew to Jeddah and donned our pilgrims' garbs there before traveling to Mecca.

Recently, my daughter Ladan and my younger sister Nayer visited the House of God (Kaaba) traveling from the United States. Of course, the facilities and hotels in Mecca today are very different to how they were in 1967 (1346), when I was there, or 1941 (1320) when Shajan made the pilgrimage. Her trip lasted three months, and if we go even further back, the pilgrimage made by our grandparents, Abolhassan Fakhr al-Molk and Princess Valieh, who traveled with their retinue and their two sons by boat and train, took nine months to complete. My trip was over in seventeen days and my daughter and sister did a round trip from San Francisco in only eleven days. It is good to know that the younger generation still maintains its faith.

During the seven trips between Safa and Marwa,[18] we kept crossing paths with Ibn Saud, the ruler of Saudi Arabia, whom I remember as distinguished-looking and somewhat somber. While we were praying at night to Ibrahim, Ibn Saud was also saying his prayers just across from us. After completing our Hajj, we returned to Jeddah, where arrangements were made to fly to Medina. We were told early one morning to prepare to leave. Jeddah airport in those days was simply a desert hut with a roof; there wasn't a chair or bench to sit on and passengers squatted on the floor for hours while waiting for their flights, which were regularly delayed.

---

18. Safa and Marwa are two small hills, connected to larger mountains in Mecca, Saudi Arabia, now made part of the Masjid al-Haram, or Great Mosque of Mecca. Muslims travel back and forth between them seven times in what is known as Sa'ee ("seeking/searching or walking") ritual pilgrimages of Hajj and Umrah (see footnote 33 on page 87).

Mehri was really ill that day and couldn't stand for long. Hours passed and no one thought about the passengers. Our tour leader, Mr. Assem, appeared helpless to do anything. An airline employee, a foreign gentleman, possibly a Texan, to judge by his boots, stood at a counter with one foot on the conveyor belt. He paid no attention to all the complaints and protests of the passengers. I looked around to find the person in charge at the airport. At the very end of this covered space, I saw another airline employee busy eating a tomato omelet. I couldn't decide whether this was breakfast or lunch, or both, as it was 11 a.m. and we had been waiting there since 6 a.m.

Banging on his table in frustration, I asked him in English, "Who is in charge of this wilderness?" The poor man couldn't swallow; he looked up to find a woman in a chador talking to him. He tried to send me away, but I didn't give him a chance and said, "My sister is very ill; we have been waiting here for five hours when we could have been resting in our hotel. What are we to do?" He then got up and led me to a staircase. He told me to go upstairs and turn right, where I would find the office of the airport manager. I did as he had directed and knocked on the door. I greeted the manager and repeated my problem, adding that if he didn't help us, I would lodge a formal complaint to his embassy as soon as I reached Tehran.

He asked how many we were. I replied that we were four, but that there were many more Iranians—young and old—who have been stranded for many hours and we would refuse to leave until everyone was looked after. He realized that I was adamant. The booted foreigner was still at the reception booth. Looking straight at him, I said, "You need to improve your manners." Then, addressing the numerous Iranians who were there, I said, "You will all be able to board soon and we will stay together as a group." There were a few turbaned mullahs among the group. One of them said in a loud voice, "Praise be to God; you are called a weak woman and we are supposed to be the men?"

By the time they called us, the American had disappeared and we never saw him again. All the Iranians boarded and we joined them too. The plane left for Medina amid cries of "Praise be to Allah." Writing these lines now, it occurs to me that we have short memories. In those days, turbaned mullahs, men with neckties, and women with headscarves or chadors lived side by side with those who did not wear hijab. In those days, turbaned mullahs and women in headscarves or chadors lived side by side with men in neckties and women who did not wear the hijab. Nowadays, you don't see a turban or an *abba* any more in the streets of Tehran; the clergy all ride in Mercedes with tinted windows! And women are second-class citizens, simply content that they are represented in parliament. Everyone has turned away from Islam and the clergy are busy acquiring property—no doubt as insurance for the day of reckoning! But more about this later.

Medina and a Pilgrimage to the Prophet's Mosque

In Medina, we stayed at the Altair Hotel. Mehri was burning with fever and passed out once she was in bed. Queen Turan, the mother of Prince Abdolreza and Prince Gholamreza Pahlavi, half-brothers of the Shah, was staying at the same hotel. For two consecutive nights, they cleared the mosque for her party. We were also invited to join their group and visit the mosque—we were twenty-five in all. It was an amazing experience to be in this holy place with such a small group. I sat at the foot of the dais and prayed for everyone, remembering all those who were absent. I prayed for my husband and my children, for our life and their good fortune. I prayed for my sick sister and her family, for our friends, for the good and for those who are not so good in our eyes. I wished for everyone's well-being and for their redemption; it was an unforgettable night!

The following night, my sister was better and was able to join us and take advantage of the quiet in the mosque. On Eid-e Ghadir, Mr. Assem contacted me to arrange a small celebration and assured me that there would be no shortage of food. I therefore invited all the Iranians in the hotel by leaving a note under their doors. We gathered around a large table in a reception hall. Queen Turan was also with us, as well as Mrs. Azar Ebtehaj (the wife of the prominent banker and economic planner Abolhasan Ebtehaj) who was staying there.

The hotel staff also benefited from this occasion, receiving bags of fruit and pastries as well as tips. We finally returned to Tehran; it had snowed heavily in April and it was very cold. We were happy to be reunited with the family. Mohsen jokingly said, "Living with a grandmother who is now also a *hajieh* will be difficult." He had forgotten that he too was now a grandfather. There is a grain of truth in every joke, but I was oblivious to this at that time.

An Audience with the Shahbanu and Construction of the Convalescence Home

The winning blueprints for the children's convalescence home were ready and the Nowruz holiday was over. I requested an audience with the Shahbanu to thank her for the gift of the piece of land. I had been suffering from severe back pain for a while and would lie flat on the floor for relief. My American colleague Mrs. Ruth Hall, who was responsible for the monthly newsletter in English, was busy taking notes on the items to include when the phone rang. I was informed that it was Mr. Nabil from the office of Shahbanu Farah to speak to me. I went to the phone. Mr. Nabil said we had been granted an audience the following Monday at noon; he asked me for the names of all those who would be present on this occasion. I gave him the names of the vice-presidents and our Persian and American secretaries as well as the treasurer. I didn't even mention the name of my daughter Mariam, who had, after all, designed the winning design.

Mrs. Hall didn't speak Persian but understood what was going on and had given the good news to Mrs. Alice Meyer as one of the vice-presidents. The following day, I received a letter from her, announcing her resignation from the board. We were in the habit of addressing each other by our first names, but this letter was addressed to "Mrs. Moghadam"! Shocked at receiving this short, curt note, I replied immediately: "Mrs. Meyer, so long as you haven't informed the board of the reason for your decision, your resignation is not accepted. Signed: President . . ."

That same day, there was a reception at the French embassy. I handed the letter to the guard at the American embassy on my way to the reception, where I tried to avoid Mrs. Meyer. I then stayed for about an hour out of politeness and came home. I felt that Alice Meyer wanted to get her own back following our refusal to join the Women's Organization and the rejection of the plans drawn up by the Peace Corps. She believed I was responsible for these two events. Later that same evening, she had been at dinner somewhere with my brother Bagher and had complained to him that Houri used the Meyer name to get an appointment with the Shahbanu.

My brother was unaware of the situation. On his return home, noticing the lights were still on next door, he came over and told me how unhappy Mrs. Meyer had been. When I explained the whole story to him, he was shocked. Mohsen was also present. My brother asked me to get in touch with Mrs. Meyer immediately. I protested that it was late but he insisted and said that Alice will be waiting for this call. I dialed the U.S. ambassador's residence, and Alice picked up the phone. I told her that I had never used her name or that of any of our other colleagues in my letter to Her Majesty. I had requested an audience simply as president of the IWC, just as I had done the previous year when she was elected vice-president.

Bagher and Mohsen both witnessed this conversation; Alice Meyer had nothing to say in response to my clear reasoning. I also reminded her that she was welcome to join the rest of the board at the audience, and I promised to send her a copy of my letter to the office of Her Majesty as she had already specifically asked to see this. I can imagine her disappointment when she saw that the letters from the previous year and this year were essentially exactly the same.

Monday arrived; I was still in mourning dress for my brother Nasrollah. Guity Fallah and I went together to Niavaran Palace. The other board members were already there, including Mrs. Meyer, the vice-president who had wanted to resign! We all greeted each other and went over what we wanted to tell Her Majesty; I invited Mrs. Meyer to speak about our increased revenues. I then asked Mrs. Lois Harlan, our treasurer, about our bank balance. My estimate differed by only one rial from her figures! I knew exactly what we could budget for the construction project. Guity Fallah was in charge of the food for the children and I was the one to speak about the plans.

Since Alice Meyer had complained to my brother that "Houri speaks Persian and we don't understand," I reminded my colleagues that we would wait for Her Majesty to start the conversation. She would normally do so in Persian and ask the president questions; then, after some pleasantries, the conversation would switch to English. It was exactly so when we first had an audience with the Shahbanu and all had passed very successfully. As before, each person responded to her questions. At the end of the meeting, I reported that Mrs. Silvia Warder would be leaving Iran and expressed gratitude for the contributions of this modest and philanthropic lady.

Silvia had worked for many years as a volunteer in the children's hospital. Before leaving Iran, she confessed that Mrs. Meyer had called her while on a tour of southern Iran in the company of her husband and wanted to share her plan to boycott the meeting with Her Majesty. Silvia had replied that it was an honor for her to be included in the meeting and that she was definitely planning to attend. Our other vice-president, Mrs. Alice Eqbal, was on vacation with her husband and returned to Tehran that very morning. Apparently, Mrs. Meyer had called her at 8 a.m. that morning to dissuade her too from attending. Mrs. Eqbal had replied that she was not expected to attend and had not been informed of the meeting due to her absence.

The U.S. Embassy Charity Bazaar

In late spring, Alice Meyer and our other Iranian and American colleagues organized a large charity bazaar, to be held at the U.S. embassy. Various committees were formed. The other vice-president, Mrs. Eqbal, and I were responsible for running the Iran booth. We approached a handicraft center situated across the street from the U.S. embassy, having first obtained the permission of the Ministry of Arts and Culture, and were given goods to the value of 3,000 tomans. Mrs. Eqbal was a quiet and kind lady and very down to earth; a deep friendship had formed between us that endured for many years. A modest lady, with no airs and graces, she never acted like the wife of a former prime minister, or the spouse of the head of National Iranian Oil Company, and didn't mind accompanying me to the different stores.

Alice Meyer had invited Mr. Hoveyda, the prime minister, to attend this event. I was at my post behind the Iran booth when Mr. Armin Meyer, the U.S. ambassador, approached and told me the prime minister was on his way. "Houri, you are the president and you should greet him at the door." I thanked him and replied, "We are in the U.S. embassy and you are the ambassador and our host. It should be you who greets him at the door. I will approach him when he reaches the Iran booth and greet him privately and you will not be alone since Mrs. Alice Eqbal will be at your side." Soon after this, Mr. Hoveyda appeared and actually made several purchases from our stand. He was not carrying any money on him to pay for his purchases and later sent us a check as a donation.

They had set up a disco in another corner of the grounds for the younger people where you could hear all the latest hits. The total proceeds from this event, including the international stall, the U.S. booth, lottery, and games were substantial. I had had good reason to introduce Mrs. Meyer to Shahbanu Farah as the person responsible for increasing our revenue! Our spring event, the U.S. Embassy Garden Party, had been a great success. The highest sales belonged to the Iran booth; Mohsen purchased a painting by the contemporary artist Iran Daroudi. My sister Mehri paid twice the retail price for a set of turquoise plates and bowls that we had been given by the handicrafts store for free—Alice Eqbal was in charge of wrapping up Mehri's purchase! Everyone cooperated and the event passed without a single unpleasant incident. We invited several bids for the construction of the convalescence home, with the help of the Ministry of Housing, and chose one of the contractors.

Expo 67

The summer of 1967 (1346) had arrived. Ladan was in the U.S., studying at Wilson College, and wanted to stay on for another month to take a dance class with the celebrated Martha Graham. She was keen on dance and headed the college dance group. I wanted to visit the 1967 International and Universal Exposition in Montreal and decided to plan a short trip with eleven-year-old Hamid to North America—with Mohsen's blessing. It was Hamid's first trip to the U.S.; we joined Ladan in New York and traveled together to Montreal. Expo 67 was being held a little way outside the city center, near the St. Laurence river, and we had reserved rooms in a motel nearby, where we could travel to and from the exhibition by shuttle bus.

On the first day, we visited the Iran stand, which was managed by the National Iranian Oil Company. We were warmly received; the VIP treatment including the right to visit all the other stands without having to wait in line. These were some of the privileges offered us without even asking. At the time, Iran had a high standing in the international community. In front of the large exhibits of Canada, Czechoslovakia, France, UK, and Germany, the lines were very long. Accompanied by the two children, we were given access through private entrances and could visit everywhere we wanted.

For the first time, exhibits were voted on by the participants by pushing a red or green button. The main theme for the expo was "Man and His World". In my opinion, the Czech stand was the best of all. The creative Czechs had made a film that incorporated a live theater act; a person would emerge from the screen and continue the story of the film in a live performance.

New York–Tyler, Texas

After a week in Montreal, we returned to New York, where we said goodbye to Ladan. Hamid and I were invited by my sister Nayer in Tyler, Texas, to visit her. Hamid had a chance to get to know his two cousins, Jamie and Jan, the first two years older and the second only six months older than him. They had of course met before in Tehran. My sister gave two large receptions in my honor and invited her many friends and acquaintances.

The San Francisco Conference

After New York and Tyler, we visited San Francisco, where the International Women's Organizations held a large conference every two years. The conference that year was at the Hilton Hotel and we had reserved rooms there. After twenty-four hours in the hotel, Hamid was invited by Mr. Farrokh Panahi-Izadi, his mother Razieh Khanum, and her grandson Nader, to San Rafael for a few days. Nader and Hamid were only two weeks apart in age; this kind lady was my friend and I was sure Hamid would have a good time with them.

As the president of the IWC of Iran, a member of the international body, I was invited to be a guest speaker to talk about the new activities of our club, which included the children's convalescence home. I wanted to honor the founder of our club, Mrs. O'Grady, the wife of the former U.S. ambassador to Iran. Although I didn't know her personally, I was aware that she had a special interest in Iran. For this reason, we invited her to the conference to be our guest for lunch and to hear the presentation. At the end of the presentation, I asked Mrs. O'Grady to stand up and everyone applauded her. We were able to have a few words at the end of the meeting, during which she thanked me for inviting her.

The conference was very well planned. One of the speakers was Jack Valenti, one of the greats of the cinema at that time, who had arrived in his private plane from LA. I also met a lady who had traveled from the East Coast by a plane that she had personally piloted. She invited me to the top of Mark Hopkins Hotel, from which you could see the whole of San Francisco, the Golden Gate and Bay bridges, and the Atlantic Ocean spread out below. An interesting young woman, she was also intrigued to meet someone from the Middle East.

Washington DC

We left Los Angeles for Washington DC. My brother-in-law Reza, his wife Mariam, and their young son Kamran were living in Chevy Chase and we stayed a few days with them. During our stay, Houshang Ansari, the Iranian ambassador in Washington at the time, invited us all to dinner. The senator from Texas, Mr. Yarborough, whom we had met in Tehran, invited me to attend the Senate for a sumptuous lunch as his guest, together with my sister-in-law Mariam. Senator Yarborough and his wife, Opal, were my sister Nayer's friends from Houston and had been our guests one evening in Tehran. He had called to invite me by phone a month earlier while I was in Tyler.

Washington–Tehran

Accompanied by Hamid and Ladan, who had joined us, we left for Tehran. Our arrival caused much excitement at home. Mohsen seemed happy and friends and family paid us visits. Leila, our granddaughter, had grown and was a source of great joy for us. Our son-in-law, Fari Safinia, was setting up his private practice in Tehran—having decided to return home from England. At the same time, he was teaching at the National University of Iran. The wheel of life was turning; it was the end of summer with a little time remaining before the start of the school year.

Building and Equipping the Children's Convalescence Home

I would pay regular visits to the construction site of the children's convalescence home, where work seemed to be proceeding well. At the same time, I had asked a group of members to help with equipping the home, each accepting responsibility for one aspect of this. We formed different committees, and it was decided to call each each of the six dormitories after a flower. We were well supported, with gifts arriving from different members and other organizations. Marina Khabir accepted the task of providing the curtains for the dormitories while I adopted the design of our own kitchen, which had recently been built by Mr. Aftandelian, and simply enlarged the scale. The large hall intended for the club meetings and children's gatherings was now ready. Guity Fallah, the club secretary, had donated the fabric for the curtains. Small flags representing the different member nations had been ordered and donated by the Iranian representative of the UN.

Beds and bedding miraculously arrived in a very short time. The garden committee was headed by Beenie Thatcher, a truly good friend. She produced a beautiful design that was instantly accepted. Mr. Bonakdarpour, a professional garden designer, offered his services free of charge and with the help of a green-fingered club member, Mrs. Zari Taheri, the garden started to take shape. Other members volunteered their time and donated trees and shrubs. Many institutions and members paid for the beds, to the tune of 10,000 tomans each, which helped considerably in the equipping of the home. The IWC, which would now be meeting at the home, had its own, new address.

The Coronation

October 1967 (Mehr 1346) was a busy month for all Iranians. The Shah was being crowned after twenty-six years on the throne and more importantly, Shahbanu Farah, was assuming the role of regent up to the time the crown prince reached maturity. It was suggested that, as the chief of protocol of the court was our neighbor and his wife a friend, she might expect me to write him a letter. It wasn't a bad idea, but I suggested that Guity write the letter on behalf of the IWC. This resulted in two invitations arriving for Guity and myself.

On the day of the coronation, we participated in the sumptuous event; we had good seats in the exterior of the Golestan Palace. Inside the palace were the members of the royal family, the prime minister and cabinet ministers, foreign dignitaries, military chiefs and close friends of Their Majesties. Everyone else, heads of banks, CEOs of companies, both private and public, university professors, industrialists, and members of the government were seated outside, where they could observe Their Majesties leaving the palace and getting into the royal coaches.

The crown prince was just seven years old and walked with great dignity in the procession. People applauded him. The men were dressed in tails and the ladies wore long dresses and gloves. Designed in Paris and made in Tehran, the Shahbanu's outfit was magnificent. It was a day of celebration, and I must emphasize here that, at that time, the royal family were much beloved by the people.

Teaching English at the National University of Iran

Located in the hills of Shemiran, the National University of Iran, founded in 1959, was still in its infancy. I was invited to teach English in the faculty of sciences, which included teaching science and medical students to write scientific texts in English. I took on eight hours of classes a week, for which I was paid 35 tomans an hour, my monthly pay equivalent to what I paid our cook. I worked only thirty-four hours a month but marking papers and other work done at home had to be included in this. Each class consisted of twenty-five students. They came from Tehran and the provinces, from different social classes and with differing levels of knowledge of English. International students from the Tehran American School mixed with students from far-flung parts of the country.

In those days there was not a headscarf to be seen, the classes were peaceful, and there was no sign of political activity. From 1970 (1349) onward, however, I noticed a few young women wearing small headscarves that didn't cover all their hair. Gradually, the scarves grew larger until it was the turn of *maghnae* (a face covering) and black chadors! In spite of my family's devotion to traditional values, I was not happy to see young university students wearing a chador. Reza Shah had abolished the veil and opened the doors of the university to women. Now, after thirty-five years, we were stepping back in time—this could not be called progress. I tried to keep my thoughts to myself and not allow my feelings to show in class.

One day, as I entered the classroom, I saw a scene that gave me food for thought. A young woman wearing a black chador was sitting next to a young man called Albert. Albert, who spoke good English, had been a student at Iran Zamin School, a combined Iranian and American international establishment, and was dressed in the latest fashion with a shirt unbuttoned to his navel and a large silver cross hanging around his neck. Veiled girls would usually sit at the back of the room. On this occasion, the young woman had arrived late and the only seat available was next to Albert. I asked him to button up his shirt out of respect for the young woman sitting next to him, and he immediately obeyed. Albert spoke good English; the veiled women were also good English speakers. Trained in Islamic schools located in old buildings in the furthest corners of the city, many of them were academically far superior to the well-heeled, fashionably dressed young women students.

In November (Aban), the students commemorated the death of two students at the University of Tehran and refrained from attending classes. Most of the time, my students would share this information with me in advance and request that I go along with their wishes. One of the student leaders would open the class door and I would nod to allow the students to leave and smilingly would say, "I have dinner guests tonight and this is a good opportunity for me to go home and prepare for them!"

My University Students

In all my thirty-nine years of teaching in a high school and later at the university, I can honestly remember only two occasions when I had some friction with a student, for I respected my students and university colleagues. It was in the first two weeks of term and the class was in full swing, when a tall young man entered and went to take a seat. Not recognizing him, I asked what he was doing in the class. He replied that he had come to study English. I reminded him that the course had started two weeks before and this session had already been going for a half hour. Where had he been until now? He replied that he had been a student for five years. I replied, "How many more years do you intend to stay? You are taking up the space of all those students who did not gain admittance; a BA is supposed to take four years."

I told him to listen up and never step into this room again. I was not prepared to accept a student who was not willing to apply himself. He had no choice but to leave. I apologized to the students for the interruption and continued with the class. The following day I received a note from the head of the department requesting that I re-admit the young man to my class. I replied, writing at the bottom of the same note, "This student does not belong in my classroom. He is a time waster and I am sure there are other classes he can choose to attend." That was the end of that episode.

I am getting ahead of myself. In 1976, toward the end of the academic year, I went on a short trip abroad; as a result, I was going to miss the final English exams. The multiple-choice questions were set by the head of the department; they were corrected automatically and my presence was not really necessary. On my return, I went to the office to see the results of the exams and found a few of our veiled women students who were complaining of having failed the exam.

I asked to see their exam papers and realized that they had done badly in the exam and were correctly graded. I then looked at their grades during the term and found the median between the two grades, as a result of which some had passed and some hadn't. I adjusted the final grade at the bottom of the exam papers and signed them. This was quite risky, and I was the only person with the authority to change the grade; if by chance I had made an error, I would have had to face the consequences.

I saw a few of them outside in the corridor and informed them that now they had a passing grade. I also reminded them that they owed this to their efforts during the academic year and not to their performance in the final exam. They admitted that they had neglected to revise properly and had put their effort in preparing for other subjects. I wish I knew what eventually happened to these students of mine as some of them were truly smart, hard-working, and serious about their studies. For now, the country is in the hands of a bunch of incompetent illiterates.

Hamid and Alborz High School

Life went on. Ladan was in the last year of Wilson College and Hamid had left Safinia School and was attending Alborz High School in the city. At lunchtime, a driver would bring him home to Shemiran and would then take him back to school. A commute of 50 kilometers a day to attend school, including the round trip at lunchtime, wasn't very practical, however, and seemed a big waste of time. The main issue was that there was a two-hour break for lunch between the morning and afternoon sessions. Unlike Hamid, most of the students stayed in school or only went home for lunch if they lived nearby. Some would leave school to buy lunch as there was not an adequate school cafeteria. In addition, the school didn't have enough playgrounds for the number of students. In my opinion, this two-hour break was a waste of time and, what's more, gave the boys plenty of opportunity for getting into trouble.

I discussed this with Dr. Mojtahedi, the school principal, on a couple of occasions and suggested a shortening of the lunch break. Instead, they could end the day earlier, especially in the fall and winter when the days were short. But my comments seemed to fall on deaf ears.

Hamid finished seventh and eighth grade with this long commute. He was among the best in his class as he was very good at math and English, but when I saw his report card for the second term of eighth grade, I noticed he had only a 10 (out of 20) for history. Even then, TV in the evenings was a major distraction for school-age children and certainly did not give Hamid enough time to study and memorize much of the history textbook. Nevertheless, a grade of 10 was unacceptable in our household. When the end-of-year exams grew near, I kept him under strict surveillance and made him work hard. I told him, "Your grandfather is a historian and used to teach history at the law school. Your low grade is a dishonor to his name and mine." His history grade improved to 14!

I admit that the teaching method and the expectation that a student should simply memorize facts about battles and victories without understanding the causes or effects of those events doesn't leave much of an impression on a young mind. Even if a test question is so designed that students may refer to a textbook, they still may not be able to answer it unless they have understood the underlying cause.

In the third year of high school (ninth grade) and with Mohsen's approval, we sent Hamid to Iran Zamin School, which had a forty-five-minute lunch break, so that day ended early and the students came home at 3 p.m. When I went to see Mr. Moussavi, the deputy principal of Alborz High School, to get Hamid's record, he asked me, "Khanum, all the other parents wish their sons had been accepted to the class Hamid was eligible for, and yet you are transferring him to another school?" I replied, "Maybe those parents are not aware of the damaging effect of this two-hour break in the life of an impressionable boy. I am a teacher myself and I know full well how much trouble a boy can get into during even a short period of time.

From left: Hamid, Leila, Houri, Mariam, and Mohsen

Problems don't arise when the boys are in the classroom; you are not paying enough attention to what they might be doing outside class." Hamid spent his ninth grade at Iran Zamin School. The problem of idle time was resolved but there were other problems—more about these later.

A Trip to India and Ceylon (Sri Lanka)

I took advantage of the break between two terms at the National University and, with Mohsen's approval, I joined five members of the International Women's Club on a remarkable trip to India and Ceylon. The trip lasted for twenty-five days. My companions were Mrs. Farangis Shadman, Mariam Arfaa, and three German ladies who were members of the club. The trip was well organized and included visits to New Delhi, Agra, Aurangabad, Ajanta, Ellora, Bangalore, Mysore, Bombay, Madras, Jaipur, and Udaipur.

We spent a few days in the Indian capital, New Delhi. Mr. Jalal Abdo, the Iranian ambassador to India at the time, invited our group to a luncheon at the embassy. There were innumerable sites to visit around the city. We spent most of the days visiting historical sites in New Delhi, traveling in two cars with two guides, one of whom was Persian but knew several Indian languages while the other was Indian and spoke perfect English. Being a tourist involves a great deal of walking and we had walked for miles that day. In anticipation of the luncheon at the embassy with Mrs. Abdo, I had a spare pair of smart black shoes in the car so I could change before seeing her and appear more respectable!

The following day, we traveled to Agra and visited the Taj Mahal, a magnificent structure built in the mid seventeenth century as a burial place for Mumtaz Mahal, the favorite consort of Shah Jahan. Mumtaz Mahal, the daughter of an Isfahani merchant, was born in India and married Shah Jahan. When she died, her husband asked the architect Issa Isfahani, whose name is inscribed in marble close to the name of the royal couple, to build what is considered to be one of the most beautiful pieces of architecture in the world.

In Udaipur, there were many other magnificent sites, one of which was the fabulous Lake Palace Hotel, formerly the home of a maharaja. We were lucky to be able to spend a few days there, from where we would take a boat to the shore to visit the city. In the maharaja's own quarters, all the furniture, including his bed and chairs, tables and the entire contents of the room, were made out of crystal. We celebrated Gregorian New Year's Eve 1968 (1347) there. Purple and orange bougainvillea covered the walls of this spectacular building constructed in the middle of a large manmade lake—an unforgettable experience.

From Udaipur we flew to Aurangabad and checked into our hotel. Our Persian guide, who had organized the entire trip from Iran, had lived in Germany for many years where he had worked as an announcer of Persian news on the radio. He was extremely efficient and did everything to make our trip as enjoyable as possible. The day after our arrival, we visited the Ajanta caves, discovered early in the nineteenth century by a British officer. We were told that this officer had lost his way and was separated from his platoon. Losing control of his horse in the dense forest surrounding the caves, he suddenly found himself in a clearing where, to his amazement, he discovered several extraordinary caves carved out of the low hills. When he eventually found his way back to his barracks, he prepared a report about his discovery and returned to the site armed with tools and experts.

What we were able to see in that one day was quite amazing. There were twenty numbered caves in which were raised images carved out of stone that told the story of the Buddha from when he lived as a wealthy prince to the day when he announced to his family that he was abandoning all his wealth and power to live in the wilderness. We were told that, if the Hindus had found these caves, they would have been destroyed. It was sheer luck that these marvels had remained undiscovered and later found by those who appreciated their history and craftsmanship. To visit all twenty caves, we had to climb many staircases, specially built for this purpose. Mrs. Shadman, who was not in the best of health, had no choice but to be helped by being carried up and down the stairs.

The next day we drove to Ellora and visited the Hindu temples carved out of stone, with a number of scenes depicting naked men and women engaged in different forms of sexual intercourse in addition to events from the major epics of Hindu literature. Unfortunately, our visit was cut short because Mrs. Shadman became unwell; I returned with her to the hotel and spent the next day at her bedside. An Indian doctor visited her and ordered complete rest. Our group then traveled to Bombay where Mrs. Shadman was hospitalized. We stayed a few days in Bombay and visited Elephanta Island situated in the Indian Ocean.

On the island, we were told the story of Shiva, his consort Parvati, and their son Ganesh, in a series of scenes all carved in stone. How Ganesh acquired his elephant head is quite a story in itself. Shiva had gone away, unaware that his wife Parvati was with child, who was born a few months later. Shiva's travels lasted several years; when he returned home unannounced after this long time, he saw a little boy. Thinking that his wife had been unfaithful to him, he beheaded the child. At that moment his wife emerged from her bath and cried out, "You just murdered your son! I was pregnant when you left."

Shiva, horrified and contrite, ran out of the house in the hope of finding another head to connect to his son's lifeless body. Just then he spotted an elephant coming toward him. He then beheaded the elephant and connected its head to his son's body (of course, only gods are capable of such miracles!). This is how Ganesh ended up with a human body and an elephant's head.

In Bombay, we visited the Taj Mahal Palace Hotel and the Gateway of India, among other sites. The staff in the hotels still followed British protocols. We found the hills around Bombay green and lush; of particular interest were the mounds created by ants with their saliva. With some as tall as a ten-year-old child, the mounds were so solidly built that you could not demolish them even with a pickaxe. One night in Bangalore, we were taken to see a classical dance performance, in which, as our guide explained, every twitch of the eye, eyebrow, hand, or foot by the young dancer had some religious significance. Street vendors visited the hotel every evening and offered beautiful hand-embroidered tablecloths at very reasonable prices. We could shop right there and didn't need to visit stores.

The contrast between the opulence on the one hand and the extreme poverty and misery on the other created an enormous contradiction. We saw children who were naked, some just wearing a rope around their waist; they ate whatever they could find. What I learned during those few days was that Indians love Iranians and respect them even though Nader Shah[19] was considered an invader who had robbed India of the Peacock Throne as well as much priceless jewelry. Although our Indian guide had a master's degree, it wasn't enough to feed a family, as I found out later; salaries were meager and expenses high. This is why he had become a tour guide to earn extra money.

In Bangalore, we visited the public gardens in the evenings as they were lit up and beautifully decorated. In addition, being wintertime, the weather was most pleasant. After twenty days in India, we flew to Ceylon, as it was called in those days. Mrs. Shadman stayed in Bombay and joined us at the airport on our way back home. We stayed in Colombo, the capital. The weather was so pleasant that we even swam in the Indian Ocean before leaving by car for Kandy. On the way, we passed lush tea plantations. Traveling by car has the advantage of allowing one to see

---

19. Ruler of Iran from 1736 to 1747, Nader Shah (1688–1747) rose from obscurity to control an empire that briefly stretched across Iran, northern India, and parts of Central Asia. He developed a reputation as a skilled military commander and succeeded in battle against numerous opponents, including the Ottomans and the Mughals. The decade of Nader's own tumultuous reign was marked by conflict, chaos, and oppressive rule. Nader's troops assassinated him in 1747, after he had come to be regarded as a cruel and capricious tyrant. His empire quickly collapsed, and the resulting fragmentation of Iran into several separate domains lasted until the rise of the Qajars decades later.

everything close up. We would rest and eat in guest houses hat had been reserved for us. We were astounded to see the three larger-than-life Buddhas: standing, sitting, and sleeping. At the time, Korean experts were injecting chemicals and working to preserve these 1,500-year-old ancient monuments carved out of the mountainside.

We were told that the government had put a stop to the peddlers who would congregate around these sites and sell souvenirs to tourists. As they couldn't earn a proper living that way, they would come in the dark and hack away at the images of the gods carved in the stone, causing great damage to them. As a result, the historic sites were surrounded by barbed wire and experts had been appointed by UNESCO to repair the damage. It is sobering to think that if those who were against the teaching of Buddha had got their hands on these monuments, none of them would have been preserved.

On the way back from Kandy, we stayed one night at the place where they filmed *Bridge over the River Kwai*, chosen because of its resemblance to the actual River Kwai which the film makers could not use. In fact, the hotel where we stayed was built for the crew at the time of filming and later turned into a hotel. I woke up really early one morning before sunrise and crossed the river in a canoe. I bought souvenirs and postcards everywhere. Among the gifts from Ceylon, to bring back home I bought two pineapples for a dollar each. We were finally united with our friend Mrs. Shadman at Bombay airport; she was feeling much better and we flew back together to Tehran.

Back in Tehran

On my return, I threw a big party and invited family from both sides. It was good to see everyone. To celebrate, I cut open the two pineapples and shared the fruit, regarded then as an exotic novelty. Winter was almost over and Nowruz (1347/1968) around the corner. Mohsen was preparing for a trip as the problems with Reema had not given him an opportunity to get away for a while. I was planning to stay in Tehran with Hamid. One night there was a grand reception given by the National Iranian Petrochemical Company, of which my brother Bagher was the managing director, at the Hilton Hotel to which we had also been invited.

After dinner, just as Mariam was getting up from the table, she passed out. If her husband hadn't caught her, she might have suffered a concussion hitting her head on the wooden floor. Even though she seemed to recover quickly and got up, I was really worried. We decided it would be a good idea to send her to London for further investigation. As her husband was doing his military service at that time, Mohsen agreed to accompany her to London. It was strange that, in spite of his great love for his children, he seemed at first reluctant to do this.

Our granddaughter Leila's second birthday came around. The party was held at my sister Mehri's house, where Fari and Mariam were living, and two-year-old Leila wore a beautiful pink outfit. We all attended the party and Mohsen left straight for the airport from there. Mariam was due to fly out the next day and Mohsen would meet her at Heathrow airport. Unable to accompany Mariam, as I couldn't leave Hamid behind, I was very anxious and decided to make a pilgrimage to the holy city of Najaf to pray for my daughter's recovery. I discussed this with Mohsen before he left. He didn't seem too happy about this and accused me of taking too many trips; I was surprised that he considered this a vacation! Eventually he consented and I decided to take our cook, Fatemeh, with me and Hamid.

The Pilgrimage to Najaf

We left the house in Ghasem's care and I got a passport for Fatemeh. The plan was for her to travel by bus; we would fly and join her at the destination. Initially she was really overjoyed at the prospect of the trip, but later she came to me and said, "Khanum, I will lose face among my family and friends if they find out that I didn't fly with you. Please take me with you and deduct the difference in price between a bus and airline ticket from my wages." I assured her that there would be no need for that and she could fly with us anyway.

After Mohsen and Mariam had left, we departed for Baghdad, where we spent the Persian New Year's Eve at the home of the Iranian ambassador, Mr. Ezzatollah Ameli, and his wife. I couldn't help thinking of my father, who had been so excited to be appointed to this same post. Unfortunately, the Iraqi foreign ministry had not approved his appointment, which was not surprising given the books my father had written, revealing the duplicity of the British and the Russians.

Hamid was not too happy about this unexpected trip. A religious pilgrimage couldn't have been too exciting a prospect for a twelve-year-old boy. Maybe he would have preferred to have gone away with his father. I pretended not to notice. Fatemeh, Hamid, and I stayed in Baghdad's best hotel; I did some shopping, but Fatemeh bought twice as much—to the point where I had to pay excess baggage for her. We visited many places outside Baghdad, especially sites with Iranian artifacts, and of course we regretted having lost that territory. In the holy city of Najaf, we were invited to the house where my mother-in-law and sister-in-law were staying. Molouk Kashani and I often prayed for Mariam and shed many tears. Those two ladies truly shared my unhappiness and sincerely prayed for Mariam's recovery. Soon we were on our way back to Tehran.

Mariam and Ladan Come Home

The specialist in London told Mariam that she had to be careful when standing up as she had a serious fluctuating blood-pressure problem, which had caused her fainting spell. He also asked her to stop smoking and Mariam listened to his advice. She returned to Tehran after a few days as she had left Leila behind. At the time she had two jobs: at Reema with her father and as a teacher at the Safinia School. Her students both loved and were in awe of her.

Life got back to normal and Mohsen returned from his travels. The academic year also came to an end and Ladan graduated from Wilson College with a BA. None of us was able to be there for her graduation; luckily my brother Bagher, who was in the U.S. on business at the time, made his way to the small town of Chambersburg to represent the family. Ladan headed a ballet group called the Orchesis Dance Company and they had put on a wonderful performance. She returned home and livened up our lives considerably. A beautiful young woman, with a great sense of style and a strong sense of purpose, she wanted to prepare herself for an MA at Columbia University in New York.

She left for New York at the end of summer having decided to continue her studies in economics. We communicated only through letters; making long-distance phone calls was very rare in those days. Ladan has beautiful handwriting, both in English and in Persian. Mariam writes too quickly; her brain works faster than her hands and her handwriting resembles geometric shapes—which is another way of saying she has really bad handwriting! Hamid is somewhere in between and has acceptable penmanship. Mohsen had beautiful handwriting; all you can say about mine is that it is legible.

The Formal Inauguration of the Children's Convalescence Home

Her Majesty Farah Pahlavi formally opened the children's convalescence home. Mrs. Khonsari, president of the IWC at the time, welcomed Her Majesty along with the board members of the club. After the Shahbanu had finished inspecting the dormitories and other facilities, she approached me as she re-entered the main hall. Shaking hands with me, she said, "I know how much work goes into establishing a place like this." This was her way of acknowledging my efforts.

A little while later, a crack appeared in the building. I am sure that in the initial stages of the construction, when I was away, and not able to supervise the project, the contractor had been negligent. I contacted Mrs. Khonsari and told her that this building was my project and I would accept responsibility for its structural problems. I visited Mr. Yeganeh, the minister of works at the time, and was received by him. I explained that the contractor had been chosen under the direction of the Ministry of Works and was on the list of approved contractors, but apparently he had then given the job to a less experienced subcontractor. It seemed that the problem was in the laying of the foundation of the building.

After I had related the story, Mr. Yeganeh shook his head and said, "I am glad to hear your account. It is our responsibility to ensure the original contractor makes good the damage by demolishing part of the left side of

The Shahbanu visits the children's convalescence home, 1966. From left: Mrs. Shadman (second from left) Mehri, the Shahbanou, Mariam, Houri, and Silvia Warder (shaking hands)

the structure and rebuilding it according to building regulations. Otherwise his company will be blacklisted." We managed to contact the original contractor with the help of Mr. Yeganeh's deputy, and he realized that it was in his interest to make good the damage. The part of the building that had suffered settlement was rebuilt as a result of cooperation between the ministry, the contractor, and the club. As long as there is goodwill on all sides, every problem can eventually be resolved.

Fall 1968 (1347)

The long weekend in October (Mehr) gave Mohsen, Hamid, and myself an opportunity to visit Isfahan, together with Mariam, her husband Fari, and their daughter Leila. We stayed at the magnificent Shah Abbas Hotel, a unique blend of old and new—a creative conversion of an old caravanserai into a modern hotel. We had a really enjoyable time with our two children, Hamid and Mariam, though we missed having Ladan, now at Columbia University in New York, with us too. Isfahan is a beautiful old city; our hotel had recently been inaugurated and everything was new. Years later when I traveled to Isfahan and visited the hotel, dust had settled on its beautiful chandeliers, the sheets were old and the beds dilapidated. Much had changed between 1968 and 1992 (1347 and 1371)! The quality of the food was atrocious too, but I digress . . .

The three days were soon over and we returned to Tehran. That night, on the occasion of the coronation, there was a gala performance at the Rudaki Concert Hall with Margot Fonteyn, the British dancer, and Rudolph Nureyev, a Russian exile living in the U.S. They performed the pas de deux from *Don Quixote* as well as excerpts from several other famous ballets. We made it in the nick of time, having raced home to change and arriving just as the doors of the hall were closing for the arrival of Their Majesties. We had excellent balcony seats that I had purchased months in advance and the best view of the stage as well as of the royal party. It was a formal occasion and the audience wore evening gowns and dinner jackets. Although Rudolf Nureyev was a young man and Margot Fonteyn must have been around fifty at the time, it was an unforgettable performance by the world-famous prima ballerina and this young virtuoso who had had to leave his country.

Nowruz 1348 (1969)

Mohsen had been talking about a visit to the U.S. for some time and the possibility of taking a round-the-world trip, though there was no indication that we would be traveling together. Business was running more smoothly and the company was performing well. Ladan was at Columbia and Mohsen wanted to visit her and possibly have her accompany him for part of the trip. Easter break coincided with the Nowruz holidays. Twelve-year-old Hamid had never traveled with his father, although he had accompanied me to Europe, the U.S., and the pilgrimage to Najaf. He was hoping that this would be a family trip, but it didn't turn out that way. Mohsen packed his bags and started his journey by visiting the Far East. Flights to the Far East always left late at night from Tehran and so neither of us went to the airport with him. Hamid and I were stuck in Tehran on our own during the holidays and, for the second year, my husband would be traveling without us at Nowruz.

Setting a Trend

A few years before, Mr. Clements, the American oil magnate, had entered into a joint venture and established a company by the name of Southeastern, of which Mohsen was a shareholder and Mehdi Mashayekhi the CEO. Mohsen didn't want, nor did he have the time, to be involved in the company other than to attend board meetings. A gentleman from the company by the name of Etherington would visit Iran, and on these visits, social events were held in his honor. I had heard that he was recently divorced from his wife and had married a young woman who was a flight attendant. It seems as if men going through the male menopause find a solution by changing their partners and starting a new life.

Mohsen used to joke how this middle-aged gentleman, now a father all over again, carried a picture of the baby in his back pocket, taking it out and showing off to everyone! The new couple came to Iran in 1968. I found it very difficult to welcome this young woman because I had known Etherington's first wife, so Mr. Mashayekhi organized a big dinner at the Hilton Hotel to welcome the new couple. At Mohsen's insistence, I also attended the event. Later, on a trip to Isfahan, I was obliged to buy a wedding present for them. Etherington had invited himself to our home and so, faced with the inevitable, I bought a traditional bronze picture for them, similar to ones I had at home and which he had admired on a previous occasion.

There was a small inscription at the bottom of this picture that said, "Wherever you find peace, there is heaven." A few years later, Mohsen, Clements, and Etherington had disagreements and Mohsen decided to leave the company. He discussed the situation with me, saying he had originally invested 20,000 tomans and his share was now worth 500,000 tomans. Nevertheless, he was willing to forgo this profit in order to disengage from the company.

It had been years since Mohsen had consulted me about business. I don't know what came over me, I responded, "If I were you, I would ask for the value of your shares after all the time and effort you contributed to the success of the company." Maybe he would have done this anyway but didn't want to appear greedy! I later found out that Clements had also divorced his wife and given her half his assets before he then married someone else. Of the three board members of Southeastern, two had started new lives, I wondered if Mohsen would be the third?

The Summer of 1969 (1348)

Ladan completed her postgraduate studies at Columbia and decided to return to Iran, where she got a job at the Ministry of Science at the same time as she was working on her thesis. As part of her thesis, entitled "The Profitability of Selected Fields of Higher Education in Iran," she prepared questionnaires that former students in different fields had to complete, stating to what extent they were using the subjects they had studied at university in their careers. This was to discover if time and money had been efficiently used. I was very happy that both daughters were back in Iran and Hamid was now at the Iran Zamin School. Mariam and Fari had bought a beautiful house in Hyde Park Avenue with financial help from their parents on both sides. I had come across this particular house by chance through a friend; it belonged to a young couple who were moving to the U.S. and who had recently bought and furnished the house.

Our social life continued. Once a month there was a gathering of about forty members of the Ardalan family—aunts, uncles, cousins, and all their children. These occasions were jolly and noisy and a lot of fun. We had another monthly gathering of around twenty friends from the Esfandiary side of the family. We also tried to start a regular gathering of the Mostofi family, but this soon petered out due to different members being away on their travels. There was no gambling at these parties, only jokes and conversation. Our life seemed to be peaceful and happy; by now Leila was three years old and a source of great joy for the family.

This was when Mohsen was dubbed "husband of the year" because, quite unexpectedly, he brought me several very valuable precious stones. Accompanied by my old friend Pari A——, I took them to Reuben the jeweler to be set into a ring. It was she who decided to award Mohsen with this title for being the perfect husband in displaying such generosity to his wife. Mohsen was also considering buying a piece of land and building a grander home.

We kept searching in our neighborhood for such a plot and finally found an ideal piece of land—6,000 square meters in Boustan Street, just north of our house. We bought it for 3 million tomans. The land consisted of three separate plots—each measuring 2,000 square meters. Since Hamid was a minor, one of the three plots, which had a pool in it, was bought in his name. I used to take walks with Mohsen in the neighborhood, unaware that the silence between us contained so many secrets about which I knew nothing or maybe chose not to know.

An Invitation to the Romanian Embassy

I finally returned home after a work trip to Romania and Czechoslovakia that had lasted forty days. Following my trip, I wrote an extensive report and presented it to the Foreign Ministry; then I started teaching again. On seeing my name as Iran's representative to Romania, Moushka Daftari, in charge of international affairs at the Foreign Ministry, had apparently remarked, "Finally they had the intelligence to choose someone of Houri's caliber to do our country proud!"

That year we had a hard winter with lots of snow and freezing weather. One night we were invited by the Romanian ambassador to dinner; this was a select occasion to welcome the new American ambassador, Mr. MacArthur, and his wife, who were replacing the Meyers. It was late and Mohsen was still not home. When he did arrive, he announced that he had no intention of going to the party even though we had already accepted. I didn't react to this but, realizing that I couldn't drive in the deep snow, I called the embassy and apologized, giving the bad weather as an excuse. The Romanian ambassador's wife replied, "You are one of the guests of honor and I will send my driver to bring you here." I accepted the offer and arrived slightly late to the party. Mrs. MacArthur said she had been looking forward to meeting me; I reciprocated the compliment. I was sure that she knew something of the difficulties between Alice Meyer and myself. The MacArthurs stayed in Tehran for two years before being replaced.

A Painful Secret is Uncovered

For Nowruz 1349 (1970) we went on a family vacation for the first time in years. Mohsen, Ladan, Hamid, and I, together with my sister Mehri and a group of our close friends, took a tour of the Far East and arrived in Bombay just in time for the Persian New Year.

Our tour ended in Hong Kong and we returned to Tehran. The following week, on Monday, Mohsen announced that he would not be coming home for lunch that day, so I made arrangements to have lunch with Ladan at a restaurant close to Mohsen's office. I remember exactly what I was wearing—a beige outfit that I had bought in Milan, along with a double-strand pearl necklace from

Tokyo and the very expensive ring that had earned Mohsen the title of "husband of the year"!

Ladan and I were talking about her thesis and the difficulties she had with the responses she was getting to her questionnaires. For some reason I felt anxious. Mohsen was a very disciplined person and loved a regular routine. It was rare for him not to come home for lunch or to return late in the evening. After lunch, I dropped Ladan off at her office and started off for Shemiran.

It had been a while since I had seen my friend Ghodsi Foroud, and since she hadn't replied to my telephone call inviting her to bridge and lunch the following day, I decided to drop by her new home, located in a narrow street, and leave her a note. I had never been to that street before; if felt as if someone was telling me not to drive there, but I paid no attention to that inner voice. I left a note for her and, as the street was too narrow to turn around, I proceeded to a bridge where I could do a U-turn.

I was almost at the end of the street when I saw my husband's car parked under a tree, next to a Rambler (an American car made in Iran). My heart fell; I was trembling. With great effort, I managed to turn the car around and drive home. My tears blinded me; I just pressed hard on the accelerator, nothing else seeming to matter at that moment. I turned into our street and stopped at my mother-in-law's house, where she had recently moved, to be close to us. I rang the bell; her maid came to the door and said, "Khanum is taking a bath." I turned around and went home and locked myself in my bedroom.

I was lost in thought, remembering all the trips he had taken without us. Even in this last trip we had taken with the family, he seemed to be somewhere else. I reflected on the artificial smiles and on my six-month trip to the U.S., which, in retrospect, seemed to have been a warning sign about the state of our marriage. We were both just turning forty and had a long life ahead of us. How long could we go on playing the part of the happy couple?

The Beginning of My Depression

The following day—a Tuesday—was my lunch party. My friend Ghodsi Foroud had not yet returned from a trip to Pakistan, as I later discovered, and hence never got the note I had left. Other friends arrived and we started to play bridge after lunch, accompanied by the usual chatter. The week dragged on slowly. On Thursday afternoons Mohsen used to stay home and, as it happened, that Thursday our cook had a day off. Mariam, Fari, and Leila were in London at the time, Hamid was at school, and Ladan had gone to have her hair done. I sent Ghasem away on an errand and took advantage of the empty house after lunch.

I asked Mohsen to come to the living room as I had something to discuss. Monday to Thursday felt like an eternity! At first, he said he wanted to rest, but I insisted that what I had to say was important, so he came to the living room. I related all that had happened on Monday without leaving out any details. I somehow was able to speak in a calm manner; I didn't want to make a scene. I asked him whose house that was and what he was doing there. I addressed him as *shoma* (the formal pronoun in Persian for "you"). He didn't reply. I warned him that, if he didn't tell me everything, I would hire a private detective at his expense and find out all that had been happening.

He said, "It involves a woman." I asked him about his relationship with this woman, surprising myself at my ability to control my feelings and my tongue. I wasn't angry; I had spent almost twenty-eight years of marriage without resorting to anger or drama. Only my tears betrayed how I was feeling. It seems unbelievable, doesn't it? I was a person who defended the weak, I was known for my fearlessness outside the home—at school and in society. But at home I was quiet, obedient, and almost helpless. Maybe this was a reaction to Shajan, who had ruled our house boldly, causing me to promise myself not to be a bossy wife, and to allow my husband to rule our home. Maybe I was like my father, who was quiet and conciliatory at home and a lion outside.

Up to that day, I had never questioned my husband, even though there were many issues to question. Now, as I write these lines, years have passed since that fateful day and many years have gone by since Mohsen passed away. I don't want to speak badly of someone who cannot defend himself; it wouldn't be fair. But I was incapable of ignoring this important part of my life—my best years—and continue to live as if nothing had happened.

Today is 28 December 1999 (7 Dey 1378) and I am fasting as it is Ramadan. I sit on the ninth floor of this building overlooking San Francisco Bay; I am talking to myself and to God who created us all. Above all I want to be fair. In the past, it was common for men to have many affairs while living respectful lives. It was common for women to be long-suffering, to tolerate their depression and rarely retaliate. If, God forbid, a woman strayed, the culture and tradition automatically found her guilty. Mohsen had taken advantage of his rights as a male. But we were living at the end of the twentieth century. Wasn't this a betrayal? Wasn't it a lie? My pen is once again running away with itself.

Back on that fateful day, my husband paused and then replied, "It is nothing important. Most men have mistresses and I am one of them. I didn't think you would care." I persisted: "You haven't answered my question. What is the nature of your relationship with this woman?" With apparent calmness, he replied, "She doesn't have anything on me. But I cannot act immorally either; we have nothing on paper." He repeated, "She doesn't have anything in writing from me. I can stop visiting her anytime I want and never look back, though this woman has an amazing history."

I sensed he was going to present this woman as some sort of heroine to me, as though I should be impressed by her. I asked her name. Shahla. How old was she? Nineteen years younger than me. I was choking on my tears. I told him, "This woman doesn't love you; she is in love with your wealth. She is in love with the trips to Europe and around the world. She is in love with the house, the furniture, and the car you have bought her. It would be the same if a woman was with a man nineteen years her junior. The only difference is that women are ridiculed when they pair off with younger men, while men are proud of their conquest of a younger woman. I hope you will walk in on her one day and find a younger and stronger man in her bed; then you will remember how you made me feel."

He became defensive and said, "Why did you become president of the IWC? Why did you build the convalescence home?" I replied, "You had all the invitations and programs printed at your own expense; you contributed 30,000 tomans in the name of your three children to the home. You are still making donations. My service to this organization should make you proud, not a reason to look elsewhere. Don't look for excuses for your behavior. Shajan's prophecy came true; the apple didn't fall far from the tree." I retreated to the bedroom and passed out with a raging fever.

Mariam and Family Return from England

Ladan returned from the hairdresser, Hamid from school, and Ghasem from shopping. That same evening Mariam, Fari, and three-year-old Leila were returning from their trip to London. I didn't go to meet them as I was suffering both physically and emotionally. Mohsen and Ladan went to the airport to bring them home. Ten days passed. My daughters were concerned about me, since they had never seen me weak and unwell.

I told them that, while I was in Romania, a doctor had found a tumor in my stomach. I told this lie so as not to involve them in the tragedy that was now unraveling. Ladan insisted I should see a specialist and made an appointment with a doctor for me. After resisting for ten days, I finally came clean. Mariam had such confidence in her father that she was appalled at this accusation and told me I was being unnecessarily suspicious!

She made a date to see her father the following day on the pretext of visiting the Saltanatabad construction project that he was supervising at the time. It appeared that Mohsen corroborated what I had related, adding that he had always been a good father to his children and now it was time to think about himself. No one had the right to interfere in his private affairs. Maybe he had forgotten that his private life included a partner—what was to become of her?

Mariam came home dejected; the father she adored had surprised her with his response. The emotional toll these events took upon her surfaced much later in her life, but at this moment she had her own family to look after and was not immediately involved. Ladan, at twenty-two years old, was of course all too aware of what was going on, while Hamid was just a witness to the strange events. At thirteen years of age and approaching puberty, he too was still in love with his father. The "imperial family" and "husband of the year" had become the victim of the "evil eye"!

As time passed, my physical condition deteriorated. My mind was in turmoil, my stomach in a permanent cramp, and the world had turned very dark in my eyes. In addition,

I had developed insomnia. Yet I kept up appearances and tried to save face at all cost. What injustices have been done under the cover of "saving face"! I was tormented by the realization that Mohsen had been unfaithful to me for many years and I had turned a blind eye to it. And now, when I had discovered the truth, it was tearing my family apart. I was no longer the quiet and meek Houri at home; we had many arguments. I was wounded and wished myself dead. My shoulders drooped and I lost a lot of weight in the space of just a month.

Cancer of the Soul

I was due to go on a group trip to Abadan and Kharg Island. Initially, I wanted to back out but the girls forced me to go away for a few days. Now that his guilty secret was out, Mohsen seemed kinder and would try to appease me; he even offered to drive me to the airport. I replied that it was not necessary; I would be picked up by another member of the group. I was really ill and of course I couldn't tell anyone the cause. I suddenly realized that there was nothing left of the Houri everyone knew, of the optimist, energetic, and happy woman.

On the way back, the plane developed technical problems. Everyone was anxious and afraid; privately I welcomed the possibility that my life would end and I would be liberated from the impossible situation in which I found myself. Mohsen would also be free to pursue his life.

And then I suddenly remembered all the other passengers; did they also deserve to die? I was ashamed of my own thoughts. This short trip not only hadn't brought me peace; it had actually weakened me morally and physically.

I was still teaching at the university. One day I became really ill in class and had to go to the bathroom to throw up. I noticed several students standing behind me to make sure I didn't faint. I was no longer capable of behaving normally; I was suffering from cancer of the soul, a name I had given my condition. One day we had another argument at home and I told Mohsen I would leave, since I just couldn't go on any more. That same afternoon, his brother who had recently joined him at Reema, came to the house, packed Mohsen's personal effects in a suitcase, and said, "My brother has moved into a hotel and will need these." This was the first time Mohsen had left home except when he was away on a business trip.

Mehr Hospital

There was no news of Mohsen the following day. I told the girls, "I will stay with Mehri *joon* and visit a doctor. Call your father and tell him he can come home; I don't want Ladan and Hamid to be alone." Mohsen returned that same night. I stayed with my sister for a few days, but my condition was rapidly deteriorating. Finally, I was taken to Mehr Hospital. Dr. Sadr, the hospital director, and his wife were close friends and really took excellent care of me. I asked the girls not to let anyone know where I was; and I wanted no visitors except them. I was visited by a psychiatrist, who came to talk to me; apparently Mohsen had also consulted him. I was under sedation, but sleep had abandoned me. Dr. Sadr visited me every day and remarked, "An elephant would have succumbed by now if we had given him the medication you are taking." After a week Mohsen decided to come and visit me. He had promised the psychiatrist that he would resolve the problem, given a bit of time, though afterward I realized he was just buying time so I would get used to the situation and accept it.

When Mohsen arrived, he looked sheepish and tried to persuade me to return home. Our problems had still not been made public and it would be best to keep up the pretense. I agreed to return home on the condition that Hamid would be sent to a boarding school—Aiglon in Switzerland. I explained that our son would soon be fourteen and didn't deserve to live in such a troubled environment. Finally, after twelve days, I returned home and tried really hard to remain calm—at least on the surface. Ladan's birthday was approaching and, as always, I planned a big party for her despite all the medication I was taking.

When I took the anti-depressants, life would brighten up for a couple of hours, but soon the depression would return in full force, making me feel worse than before. After five sessions with the therapist, I decided to take myself in hand. I threw away all the medication; two hours of peace was not worth twenty-two hours of depression. I read a lot—biographies of artists, writers, and politicians who had endured great difficulties in life and overcome adversity. Sometimes I would read novels; in the end I resorted to reading the Qur'an. As soon as I felt the depression coming on, I would open the Qur'an at random, with the Persian translation on one page and the original Arabic on the facing page. At times, I saw a divine message in those lines and this would calm me down. I kept asking, "Why did this happen to our family?"

A Desperate Act

All the conversations and arguments we'd had, and all the letters we sent to each other had changed nothing, as far as I was concerned. Mohsen had forgotten his promise to me and clearly felt that he had the right to behave exactly as he desired, expecting everything to remain the same at home. One Friday, we were invited to lunch at his brother Reza's home. The night before, when he came home, we had an argument. I was so agitated by this that I went into my room and swallowed eight 5 mg Valium pills. Upon discovering what I'd done, Mohsen was furious. He woke Ladan up and apparently told her, "I hope she dies and gives me my freedom."

I know that when he said these words he didn't actually mean them, yet I've never understood what exactly he expected me to do. Did he really think I could behave like a wife from the previous century? Maybe he didn't know me well enough. Just because I kept the peace in our private life didn't mean that I was weak. Quite the opposite: I was trying desperately to keep my family together.

Ladan, who had just woken up, immediately called her sister. Mariam, who had not told her husband anything up until that moment, then had no choice but to relate the whole sad story that night to explain why I had taken an overdose. She and Fari drove me to a clinic. I was so frustrated at Mohsen's indifference that I asked Mariam to call Reza even at that very late hour. Very soon, Reza and Mohsen arrived at my bedside; at that moment, our secret was out. My stomach was pumped and I was taken home by Mariam and Fari. They put me to bed and gave me strong coffee to drink. Mohsen picked up his pillow and blanket and went into the other room. I confess that it was wrong to do what I did. At that point, I was in such despair that I had no reason to continue living.

Mohsen and I had been leading parallel lives for years and I was used to his lack of attention. Therefore I was surprised at how let down I felt, given the state of our relationship. Thirty or so years have passed since that time and I still don't have an answer to why I felt as strongly as I did. Maybe I regretted the patience and tolerance I had exercised all those years. Maybe I was shaken by my children's distress. Maybe I cared about what people thought, the schadenfreude of the envious, the sadness of close friends. No, it wasn't any of these things. I realize now that I was chiefly disappointed in myself and had lost my self-confidence. Pride, which had kept me on the straight and narrow, this pride was hurt and it seemed there was no way to heal it.

My daughters watched me anxiously; Hamid was silent. My devoted staff hovered over me. I wanted to go back to being the person I had been, but there seemed no hope of that. I wanted peace to return to our lives, but that seemed impossible too. Our life was shattered as a result of a selfish act and everything was falling apart. The following day, Mohsen's other brother, Agha Bozorg who seemed to be charged with being the bearer of bad news, came to the house and again packed a suitcase for him. It wasn't his fault, he was just the messenger. My mother-in-law, a woman who had also been humiliated and wronged and had kept silent for many years, was grief-stricken.

One can criticize and complain about one's husband; it is much more difficult to say such things about one's son. I felt sorry for her. My sister-in-law Ezzat said, "I am so glad you didn't hear about Mohsen from us; we have known about it for a long time." Mohsen's brother-in-law Kazem then came to see me. I was sick in bed and hiding under the covers, ashamed to look anyone in the eye, but it seemed that he had something to share as well. "Houri, the same thing happened in my family," he said. "We suffered greatly as a result and our lives were never the same again." He was speaking of his own parents.

Dreaming at Dawn

Mohsen was staying at the Palace Hotel and would meet the children in his office. Mariam was less in touch with him, however; she hadn't expected this reaction from her father. I sometimes have dreams that later come true. A while back I had dreamt that I was wearing a formal outfit but with no shoes and my toes seem to be cut off. Apparently in dreams, shoes represent a husband and so no shoes means the opposite. The dream came true with the events that ensued.

One day, after my morning prayer, I went back to sleep again and dreamt that I was driving a huge truck and trying to cross a rickety bridge that spanned a deep ravine, wondering how I was going to do this. A voice was telling me, "Continue the way you are going." At that moment, Ladan entered my room and I woke up. I remember the details of the dream because just as I woke up I was asking myself, " Which way I was going?" Then I remembered that I always forgave, I always compromised and always surrendered; I would always extend a hand in friendship and give another chance to anyone who had wronged me.

It was 7 a.m. when I called the Palace Hotel, where Mohsen had been living for the past two weeks, and asked to be connected to his room. When he picked up the phone, I asked, "Did I wake you up?" To which he replied, "No, I haven't been able to sleep at all." That surprised me since Mohsen was always a sound sleeper. Clearly, he was troubled. I told him about my early-morning dream. I said I wanted to come and pick him up. It was the weekend. I drove to the hotel and found him ready in his room, with his bags packed. We returned home in two separate cars. Everyone was overjoyed at seeing Mohsen. There and then, he promised me he would leave that woman and added that she had become quite demanding of late. Apparently, she wanted things that were not in his power to give. He said, "You have to give me time."

That evening we all celebrated by going out to a poolside dinner at the Hilton Hotel. Yet it seemed that my optimism was misplaced. I kept hoping that this cracked plate would hold together, but the promises never materialized. Poor Mohsen was trapped. He, who was so clever, had fallen prey to someone who had ensnared him. She had threatened to tell all, to disgrace him. So Mohsen started seeing her again and all his promises were forgotten.

Geneva–Montreux

My depression was directly linked to the situation we were in. I had lost control of both mind and body. Mohsen couldn't accept the advice of his brothers, sisters, and mother; he was treading a path to nowhere. Taking advantage of the fact that Hamid, who was just turning fourteen, would soon be starting at Aiglon College in Switzerland, I decided to leave for Geneva a bit earlier with Hamid, an almost empty suitcase, and $8,000 that Mohsen had given me. Mohsen and the girls saw us off at the airport.

In Geneva, we stayed in a beautiful hotel that had recently opened. We had a big color TV in our room and Hamid seemed happy. We would spend the mornings shopping for items on the school list. But the nights were difficult. Depression would descend on me despite my efforts not to upset my son. Undeceived, he said to me one day: "Mummy, the world hasn't come to an end. Why are you doing this to yourself?"

My sister Mehri was in Europe at the time and came to Geneva to visit me. I had planned a trip with Hamid to Portugal, but she dissuaded me from going, saying that it wouldn't be advisable to go to an unfamiliar place in the state that I was in. When we finished Hamid's shopping for school supplies, we went to Montreux and stayed at the magnificent Montreux Palace Hotel in a luxurious two-room suite. Hamid and I enjoyed the pool and played tennis during the day. In the evenings I would be busy sewing name tags on Hamid's clothes.

I had invited my aunt Valieh Azam, who lived in Geneva, to spend a few days with us since we had plenty of room. One day after I visited the hotel hairdresser, my aunt said, "Is it possible that your hair has also become sick? One can't tell you have just had it done!" It was the truth. I was deeply wounded and needed a long time to heal. The day finally arrived when Hamid and I would have to part. We packed and left by train for Villars.

Aiglon College, Switzerland

Aiglon College is situated in the Swiss Alps, high up above the village of Villars. To reach it, we took a taxi from the train station. It was raining and the road had many twists and turns. All the while, I was trying to remain cool and calm and not allow the tears to fall. The taxi stopped outside the school and waited for me as Hamid's two suitcases were taken in and I accompanied him. Inside the school, I met the principal, a retired British army officer, for the first time. I explained that, since there was a big age difference between Hamid and his sisters, I didn't want him to grow up as an only child. "We teach our students core values here," he replied, then added: "Of course, the academic side is also very important, but you can study anywhere. These days, human values are not respected everywhere."

Agitated and afraid that my trembling voice would give me away, I joined Hamid in the corridor. His housemaster Mr. Sena took us to Hamid's room. It was small, bare, and contained a bunk bed and a single bed. The closet was very narrow and I could see from Hamid's expression that he was wondering where he would hang his clothes. He was quiet, otherwise, and appeared calm. I left him in Mr. Sena's care and with a heavy heart got back into the taxi.

I remembered Mohsen telling me that he was not happy about sending Hamid away to boarding school and wanted me to keep him at home until he had graduated from high school. Exhibiting none of my usual restraint, I shouted, "You want him to stay here and become a hostage to our ruined family life! I have to take him away from this toxic atmosphere so he doesn't become tainted by it." Mohsen was no position to disagree. Now I was leaving my son in the care of a stranger and in God's hands. The rain was falling hard and fast, rolling down the windscreen of the taxi, just as the tears were falling down my cheeks. The driver left me and my only suitcase at the train station, from which I would travel to Berne before flying to the UK.

Troubled Thoughts

My nephew Khosrow Safinia picked me up from Heathrow airport in his Morris Minor and took me to his apartment in London. It was here that I tried to take stock of my life. In the mornings, I would walk in Hyde Park, lost in thought. I was not a helpless woman, I told myself; I was not destitute. I had spent the best years of my life raising a family and investing in my children. While the breakup of the family was painful, continuation of the status quo was out of the question. I couldn't be bought with money—our family's capital did not lie in money, but in truth, dignity, and right action.

I kept telling myself I had to somehow clean this stain from our reputation. In those days, society did not accept a man with two wives; Mohsen was destroying himself and couldn't see it. My daughters were shame-faced; Hamid had lost face among his cousins, who were all about the same age. We had worked so hard for this picture-perfect family, sacrificed so much. It seemed unreal that all this had been shattered with one blow. As I walked, I would suddenly come to myself and realize that I had been talking aloud in Persian. Fortunately, there were many strange people in Hyde Park and many speakers without an audience! Some days I would spend time in Harrods, buying clothes I wouldn't wear. Life had lost its taste. Nothing seemed to assuage my troubled thoughts. How could I come to terms with my own conscience?

While I was in London, Hamid would write to me in Persian from his school in Switzerland. He didn't complain but related how every morning they had to run through the village in their gym clothes before taking a cold shower, since the hot water was turned off on purpose. While we had been together, he would occasionally send his father a postcard, whereas I did not try to contact Mohsen. Mohsen complained about this, wondering why I would not communicate with him even though he had accompanied me to the airport! I was astonished that a man who considered himself to be so smart could be so blind. These were not his words; they merely reflected the self-deception that had turned him into a stranger to himself.

Another month passed. One day Khosrow handed me a letter that had arrived from Tehran. I recognized Mohsen's handwriting on the envelope, which I opened with some trepidation. It was several pages long. He wrote about Ladan's bad behavior toward him and the fact that she had left home and gone to stay with Mariam. He implored me to return home and take control of our lives once again. As if nothing had happened!

Although it was late, Khosrow was still awake. After keeping quiet about all this for a month, I showed him the letter. The young man read the letter carefully and then I told him the whole sordid tale, though I have a feeling he already had some idea about the incident; we talked through the night. Khosrow loved Mohsen; he had really good memories of him during his stay with us for the eight months when his parents were in England for Mr. Safinia's treatment. Mohsen had treated him kindly and warmly. Khosrow was surprised at the sudden change that had caused so much pain to the family. Mohsen never received a reply from me to that letter.

An Unexpected Phone Call

One day Ladan called from Tehran; she was speaking from our own house and wanted to let me know that she had returned home. She also added that Mohsen was sick and had been hospitalized, although he was feeling a little better now. I didn't react to the news; it was as if she was speaking about a stranger or a friend I was trying to forget. She also had some other news.

Ali Lari had proposed to her and she wanted my blessing. I had only met the young man once at the party for Ladan's twenty-second birthday but I knew his sister Parvaneh. I told Ladan, "I hope this decision of yours is not precipitated by the problems between your father and me. You still have time, you know, and you need to finish your education." She replied, "I have finished my thesis and my decision to marry is not because I want to get away from our problems." I told her that if she and her father were happy, I would congratulate her and wish her well.

Ladan then put me on to Mohsen, saying, "Baba wants to talk to you." We greeted each other formally. He explained that he had fainted while attending a funeral and had been hospitalized, but that it was nothing important. Our conversation ended. Ladan then announced the date and time of her arrival in London; we were to travel together to New York where she would present her thesis to Columbia University and we could do some shopping for the wedding. My time in London now over, I thanked Khosrow for his friendship and advice, and his hospitality, and returned home. Ladan and I then departed for New York.

Ladan Presents Her Thesis at Columbia

We stayed at the St. Moritz Hotel in New York. The following day we went to Columbia University, where we discovered that her professor and adviser had transferred to Syracuse University—so the next day we had to fly there. Her professor met us at the airport and took us to his house as it was the weekend and Ladan didn't have much time left to present her 350-page thesis. He took one look at the impressively thick document and said that the thesis was too advanced for a master's degree.

If Ladan enrolled in a doctorate program in economics, she could use this thesis without needing to write another at the end of the course. Ladan thanked him for the compliment and replied that, as she was about to get married, she was happy with a master's degree. Although surprised at her response, he nevertheless signed off the thesis. We stayed there for lunch and, in the afternoon, flew back to New York.

The following day was the deadline for submission of her thesis to Columbia; we made it with only minutes to spare. Ladan is a perfectionist but she does have a tendency to leave things to the last minute. We were finally able to relax and turn our attention to the Fifth Avenue shops!

After spending some time in San Francisco and Los Angeles, the Christmas holidays were upon us. We flew to Switzerland and picked Hamid up from Aiglon College, bringing him to our hotel. This time it was for him that we shopped so that he could at least participate in his sister's engagement party. The three of us left for Tehran after being away for four months. At the airport, Mohsen and members of his family, together with Mariam and her husband, had all come to meet us.

Planning Ladan and Ali's Wedding

The household staff were happy to see me back. I appeared to have gained control over my depression, although the damage our family had suffered was by no means over. While I continued to wrestle with my emotional ups and downs, my life had become so busy that I had less time to dwell on my problems. Our future son-in-law came to visit me. We decided to hold the *aqd* and the wedding reception on the same day. There wasn't much time left for planning; we had only six weeks to arrange the engagement party, find the young couple an apartment and furnish it, and hold the formal ceremony and the wedding reception. Today, after almost twenty-nine years, Ladan is faced with the same responsibility for her grown-up daughter, Firouzeh, and she has spent almost a year planning the wedding.

The first thing I did was to host an engagement party at our house to which we invited the families on both sides. Everything was prepared at home and the two families formally met. Ali had been searching for an apartment, and luckily found one in a building owned by one of Mohsen's cousins that overlooked Saii Park. We visited it and found it suitable, as did the young couple, especially since it had beautiful views. We just needed time to furnish it. Ladan knew that the only reason I had returned to Iran was to make sure she got a good start in her married life; I had otherwise decided to live in Geneva, close to Hamid, forgetting about my life in Iran altogether.

The wedding invitations were ready. The reception was to be at the Hilton Hotel with the *aqd* to take place at our home. I was no longer the old Houri but mechanically went through the arrangements with Mr. Fillipedes, the general manager at the Hilton—Mohsen agreed to everything. We furnished the young couple's apartment beautifully.

We planned the seated dinner menu with the Hilton's Swiss chef, which required much more careful planning than a buffet dinner, which I didn't want. Somehow whenever dinner was served buffet-style, people forgot their manners, I always found. However, the hotel couldn't manage a seated dinner for 560 guests; the most they had accommodated in the past was 300, and we had almost double those numbers. I suggested that we forget about round tables and use rectangular ones instead; in this way, all the guests would be accommodated and everyone would have an equally good view of the whole hall.

Nowruz 1350 (1971)

Nowruz was once again upon us and Hamid's vacation coincided with it. Our situation was uncertain. My mother-in-law was really disappointed in Mohsen's behavior though she pretended otherwise. As I told her, "If Mohsen decides to travel alone once again, he will have to forget any chance of keeping our family together. I only returned to Iran for Ladan's wedding; otherwise, there is no way I would put up with this humiliation; I absolutely won't." We decided

The Wedding of Ladan and Ali Lari, 1971. From left: Houri, Mohsen, Ladan, Ali, and Arasteh Lari (Ali's mother)

to spend the vacation at the Caspian and stay in Villa Hamid, as we had named the house we had recently bought for our son, situated near Chalous. Hamid returned from Switzerland; we met him at the airport and drove to the Caspian.

Our life had become empty and artificial, both of us walking constantly on eggshells. Mariam and Ladan each had their own lives but still worried about us. Hamid was with us for a short time, so we continued this imitation of our former life. I, who loved the truth, had been living a lie for such a long time. It seemed as though laughter, joy, and hope for the future had turned their backs on us. I asked myself how long this sad comedy could last.

The day after our arrival at the Caspian, Mohsen left for Tehran without any explanation even though Hamid had just arrived the night before. So, I was left with Hamid and our cook Fatemeh, who actually hated being there since she couldn't get along with the resident gardener and his family. Seeing the state I was in, she didn't complain, however. Mohsen returned at the weekend with Mrs. Lari (Ali's mother) and her youngest daughter, Shohreh. We all returned to the city after two days and Hamid left a couple of days after that for Aiglon College.

Before he left for Switzerland, Hamid asked his father to buy him a fancy motorboat that would have cost around 40,000 tomans, and so one day we all went boat-shopping together. I was against this purchase and believed that we shouldn't indulge this request because owning a boat required being an excellent swimmer, which none of us were. We therefore needed to have a lifeguard and, for the short period we could use the boat, it was not practical. I am sure Hamid wasn't happy about my objections but I managed to convince him that it wasn't a reasonable idea. I knew his father wanted to please him, though I was surprised that a cautious man like him would even contemplate such a project. I suggested instead that we buy Hamid a Honda motorcycle that he could use in the summertime in the garden as well as on the beach.

After Hamid left, life became even more miserable. I just spent my time reading and teaching. I had asked Mariam, my sister-in-law, to teach in my place while I was away and she had done a great job. Ladan was now teaching at the National University, but Mariam had left her job at the university. She also worked with her father for a while but then decided not to stay at Reema. I was sorry that she was not using her education, although later on this young woman turned out to be a successful entrepreneur. For the time being, she preferred to stay home and take care of her family. She was also expecting her second child and needed to take it easy as she had had a miscarriage a couple of years before.

An Untimely Trip and Applying for a Divorce

It was now April (Ordibehesht). Looking through my passport one day, I found a note that had been overlooked for months. I decided to deliver it to a lady I knew who worked at the American consulate. The waiting room was full when I got there; I suddenly spotted Mohsen and asked him what in the world he was doing there at 10 a.m. on a weekday. He smiled and said he was there to get a visa. I replied, "Are you planning to go to the U.S. at this time of year when it is peak construction season?" My blood was boiling and, without waiting for the lady I had come to see, I left.

When I arrived home, I was told Mariam was in the hospital. Hurriedly, I packed a bag and went back to the city. She needed a small procedure in order to avoid another miscarriage and had been anesthetized and taken to the operating room; I started to pray for her recovery. The procedure was quite short and she was returned to the ward. Semi-conscious and talking to herself, she kept opening her eyes and closing them again.

Then she suddenly opened her eyes fully and, on seeing me, she said, "Why are you so worried; it was a simple operation." She then closed her eyes again. The next time she opened them she asked, "What has happened? You look unwell again." I didn't tell her what had happened, but she kept shaking her head and saying, "You don't look right; something must have happened." Despite her groggy state, my poor girl knew her mother and was aware of what was going on with me.

After a little while, her father arrived. I asked him for the phone number of our lawyer, Dr. N——. Reluctantly he wrote the phone number and address on a piece of paper and gave it to me. I contacted the lawyer and asked him to arrange a divorce. I told him I needed to cleanse my family of this shameful situation and I didn't want anything from Mohsen. Writing these lines now in the U.S., I am reminded of the expectations of American women and wondered why we Iranian women gave up our rights so easily.

If a woman like me can be so badly treated, what about younger women who have no support system, are not financially independent, and have no choice but to put up with the situation? Here I would like to apologize to all the faithful and reasonable husbands out there; and there are plenty of them. I also apologize to Mohsen for speaking out in this way. He became a victim of his desires, his stubbornness, and his wealth. A rich man is an obvious target in the just the same way as a young and beautiful woman.

Dr. N—— tried to get me to change my mind. I told him he needed to be professional and put our friendship aside. The following day my sister Mehri and brother-in-law Reza came to visit me. I signed the divorce papers but Mohsen refused to sign, telling his brother, "I know Houri will not remarry; what is the use of this piece of paper?" Mehri took my copy from me and said, "I will keep this document and I know Houri will not contradict her older sister." Our legal divorce remained unfinished.

I was sick the next day; the depression had returned. I took refuge in Hamid's bedroom. My two lovely sisters-in-law Simin and Mariam came to visit. I was miserable. They sat on the floor and joined me in my grief.

Leaving the House and the Family

My sister Mehri came to see me that same evening; she was my rock and we were very close. It wasn't just my own family that had been affected; my sisters-in-law confessed that they had arguments at home every night, to the point that they had made a decision not to bring up the subject so as not to damage their own relationships. Mohsen came home late and went straight to his dressing room.

He brought down his suitcases and started to pack. I was lying down on Hamid's bed and my sister was still with me. Ghasem helped put the suitcases in his car; it was 10 p.m. We hadn't had dinner yet. I got up and asked Mohsen not to leave without eating, ingrained habits dying hard. He ignored me and left. Mehri was our witness and said, "You have no pride. The man who has brought all this into your life is leaving and you are worried that he might be hungry!"

Two days later, I heard he had left for Europe and probably on his own—since Ladan and Ali had taken him to the airport. It was the second spring I was grappling with depression. The roses were blooming in the garden, the sky was blue, and the trees full of young leaves, but I saw everything darkly and was just surviving. I taught all my classes, however, and was in touch with both my daughters, who were concerned and caring.

The Summer of 1971 (1350)

For the first time in years, I volunteered to teach summer classes at the university; I needed to keep busy and took classes for eight hours a week. On the other days, I would visit the children's convalescence home. A new board had been elected at the IWC. I was reinstated as president, and, at my invitation, my friend Guity once again agreed to act as club secretary; our treasurer was Ann Rattray. The vice-presidents were Lady Frances Ramsbotham, the wife of the British ambassador; Thea Van Reeven, the wife of the CEO of the oil consortium, who was Dutch; and Maggie Cassals, the wife of the Argentinian ambassador. We had a two-month break in the summer and no monthly gatherings. However, there was much excitement about the 2,500-year celebration of monarchy, in which we had as yet no part.

After Ladan's wedding, I had become friends with Vanna Fillipedes, the wife of the general manager of the Hilton Hotel; she was also a club member. Vanna suggested that we organize a gala dinner at the Hilton and have a fashion show of a few Qajar outfits alongside modern clothes by Iranian designers. In the past, we had organized a fashion show of Dior outfits as a fundraiser for the club and I didn't think we should repeat this.

On that previous occasion, we had very little preparation time; the dresses were ready and we had been asked by the Shahbanu's office to organize the event. Vanna's suggestion inspired me to investigate women's dress from much further back in history. That summer I requested a meeting with the minister of culture, Mr. Pahlbod, and asked him to authorize us to photograph ancient artifacts and etchings in the Iran Bastan Museum. The minister welcomed my suggestion and put a photographer at our disposal. In addition, he introduced Mr. Yahya Zoka to us, who was an authority on the subject of men and women's dress over the centuries.

Research on Women's Clothes

I spent those long and hot summer days in the company of Mr. Zoka and the photographer, while everyone else was thinking about attending the 2,500-year celebrations. We visited the Iran Bastan Museum and photographed a range of objects, from tiles and chalices to miniatures and statues. We organized a committee of club members for this purpose, chosen for their knowledge of design, and which included Vanna Fillipedes, whose idea it was, and Homa Fattollah-Zadeh, a talented dress designer.

We were hoping to choose twenty outfits from the hundreds of photographs we had taken in order to represent twelve periods of Persian history, and we wanted to do everything without spending a cent of the club money. I asked Lady Ramsbotham to arrange a gathering at the British ambassador's residence and I invited a few members of the club to be there.

Having previously discussed with them what we needed, they arrived with exquisite fabrics and cash donations ranging from 300 to 3,000 tomans—our budget was almost reached. At that same meeting, we chose the twenty members who were to model the outfits. Our hostess also agreed to wear a traditional costume and appear on the stage. We invited our non-Iranian members to model the more recent outfits from the time when foreign women started to arrive in Iran. Our effort was to produce a show that was authentic and backed up by reliable sources. Guity made a brilliant suggestion, which was to enlist the help of our top dressmakers on a voluntary basis.

The First Dress–"Goddess of Susa"

Our first resource was a silver cup from Marvdasht from 3000 BCE with the image of a woman in relief that Homa Fatollah-Zadeh sketched on a large sheet of paper. We then pondered over the color of the dress and the type of fabric to use. Each member made a suggestion, as well as Mr. Zoka. I had seen the cup up close at the museum and decided that the fabric should be a greyish taffeta from Yazd, which bore a resemblance to the original. We decided to call the dress "Goddess of Susa." Fortunately, my suggestion was unanimously approved. The following day, it had snowed heavily and I drove from Shemiran to the Grand Bazaar and bought a whole roll of this fabric for 60 tomans (8 dollars).

The next day, we took the fabric to the studio of the dress designer Mrs. Parvin F—— and asked her whether she would be prepared to make the dress for us without

The Marvdasht silver cup from 3000 BCE *that inspired the "Goddess of Susa" costume*

charging. She kindly replied, "I make so many dresses each year that are worn once or twice and remain forgotten in closets. You say these dresses will be donated to a museum. It would be an honor for me to offer my services as a gift to the club." We left the fabric with her; it had been a perfect choice especially since the model would be Lily A——, who was tall and actually resembled the image on the cup.

Our first outfit turned out to be a masterpiece and it had all come about as the result of amazing teamwork. Other dress designers gladly agreed to participate, creating from one to four outfits each. The embroidery and decorative detail of the outfits were done by friends of Homa, all free of charge. Many of the fabrics were gifts from our members, most from the Iranian handicraft stores; on two occasions we used fabrics from Greece, with the help of Vanna.

A Private Audience with the Shahbanu

Toward the end of January 1971 (Dey 1349), I requested an audience with the Shahbanu. Her private secretary, Mr. Karim Bahadori, made an appointment for me and the dress committee. He mentioned a delegation of Iranian women that would be traveling to France to attend a hair and beauty show at the Palace of Versailles, and suggested that these ladies wear some of the dresses we were making. I immediately replied, "We haven't even started making the dresses and, even if they were ready, they would be worn for the first time by members of the club in Tehran."

I am not sure if Mr. Bahadori was expecting such a reply. He didn't make a comment and just added that since the Shahbanu was traveling the next day, she would only be able to give us a few minutes. I replied, "We will leave as soon as she asks us to. At the same time, I would like the designer of all the dresses to accompany the dress committee to this meeting." It was the beginning of February (Bahman) and the weather was very cold. Niavaran Palace, where we were, was covered in snow.

We entered with a suitcase full of fabrics and the designs of the dresses. Our turn came and we were ushered into Her Majesty's room, which was on the upper floor. She greeted us warmly. I opened the white suitcase and, since there wasn't enough room on the desk, I sat on the floor and showed her the fabrics one by one. Her Majesty glanced at her watch and said, "The American ambassador and his wife are coming to say farewell. Please stay here; I will leave you for fifteen minutes and be back." She kept her word and returned shortly. I asked her to promise us that she would attend the gala fashion show. Homa was delighted that I had asked her to join us and said, "I have been involved with many voluntary projects, but this is the first time my contribution has been truly appreciated."

The Wanderer Returns Home

That year, we had an especially hard winter; everywhere was covered with ice and snow, making walking dangerous. One day, my brother Bagher, who was also our neighbor, came to see me. He told me that Reza had spoken to him and asked him to be an intermediary between Mohsen and myself. I replied, "My dearest brother, please don't interfere in this affair." He was surprised and asked me why. I then explained: "If things go wrong again, everyone will say you took the first step and insisted on a reconciliation. Why doesn't Reza himself take on this role?"

The following day, Reza called me after dinner and said he wanted to see me. We lived very close to each other. Even though snow was thick on the ground, he was keen to come over. We had a lot to talk about. He told me that his brother was very unhappy with his life; he would lose his temper over small issues at work and it was time to help him to come home again. "What are your conditions?" he asked.

I replied, "You are like a younger brother to me; I never sent Mohsen away from home. He left to go on a trip with his preferred companion and decided to stay with her." He said, "I know all this. Mohsen was under great pressure; it was not his choice to go away right at the peak of the construction season. The trip was imposed on him." He asked me again about my conditions. I replied, "My only condition is that this stain be removed from our family. I have no other conditions."

For the next month, Reza would come over once or twice a week after dinner to talk. One Friday, he and his wife Mariam invited me to lunch at their house and told me Mohsen would also be there. Eight months had passed since I had seen him. I arrived on time at Reza's, where the small talk was all about the weather. After lunch, at which my mother-in-law was also present, the conversation turned to the new house we were building in Boustan Street. The designs for the house were spread on the dining table, and Mrs. Moghadam asked me to have a look at them. I thanked her and said, "There will be plenty of time for that." Mohsen appeared calm but I could sense that he wasn't really.

When I returned home that evening, my daughter Mariam came to see me and asked where I had been for lunch. I hadn't told anyone where I was going. I explained that I had been in discussion with Reza for the past month and today I was a guest at his house for lunch. Mariam looked at me and said, "You want to take Baba back? But you must know that he won't change." I replied, "But I thought you would be happy about this possibility." Mariam said nothing. A few days later, Reza called and reported that his brother had moved to the Hilton and that he was going to collect him from there. I said, "I will come with you." The two of us went to Mohsen's room. His suitcase was packed; we came home together.

The news of Mohsen's return spread really fast. That evening the whole family came to our house for dinner. His sisters and brothers, and especially his mother, were all very happy. The following day, I had many calls from friends congratulating Mohsen on his good decision. On another evening, Reza and Mariam gave a dinner for the three brothers and their wives. My state of mind was neither happy nor sad—but something in between. I was kind and polite; I felt Mohsen was not well and that I had to help him. The staff were happy that Agha had returned and made sure everything went smoothly. Our daughters were also reasonably happy; they loved their father and respected him. During the past eight months, they had only visited him at his office.

A Skiing Accident in the Swiss Alps

One day Mohsen came home for lunch and said we should call Hamid. In those days, it was not common to make an nternational call except in an emergency. Instead, Hamid wrote us letters in Persian, letting us know how he was getting along. I asked Mohsen if anything had happened. He replied, "It seems he hurt his leg while skiing." I went straight to the phone and called Hamid, who explained what had happened and said that his leg was in a cast. It was the middle of March (Esfand); Mohsen insisted that I fly to Switzerland immediately. I replied, "There is nothing to be done now; let us wait and visit him together in the spring."

Nowruz 1351 (1972)

While Reza was mediating between Mohsen and me, I told him that I was once again the president of the IWC and we had a big project ahead in the form of the fashion show. If Mohsen objected to this, I was prepared to resign while there was time for someone else to take over. Reza apparently discussed this with his brother, who replied that he was happy that I was busy and wished me success with the project. My time was divided between the National University, running the house, and the dress committee, leaving me little time to plan for the future.

Rehearsing for the Gala Fashion Show

One of the responsibilities of the dress committee was to organize a rehearsal for the models wearing the dresses. The accompanying music was chosen; and the composer Loris Cheknavarian wrote and recorded a different piece for each dress. After seeing the rehearsal, I suggested a few changes, in particular the way each wearer would greet the audience on arrival. Lady Ramsbotham showed the models the European way of saluting; I enlisted Mr. Zoka's help to find the traditional salute of those ancient days in Iran. The Goddess of Susa was the first on the stage and she needed a special greeting. I explained to Lily A—— that, being a goddess and high-ranking, all she had to do was to incline her head very slightly. She would be carrying an ancient scroll in each hand; in this way, we resurrected the image on the silver cup of Marvdasht!

We had a problem with two of our models. One was a prominent lady who didn't walk like a model, but no one wanted to tell her this. I spoke gently to her and suggested that it might be better if her daughter wore the dress instead. This young girl had just returned from Europe and all we had to do was to take in the dress a little. Unfortunately, she also walked with too much of a swagger and fell somewhat short of our expectations on the catwalk. While none of these ladies were professional models, we wanted the show to meet the highest standards.

I had the same problem with another lady, who listened to what I had to say and gave her place to another. Mrs. Cassals, the Argentinian ambassador's wife and my deputy, came to me and said, "The Zoroastrian ladies chosen are rather large; models should be slim." What she said seemed reasonable. I consulted Mrs. Morvarid Yeganegi, who had accompanied the two Zoroastrian ladies. In her charming accent, she replied, "We Zoroastrians prefer our women to be large as they show off the dresses better. Let these two ladies put on the outfits and their full regalia and jewelry and then decide."

The following day, the two ladies turned up in the wedding dresses of their grandmothers—the outfits chosen to be displayed. Maggie Cassals was present and we both agreed that Mrs. Yeganegi had been right; the models looked perfect in the outfits. She explained that when a baby girl was born in a Zoroastrian family, they would start to prepare her wedding dress right then and there. All the dresses were handmade and each one often took sixteen years to complete—in good time for the marriage.

The preparation of the hats and shoes was another story. In my absence, Homa and Vanna had agreed terms with professional hat and shoe makers, at a cost of 5,000 tomans, since these people could not afford to work for free. They were worried about telling me and had decided that, if it met with my disapproval, they would pay for it out of their own pockets. I assured them that we had enough funds to cover these expenses; money was there to be spent in the right place. While our successful dressmakers could afford to work for us without payment, the artisans of Rudaki Hall could not be expected to do the same.

Ticket Sales and Seating Arrangements

The wife of the Australian ambassador, Mrs. Hall, was responsible for ticket sales and table arrangements. On the day, when the 200-toman tickets were ready, along with the room and table plans, we had a meeting. Mrs. Hall asked me to be the first to choose and buy a table. I chose two tables of eight each and paid for the sixteen tickets by check. The other members of the committee also chose and paid for their tickets. In this, Mrs. Hall was helped by the Hilton staff. We decided on the menu based on Ladan's wedding with slight alterations as we wanted to be economical so there would be some funds left over for the convalescence home.

Except for the Shahbanu and Princess Fatemeh, who were guests of the club, all the participants and even the models had to pay for their tickets.

We sent one free ticket to each dress designer; and we were sold out in a very short time. I was asked by the deputy foreign minister, a former neighbor, for a ticket but I couldn't accommodate him. We had given priority to all those who had helped to make this event happen; dignitaries did not have the same privileges to which were accustomed to on other occasions. My sixteen tickets were divided between my side of the family and Mohsen's, plus one lady who had made a sizeable contribution to us to the event.

The Evening Before the Fashion Show

Richard Nixon and his wife were guests of Their Majesties on their way back from their historic trip to China. One of their bodyguards was John Glenn—the younger brother of Nayer's husband, Kirk—who had arrived in Tehran a few days before. The British ambassador asked me to sit at his table since his wife was one of the models and currently backstage. Mr. Davis, the British secretary of state for trade and industry and the guest of his Iranian counterpart, Mr. H. Ansari, the minister of economy, was also seated at this table. I welcomed this unexpected invitation and was able to give the place at my table to John Glenn.

The night before the show, I had a very long telephone conversation with Guity, who was unhappy about her own dress, which she considered to be too plain. She wanted me to find someone else to model it. I persuaded her that the dress looked perfect on her and that it would, in any case, be a pity to find someone else at the last minute to replace her. Fortunately, she listened to me and her dress, "Mandana," made out of an orange taffeta, was one of the most beautiful. The following day, she sent me an apologetic and loving note, together with a big basket of flowers.

The Night of the Show

The next morning, Mohsen announced that, after a long search, he couldn't find his ticket, no. 101 (the tickets were numbered, beginning with 101). I told him not to worry as the seats were numbered and no one else could use his ticket: "I will give you my ticket, no. 102, since no one will stop me entering the hall." Problem solved. I arrived at the Hilton an hour before the start of the event; Mohsen promised to be there on time. It was a formal affair with the men in black tie and the ladies in long gowns. Having recently undergone renovations, the hotel could now accommodate 700 guests for a seated dinner.

The Shahbanu and Princess Fatemeh entered through a special entrance; the guests were all seated and the photographers were busy. After preliminary greetings, Her Majesty asked me, "Did you have any problems dealing with so many ladies?" I smiled and said, "I am perfectly happy with the team of fifty who worked with me." I have a feeling that complaints may have reached her.

The Shahbanu complimented me on my dress, which I had bought for Mariam to wear at Ladan's wedding. Fortunately, Pari Abasalti approached just at that moment and so I didn't have to confess that it was borrowed finery. I asked Her Majesty to stand in front of the beautiful tilework being used as a spectacular background for the photographs. One of her staff whispered that I shouldn't have asked Her Majesty to this. I whispered back, "I am sure if the Shahbanu had disagreed with my suggestion, she would have simply ignored it. Tomorrow when the pictures come out in all the papers, you will see the result."

We entered the main hall, and the Shahbanu and her guests took their places. I sat at the British ambassador's table sandwiched between the two government ministers, Mr. Davis and Mr. Ansari. The tables each seated eight; I became aware that two people were standing by one chair at the table opposite. Khodadad F——, the head of the Plan Organization, who had broken his leg skiing and was on crutches, was standing by his seat while a lady who had forgotten to collect her tickets from me was also standing there. How was I to explain to this lady that it wasn't her seat without creating a scene?

I called a waiter and asked him to bring another chair and a place setting for the lady, while inviting the injured gentleman to take his seat. The waiter immediately did as I had asked. "That is interesting," commented Mr. Ansari wryly. "I have been arguing with the same waiter to do the exact same thing and he refuses, saying he doesn't have permission. How come you spoke two words and he immediately obeyed?" I smiled and said, "You are in the habit of signing the checks in your job but tonight I will be the one signing the check. The staff have been told if a single chair is added without my permission, I will not sign the check!"

Dinner was served; I stood up before dessert arrived and made a short welcoming speech in Persian. There were translations of my speech on all the tables for the non-Persian speakers, together with the names of each dress and its historical period. We were in Iran and there was no reason for me to speak in English. I then returned to my seat.

The first model, Lily A—— as the Goddess of Susa, entered with great dignity. The second dress representing Rudabeh, the mother of Rostam,[20] was worn by M. B——. She was so nervous that the sheaf of wheat she was carrying shook in her hands. I left my seat and placed myself behind the Shahbanu thinking that if the models could see me, they would be more confident. We reached the period after Islam. Two young girls entered wearing outfits with green armbands covered in Arabic writing. Then our young pianist friend entered wearing her spectacular outfit.

One by one the dresses being modelled advanced through history. On arriving at the Pahlavi era, Her Majesty expressed concern saying, "What now?" I assured her that she would not be disappointed with what was to come. Iran

---

20. *A princess of Kabul, Rudabeh is a Persian mythological figure in Ferdowsi's* Shahnameh *(Book of Kings). She falls in love with and marries Zal. Their child is Rostam, who becomes the legendary hero par excellence of the* Shahnameh *epic (see footnote 20 on p. 40).*

Ala's collection of beautiful evening dresses made in traditional fabrics to original designs were followed by outfits from the different parts of Iran. The show ended with great applause filling every Iranian woman there with pride.

What We Raised from the Fashion Show

After settling the bill for the Hilton, we were left with a considerable profit. The oil consortium had promised to match what we had raised. The following day I had a phone call from the minister of arts and culture, who congratulated me, saying that after the procession at Persepolis,[21] this had been the most outstanding cultural event in living memory. He added that, if we agreed, the ministry wished to film the show. I signaled my agreement, so long as we retained full artistic control. But when he suggested that I could be the director of the documentary, I replied that my directing days had just ended!

Shortly afterward, I had a meeting at my house with the media director, who was accompanied by a young filmmaker. We had promised to hand over the twenty outfits, produced by our dressmakers, to a museum in exchange for

---

21. The celebration of the 2,500th anniversary of the founding of the Persian empire by Cyrus the Great was a national event in Iran. Consisting of an elaborate series of grand festivities held during October 1971, it was intended to highlight Iran's ancient civilization and history as well as to showcase its contemporary advances under the Shah. The celebrations highlighted in particular the pre-Islamic origins of the country, promoting Cyrus the Great as a national hero. Some historians argue that this massive spectacle, out of touch with the Iranian people, contributed to events that culminated in the Islamic Revolution of 1979.

200,000 tomans. The oil consortium kept their word and sent us a check for 200,000 tomans. The Ministry of Arts and Culture asked me to collect the check for the dresses. In response, I suggested they bring the check to me and I would hand over the dresses there and then, in addition to inviting the bearer of the check to lunch!

Later, when the book about the show, *Negar-e-Zan* (Portrait of Woman), was published and a number of copies had been sold, the total we had made for the club rose to 700,000 tomans ($100,000 in those days). Who knows what happened to this money after the revolution when the convalescence home was taken over—once again, I am getting ahead of myself, however.

Mysterious Letter, Mysterious Location

One day a letter arrived requiring me to turn up at a specific address on a specific day. When I asked Mohsen if he knew anything about this, he said that he didn't. I didn't know whether to take the letter seriously and turn up for the appointment or to simply ignore it. It had been hand delivered and didn't have a stamp; I decided in the end that it would be better if I turned up. I parked the car at the top of the street, which was deserted, with no one around to ask for directions. I arrived at the address, and found the door open.

I walked through a small front yard and entered the two-story building. A man was sitting at a desk in the entrance. I asked him if I had come to the right place; he nodded and pointed to floor above. Upstairs, there was another man behind a desk who directed me to a small room with two men sitting at desks facing each other, one of them at a typewriter. I showed the second man the letter and he signaled that I should take a seat.

I was then subjected to a barrage of questions—name, surname, address, and so on—the typist busy recording everything. By the time he had started on a third sheet of paper, the questions had turned to my family background and positions I had held. The two men appeared to be listening intently to my replies, until the second man suddenly interrupted and said, "All these are just formalities. We know who you are and we know all about your family background and their service to this country." He then turned to the typist and said, "You can stop typing and in fact you can tear up the pages you have already typed. We don't need them anymore."

I was left wondering about the point of the whole charade if they already knew all this about me, but I didn't say anything. The second man then introduced himself and said, "We need your help. You are a prominent personality, which is why we wanted to speak to you." I pretended to be listening, all the while asking myself, "What am I doing in this deserted place? Why should I care what you think of me?" He asked me to work with them as an informer and said, "Khanum, we know everything that is happening in this country. We are the Shah's eyes and ears. He does not know what is happening with the people. We prepare reports and send them to him; he makes decisions based on these."

I replied, "Thank you and your colleagues very much for your favorable view of me. But I am a teacher, that's all. My public service is soon coming to an end, and I will have no official post. Above all, as a teacher I am very talkative, and my life is like an open book. Allow me to talk to my husband. If you can give me a phone number, I will call you back."

The second man continued: "Khanum, all the ministers and public servants have to pass our scrutiny. Unless we approve, the Shah does not appoint them." I took in what he was saying, already with some inkling about this. I then stood up, nodded goodbye, and left the building. The second man had seemed polite and reasonable, but neither man was familiar to me and I never saw them again.

At lunch, I told Mohsen everything and asked his advice. He replied, "It is up to you." I told him, "I cannot do what they ask; I will call and tell them so." The following day I called and politely refused their offer. No one ever got in touch with me after that, nor was I ever troubled again.

The Ups and Downs of Movie Making

The first footage of the documentary about the fashion show was shot in our house. Homa Fatollah-Zadeh was planning a trip to the U.S. and it made sense to film her before she left, wearing her costume, "Ubal," which belonged to the

Parthian era. The "Goddess of Susa" was filmed in the land close to our house with its huge trees. I was always present to supervise the proceedings since the director wasn't too bothered about details. Maggie Cassals was leaving Iran as her husband's post had come to an end after seven years. We filmed her in the garden of the summer residence of the British embassy under a traditional and very beautiful tent.

Sometimes the director wouldn't listen to my advice. For example, it didn't occur to him to remove the modern chairs that were outside this tent; then I had no choice but to put my foot down. Unfortunately, Vanna would take his side and say, "These are minor details and unimportant." I believed that it was precisely such details that could make or break the film. I had been a photographer since my youth and always paid a lot of attention to the background of the shot. Our director didn't know the difference between the Sasanians and the Samanians, hadn't seen the dresses before, and was largely unfamiliar with Iranian history; how could I let him do whatever he wanted?

The filming took almost a year. When they traveled to Isfahan and Shiraz, Vanna would accompany them; I had to step in whenever there was a problem. The director decided to start the film with shots of the bazaar and the streets of modern-day Tehran. I had different ideas and wanted to start from the Iran Bastan Museum, showing its artifacts and library. I had envisioned a hand opening a book and, one by one, the dresses appearing in historical order and in a setting appropriate to their period.

It was to be a story of upper-class women's dress and adornment. But since I didn't want to travel with the group, I had delegated my supervisory role to Vanna. She was convinced by the director that the film should start with shots of everyday life and common people, while everything in the film was showcasing the jewelry, headdresses, adornments, and exquisite clothing of high-ranking women of their time. It was then that I regretted not having accepted the minister's suggestion to direct the film myself and allowing it to be entrusted it to another. Thirty years later, the book about the show, by contrast, stands as a valuable work of art. Written in both Persian and English, and published in Iran, *Negar-e Zan* was admired by everyone.

Working on *Negar-e Zan*, 1972–3 (1351–2)

While the filming was going on, I set about collecting documents and photographs for the book. It had seemed a fairly straightforward process, but writing a book in Persian and English, giving descriptions of each model in both languages, on facing pages, could not be done casually. I asked Mr. Zoka to note the history of each period in a few lines. Everything to do with the background of the project as well as the artistic, social, and cultural contributions of the club I wrote myself. I chose the best out of dozens of photos of each dress. The cover of the book is an image we obtained from the Louvre Museum via the Iran Bastan Museum; it is the statue of Napir-Asu. Mr. Zoka's notes were edited and then translated into English by Gregory Lima, a journalist and author living in Iran at the time. I was also greatly helped by the advice of my friend and the former IWC president Mrs. Farangis Shadman.

One day, I was speaking to a colleague, Tooran Bahrami, who was a gifted poet. Although she had not seen the dresses, she composed a two-line poem for each outfit, simply based on the photographs—again in the language and style of the period. Each morning Tooran would call me with the poem she had composed for one of the dresses and, with one or suggestions from me, we would agree on the final version. It was a delightful partnership and we were both happy with the outcome. In this way, all the Persian notes about the outfits came to life. Had we had more time, we might have translated the poems into English, but I decided that the English translation of the historical background to each outfit should be part of the introduction. I am getting ahead of myself again.

At the Louvre, life-size bronze-and-copper statue of Queen Napir-Asu, wife of the Elamite king Untash-Napirisha, used for the front cover of Negar-e Zan

An Unexpected Letter

It was the summer of 1972 (1351) and Mariam was recovering from an appendectomy. Ladan was expecting a baby and experiencing a difficult pregnancy since she could not eat and had lost a lot of weight. I tried my best to attend to both. Hamid was still at Aiglon College and due to come home for the holidays. I tried to keep myself busy and not think too much since the future was unpredictable. As Ladan wasn't feeling well, we went to visit her one evening; Mohsen invited her to have lunch with us the following day.

The next day, I had breakfast with Mohsen, who appeared very pale; I noticed his hands were shaking. After he had left, I got ready to go to a bridge party. I told the cook we would be three people for lunch, but when I got back after the game, I saw the table was set for just two. Ghasem informed me that Mohsen had said he wouldn't be home for lunch. I was surprised since Mohsen had invited Ladan himself and now he wasn't going to be home. I then went into my office and found an envelope with Mohsen's handwriting propped on my desk. I opened it and read the letter, which I still have. In the letter he said that he apologized but that he was leaving the house for good.

I hid the letter just as Ladan arrived. I pretended all was well and we had lunch, though she could barely keep her food down. I took her to her old bedroom and told her to rest. I opened Mohsen's dressing room and found it empty; he had taken all his belongings. I reread the letter and called Reza at work asking him to come to our house before returning home that evening. I told him that something important had happened. He promised he would come round.

Ladan rested for an hour and decided to return home; I said nothing, not wanting to upset her. After she left, I called Fatemeh and Ghasem. They told me that Mohsen had returned home after I left for the bridge game and packed his suitcases. He had told them he wasn't feeling well and couldn't carry on anymore and asked them to look after me.

Early that evening, Reza came to see me. I showed him the letter, which he read carefully, then he shook his head and said, "Houri, I apologize if I disturbed your peace by encouraging you both to get back together. Mohsen is the loser here." I replied, "It isn't a question of loss or gain. Your brother is not the same man anymore; he will be unsettled wherever he goes. He once told me, 'Ever since you found out, I don't have a life anymore and I am miserable everywhere.'"

I had become so hardened to the situation that I was able to keep up appearances. Each time sadness or depression appeared, I would take refuge in the Qur'an. The girls found out; Mariam had been right; Mohsen had been unable to change. Hamid knew nothing yet. He would have plenty of time to grieve later; I awaited his return.

Alone and Dejected

Depression, that cancer of the soul, returned and would not leave me alone. My heart was broken. Privately I shed many tears; publicly I kept up appearances. My sister Mehri was worried about me. Apparently, she had spoken to the prime minister, Mr. Hoveyda, about me. One day, I received a call to visit him at 10 a.m. Hoveyda didn't have much of a personal life; I found out later that his wife had left him at around the same time. He suggested that I should take up the post of Iran's representative at UNESCO in Paris. "You are fluent in both English and French and you can represent our culture and our society," he said. "It might be good for you to move away from here." When I asked him whom would I be replacing, he replied, "Fereydoun Ardalan."

I replied, "You want to replace an Ardalan with a Mostofi? If you are happy with his performance, it wouldn't be fair for me to replace him, especially since you don't have another job lined up for him." He just shook his head and said nothing. I thanked him, but declined the offer, saying that I had children and grandchildren here in Iran and they might need me. Later, I wondered if it wouldn't have been wiser to accept the post. Fereydoun was a second cousin and we knew each other. He remained in that post for many years until the revolution.

Living on My Own

Ladan's birthday was on 11 July (20 Tir) and I had organized a big birthday party for her as her apartment couldn't accommodate a large group. I suggested that she invite her father since all the members of the family on both sides had been invited. I never discussed our situation with anyone and luckily no one asked me any questions. I found it difficult to attend large gatherings on my own, but the responsibilities of the club made it impossible to refuse certain invitations. The first time, having been invited to dinner at the Australian embassy, I asked a friend and her husband to accompany me. But gradually I got used to living on my own. I would always ask a friend to follow my car to my house, although, in those days, Tehran was a very safe city. I had lost my self-confidence. Fortunately, the passage of time remedied this too.

Hamid, now returned from Aiglon College, would occasionally go to the office to see his father. I never asked him any details and he never volunteered any. I never belittled Mohsen in front of the children and I never spoke badly about him. Hamid's injured leg that had been operated on looked very thin, owing to the lack of exercise, and completely different from his other leg. His report cards from Aiglon were excellent and he had not wasted the last two years. In spite of all that had happened in the family, he carried on with his studies and extracurricular activities.

Hamid and Cars

One day Hamid brought up the subject of a new car, saying my car was too old. He consulted his father and together they ordered a beautiful new one for me. Hamid was young and loved sports cars. They ordered a BMW in a metallic light blue, fully equipped with all the latest gadgets—at the exorbitant price of 205,000 tomans. I remember the importers asking for an initial and separate, personal payment to them of 50,000 tomans; this was their pure profit. The balance was paid in a check written to the company. As beautiful as this car was, it gave me much grief. Like a beautiful and fickle woman, it was completely unreliable, stalling several times in the city. This was my last car in Iran. After the revolution, I got around using buses, the metro, and occasionally a taxi.

When Hamid reached the age when he could drive, and while studying at MIT, we ordered a Jeep Renegade for him. When the car arrived and was held up at customs, I asked him if he wanted me to step in and help, but he said no—he would deal with it himself. He was a responsible adult now. Accompanied by a driver, he left every morning in my car for the customs office, which was out of town, and returned, exhausted and dripping with perspiration, at 2 p.m.—empty-handed. Eventually he did ask for my help.

Having heard of the name of the head of customs, I found his phone number and spoke to his secretary, introducing myself and asking to speak to him. She first asked me where I was calling from. I replied, "Whether I'm calling from the prime minister's office or a public payphone, what difference does it make to you? You have my name." She was continuing to argue with me when our conversation was interrupted by a new voice that asked, "Khanum, what can I do for you?" I realized the boss was on the phone.

After preliminary introductions, I started my complaint and said, "My son is only here for six weeks' vacation from university in the U.S. He wants to pay his dues and get his car out of customs. They are giving him the run-around and he comes home every day, empty-handed. And you wonder why students studying abroad become revolutionaries? My son is not interested in politics, but this policy does not have a good effect on the young."

He listened to me carefully, asking for our details, and suggested that we see someone the following day who would arrange everything. The next day Hamid and the driver went in my car to the customs office and returned at noon with the Renegade. He had paid 20,000 tomans in dues. Ghasem, who had overheard my telephone conversation, later commented, "Khanum, you can speak to people in authority in this way and not get into trouble. If I had complained in the same way, I would get into serious trouble and be labeled a dissident."

When I returned to Iran many years after the revolution and came across a taxi driver or shopkeeper who complained about his lot, I remembered what Ghasem had said. Now the tables had turned. This kind of person would not get into trouble for openly criticizing the system, but if someone like me had commented negatively, we would end up in jail and be tortured.

The International Conference in Rome with My Sister Mehri

My sister Mehri, now a member of parliament, was participating in an international conference in Rome. Most delegates were accompanied by their spouses and I was to be her plus one! I arrived in Rome after a few hours' delay and made my way to the hotel where Mehri was awaiting me. Two thousand dignitaries from around the world, including senators, members of parliament, and their spouses were gathered there. My sister was one of the speakers and I hope I'm not being biased when I say that everyone thought hers was one of the best presentations. She spoke in English and the guests could listen to a translation in their mother tongue through earphones. In between sessions, we were treated to delicious cappuccinos.

One night, dinner was at the Palazzo Orsini on the outskirts of Rome. Tables were arranged in the different reception rooms of this museum-like building and dinner was served buffet-style. The high walls surrounding the palace were dotted with torches that lit up the gardens in which the guests were free to roam. In one corner of the garden, there was a pizzeria. Wearing long white aprons and tall hats, the chefs made pizzas to order in large ovens. All the dignitaries lining up for pizza was quite a sight! It was an unforgettable night and most enjoyable.

One day we were invited to the Vatican by Pope Paul VI. An academic and writer had recently given a speech at the United Nations, stressing the important role of this organization in improving conditions around the world. The transcripts of this speech were distributed among the guests. The pope walked among us and shook hands right and left. I was wearing a chiffon headscarf out of respect. The following day my picture with the pope appeared on the bulletin board. Unfortunately, this important photo remained in Iran and I have no idea what became of it. The conference over, it was time to return to Tehran and the start of another academic year.

Back in the Daily Routine

Classes had started. The IWC had also taken up its activities and our monthly meetings continued to be held at the homes of our members, alternating between those of the Iranian and non-Iranian ladies. Running the children's convalescence home required constant attention. At the same time, work continued on the writing and editing of *Negar-e Zan*. They were in the process of filming the Qajar-period dresses at the Golestan Palace under my supervision. Those of Safavid period had been filmed at the Sepah-Salar School and in front of the mosque of the same name in Baharestan Square. Based on sketches done by foreigners visiting Iran and published in various books about the country, the dresses were modeled by members of the club. Young seminaries were sitting on the steps of the mosque watching the proceedings while some were strolling through the large central garden. It occurred to me that our models were more modestly dressed than the women in the streets in those days.

Finally, the filming was over. I was unhappy with the beginning of the film, which had been the brainchild of our young director, recently graduated from Berkeley—known jokingly at the time as the People's Republic of Berkeley. Nowadays this university is much more mainstream and my first grandchild is a graduate. She is a disciplined and capable young woman, so I don't wish to insult the university.

Since the fashion show had been such a success, it was decided to have a repeat performance at the Hilton Hotel before handing over the dresses to the museum. Some of our models were away and we had to find replacements. This show was held in the afternoon to an audience of a thousand. The minister of arts and culture, who had not been able to attend the first show, was our guest of honor and accompanied by one of his sons. The minister of economy decided to attend for a second time and promised that he would have something interesting for the club. We never heard from him again!

I heard that Mohsen was not well and had gone to England for treatment. By contrast, I was feeling much better. The passage of time and my efforts had lifted the depression and I stopped taking the medication; I had become my own physician. Socrates tells us to know ourselves; we say self-knowledge is knowing God. My children did their best not to remind me of the past; even now, after many decades, they still try to keep sad news from me, despite my saying to them, "Since I will find out eventually, please tell me the truth."

It was back to routine: university, the book, the film, running the house, and spending time with my grandchildren, then one day Reza came to see me and said, "Mohsen is very sick and is going to England for a second time. I would suggest the girls or at least Mariam should accompany him." I replied, "The girls must make up their own minds; I am happy to look after their children while they are away. But I do know they would not want to meet the woman who destroyed their family. Maybe you should suggest that Mohsen goes alone this time and then the girls would be happy to accompany him." Reza said he had suggested the same to his brother—unfortunately to no avail. He added, "Houri, you know this woman is just looking after her own interests."

That summer Mariam and Fari were planning a trip to Greece, after which they would go to meet Mohsen in London. Leila went with them while I looked after their daughter Marjan in their absence. She was eighteen months old and Firouzeh, Ladan's baby, was six months old.

Mohsen's Illness

Mohsen was being treated by a British physician called Dr. Sheila Sherlock. Much later, Fari told me how, some time before, he had received a call one day from Mohsen complaining that he had vomited blood. Fari had made an appointment for him to see a hematologist, who examined him and recommended he go to London. Mohsen's regular physician in Tehran was a pulmonary disease specialist and not a liver specialist—more of a businessman than a caring doctor.

Fari's recommendation was the only intervention by the family. After that, even the hematologist didn't receive any news, since the medical reports from London were being sent to Mohsen's regular doctor in Tehran. Our family had no idea about the progress of the treatment or of the illness. Mohsen didn't trust anyone, and he was so busy with the company, all the issues surrounding the work at Saltanatabad, and the new house, that he had neglected his own health.

In the summer, Hamid returned from Aiglon College. Fari and Mariam arrived in London after their trip to Greece and, rather than meeting Mohsen as they had expected, found a letter from him. In it, he told them that he had been discharged from the hospital and was going to Paris to have some suits altered as he had lost so much weight! Mariam was disappointed not to have seen her father in London. It seemed he then left for Tehran a few days later. Ladan and Hamid went to visit him at the office.

One day, my granddaughter Firouzeh was really sick and I went to visit her at home. I had been there for a half hour when Mohsen arrived; I was shocked to see him. He was really thin and ill-looking. I pretended all was well and asked him how he was. He sighed and said, "Thank God, I am well," though this was clearly untrue. Happy to see the baby, he added, "These little ones are a balm to my soul." I wanted to speak to him about Hamid and remind him that our son had nothing to do in the summer and maybe we should think of something for him, but he changed the subject and shortly afterward I took my leave.

It seemed Mohsen was on a strict no-salt diet. Ladan would bake no-salt bread at home and send it to the office. A week later, Hamid went to the Caspian with his father; I had prepared food for them at home. Mohsen wanted to drive, but Reza persuaded him to take a driver along. Hamid and a cousin accompanied Mohsen, but they stayed for only two days before returning to Tehran. Hamid didn't talk much, although he was never much of talker—I used to call him monosyllabic!

The following day I dropped him off at the office and went to my publishers. The book *Negar-e Zan* was almost ready to be printed and just needed a final edit. Around noon I called home to find out if Hamid had returned. Ghasem replied, "Hamid came back almost straight away; then Miss Ladan came and they went to Pars Hospital together. Sir has been hospitalized." I raced from the publishers to the hospital, where I met Mr. Javad K——, Mohsen's brother-in-law, by the elevator. I asked him if I could visit the patient. He nodded and said of course.

As I entered the room, I saw Mohsen's mother, brothers and sisters and their children, as well as Ladan and Hamid, all gathered around his bed. Mohsen was the color of a bright yellow canary and had an oxygen mask on his face. I leaned down and said, "Inshallah, when you are recovered, we will go on a pilgrimage to Mecca together." He held both my hands and kissed them. He was a proud man and had never done that before. The whites of his eyes were also yellow and very little showed of his pupils, but tears were streaming down his face.

I had never seen Mohsen's tears before. When our baby Iraj died, he didn't cry. Nor did he when his father died. These tears and kissing my hands were something else. For the first time, he seemed to be asking for my forgiveness.

Cut Down in His Prime

Seconds, minutes, hours went by. Mohsen was still conscious. They took him to the ICU and we had to vacate the room and congregate in the waiting room. Time passed slowly. Mr. Javad K—— came to me and said, "It is almost over now. Why don't you make up with him?" I replied that there was nothing to make up. Then I realized what he was implying. I replied, "With respect, I just came to see him and now I will take my leave." Mohsen's brother Agha Bozorg arrived and said, "In the ambulance coming here, Mohsen said he was never returning to this woman's house: 'Please tell Houri and my children not to disgrace me.'"

With tears in my eyes and a lump in my throat, I said, "Mohsen asked you and you are asking me? I don't have any expectations, but if you would like his dignity to remain intact, we must forget that this other person ever existed. In life, we have choices and our choices have consequences.

He made a mistake. Maybe he was duped; we must put this behind us. I saw remorse in his eyes." At this point, Mohsen's brother-in-law Kazem K—— arrived and joined in the conversation. It was getting late; I sent Ladan home to her little one. Hamid was quiet and witnessing everything. At my insistence, he also went home.

I brought out a small copy of the Qur'an from my handbag. Mohsen's sisters were with me but his poor mother had been taken home. As the night ended, and just before the break of day, we would go into the ICU in turns and check on the patient, who was now in a coma; we would each say a prayer and leave. At some point, I don't remember the time, the oscillating lines on the monitor turned into a straight line. It was indeed the end of the line—a journey that everyone will take.

I was paralyzed, in shock—I could not move. It was dawn when I returned home; my sisters-in-law also went home. Mohsen was buried that same day. We all gathered in the library of Pars Hospital and drove from there to the Behesht-e Zahra cemetery. His family had bought a mausoleum which was yet to be built. In the heat of that day—25 July 1973 (3 Mordad 1352)—I saw the mound of dirt piled next to the spot that would be his final resting place and I said to myself, "Dear God, this meticulous man, who would have his car washed twice a day and would not eat off a plate until he had wiped it himself with a napkin, how can he be buried under this pile of dirt?" I reflected on the meaninglessness of life, on his premature death, at just fifty-two years of age. It was a tragic sight.

And there were more surprises in store for us; the Chinese fortune teller we had once visited had indicated there would be. Mohsen's lifeline was short. His funeral and the memorial ceremonies a week later were held at our house and his mother's. They were dignified occasions. Mariam, Fari, and Leila returned to Tehran. Mariam had not seen her father in London and was not able to be there at the end; she was truly devastated. Indeed, she appeared to change after that, becoming very spiritual. Before any of us, at the age of twenty-nine, she let go of all attachment to material objects, and to this day she is indifferent to the superficial aspects of life.

Death doesn't solve any problems; sometimes it makes things worse. After the revolution and the death of the Shah at the age of sixty, I often thought of these two men and compared their lives. When the Shah died, the people of Iran lost their joy and our country was destroyed. After the death of Mohsen, the happiness that had left us a while back never returned. Hamid, aged only seventeen, became a man overnight. Ladan and I both descended into depression. Reema was destroyed; it had been a one-man show. The fruit of thirty years' hard work simply melted away like a snowman in the sun. It was like a play written for just one actor, and when he was no more, all he had built fell apart.

There followed some family disputes that lost their importance after the revolution; they were mostly related to the material aspect of things, which is always easier to forget. After a while, the mausoleum was built. The interior walls were covered in Safavid tiling from floor to ceiling, with two verses from the Qur'an inscribed at a high level.

When the revolution came, the revolutionaries didn't spare the dead; they stole the beautiful blue chandelier and the Qur'an together with its stand and the candlesticks. Fourteen years after the revolution, when I returned to Iran, we had no choice but to replace the main door with a steel one to safeguard the resting place. Luckily the Qur'anic verses and the tiles were set into the walls, otherwise they would have been taken too.

The Summer of 1973 (1352)

It was a sad summer. For my birthday on 18 August (27 Mordad) the girls brought me gifts; we were all wearing black, as dark and somber as our hearts. Having been accepted at MIT at the age of seventeen, Hamid was preparing to leave for the U.S. Before he left, I took him to say goodbye to his grandmother, aunts, and uncles; I always believed that one should not destroy bridges one. After he left, the unity we had enjoyed for so many years turned into bitter separation, which was painful for me.

Thirty years' investment in this family seemed to have come to nothing; I gradually learned to put my faith only in God and myself. The depression was back, although I strove to appear calm on the surface. The girls worried about me and I worried about them. I tried hard to overcome my fragility and weakness and to regain my strength. The fortieth day of mourning[22] was held at the graveside and no longer at home; we also made a donation to Kahrizak Foundation in his name.

On Fridays, we usually got together as a family. Seeing my daughters and the grandchildren brought joy into my life. At the suggestion of the girls, I planned a trip to Boston to see Hamid's new life for myself. On the way, I stopped in Beirut for a few days and was able to visit the historic sites of this ancient land, though I was shocked at the tents of the displaced Palestinians, victims of the Arab–Israeli conflict. Our driver and guide reminded the group I was traveling with that the government was willing to house these people, but the Palestinians preferred to live in tents so the world would not forget their plight. From the clothes hanging on the washing lines, you could tell that these people had means; their condition was the form of political protest they had chosen.

I then visited Damascus, accompanied by a friend. On the way from Lebanon to Syria, you could see signs of warfare—military installations, soldiers in camouflage, and military jeeps. In Damascus, we visited the shrine of Zeinab, an important destination of religious pilgrimage for the Shia. We also visited the world-famous Bazar-e Shaam, humming with activity— people, animals, cars, carts, porters all jostling together. The stalls were piled

---

22. *The observation during mourning of the fortieth day after death occurs in Islam and the Eastern Orthodox tradition. The ritual represents spiritual intercession on the part of the dead, who are believed to collectively await the Day of Judgment.*

high with all kinds of goods; it was a miracle that anyone could find what they were looking for in the chaos. I then returned to Beirut and caught a flight from there to Boston, via London.

Hamid lived in a dorm and went to the campus on foot as I had asked him to wait until he was eighteen before buying a car. "How come I am old enough to go to MIT but not old enough to drive a car?" he had protested, but he listened to me even so. Years later, when the first thing my grandchildren did on turning sixteen was to buy a car, I was sorry for imposing this condition on Hamid. He confessed later that he would occasionally borrow and drive friends' cars and hadn't been as obedient as I had imagined.

From One Presidency to Another

At the beginning of the month of Aban (November), the IWC held their elections. My friend and colleague Guity Fallah was elected president without opposition and I was able to hand over the reins to her. Soon after that, *Negar-e Zan* was published. After two and a half years in gestation, the book was very well received; I was responsible for its distribution and sales.

With more time on my hands, my friends urged me to accept responsibility for the Tehran Zonta Club. Mrs. Ezzat Malek Soudavar insisted that I replace her as president and I accepted. The Zonta Club is similar to the Rotary Club, but for professional women. Our branch was a chapter of Zonta International, which has branches around the world.[23] Every two years, there is a large international gathering in one of the member countries with the aim of helping women in underdeveloped countries. At a meeting at the Iranian Bank hosted by Mrs. Ebtehaj, wife of the bank's president, the gavel was passed on to me. This club was a much simpler organization to run. The monthly lunchtime meetings were usually held at the Marmar or Intercontinental Hotel. Each member paid for herself; the club secretary simply had to send out the invitations to each meeting and there would normally be a guest speaker.

I got in touch with various companies to see if we could hold meetings at the company, inviting company employees to attend. On this basis, we visited the Melli Shoe Company, the *Kayhan* newspaper, and the Malek National Museum and Library, situated in those days at the end of the Grand Bazaar. At the invitation of the Iran Petrochemical Company, we flew as a group to Kharg Island. The members continued to pay for their lunches or trips to the club treasury and this money was then used for charitable causes.

Our problem was the Women's Organization of Iran, which showed great interest in the two clubs with which

---

23. The first Zonta Club was founded in Buffalo, New York, USA, on 8 November 1919, by a group of businesswomen under the leadership of playwright and journalist Marian de Forest. Membership is based on a classification system, inspired by the Rotary Club. Zonta International envisions a world in which women's rights are recognized as human rights and every woman is able to achieve her full potential. In such a world, women have access to all resources and are represented in decision-making positions on an equal basis with men. In such a world, no woman lives in fear of violence.

I was involved. A few days after the second fashion show, a member of the organization, Mrs. H. Z——, invited me to lunch. Guessing her reason for inviting me, I said, "I will accept your invitation to have lunch with pleasure. However, you must know that our organization cannot join yours." Apparently, the sudden fame of the IWC following the fashion show had made our club a desirable acquisition. But now there was pressure from senior members of the Women's Organization of Iran concerning Zonta; and after consultation with our members, we agreed to merge Zonta with the Women's Organization with the proviso that there would be no interference in our affairs.

Neither of the two clubs with which I was associated had any political agenda; if they had, we would not have been able to register them as charities. One of the club projects was to encourage young women to become pilots, and our first scholarship was named after the pioneering aviator Amelia Earhart. Interestingly, two Iranian women were the recipients of this award on two different occasions.

The Winter of 1973 (1352)

That winter following Mohsen's death was particularly harsh; freezing weather and constant snow made life difficult. Ladan would go skiing on Sundays. Once she returned with a broken leg; at the same time, Firouzeh had come down with a really bad cold and her nanny was on pilgrimage to

Mecca. To top this all, Ali had gone hunting and the replacement nanny was unfamiliar with the baby. Even though I had snow tires, driving was dangerous and there was no way I could walk the distance between our house and Ladan's. So, I hitch-hiked a ride in a tanker truck that was going close to Ladan's house and walked the rest of the way! Ladan's leg was in plaster, and she couldn't move. At this point, Ali returned with a large deer he had shot, and shortly after that the original nanny, who was now a *hajieh*, also returned, and so all was well.

One day, we discovered that a shareholders meeting was being held in a bank that had been established with a substantial investment from Mohsen to elect someone else to replace him on the board. The family were among the major shareholders of the bank and yet no one had told us about the meeting. Despite the freezing weather and the treacherous driving conditions, all of us shareholders in the family, except for Hamid who was in the U.S. and for whom I had power of attorney, managed to turn up. Even Ladan did, with her leg in plaster.

Seeing us, the person who was hoping to replace Mohsen backed out and all of us voted for Mariam, who won the ballot with the millions of shares we had as a family and took her father's place on the board. While her responsibilities weren't onerous—attending a board meeting twice a year, after which she was treated to a sumptuous lunch and rewarded with a handsome honorarium—but this was just one of the issues we had to face after the death of Mohsen; nothing was straightforward anymore.

An Offer to Buy the New House in Elahieh

The big new house in Elahieh remained unfinished. All the plans, even the color of the marble, had been chosen and samples lay on the floor of a tent in the garden, but none of it came to fruition. The main structure of this house lasted for many years under the elements, until it fell into the hands of the revolutionaries. The Japanese ambassador Mr. Ikawa and his wife were friends of ours and were keen to buy this piece of land. At the time they offered us $2 million, but Mohsen, in a handwritten will, of which we had a photocopy, had asked that the building should not be sold; maybe he hoped Hamid would finish it.

Our inheritance laws, based on Islamic tradition, deem that a wife cannot inherit land but only buildings, trees, furniture, and cash, while a parent of the deceased, by contrast, inherits a sixth of everything including the land. I had little interest in the house, however, and pretended not to mind about the unjust nature of such laws. I replied to Mr. Ikawa that we didn't want to sell because we wouldn't know what to do with the money; in addition, my husband had indicated in his will that the property should not be sold.

I didn't even consider selling the 2,000 square meters that had separate deeds and was in Hamid's name, even though I had a power of attorney for Hamid. We were Iranians and everything we had was in this country. I didn't even have a simple bank account abroad except for the small amount that Hamid needed for his college. Even this we returned to Iran as interest rates were very low in the U.S.

Remodeling My House

Our house needed renovation and remodeling. I asked Me'mar our contractor, to help me with this and we added 50 square meters to the living and dining room by incorporating the terrace into the house. We then pushed out into the back yard and created a new terrace. The floors were parquet, and we renovated the rest of the house too. For eight months, I lived with the workmen.

During the month of Ramadan, I invited all the workmen who were fasting to break their fast as our guests. The cook, Fatemeh, prepared delicious food for them and, with Ghasem's help, they served the workmen while I broke my fast in the small dining room. At the end of Ramadan, the structure was complete, and they started work on the finishing. At times when the floors were still unfinished, I would say my prayers standing on my bed! It was a huge undertaking.

The Strangest Dream

Every day at dawn, Fatemeh would come to my room to let me know that *Sahari*, the last meal before starting the fast, was ready. When I finished eating, I returned to my bedroom, locking the door of the corridor between the bedrooms and the rest of the house. I then read from the Qur'an until it was time for my prayers—the same copy of the Qur'an that had saved me from depression. It was the end of Ramadan and I had reached the final verses. After saying my prayers, I went to bed again. It was six a.m. When I woke up crying a little later, the clock said 6:30 a.m. I have related the dream that I had during that half hour many times to those close to me, but at the time I wasn't sure whether I was dreaming or not.

In the dream, someone entered the bedroom quietly. I asked myself who it could be. Hamid would sometimes fling himself on my bed, but I then remembered that he was in the U.S. I looked again, and realized that it was Mohsen, who now sitting in the high-backed armchair in the corner of the room. Aware of a vague unhappiness stirring within me, I asked him what he was doing there, reminding him that I had locked the door of the corridor. He smiled and said, "Doors and locks are not an issue for us." He then put his hand in his pocket and brought out a blue velvet box. I told him I didn't want anything from him. Then I noticed I was wearing a ring that I hadn't seen before. It had three stones—two sapphires and one diamond. The stones sparkled; the ring was spectacular.

Suddenly Mohsen stood up, and I asked myself, "Am I dreaming or is this actually happening?" I thought that if I heard the bells attached to the front door, I would know I was not dreaming. Just then I heard the sound of the bells. I hurried to the front door and saw him leaving the house. I asked him to come back. It was then I realized he was not of this world. But he came back, and we sat together on the old seat next to the hall telephone—somehow, we both fit on that small sofa. Fatemeh and Ghasem were standing at some way distance near the living room. They were crying. I asked Mohsen to stay, but he shook his head and said, "You know I can't." It was then I woke up from my early-morning nap, sobbing.

I jumped out of bed; it was 6:30 a.m. I tried the door of the corridor and found it still locked. I unlocked the door and searched the entrance hall. The front door was also closed. Everyone was asleep. We had received a visit from an unexpected guest who had come and gone. I still couldn't believe that this was just a dream. Years later, when we reluctantly left Iran, I suddenly remembered the dream about Mohsen and the ring. That beautiful ring with its three precious stones represented my three children, I now realize; this priceless legacy was the capital their father had entrusted to me for safekeeping.

Otherwise, when the revolution came, we left our country practically empty-handed and with no plans—just like thousands of others who were forced to leave and never went back to Iran. Hamid was a university student; the girls had left the country temporarily to escape the cold winter, the power cuts, and the violence for the sake of their young children. We all expected to return. In fact, Ladan and her family did go back that same year and tasted the revolution for a few years before leaving Iran in a journey fraught with danger and great difficulty.

Warned in Another Dream

I was busy in the spring and summer of 1974 (1353) with the remodeling of the house. Hamid came home for the summer holidays and promptly fell ill. Although he was eighteen by then, and no longer a child, he was still registered with our pediatrician Dr. Mostofi. I called the doctor and followed his instructions to the letter; I was the round-the-clock nurse feeding my son chicken soup and endless glasses of freshly squeezed juice from the oranges of Villa Hamid. One day I was so exhausted, I fell asleep on my bed just before lunch. I had been asleep no more than ten minutes when I saw Mohsen on the balcony outside leaning against one of the columns and pointing to the sliding windows of Hamid's room. He kept looking at me and then turning his gaze toward our son's room.

I woke up at once and ran to Hamid's room, where I found him unconscious. I put a thermometer in his mouth; it was above 40 degrees. I called Dr. Mostofi. He ordered us to prepare a cold foot bath for Hamid and to persevere with this until his arrival. We followed his instructions and Hamid gradually opened his eyes. Dr. Mostofi had come to our aid and God had helped us. I have no idea what would have happened if I had stayed asleep. Mohsen's frightened look had alerted me to the patient's serious condition. He and I had this strange telepathy, it seemed, and, on many other occasions, he came to warn us of impending danger.

Sorting Out the Family Finances

From the start of the year 1974 (1353), Reema began to go downhill; its finances were in bad shape and everything was falling apart after the death of its founder. I agreed to stop receiving a monthly stipend. Mohsen's mother and the other woman also received a monthly check. If I stopped receiving mine, then the others would also have no claim. On the other hand, the bank, whose CEO was Mohsen's brother Reza, was doing very well and once probate was granted, Mariam decided to divide Mohsen's bank shares between the heirs.

But first taxes had to be paid; our immediate family paid the equivalent of $300,000 in inheritance taxes and Mohsen's shares were divided between us. When he was alive, Mohsen had put roughly 2 million tomans in shares each for the girls and me, and 4.5 million for Hamid. After Mohsen's shares were divided, each of us ended up with a larger number of shares overall. This was the only part of Mohsen's assets that were divisible and did not depend on the agreement of all the heirs. Everything else, including land, the factory, the new house, and Reema, remained as it was; and then it was too late—the revolution had already happened.

Mariam divided her shares between her husband, her two daughters, and herself. Ladan borrowed money to buy more shares since the dividends were substantial. The cost of Hamid's education at MIT was considerable and was paid out of the dividends on his shares. I am relating all this to show that the heirs were in no financial difficulty and had no expectations from Reema—which was now a failing company. We were happy if it could cover its own expenses. I did visit the company a couple of times after Mohsen's death, but when I saw someone else had taken his place, I never set foot there again.

Money was never high on my list of priorities. But in spite of my indifference to financial wealth, I have always been provided for and have managed to live a dignified life. After the revolution, many kowtowed to the zeros after a person's bank balance; it made me laugh and sometimes cry. In the past, if a young man asked for a girl's hand in marriage, he would be asked about his family background and how well educated he was. These days as long as there is plenty of money, nothing else seems to matter, but I digress . . .

Today is Sunday 23 January 2000. I am sitting in bed listening to *La Traviata* and the soaring voice of Luciano Pavarotti as I pour my heart out onto the pages of this journal. Where were we? Back in 1974 (1353), Hamid came home for the New Year holidays and brightened our lives. Firouzeh was a little older and Ladan had moved from the Saii Park apartment to a lovely house in Kamranieh. Their little family was happy. Hamid had cut his hair, which had grown long, and was now a handsome young man. He was very attached to his young nieces and loved all children—just like his father.

More Building Projects

Fari and Mariam had bought a piece of land in Elahieh sometime before and were now busy building; their new house was very close to mine. We all got together on Fridays and relative peace had returned to our family. The grandchildren and their nannies (young women from the Philippines who had recently come to Iran and were being hired by wealthy families) would gather around the breakfast table while the older family members sat at the dining table. My sister and brother would often join us with their children. Fridays were family days, and we were happy to get together at one of our houses.

For Nowruz 1354 (1975), we stayed in Iran and visited the Caspian where we stayed at Mariam's villa in Alamdeh for a week. This gave me an opportunity to visit Villa Hamid; and I decided to make some changes to the house. Mariam drew up some plans and we set about modernizing the single-story structure. Managing things long distance was difficult, which meant I spent that whole summer traveling back and forth. We added a bathroom and created a fireplace; the construction took six months. Toward the end of the summer, we were able to stay there for a few days. Hamid invited some of his friends and cousins to spend time with him.

Hamid was now nineteen and drove his own car. Once when I wanted to check on the work, he drove all the way from our house in Elahieh to Villa Hamid in under three hours. It's a dangerous and windy road and I was convinced

I must be about to have a heart attack! But it is impossible to argue with the young and I never uttered a word. We stayed one night and returned the next day to Tehran; this time the trip took even less time.

Activities of the Zonta Club in Tehran

We organized a gala dinner at the Intercontinental Hotel and made a good profit through ticket sales as part of the celebrations for Greek Week. The Greek ambassador had intended for the proceeds of that evening to be donated to the Physical Education Organization, headed by Prince Gholamreza. I called that office and said that as it would be beneath the dignity of that organization with its vast budget to accept such a small donation, we would instead love to invite the prince and Princess Manijeh, his wife, to the event itself.

The final event of the Greek week was in aid of Zonta. The renowned Greek goldsmith Ilias Lalaounis had prepared a most interesting film of his jewelry show and the Greek fashion designer Yannis Tseklenis had designed and made many outfits in Persian-inspired silks, displayed by Greek models. We organized an afternoon event and the tickets were reasonably priced, so all could come. We also invited Mrs. Farideh Diba to honor us with her presence. The Intercontinental had prepared a fabulous spread for afternoon tea. The event was sold out and it was standing room only after that—400 ladies attended. I opened the afternoon by thanking the two Greek designers, followed by a brief summary of the work of the Zonta Club. Mr. Lalaounis then presented Mrs. Diba and myself each with a gold cup, and the show began.

The models walked in against a backdrop of a scene from Persepolis, wearing very simple outfits to show off the pieces, which were inspired by the ancient jewelry of Iran; the accompanying music was soft. Ancient and modern Iran had come together and were parading in front of us and the effect was spellbinding. You could hear a pin drop in the hall. After that, it was the turn of the silk dresses in designs copied from Persian carpets. The background consisted of the carpets themselves and the tilework of Isfahan, with the models gliding in front of these images.

The show was very well received; the newspapers were full of praise for the event. The considerable proceeds went to the Zonta Club, to be distributed among the various charities we supported. Tseklenis sent me a beautiful silk scarf; I hadn't realized that the outfit I had once bought in Rhodes—and as a result nearly missed catching the boat from the island—was the work of this same designer. Interestingly, I still have the two gifts with me—the golden cup and the scarf—while everything else I owned was left behind in Iran.

Fatemeh Goes on Hajj

Fatemeh had been preparing herself to go to Mecca for some time now. While she was away, Ghasem and his brothers took care of me and the house. She returned a *hajieh khanum* and stayed at her own house for ten days while all her family and neighbors came to pay their respects. If one sheep had been sacrificed for me, she had two sheep slaughtered to feed all the guests. When Fatemeh eventually returned to work, I asked her how I should address her now. She replied that she wanted to be called "Hajieh Khanum" and so she was. She had brought presents for everyone and, since her return, had become quite a personality.

Sometimes she and her younger brother, who was married and had children, would have a disagreement. Her brother would mock her saying, "Who do you think you are? Mrs. Moghadam? You have too many airs; she is far humbler than you!" Hajieh Khanum didn't have children and devoted herself to other things instead; she loved a clean house, good food, and nice clothes, and was an expert at cooking and ironing.

It seemed that she was not only an important person among her neighbors but was also well known in Elahieh. She had a radio and a small TV in the kitchen, which overlooked the street, was well informed about the news and liked to air her political opinions. I tried hard to teach her to read and write, but I finally gave up. By contrast, her colleague Ghasem had made good progress and finished primary school. Hajieh Khanum had an amazing memory for her recipes and would never forget an ingredient. She was highly intelligent—just not interested in becoming literate.

One winter's day, I came home to find the outside door to the kitchen open, the lights, radio and TV all on, and the kettle boiling on the stove. At that moment, Hajieh Khanum entered the kitchen from the garden with some herbs she had cut for lunch. After greeting her, I asked her to sit down as I had something to tell her. I had to be very tactful if I needed to mention something as she was extremely sensitive and didn't take kindly to criticism. This was during the presidency of Jimmy Carter, who was an advocate of human rights and energy conservation.

I said, "Hajieh Khanum, do you know what is meant by energy?" She replied, "Everyone talks about it." I said, "Today, you wasted energy in various ways. The sun is shining and you have the lights on; the TV and radio are both on and the kettle is boiling merrily on the stove. At the same time, the central heating is being wasted since the kitchen door is wide open and you are in the garden. This is a waste of energy." Realizing that what I was saying made sense, she didn't take offense but just laughed and said, "Khanum, you have so much. Why are you worried about small savings?" I didn't reply and turned to go to my room.

A few weeks later we had a major power cut; the house was dark and the food in the freezer was defrosting. Hajieh Khanum was really upset and begged me to do something about it. She wanted me to call someone. I said, "You have answered your own question today. There are times when money is available but there is no power; this is why we must not waste energy."

One morning when I was hurrying to go to the university, I told her that the tea that day was excellent. "Are you joking?" she replied. "No," I reiterated. "One has to give credit where credit is due." She then said, "Last night after the guests had left there was some tea left, so I warmed it for you this morning. You see, I too, know how to 'waste not, want not'!"

Sometime later, I traveled to Russia. On my return, I noticed that she had become a libertarian and kept repeating things she had heard on the radio and TV. Once again, I sat her down and said, "Hajieh Khanum, I have just returned from a country where you need permission if you so much as want to put a nail in the wall. People are hungry and poorly dressed; they live on black bread and borsht. If the regime changes in this country, our lives will be affected. Your life will deteriorate. Don't believe everything you hear. You have a comfortable life now, for which you should be grateful." In those days, we were afraid of communism. Years later, after the revolution, she said to me on the phone, "Khanum, you were right. The revolution was a disaster."

One morning she said, "I dreamt last night that you gave me your agate ring inscribed with the names of the five imams." I replied that, since I only had this one agate ring, I would give it to her as soon as I bought another. Soon after, I went to Isfahan with Mrs. Soudavar and bought a beautiful agate stone in the Grand Bazaar, which I had Nassib jewelers set into a ring for me. I then gave her the ring she wanted. Dreams seemed to be big in her family; with a tendency to come true once her niece had dreamt that her aunt had given her a beautiful carpet from right under her feet!

A year after Mohsen died, Ghasem asked to be transferred to the Petrochemical Company to work there as a waiter. He would come home at the weekends and deal with the heavier chores; the rest of the week, Hajieh Khanum managed by herself, but she missed her colleague. I suggested that she take on someone she could get along with to replace Ghasem. Resistant to this suggestion, she replied, "These days you can't trust anyone."

But I persevered until finally, we employed a young man from Sri Lanka. He was smart and capable, and spoke English fluently. He knew how to drive and once drove all the way to the Caspian, but there was something strange about him. He was almost too good to be true; he was so willing and able that I became suspicious, but, more importantly, he didn't pander to Hajieh Khanum. He didn't last long in our household.

After that, we found someone from Bangladesh on the recommendation of the Iranian ambassador to that country. Once again, Hajieh Khanum was not happy and would say, "Is this going to be my destiny? To wake up to a foreign face every morning; it spoils my whole day." She would cry all the time and complained incessantly. The situation was untenable. The day I left Tehran for medical treatment in the U.S., Mohammad Ali was still in our house. But after the revolution, he was sent back to his country and Hajieh Khanum breathed a sigh of relief; her wish had been granted.

Eventually, I ended up living in Paris and Hajieh Khanum was left by herself in the house. For two years, she was in charge; after that we thanked her for the many years of devoted service, gave her a big bonus, and sent her home, which was well furnished and comfortable as I had offered her whatever she wanted from my house. A little while after that, she developed cataracts, and Hamid sent her money for treatment. The Islamic Republic of Iran, which was supposedly on the side of the dispossessed, charged her a huge amount of money for her treatment at the Sina Hospital. When I returned to Iran after fourteen years, Hajieh Khanum, Ghasem, and his two brothers came to visit me with a beautiful bouquet of gladioli and a big sack of fresh walnuts from Ghasem's farm. They had nothing but complaints about the regime.

Sadly, Hajieh Khanum didn't live long after that; she passed away in her own home surrounded by her family. May she rest in peace. She achieved what she wanted in life but didn't live long enough to enjoy it all. Ghasem told me that she had at least 20 million tomans to her name; but after her death, her brothers didn't even buy her a headstone. She was buried in Behesht-e Zahra. Such is the way of the world; this brother was her only heir.

Ghasem Agha

Today, 18 January 2000, Ladan brought me sad news I should have been told a month ago, but she had hidden it from me. Ghasem, my faithful and dependable aide, had died of a sudden heart attack at the age of fifty-six. A fine human being who spent his life working hard and serving others, he didn't live long enough to enjoy the fruits of his labors. I was so upset that I burst into tears. I cried for this gentle individual, the likes of whom are rare. I cried for his devoted wife and for his three sons aged twenty-two, seventeen, and six. He never had enough time to be with them but supported them to the best of his ability. His oldest son had graduated from college, his father paying his college fees. What had happened to all the promises of the revolutionaries?

The day I had left Tehran for treatment at the Mayo Clinic, Ghasem held the Qur'an for me to pass under. I remember telling him, "Ghasem, our time is over. In future, maybe you will come to our aid." My trip, which was planned for one month, lasted fourteen years. When I returned to Iran in November 1992 (Aban 1371), having been away for fourteen years in the U.S., Ghasem came to see me. Not wanting to sit, he kneeled by my chair and said, "Khanum, they lied to us and tricked us—and we believed them." I didn't have to ask him who "they" were.

When Ghasem, aged sixteen, was sent from the Reema factory to deliver building materials for the prefabricated house we were building in Elahieh, he used to sleep in the building site while construction was going on. When the house was finished, he started work in the garden; gradually he started to help in the house. As well as learning to read and write, he learned to bake cakes, clean chandeliers, garden, cook, and eventually to drive—he became a jack of all trades.

He would take phone messages; he almost became my secretary. He played a big part in the building children's convalescence home, although he never set foot in it! Later he married his cousin and bought a piece of land in Gheytarieh with his savings. Hajieh Khanum would sometimes cover for him when he was absent. If any of my belongings were salvaged after the revolution, it was thanks to Ghasem and his brothers, who hid some of my carpets in their own homes and saved them from being looted.

A year after the death of his employer, Mohsen, I contacted the HR department of the Petrochemical Company and asked them to give him a position. I told them that this young man was a gem, and that they should appreciate him. He started work there as a waiter. He had done two years of military service but I warned him not to let on that he was a skilled cook and knew housework. I wanted him to learn to drive since it would give him more options in the future. But they found out about his skills and he was seconded to work in the home of a four-star general. Everyone admired this young man's talents; he worked tirelessly in that household for two years in the hope that he would later find a permanent position in the army—but that never happened.

At the Petrochemical Company, they valued his service, and he was responsible for serving at important social occasions. After the revolution, although he was on a good salary, so he worked nights in people's homes as a waiter while his wife took care of the house and family. Ghasem was principled, generous, and caring. If I gave him a new suit, he would immediately donate his old suit to someone. He helped his brothers leave their village and find work at Reema; one became a skilled driver and was eventually employed at the municipality.

The other brother, Ali, who was the most educated, worked for Reza for some time. After they left for the U.S., and while Ghasem was doing his military service, he came to work for us. He was quiet and responsible and he too had learned all the household duties. His only weakness was that he was a heavy sleeper. I often talked about it to him, reminding him that this kind of deep sleep—being dead to the world—was not good for him. Eventually, he managed to overcome the problem.

One night I had gone out with Mohsen, Reza, and my sister-in-law Mariam. As we approached the house, Mohsen sounded the horn very gently. Ali's room was close to the gate and he immediately jumped up and opened it. Reza was surprised and said, "Houri, this is a miracle. When he was with us, you could sew him to his sheet and blanket and he wouldn't wake up." I replied that the miracle was in having awoken this young man's sense of responsibility; he had found the willpower to deal with the issue.

These boys came from a village where their parents couldn't support them and so they were sent one by one to the city, where they eventually managed to make a life for themselves. The third brother, Hashem, worked for a while at the Reema factory and then returned to his village where he started work as the manager of a cooperative. The sons would each send money to the parents, who were able to live in this way, with their sons' support, not being particularly ambitious or hard-working themselves. They would occasionally come to the city and stay with us, Ghasem's mother in traditional Kurdish dress. She was grateful to us, saying, "You have been like a mother to my sons."

When I returned to Iran after the revolution, Ghasem and his family invited me to lunch. One of his cousins drove a taxi—despite being employed by the municipality as a garbage truck driver—and came to collect me. "Khanum, you have bought this car that I drive as a taxi," he said. "But I have been away these past fourteen years," I said, and he replied: "Nevertheless it was with your help and Miss Ladan's that I managed to buy a car."

I entered the home of Ghasem and his wife Sakineh. All their neighbors came to greet me; the women would try to kiss my hands and face. Sakineh Khanum had also invited Hajieh Khanum. A large tablecloth was spread on the carpet. Ghasem smiled and said, "Khanum, this carpet is factory-made and is more than enough for us." A large stove was burning and the best dishes had been prepared—enough for thirty people. After lunch, some neighbors joined us and, after bowing or shaking my hand, took their place on the carpet beside us.

One was Ghasem's sister. "Khanum, we owe everything to you," she said. "But I haven't done anything for you," I replied. "We had a small grocery store that the municipality wanted to demolish," she continued. "We came to you. You called and spoke to the mayor and persuaded them not to do this. We have been working here for many years."

Ghasem jokingly said that, since his brother-in-law was self-employed, he and his sister must be rich. Hajieh Khanum, who was quite self-important, sat at the head of the gathering at my request. It was one of the best days I had in Tehran. There was no question that they expected anything from me or that I gave them any money. They knew that my house had been taken over and that I was staying at the house of a cousin of Mohsen's. We had broken bread together and they were kind and appreciative individuals. Many families were betrayed by their angry and resentful servants; we were lucky to have lived with such good people.

Today, I write this eulogy for Ghasem and his extended family to give credit where it is due. If an employer treats his employees well, with fairness and respect, both parties enjoy a warm and harmonious relationship. Ghasem and his brothers were decent people. His life may have been short, but he could be proud of the family he had raised and the role model he had become for his sons, so that they, too, would follow in his footsteps and appreciate the sacrifices he and his wife had made. May you rest in peace, Ghasem.

Buying an Apartment in Paris, 1976 (1355)

Winter came to an end and spring arrived. I had planned a visit to France in order to buy an apartment. The Iranian government allowed transfer of currency, and as it was possible to legally take money out, everyone was buying apartments outside Iran. Hamid had stopped in Paris on his way to the U.S. and stayed with one of his Iranian friends from MIT. He asked me to buy him an apartment in Paris with the proceeds of his bank shares. I asked our friend Mr. Asghar Panahi, who had studied and worked in France and owned an apartment in Paris, to look out for an apartment for us too. On his return, he told me there were many properties for sale but a new building was going up in a first-class location, with beautiful views, and an excellent finish.

A few months before this, I had bought an apartment in Nice from a friend of Mariam—off plan and sight unseen—that was still under construction, and I now needed to visit and see it for myself. So, accompanied by my friend Aisha, we traveled first to Nice and stayed at the Meridian Hotel. We went to view the nine-story building from the outside as the staircases had not been built yet; we then went to see another block that was finished to get a better idea of the final product. The views of the city and the Mediterranean, as well as the surrounding hills, were spectacular. We spent Nowruz in Monte Carlo and had lunch at a small café overlooking the sea. The yachts, the sailboats, the flowers and the beauty of this city were famous; what a shame that some years later it was all ruined by enormous skyscrapers. The square in front of the Casino was covered in red and white cyclamen—the colors of the Monaco flag.

A few days later, in Paris, we visited a friend whose father had an apartment in the same street in which Hamid's future apartment was located. The new building was constructed on a plot that had once been the site of the American ambassador's residence before it had moved to the rue Fauberg Saint-Honoré, next to the Élysée Palace. The old building was demolished and a new, five-story apartment building, designed by the French architect Maurice Novarina, went up in its place. The upper floors were already sold, even before the structure had been completed.

I chose the second floor; since the building was constructed on a slope, it felt like the third floor. The view was beautiful. I went to see the seller, Mr. Cooperman, and told him I had only 60,000 francs on me. In those days, Iranians enjoyed excellent credit ratings and this sum was accepted as a down payment. A contract was signed and I asked Bank Melli to send Mr. Cooperman the balance. I wanted to speak to Hamid in Boston, so I woke him up at 6 a.m. and briefly explained what I was about to do. He agreed and the deal went ahead. The apartment was ready in 1977 when we took possession.

Monthly Gatherings of Friends and Family

Most of our family's social life centered on a monthly gathering or *doreh* of various groups. There was the Ardalan group, the Esfandiaris, and two bridge groups—one with friends and the other with ambassadors' wives. The Ardalans were the largest group; we were forty in number, although some would always be away traveling. The parties were loud, happy, full of jokes and laughter. This is how we kept in touch with each other's families—once a month on Sunday nights.

The Esfandiari group, around twenty-five in number, consisted of various friends. The evenings usually ended up with ladies on one side of the room and the men on the other, all exchanging the latest news and gossip. Each of us would take turns hosting the parties; occasionally we would invite one or two who were not part of the group while keeping in mind the harmony of the company. Dinner was served but the party had to end before midnight.

The friends' bridge parties were held on Tuesdays. As the gatherings were held once a week from 10 a.m. and would end around 3 or 4 p.m., lunch would be served. Occasionally there were minor disagreements, with someone adamant that she had won, finding it difficult to accept that she was wrong and blaming her opponent. But our friendships weren't affected; we all shared in each other's joys and sorrows.

There were twelve regular members of the group, including yours truly and my friends Mahin, Pari, and Aysheh. My friend Mahin was the life and soul of the party with her jokes; she was younger than the rest of us and added much to our group. I used to say to her, "It is a shame that I am not an important person; otherwise I would command you never to leave my side since your cheerfulness clears the atmosphere and makes it easier to breathe." Pari was a neighbor in Elahieh. Like Mahin, she was lively and highly capable; she remained a steadfast and generous friend.

Her daughter Shahrzad was a few months younger than Ladan and they were good friends. Both attended the Jeanne d'Arc High School and their friendship has endured after all these years. Pari was mischievous and would make up stories that she would later jokingly admit were not true. The problem was that, even when she did speak the truth, no one believed her! Both Mahin and Pari were faithful friends. Aysheh was the most serious of the group, also a good friend but quieter than the others. Her peacefulness was most noticeable when we played bridge. These three friends were the three flowers of my heart—each with a different color and scent.

Playing Bridge with the Ambassadors' Wives

I started this gathering at my house with just one bridge table and invited three other ladies to join me. The first was the wife of the then French ambassador, Fanny Charles-Roux. Born in France to a Turkish mother and a French father, she was educated and smart, and an excellent bridge player. The second was Anna Mehran, originally from Italy and married to Dr. Mehran, a former minister of education, and the third was Farangis Panahi. We played bridge once a week from 10 a.m. to 1 p.m., serving tea and coffee, cakes, and sandwiches—all homemade.

Gradually the group started to grow, with several more ladies, mostly ambassadors' wives, joining in. One of the ladies whose bridge playing improved during these gatherings was the British-born wife of the American ambassador, Mrs. Cynthia Helms. She managed to improve her game considerably during her stay by taking classes. This lady had an interesting story. I met her in Tehran; she was an honorary member of the IWC and a regular member of our bridge games. She had divorced her first husband, the father of her five children, at the age of fifty-nine and then married Richard Helms, also divorced, and with an only son. The gossip was that Cynthia's ex-husband had then married another lady who had four children herself and the whole family had gone on honeymoon together. So, the middle-aged bride and groom were chaperoned with a total of nine children. It seemed that, in the U.S., unlike Iran, middle-aged men were not necessarily after much younger women; they probably just needed a change of scenery!

A Big Mistake

But there was a more serious side to all this. The arrival of Richard Helms, former head of the CIA, as ambassador to Iran, proved to be seriously harmful for our country. Having got to know Cynthia Helms better through the bridge parties, I believe the reason for his appointment to this post was his new wife's interest in Iranian antiquities. When he was removed from the CIA, he was offered a choice of several countries as a consolation prize, where he could be appointed ambassador. Cynthia put her finger on Iran and decided that should be his choice. She had worked for many years in museums and, during their stay in Iran, she managed to visit most of the country and saw every possible historic site, from the most famous like Persepolis and Pasargadae to almost unknown places.

She traveled to Isfahan, Yazd, and many other cities; she learned to speak Persian and would consult new friends and club members for their expertise in the different fields she was interested in. She left no stone unturned. Iran was a wonderful school from which she graduated. When the Democrats returned to power and Jimmy Carter became president, the couple were recalled to Washington.

Mrs. Safieh Firouz, may she rest in peace, asked me to give a farewell lunch party for Mrs. Helms on behalf of the IWC, where she would be presented with a gift. Having invited about thirty ladies to this luncheon, I asked one of the club members to buy the present and also invited some of my bridge-playing ladies. It was a dignified occasion and pictures were taken. Hajieh Khanum had baked a cake, decorated with the flags of Iran, America, and the United Nations.

Alice Meyer had been none too pleased with individuals like me who sometimes contradicted her, and Cynthia was of the same mindset. There are many Iranians who are not sycophants, but the flatterers had spoiled some members of the diplomatic corps. In her memoir, Cynthia speaks about her desire to come to Iran; I personally wish she and her husband had chosen a different country. Richard Helms loved Iran and, when President Carter was elected, he predicted, "Things will now change between our two countries."

In my view, this Democrat president should have stayed home and run the church in Plains, Georgia. Carter was a good man but a terrible politician. Later, when he was given the Nobel Peace prize, I said to myself, "He should have received a prize for starting wars, not a peace prize." The turmoil in Iran marked the beginning of worldwide unrest; the roots of peace in the Middle East were shaken, causing the rise of terrorism everywhere. I leave it to political commentators to judge history.

Nowruz 1356 (1977)

The Nowruz vacation came to an end and everyone went back to their daily routine. Mine included the university and family, especially the grandchildren. On Fridays, we would all get together as we lived only a ten-minute walk from each other. When I think back on those days now, I become truly nostalgic. I have always been grateful for my life but the great distances between us these days makes me sad. Mariam is in London, Ladan lives a half hour from San Francisco, and my granddaughter Leila is in San Ramon, an hour away from me. Meanwhile, Hamid, who also lives in San Francisco, is always on another continent or in another state on a business trip. My sister Nayer lives in Houston, and many of my other relations are scattered all around the world.

Summertime 1977 (1356)

Once again, it was summer and time for Hamid's return from the U.S. Fari, Mariam, and their children had recently moved to their brand-new house. It had been a labor of love; a strong building, simple and beautiful. The surrounding garden was no less beautiful; a pity that they stayed there only a year and the house was auctioned off after the revolution. Ladan was busy taking care of the children and teaching at Melli University. Hamid decided to throw a big party at the house and invite all his friends. I was backstage that day, managing things, while he was the host.

There were more than fifty guests; all the food and desserts had been prepared at home by our cook and her assistants. Ghasem and his brother were the waiters and Hajieh Khanum ruled in the kitchen. Some of the young girls at the party came to my room after dinner to say hello;

their parents were our friends. The garden and the pool had been remodeled and the house sparkled. This was Hamid's first and last party in this house. Fate didn't allow us to repeat the gathering. Even though Hamid's life appeared not to have changed much after his father passed away, I am sure that his death had been a huge loss. We eventually learn that you cannot fight destiny.

In August (Shahrivar), Hamid planned to leave ahead of me for Europe. I was to follow and take possession of the apartments in Paris. In the end, we decided to go together to Nice and take delivery of all the furniture we had ordered for that apartment. Hamid had his birthday while we were in the Côte d'Azur and I invited our friends Behi and Parviz and their daughter to a restaurant in Haut-de-Cagnes. The five of us enjoyed a wonderful dinner and were invited by them in return to lunch at the Colombe d'Or in Saint-Paul de Vence. It was a wonderful time spent with friends.

After a few days, we traveled to Paris and camped out in the nearly empty apartment. The furniture was arriving piece by piece. Hamid and I would go out together to restaurants or to shop for the apartment. When it was time for him to return to Boston, my sister Mehri took his place, joining me in Paris for a few days. One day, Lois Harlan, who had been the IWC treasurer, came to visit us in the apartment. She confided in me, saying, "All the other members were full of admiration to see you stand up to the U.S. ambassador's wife." She continued, "I couldn't speak about this until today as my husband was still a diplomat. But we all suffered from this lady's behavior and could do nothing about it. We are now retired and, as a private person, I am able to criticize this lady openly." It was the last time I saw Lois, although we did correspond for a while longer.

The Opening of Zonta Clubs in Shemiran and Mashhad, 1978 (1356)

Twenty years had passed since the founding of the Tehran Zonta Club. The plans for opening branches in Shemiran and Mashhad took place during my presidency. France de la Chaise, the head of Zonta International, and Irène Bellicard, the person responsible for Europe, both French and friends of mine, were invited to Iran in March (Esfand) for the opening of the two clubs. Several American, German, Swiss, and French members also participated. A lot of effort went into preparing for the openings and careful planning was required. France de la Chaise stayed with me and Irène Bellicard was the guest of Mrs. Fatemeh P——, while other attendees stayed at Park Hotel.

I had requested an appointment to take these two ladies, together with the heads of the two new clubs, for an audience with Her Majesty Shahbanu Farah Pahlavi. She received our group of seven in her private study at Niavaran Palace and the whole meeting was of course conducted in French. The conversation centered around the activities of Zonta especially in developing countries.

After that audience, everyone came to my house for lunch where we were joined by other guests. Hajieh Khanum did her best to introduce our international friends to the finest Persian cuisine.

That same evening, the formal ceremonies for the opening of the Shemiran branch took place in the beautiful building in Bagh-e Ferdows, attended by 400 guests and graced by the presence of Mrs. Farideh Diba. We had a guest speaker who spoke about the founding of the club in 1919 and its presence everywhere except in communist and Arab countries, with a membership of professional women. The following evening, Mrs. Fatemeh P——, the head of the new branch, held a fund-raising dinner party at her home where our foreign visitors were our guests. Hospitality is one of the defining characteristics of Iranians.

The following day, a lunch was organized for 120 members of the club at the Melli Shoe Factory, at which we were served the traditional *Chelow kabab*,[24] followed by a tour of the factory. We each received a pair of slippers as a present. Our guests also had opportunities to visit historical sites, the bazaar, and the jewel collection at Bank Melli.

A couple of days later, we all flew to Mashhad and stayed at the Hyatt. The management of the hotel had prepared matchboxes inscribed with the Zonta emblem that were given to the guests. The opening ceremony was held at

24. Chelow kabab *(rice and kabab) is Iran's national dish, the equivalent of a burger and fries in the U.S. It is served everywhere, from palaces to roadside stalls, but the best* chelow kabab *is probably found in the bazaars.*

Mashhad University in the presence of the faculty and the university chancellor. This was followed by a gala dinner attended by all the members. After two days and a visit to the shrine of Imam Reza, we all returned to Tehran. Our international guests left with happy memories; a pity that less than twelve months later all, our hard work was dismantled by the Islamic Revolution.

Nowruz 1357 (1978), the Year Everything Changed

The Persian New Year brought with it a new calendar. We used to receive calendars and diaries from Bank Melli with our names inscribed on them and in which I would note my engagements and invitations. As I write these words now, I have only one of those diaries from 1357 (1978)—which at the time was marked as 2,537 imperial years. All the others were left behind in Tehran—just as all our possessions, material and emotional, were left behind. Today I have only my childhood memories to remind me of what happened so long ago, and in this account I have used up everything I can remember from that time and what I was told by parents about my childhood. From this point, I have to refer to calendars, diaries, and notes. Looking at these, I realize what a busy and active life I had led.

I returned home to a pile of New Year cards, invitations, and letters. My classes had restarted. I also had the 'friends of museums', IWC, Zonta, the Foreign Ministry

Club and of course running the household and dealing with Hajieh Khanum's endless complaints. I attended to my grandchildren when needed and followed up with Hamid at a distance. I was really busy and happy to be so. Hamid had graduated with excellent grades from MIT and obtained both his bachelor of science and master's degree; I was due to attend his graduation in Boston at the end of the academic year—three months away.

One day when I was with the wife of the Turkish ambassador, she told me that her husband was being recalled from Tehran even though they had only been at this post for two years. I arranged a farewell dinner for thirty of their friends as guests. It seemed that some of our non-Iranian friends were aware of events that we were not. This lovely couple were posted to London and stayed there for eight years. I had completely forgotten this occasion, which now comes back to me since I found my little black diary. Some days I would be invited to three dinners—a far cry from my life now. I have lived in two different worlds. Thank God, we were raised to be self-disciplined. Otherwise, the shock of the enormous changes would have been unbearable and I would not have been able to live independently in the second half of my life.

London–Boston

It was June (Khordad), the club elections were over and I was free, so I traveled to London with my sister Mehri. Our younger sister, Nayer, had arrived there with her husband and were already ensconced in Mariam and Fari's apartment. In those days, shopping in London was less expensive than in Paris. I had ordered some things for the Paris and Nice apartments, and everything was now ready. We enjoyed the time together and I left for Boston after five days.

Hamid met me at the airport and had booked a room for me at a good hotel in Cambridge. His graduation was the next day. The ceremony was quite simple; it seems the more prestigious the university, the simpler the ceremonies—it is the nonentities that seem to go for all the pomp and circumstance. Hamid's name was called out twice—first for his bachelor of science and then for his master's. I have a few pictures with Hamid gowned and hatted. We celebrated with two dinners, which included his friends.

Hamid took me out to dinner every night, and to one particular restaurant where MIT and Harvard students worked as waiters; you could tell from their demeanor and the attention they paid the guests that these were highly refined young men. My cousin Nader Ardalan and his second wife, who was pregnant, also invited us to lunch. His mother Mrs. Farangis Ardalan was in Boston at the time as Nader was receiving an award for excellence in architecture.

Hamid was returning to Iran after five years in Boston at MIT. And I had accepted the invitation of my friend and former colleague Lady Frances Ramsbotham to visit her and her husband, who was now governor of Bermuda. I asked them to book me into a hotel since I didn't want to stay at the governor's mansion. Hamid accompanied me to the airport, then packed and shipped his belongings and left for Tehran. He was accepted at Stanford to do an MBA and would be leaving for California after the summer vacation.

It was now 12 June, Queen Elizabeth II's official birthday. The governor of Bermuda, dressed in his official uniform and plumed hat, arrived in a special carriage and presided over the march-by of police and army. I went to Hamilton to watch the parade. That same afternoon there was a magnificent reception at the governor's mansion. I joined the receiving line, along with a thousand guests, to shake hands with the governor and his wife. When it was my turn, my hosts kindly invited me to stay to dinner. It was the first time I was in a gathering where I knew only the hosts; I didn't know then that this would be the story of my life from that point on.

Sir Peter Ramsbotham, who had a special love for Iran and Iranians, gave me a tour of the mansion and showed me the beautiful carpet given to him by the Shah. He told me that they had recently held a special "Iran Night" at the residence. The following day, accompanied by Lady Frances, we went for a tour of the city and had lunch together. The conversation centered around the agitations in Iran during which the governor calmly observed that this represented a serious religious and intellectual movement among the people of Iran.

He was concerned that the Shah had replaced the chief of security, who was faithful to him. I just listened and didn't really want to express an opinion. He spoke about an important issue in Bermuda that was on his mind, concerning the death sentence that had been handed down to someone who had been found guilty of treason. The man had been convicted in court and the death penalty had been issued by the previous governor. Sir Peter didn't really want to start his tenure with a hanging and kept trying to postpone the execution. I heard this news the following day at lunch from someone and still don't know the outcome. At our lunch Lady Frances introduced me to her travel agent, who was able to arrange a trip to Nassau in the Bahamas.

The Departure of Ambassadors from Tehran

I returned to Tehran on 11 July 1978 (20 Tir 1357) after being away for six weeks. Hamid had arrived just before me. On 14 July (23 Tir), there was the usual reception at the French embassy. There were also many parties held in honor of the departing Turkish ambassador. In honor of the ambassador's wife, my sister Mehri invited a group of ladies to the restaurant of the Houses of Parliament in Baharestan Square. Later, when Mehri was imprisoned by the Islamic revolutionary regime, she not only had to repay the salary she had received for four years as a member of parliament, she also had to repay the difference in the price of that subsidized lunch. This made me laugh, although in truth we should have been shedding tears.

Several ambassadors were leaving, including the Japanese ambassador, who was sent to Paris. Many farewell receptions were held in his honor, among them a beautiful dinner at the home of one of our friends. One of the guests commented that he had attended Dr. Safinia's office as a dental patient and that, while his work was excellent, his prices were high. The Japanese ambassador, at whose table I was sitting, rose to defend my son-in-law's prices and said if the work he did for me had been carried out in Japan, it would have cost three times as much and probably taken three times as long. We needed to properly value excellent workmanship. I had developed a deep friendship with this gentleman and his wife, who had both studied in France before the Second World War and spoke excellent French. We later found each other in Paris.

On Fridays, the family came for lunch and of course Hamid was there too. I threw a party for our departing diplomatic friends and invited forty guests. Hamid was at the Caspian at the time but returned for the party. After a long absence, Reza and his wife Mariam also joined us. The following day was the start of Ramadan, and I was fasting. The day after that, Hamid left for Nice and then flew on to Boston from where he was going to drive to San Francisco. I asked one of my friends to accompany him. Since I was fasting, I didn't go with Hamid to the airport. That was on 7 August (16 Mordad). Hamid packed his bags and didn't return to his homeland for fourteen years.

Ramadan on the Caspian

Once Hamid had departed, Mehri, Ghasem, and I left for Villa Hamid by the Caspian, intending to arrive there in time to break our fast in the evening. We stayed for two weeks, fasting, resting, and reading. The house was more comfortable after the improvements I had made—I didn't know this would be the last time I would stay there after all that hard work. Mariam had given me some books on the occasion of my birthday—mostly by Hermann Hesse—and these two quiet weeks gave me an opportunity to read and talk about them with my sister.

A strange incident took place while we were there. We had decided to visit our uncle Aligholi Ardalan without prior warning. On arrival at his house, we were told he was not at home and so we left. On the way back, we saw two young men who were vandalizing the public phones by the roadside and cutting the wires. When we asked them why they were doing this, they gave a vague answer that we didn't understand at the time. We had no idea about the political storm that was brewing. The changing of so many ambassadors all at the same time was just as unusual as the vandalizing of the public phones. And even though we wondered about this, we didn't put two and two together and were caught unawares by events that would turn our lives upside down.

Travels in Italy

I received an invitation to visit Padua, a city close to Venice in Italy, in honor of the seventeenth-century philosopher Elena Cornaro Piscopia, the first woman to receive a PhD in divinity from the University of Padua. Guests came from all four corners of the globe for the occasion and many of the important gatherings were held in the famous cathedral. Of course, these invitations were sent out to many, but you had to book your own place and pay for the trip yourself. I had visited Venice many years before, but I had never been to Padua, an ancient and beautiful city. When I told my friends about this trip, Aysheh volunteered to come with me. This was the second trip we had taken together. She had also just lost her husband and now lived alone.

We left for Rome on 3 September (12 Shahrivar) and from there flew to Venice, where we were taken by car to Padua and arrived very late; it had been a long and exhausting day. The following morning, the 300th anniversary of the awarding of the PhD to this notable lady, took place at the University of Padua, followed by a concert at the Basilica di Santa Giustina. Later we attended lectures by various speakers from universities in the U.S. and all over Europe. The mayor of Padua gave a reception for all the guests where we were served dinner by the nuns in the convent. A cold buffet had been prepared by these ladies and laid out in the cloisters of the church; they also provided the musical accompaniment.

On the way back, we visited Venice and the glass factory at Murano. We decided to forgo our airline tickets and instead took a train to Nice. Our friend Pari was in Nice and we visited Cannes and San Remo in Italy together. It was in the south of France that we first heard of Bloody Friday, as it was called—the start of the riots in Tehran. A French journalist was interviewing a Mr. Rouhani, whom we didn't know at the time but who spoke excellent French. Having been out of touch for a little while, the conversation caught our attention. After a few days, we returned to Paris.

Paris–Tehran

My uncle Dr. Aligholi Ardalan and his wife were to be my guests in Paris for a few days. The phone rang. Mrs. Ardalan informed me that they had been summoned to Tehran and therefore could not stay with me in Paris. I had heard the rumor that my uncle was to be appointed court minister by the Shah. They had just been to the U.S. to visit their two sons, one the Iranian consul general in San Francisco and the other working at the World Bank. Sadly, this was the last time our beloved uncle saw his two boys. The revolution scattered their family and the last eight years of his life were spent away from his children; he was even imprisoned for some months for the crime of having been court minister for a short while.

Our stay in Paris was very short. One night we invited two couples for dinner. My friend Aysheh wouldn't let me cook, saying I didn't know how and refusing to let me into the small kitchen at the apartment. So, I became the waitress on that occasion; little did I know that I would soon have to be a full-time cook. One evening we met a friend on the Champs-Elysées and, over dinner at Fouquet's, he spoke with optimism about events in Iran. He said elections were now free and true representatives of the people would now go to parliament and Iran would become heaven on earth. We had left Tehran on 3 September (12 Shahrivar); we returned on 3 October (11 Mehr).

Part Three

A Citizen of the World

(1978–1991 / 1357–1370)

Unrest in Tehran (Autumn 1978)

When Aysheh and I arrived back in Tehran, the city appeared calm. The following day, the IWC board met under the presidency of my sister Mehri, who had been recently elected. Apart from attending this meeting, I was glued to the TV; I watched the Shah speak in halting tones. In the month we had been away, he had changed; I discussed this with my sister, who said, "Everything is now upside down and we must await great changes." Despite all this, life carried on as usual. I was tired from my back-to-back trips and decided I would just concentrate on teaching. My term as president of Zonta was also coming to an end; it was time to hand over the reins to the next generation. I told myself I would stay home this year, and just read and write, but as the French saying goes, "*L'homme propose, Dieu dispose*," ("Man proposes, God disposes") or, as one might say otherwise, "If you want to make God laugh, tell him your plans."

Reception in honor of Mehri's presidency of the IWC, 1977. From Left: Houri, Mariam, Mrs. Farideh Diba (the Shahbanu's mother), and Mehri

Conversations with Students at the National University

It was the beginning of the academic year, but the university was in chaos. There was graffiti on the walls denouncing the Shah, which I found offensive. In class, the students could be divided into three groups on the right politically, men wearing black shirts and sporting beards; in the middle, moderate and fairly shy students; and, on the left, more militant individuals with communist leanings. I had experienced this kind of hostility in Nourbakhsh High School in the past. During the time of Mossadegh, there were many heated discussions among the senior-year pupils.

That day at the university, the lesson was on Darwin's theory of evolution. I wrote the word "evolution" on the board and asked the students to tell me what they understood by it. After some discussion, I added the letter "r" in front of the word and asked the students to define the difference between the two words. "In your opinion, which is the better way to develop?" I said. The leftist students immediately replied "revolution," while the rest remained silent.

"Unfortunately revolution always takes over from evolution; I wish it were the other way around," I replied. "I wish we would evolve mentally and emotionally before attempting revolution." To which the black shirts replied: "In a country where the rulers are dishonest the only way forward is revolution!" I countered this by suggesting that dishonesty came in many guises. For example, a student who cheated in an exam or a worker who shortchanged their place of employment were only two of the many forms of dishonesty. As the students started arguing among themselves, I added, "You could say that I am shirking my duties as a teacher right now as I have digressed from the subject of the class."

Someone then said, "These days we don't feel like studying and we would like to know where you stand." I replied, "If we started improving ourselves instead of criticizing others, we would turn our country into heaven on earth. Don't you think the youth in our society should first discriminate between right and wrong before taking to the streets? Even more importantly, come up with suggestions as how to improve things. Criticism is easy, but to be effective it should also include better options."

As I was leaving the class, one of the black shirts came up to me and said, "I am in agreement with what you said." As we walked down the hall, I saw a picture of Shariati[1] over a doorway. I pointed out to the student that one image had been removed and simply replaced with another. Did we always need to hero worship? That was the last time I met with my students. Classes were shut down; everyone took to the streets and teachers joined their students in shouting revolutionary slogans.

Three hundred thousand teachers who felt they had been left behind in the economic growth of the country believed that the revolution would bring about a change in their circumstances. When an individual is desperate, they can't clearly see the right way forward. And the students followed their teachers. In that year, 11 million out of a population of 35 million were students. Even if only 20 percent of them had taken to the streets, they would have present an unstoppable force.

The clergy took advantage of the discontent. Sadly, in the end the students and teachers saw no improvement

---

1. *An Iranian revolutionary and sociologist, Ali Shariati Mazinani (1933–1977) gained a PhD in sociology in 1964 from the University of Paris. Focusing on the sociology of religion, Shariati was not only a theorist but also an adherent of Islamic radicalism. He has been called the "ideologue of the Iranian Islamic Revolution," although his ideas did not end up forming the basis of the Islamic Republic.*

in their circumstances. Some even ended up losing their lives or being sent to the battlefield. Today, the situation for teachers is no better than it was before; indeed, they are forced to take on several jobs to be able to meet the rising cost of living. This group of teachers, professors, and academics has always been neglected and shortchanged in our society.

Kidney Problems

I arranged a ladies' luncheon in honor of the Japanese ambassador's wife, who was leaving for Japan. This couple were among my good friends and were Iranophiles; their grandchild had been born in Iran and they considered him Persian. A couple of days before the party, however, I became unwell and underwent a series of tests. I then visited a specialist, who prescribed a course of antibiotic injections that allowed me to recover in time for the party. Mariam and Ladan were also there and all went well. Numerous receptions were being held for this delightful couple, including a dinner at the French ambassador's residence to which I had also been invited. The Japanese ambassador, Mr. Ikawa, and his wife offered to collect me from home and we drove together to the party.

There was very light traffic that night and we arrived a little early—so we sat in the car talking. Somehow the subject of my brother Bagher came up, about whom the ambassador had only positive things to say. "I have heard that all ministries and public companies are under investigation," he said. "If they really wanted to know who takes bribes, they should ask the likes of us diplomats. After years of doing business with the Petrochemical Company the only gift your brother would accept was a box of grapes and a kilo of special Kobe beef from Japan!"

On that quiet street, we saw a cleric walking along and talking to a young man; I didn't know either of them. Anyway, it was time to go to the party and we entered the French ambassador's residence. Mr. Raoul DeLay and his wife Manon had organized an elaborate reception for our friend, the new Japanese ambassador to Paris. At the dinner table, the Moroccan ambassador sat next to me. It was a sparkling occasion, although, in retrospect, this was just the calm before the storm—something about which we still had no inkling. I was thinking how important our country had become to be regarded as a stepping stone for foreign ambassadors to the most prestigious posts in the likes of the U.S., UK, and France.

My kidney problem hadn't gone away, however. I was told that the X-rays and tests I had undergone showed a tumor on my left kidney that needed surgery. Up until then, I had never sought treatment abroad. But now it was imperative that I travel to have this problem attended to as we had regular power cuts in the city. I decided to book in to the Mayo Clinic in Rochester in the U.S.

Departing for the U.S.

I booked my air tickets to the U.S.—a return flight, as I was intending to come back in a month's time. The fateful day of my departure—24 November 1978 (3 Azar 1357)—arrived and I said farewell to my household before being taken by Mariam to the airport.

As soon as I arrived in Paris, I contacted the Mayo Clinic. I also got in touch with my French friend and Zonta colleague France de la Chaise, and we went to see the musical *Notre-Dame de Paris* together. I bought Hamid ski clothes and left for Rochester on Wednesday 29 November (8 Azar), where I stayed at the Kahler Hotel, which had the unique advantage of being connected to the hospital by an underground passage, constructed because of the extreme cold in that part of the world. The following day, I had lunch with Dr. Reza M—— and we discussed the events in Iran. Like most young people, he was a liberal and dissatisfied with the government in Iran. I shared my doubts that a revolution would necessarily improve matters. The following day I met the specialist and a complete check-up was arranged. I then took the opportunity to visit the St. Paul neighborhood and Silver Lake with its beautiful ducks.

Once the tests were done, the results were compared with the tests from Iran and consensus was reached that there was a tumor on my kidney. Consulting with the doctor, I mentioned that I had heard at least 30,000 unnecessary operations were performed in the U.S. each year and I had no intention of adding to that number. They agreed with the Iranian physicians that we should wait to see if the tumor, considered to be benign at this point, was growing or not. I stayed there for observation for almost two weeks.

I didn't like the idea of eating alone in the hotel restaurant as one night a man had approached and made me feel uncomfortable. Instead I relied on the stash of chocolates and cookies I kept in my room and just had my main meal at lunchtime. I was then put on a 1,000-calorie-a-day diet by the doctor and had to take my meals in the "diet kitchen"; I am sure that the cookies and chocolates were the culprits! I was discharged on 11 December and flew to Houston to visit my sister. I paid my bill to the Mayo Clinic, a non-profit organization. It did not seem unreasonable at the time—medical expenses have certainly sky-rocketed since then!

Houston

My sister Nayer and her husband Kirk met me at the airport. Christmas was close and Hamid, studying for his MBA at Stanford, was also invited to join us. Kirk and Nayer are amazing hosts, but I was still on my 1,000-calorie diet and couldn't enjoy my sister's cooking. Her friends arranged several gatherings for us. Hamid and I visited NASA, and one evening we went to see the ballet *The Nutcracker.*

One day Mariam called from Tehran; my daughter can always find something amusing about the most serious issues. She said, "Mummy, everyone who is anyone was mentioned in the newspaper as a 'usurper' except us! I am really disappointed that we don't rate that highly!" Ladan also called and was happy that surgery had not been necessary. I decided to celebrate this good fortune with a visit to Hawaii and so flew west after two weeks in Houston.

Hawaii

On arriving in Honolulu, I took a stroll through the city. That night I went to the movies and saw *Superman*, with Christopher Reeves in the starring role; no one could guess that this strong, young actor would become totally paralyzed a few years later after a riding accident. I visited Pearl Harbor and the coral reefs in a glass-bottomed boat. The following day I flew to Kauai and stayed at the Coco Palms Hotel. The weather was perfect, the sandy beaches stretched out, silvery gold, in the sun, and the palm trees reached for the skies; it was totally peaceful. Everyone was back from vacation and there were not many tourists about.

That same day, 12 January 1979, the heads of four nations, the U.S., UK, France, and Germany—namely Jimmy Carter, James Callaghan, Valéry Giscard d'Estaing, and Helmut Schmidt—met in Guadaloupe and decided the fate of my beloved country. As Cyrus Vance got off the plane, reporters asked him about Iran; it was a live broadcast and I heard the secretary of state say, "The Shah will leave Iran very soon."

The following day when I opened the newspapers, I saw that the normally humorous Art Buchwald had commented, "Couldn't you have let the Shah make the announcement himself—you even deprived him of this right? Mr. Carter, you used the defense of human rights to throw him into the frying pan. Wouldn't it have been a defense of human rights not to throw him from the frying pan into the fire?"

I was beside myself and don't remember much else from the trip. I returned to Paris on 14 January and was due to fly back to Tehran two days later. Early the next morning, the phone rang; Mariam was calling from London to inform me that she, Ladan, and their children were all in London, since Tehran was in turmoil. Not that things were greatly better in the UK; it was the Winter of Discontent and there were . . . There were regular power cuts and all the grandchildren were really sick as the weather was bitterly cold. She insisted that I should not go back and instead join them in London or stay in Paris. I decided to stay in Paris. On 16 January 1979 (26 Dey), a tearful Shah and Shahbanu left Iran.

In the months that followed, the international media had a field day with this event. In Neauphle-le-Château, where Ayatollah Khomeini was living during his brief period of exile before returning to Iran following the collapse of the Shah's regime, the French government installed thirty-five telephone lines to cope with all the incoming and outgoing calls. We watched the mourning ceremonies for Arba'ein[2] on French television. Bearded men sat in a circle on the floor and a mullah walked among them chanting religious verses while the men beat themselves about the head and chest. I had seen these kinds of scenes as a child in my grandfather's house but it must have been quite a shock to the French public seeing it on TV. I prayed to God to protect our country!

Depression in Paris

I had lost so much weight in two months that I couldn't wear any of my clothes anymore. The 1,000-calorie diet coupled with persistent insomnia had taken their toll. I kept in touch with my daughters and four grandchildren in London. Mariam was looking after everyone in her small apartment, including her sister-in-law Shirin, her two sons, and their Filipino nanny! The men were still in Tehran and busy with work. It was bitterly cold, and I didn't have a coat with me; I caught a bad cold and took to my bed.

I had traveled light and hadn't planned on staying in Paris for the winter. I was therefore unwilling to stock up on anything other than basic foods. One day I had a visit from my friend Mrs. Fatemeh P——. We noticed that the police had surrounded our building, being immediately next to the Iranian embassy. Pretty soon, the number of

---

2 Abra'ein is a Shiite religious observance that occurs forty days after the Day of Ashura (see footnote 9 on page 17). It commemorates the martyrdom of Hosein ibn Ali.

CRS[3] increased, and demonstrators gathered in the street. Next, the street was closed to cars and all day we heard the demonstrators shouting slogans in Persian and occasionally in French. We decided to leave the apartment.

We went to the Louvre together to see the section devoted to Persian antiquity. I am not sure what drew us to this place but it felt like visiting the grave of a loved one. We wondered what the future held for our country. That was all I could think about in those days; I wasn't worried about myself or my house back home, or even everything that I had worked for all my life. I knew that it would be impossible to go back to how things were; impossible for the new regime to maintain the standing and dignity of Iran.

My weight had dropped from 63 to 50 kilos in just three months. Since I had gone back to eating normally, this drop in weight was entirely down to my state of mind and the depression that was descending on me. To pass the time, I would visit fashion houses in the afternoons. Accepting the invitation to attend a fashion show didn't cost anything and it was a distraction for a couple of hours. My mental state was such that, when I left those places, I had no memory of what I had seen.

One day, we were invited to a show at Givenchy and had excellent seats; sitting opposite us I saw a lady in a black

---

3. The Compagnies Républicaines de Sécurité (Republican Security Corps), abbreviated CRS, are the general reserve of the French National Police. They are primarily involved in general security missions but the task for which they are best known is crowd and riot control.

coat accompanied by another whom I guessed was Princess Fatemeh, the Shah's sister. Her companion came toward us and said, "You must be Mrs. Mostofi. Her Highness would like to ask about your brother and his wife." I walked over to where she was sitting, thanked her for her concern, and told her that my brother Bagher had undergone surgery in London and was convalescing.

I added that I was really sorry about what had happened; this was the way of the world. I then returned to my seat. None of us knew about the life-threatening illness of the Shah at that time or guessed that he would die shortly. The princess left soon afterwards. In those days, it seemed that everyone had become a revolutionary, no matter what nationality they were, and a big critic of the past regime.

The Islamic Republic is Proclaimed

One of my French friends and her husband invited me to join them for a weekend in Honfleur in Normandy. They tried to do what they could to cheer me up. It was cold and raining; we arrived late in the evening by car. They had booked me a room at the Hotel de la Tour while they stayed in their studio apartment. It was 10 February (21 Bahman). My room was so cold that I couldn't sleep that night. When I came down the next morning, I noticed the look of sadness and pity on the face of the receptionist.

She asked me if I had heard the latest news; I replied I had not since I didn't have a radio and, in any case, wasn't feeling well. I was about to pay my bill when I was told that my friends had already paid it. They arrived and took me to their apartment for breakfast, buying some croissants on the way. After breakfast was over, they informed me that Iran was now officially under the rule of the Islamic Republic with Ayatollah Khomeini as the Supreme Leader.

It rained all morning but in the afternoon the sun came out and we returned to Paris via Deauville. Back home, I became really unwell and took to my bed with a high fever. In the morning, I opened the *Figaro* to images of the people executed in Tehran. I didn't know any of the victims personally, but I was seriously disturbed at the injustice and cruelty of executing anyone without a trial. My depression now returned with a vengeance; I cried every day and couldn't sleep at night.

Nowruz 1358 (1979)

I traveled to London on 2 March by train and ferry across the English Channel. Seeing my family lifted my spirits but I was still suffering. My brother Bagher was resting at home after his operation; he had also lost much weight. Ladan had moved into her apartment and tried hard to be a good host. But taking care of her children, then aged six and three, furnishing the apartment, and doing the housework didn't leave her much time. I tried to help her where I could. Mariam was also busy; her daughters were thirteen and seven at the time. We had all lived in big houses with the help of staff. Now my daughters were getting used to living in small apartments, without domestic help and with their husbands away.

One morning we heard that General M——, Shirin's father, had been executed. Shirin was Mariam's closest friend and her daughter Jamila was Leila's best friend. Jiji, as they called her, had been very close to the general since her American father had left Iran and she had been formally adopted by her grandfather. We were now truly in mourning. The general had been a career soldier, devout and with an impeccable reputation. A few weeks later, Fari Safinia arrived in London with a 10-kilo suitcase containing one suit and a few shirts—he was among the first men to leave Iran with permission. We were all really happy to see him.

One of our friends who had just arrived from Tehran related the latest joke: "The Supreme Leader is not sure whether to put the turban on his head first, then the crown, or the other way round."

It was the Persian New Year and I invited the whole family to La Carafe restaurant in London. Ali Lari had also arrived, and his family were really happy to see him. The following day we stayed home, and everyone came to visit me as the matriarch. The day after this, news came from Tehran that the revolutionaries had come for my sister, Mehri Safinia, blindfolding her and taking her from Fari's house, where she was staying. No one knew at first where she had been taken.

The day before that, my uncles Haj Ezz al-Mamalek Ardalan and Dr. Aligholi Ardalan had been imprisoned. What kind of revolution was this? Were they trying to get rid of honest, devout, public servants against whom there were no accusations? Ezz al-Mamalek had served the country all his life; he had been Amir al-hajj (commander of the pilgrimage) several times.

I suddenly remembered one of those early-morning dreams I had after my *namaz*. I dreamt I was in a large room with two beds; Amir Abbas Hoveyda was in one and I was in the other. Around us, people were whispering and telling me, "You will recover but there is no hope for the other patient." I woke up. A few hours later, Dariush, Mehri's youngest son, called to let us know of her imprisonment. Giving more details about what had happened, they described how a group of revolutionaries had forcibly entered Mariam and Fari's newly built and beautiful house in Tehran early one morning; they had caused a lot of damage, breaking open doors that had locked, before taking Mehri to an undisclosed location.

I believe in my dream I represented my sister. Hoveyda was summarily shot in the back of the head and my sister eventually released three months later. My uncles were in prison four months and barely got out with their lives. They were never able to leave Iran after that or see their families. My sister was not allowed to leave for six years;

only after repaying her four years' salary as a member of parliament was she able to leave earlier. She spent the rest of her days traveling between London and Tehran with a couple of visits to the U.S.

Worrying Times

Dark days were to follow; the news was all negative, yet we had no choice but to go on. The children were at school and coping with the cold weather and rain. They had visited England on short trips in the past, but things were different now. Mariam, always the practical one, decided to get a job immediately. She reminded us of the Paris taxi drivers, mostly white Russians who had escaped communism. At times, she spoke of opening a restaurant. On Sizdah Bedar,[4] she made a pile of sandwiches and gathered everyone together in Hyde Park.

After a while, we had news of my sister, who was in prison. Dariush had managed to visit her and we were grateful that she was alive. In the secret, handwritten record

---

4. *Ancient Iranians believed that each of the twelve constellations in the zodiac governed one of the months of the year and that each would rule the earth for a thousand years. The Nowruz celebrations, therefore, lasted twelve days, plus a thirteenth day (representing the time of chaos due to follow the twelve millennia) celebrated by going outdoors, putting order aside, and having parties. On this thirteenth day, called Sizdah Bedar ("Getting Rid of Thirteen"), entire families leave their homes to carry trays of sprouted seeds in a procession to picnic in a cool, grassy place by water. Far from home, they throw the sprouts into the water, which is thought to drive out the demons and evil spirits from the house and the household. Unmarried girls make a wish to get married by next year by tying blades of grass together. There is much singing, dancing, eating, and drinking. With this, the Nowruz celebrations are completed.*

she kept of her months in prison, she mentions how she was initially incarcerated in Alavieh High School, where she could hear the firing squads and the cries of people being hanged. The young revolutionaries who were her jailers kept threatening that her turn would come the next day.

On 6 April 1979, Nayer, my younger sister, came to London from Houston. We decided that one of us would stay at my brother's apartment.

Mysterious Phone Calls

The morning I moved to my brother's apartment I kept receiving strange phone calls. Bagher and his wife Assefeh were away. One of his former employees called to say he had brought a suitcase full of clothes for them from Tehran. He introduced himself and asked for the address of the apartment and turned up soon after that to deliver the case. I later discovered that Bagher and Assefeh had never made such a request.

A little later, there was a call from a young girl who introduced herself and asked to speak to my sister-in-law. I was surprised by this call as I knew Assefeh lived a quiet life and didn't know that many people. I told the young woman that she had better call in the afternoon when they would be back from their short trip. In fact, she did call later and arranged to see Assefeh the following day at 5 p.m.

On Sunday 8 April, we were all invited to lunch at Ladan's. I returned to my brother's flat in the early afternoon and Nayer went to visit Mariam. Bagher, Assefeh, and I walked the short distance to their apartment. The young woman arrived on time; she had long hair and was dressed simply and casually. She brought a letter from a Mr. Sharif R—— for my brother. Having read the short note, Bagher replied, "Fortunately my sister is here and can help you better than I can." He asked her how much money she had to pay for her education abroad. The girl replied that she had $30,000. My brother said that if such a sum were given to an English girl, she would find a way to work and study at the same time and save some too.

Apparently, the note requested that my brother help the young girl, who wanted to study at an English university. I asked her about her education and she replied that she had finished high school and had attended an accounting course for a year. I asked her why she had left Iran and she replied that life was very difficult there these days. I smiled and asked whether this would have happened if students like her had not demonstrated and shouted slogans to bring about the change in government. She then took a packet of cigarettes out of her bag and I noticed her hand shook as she tried to light one. I thought what a rude young woman she was light up in front of her elders, without asking their permission.

I suggested that she should find a position as an au pair in a family and attend night classes. She said goodbye and left. It was getting dark and we went to the kitchen to have supper. Nayer had sent a message not to wait for her. Just then, the doorbell rang. My brother, with a plate of salad in his hand, went to open the front door. The young woman had come to fetch the lighter she had left behind, and, having retrieved it, was accompanied to the door by my brother.

Assefeh and I were still in the kitchen when we heard the sound of loud voices and Bagher shouting for help. I ran to the entrance and saw the plate on the floor and two armed men wearing face masks struggling with my brother. There was no sign of the young woman. Throwing myself in front of Bagher, I told the young men they would have to kill me first, as my brother had young children.

One of them said, "Khanum, we are not assassins. We have come to talk." I replied, "Why are you wearing masks and carrying guns and entering people's homes by force?" My brother, who was back on his feet by now, said, "In that case, please take a seat and say what you have come to say." One of them sat down while the other continued to stand at the door of the living room. At this moment, a distraught Assefeh entered the room. The TV was still on; Bagher wanted to turn it off but they stopped him. The first man placed a small tape recorder on the table and started interrogating him: "Who is supporting you? Why did you leave Iran?"

My brother answered patiently and politely: "I studied in England and I have many friends here. I left Iran with the proper authorization to sign a contract. I then had to undergo surgery. No one supports me." The man then asked about how he had acquired his apartment, looking around, as he spoke, at the thick fitted carpets and the few photographs here and there of the 2,500-year celebrations and coronation. My brother replied, "I had inherited a house in Saltanatabad years ago, which I sold and bought this apartment with the proceeds for my retirement years."

While this was going on, the second man was inspecting the other rooms and found a bank statement. He wanted to know whose it was. I replied, "It is mine. As you can see, there is a balance of 9,000 francs in it and I am supposed to be the wealthiest in this family! The zeros are centimes—make no mistake! You came to the wrong house. There is no money here; you won't find so much as a Persian carpet or an antique vase. You have more important things to do with your time. And why did you imprison our sister? She is a hard-working public servant and devout too."

At this point, the phone rang. The second man slammed the receiver down. I reminded him that my daughter and son-in-law could arrive at any moment, saying, "You are here with guns and you will certainly be arrested." I kept my eye on them the whole time. I remembered every detail of their clothing and noticed that they spoke Persian without an accent.

The two men consulted each other. Just then the doorbell rang. I warned them that they were in big trouble now. They asked my brother to return the note the young woman had brought. Bagher put his hand in his pocket but couldn't find the note. All this time, Assefeh had her hands in the air and kept repeating, "*Bismellah al Rahman-e Rahim* [in the name of God, the merciful, the compassionate]." This had been going on for an hour and the atmosphere had become very tense. I suggested looking for the note in the master bedroom and, sure enough, there it was—on the dressing table.

This time I heard the bell to the back door, which led to the mews. I could hear Fari and Nayer outside asking why we didn't open it. I warned the young men, "My son-in-law is an angry man and if he finds you here, he will never let you go and there will be bloodshed!" I was wearing a gold Allah necklace. Pointing to it, I said, "I swear to God that I will give you time to get away. I will not pick up the phone for fifteen minutes and I will give you twenty-four hours to leave town. After that I will report the incident to the police."

One of them addressed my brother and said, "Please lead the way." Assefeh was as white as a sheet. I don't know where I got the strength to say, "Do you not understand what I am telling you? These people are outside the door and you are trapped. But I will keep my promise. Now I know you had sent that young girl to open the door for you and everything she did was just play-acting." One of them said that they didn't know her. I glared at him and said, "In that case, how do you know about the note?" They went silent, then started whispering together in some confusion. Eventually they decided to leave. Turning to my sister-in-law, they said, "Mrs. Mostofi, we apologize if we upset you," before leaving by the front door.

Only then did it occur to me that if Fari were to see the three of us so agitated and pale, there would be trouble. I told my brother that our story would be that we were having an argument between us about who was to blame for Mehri's imprisonment. Once again, I heard the doorbell. I picked up the salad dish from the floor and opened the front door. My sister Nayer and Fari entered, angrily demanding why we hadn't answered the phone or opened the door. I confessed that we had had a fight.

Bagher wasn't feeling well, so I took him to his room and put him to bed. Assefeh kept whispering her thanks to me: "Houri, if you hadn't been here, I don't know what we would have done." Fari bought our story and returned home and I didn't breathe a word to Nayer about what had really happened. That night I didn't sleep a wink, though, and the following day my brother stayed in bed.

After twenty-four hours, I went back to Ladan's house. My brother arranged to meet Sir Anthony Parsons, the last British ambassador in Iran before the revolution and now deputy foreign minister. Bagher related the whole story. Sir Anthony said, "Why did you wait so long to tell me this." My brother replied, "Houri was in charge and I was unwell." For the next six months, two secret-service men kept watch outside his apartment. After that, there was so much violence and so many assassinations that the attack on my brother's apartment seemed like a friendly visit by comparison.

Paris and Nice

I no longer felt safe on my own in the London apartment and worried whenever Ladan and the children left the flat. Ladan and Mariam decided that it would be best if I returned to France. Part of me didn't want to leave this young woman with her two small children. Depression was always waiting for me around the corner. At the same time, I felt I was imposing myself on them and their routine. So, I packed my suitcases and returned to Paris with Mariam. I had become forgetful; I needed help to cross the street. After a few days, we left for Nice, where Mariam wanted to furnish their new apartment in the simplest and most inexpensive way.

One day we went to buy a fridge and she told me, "I have so many fridges in Tehran, at the Caspian, and in London. Now I have to waste time and money to buy yet another one." We managed to furnish the apartment in ten days, then she needed to get back to her family. At the same time, she was worried about me. I reassured her that I would be OK, and that God was watching over us. My friend Behi drove her to the airport, and I was left by myself in an unfamiliar apartment, fearful and anxious. The first night I closed all the windows and blinds, yet sleep eluded me until daybreak.

Mine was an imitation of life. I would get together with neighbors and old friends who had also taken refuge in Nice. Those who had held important posts spoke critically of the Shah's regime, but I had nothing to say. I had lost the words to express myself and had no means of stopping the flow of tears. I was on autopilot and sleepwalked my way through the days. Ladan was still in London and had decided to return to Iran with the children. On her way home, she stayed with me in Nice for two weeks.

Adjusting to the New Reality

When my sister Mehri was released from prison that summer, she returned to a house turned upside down by the militia, but she said nothing, just grateful to be alive. Mariam and her family came to Nice for a month and it was a joy to see them. Her husband Fari, having left Tehran with a small suitcase, decided to stay in London and accept a job as a dental surgeon at Guy's Hospital. Many professionals restarted their careers from scratch and eventually became quite successful. Others, who had held government posts, kept waiting for a miracle. Many were too old to start again.

The women stepped up; there is no retirement for a woman. They shopped, cooked, cleaned, drove, and kept their families going. Many later returned to Iran and salvaged what they could of their lives. The men continued to have heated political discussions and watched TV for hours. Before the revolution, the ladies would get together and share tips about makeup and fashion; these days it was recipes that they shared or advice on how to get their residence permits.

That summer was a time of uncertainty. Those who had U.S. visas could still use them and many decided to make America their home. Very soon, however, as relations between Iran and the U.S. deteriorated, those privileges came to an end. I existed in a parallel universe. While on the surface it appeared as if I was adjusting to life, inside I was in a state of turmoil.

Hamid was at Stanford, Mariam in London, and Ladan had returned to Tehran. Hajieh Khanum would call from Tehran and say, "Khanum, everything you warned us about has come true. What a pity that we didn't listen." Maybe she expected the Islamic Republic to send her a big check each month. She still lived in my house and received her salary, so she was taken care of. Nevertheless, she was protesting because she had expected a big change in her circumstances after the revolution. I warned her not to say too much over the phone.

Insomnia was my biggest problem. When I watched people walking by the beach or swimming, it amazed me that life could go on so eventfully. I had developed a split personality. Some days I felt well; I would buy a ticket to the opera house in Monte Carlo and make my way there and back by bus. On other days, I felt incapable even to move or feed myself. Even on better days, I would walk by beautiful shop fronts without the slightest interest; the only money I spent was on food.

Hamid and Tina

I decided to use my still-valid, one-year airline ticket to visit Hamid in California. My cousin Ahmad Ardalan, whose term as ambassador in Moscow had ended after five years, came to the U.S. to visit his brother Majid. One night, we invited both cousins and their wives to dinner. On the way to a restaurant, Hamid stopped by an apartment building in San Francisco and soon returned with a tall young woman whom he introduced as Tina. I had no idea that one day this young woman would become my daughter-in-law.

After a short stay in San Francisco, I went to Lake Tahoe, accompanied by Ahmad, and stayed the weekend with Carol, the wife of Majid Ardalan. My next stop was Houston to see Nayer. While there, it became necessary to pay a visit to the hospital because I had discovered a lump in my breast. Fortunately, it was benign, and I was able to travel to London after a few days.

I knew that Mariam had gone to Tehran to join Ladan and, as Fari worked full time at the hospital, I felt my presence would be helpful during her absence. She was away for a month; once she was back, I returned to Paris, resolved not to continue the aimless existence I had been leading. I went to the Sorbonne without any documents showing my educational qualifications; I had an interview and was accepted by Professor René Pomeau to attend his lectures on French literature.

Studying at the Sorbonne

My days were spent at the Sorbonne; in the evenings, I attended twice-weekly sessions at the Louvre. In this way, I managed to fill the five weekdays. After some research and consultation with Professor Pomeau, I received a letter from the Sorbonne agreeing to my chosen subject for a PhD thesis. I was both surprised and happy that the university had accepted me without any proof of my previous education. Ladan eventually succeeded in sending my degree certificates with a passenger on an airplane as the postal system could not be relied upon.

My chosen subject was André Maurois; Professor Pomeau told me that little had been written about this great French author, by comparison with writers like Marcel Proust or Albert Camus, who were very popular at the time. He wrote an introductory letter to the Bibliothèque Nationale, located in the Rue de Richelieu near the Comédie Francaise, so I could make use of their resources. He also advised me to visit Nanterre University and make sure that the subject I was planning to focus on had not already been covered in another thesis.

Nanterre University had a very different feel from the Sorbonne, which was a venerable institution with historic buildings—a world apart from the modern, boxlike structure at Nanterre! I felt claustrophobic in the elevator, with fliers and notices plastered on every surface, but once I reached the room where the records were kept of all the theses that had been written, the scene changed. There, two young men, dressed properly in suits, greeted me with great respect; with their help, I was able to look through all the titles relating to André Maurois. I asked the young men about the chaotic feel of Nanterre and they responded, "Things have improved considerably; you should have seen this place not so long ago!"

The Bibliothèque Nationale

Thanks to the introductory letter from Professor Pomeau, I was immediately issued with a library card for the Bibliothèque Nationale, which allowed me fifty visits. However, there was always a line of people waiting to be allowed into the study hall. It was a world apart from any other library I had ever visited. Being there felt like visiting a museum and, in fact, a few years later all the relevant books were transferred to the François-Mitterrand Library, while the Bibliothèque Nationale is now the national repository of every work that is published in France and also holds extensive historical collections.

Studying as a Cure for Depression

At the Sorbonne I used to attend a class on comparative religion and was surprised to find that there was no mention of Islam at all. It turned out that politics had entered the university too. I, however, would proudly announce that I was an Iranian and a Muslim!

The fee I paid for the course at the Sorbonne was only 800 francs in 1980 and this permitted me to attend as many classes as I wished. I am not exaggerating when I say that my depression was cured in this way.

Facing Up to Changed Circumstances

Ladan, who had returned to Tehran full of optimism, encountered serious difficulties that I cannot even begin to relate. Hamid, who had finished his studies, was about to lose his student visa. We all had Iranian passports; even people who had green cards found themselves restricted during Carter's presidency. I had a four-year visa that had expired. When I received the invitation to Hamid's graduation from Stanford, I applied to the American embassy in Paris for a visitor visa and was promptly refused. I even needed permission to leave France to travel in Europe this entailed a long wait and I had to pay 50 francs for each neighboring country I hoped to visit. Life was difficult on all fronts and we certainly had much to learn about our changed circumstances.

I visited London for Nowruz 1359 (1980) and spent time with Mariam and her family. On my return to Paris, I was made to wait for ages at immigration; this applied to several other Iranians on our flight. The immigration officer would come by every now and then but still kept us waiting. Finally, I went up to him and asked, "Do I look like a terrorist?" He replied, "No, you don't." I continued,

"Have these other Iranians committed a crime?" Again, he said no.

I went on: "Up until last year, we were welcomed in all European countries without so much as a visa. Now we have visas; is it fair to treat us this way?" He asked to see my passport and then stamped it. My fellow travelers took advantage of the opportunity and were also allowed to leave. I felt as if he had orders from above to cause as much inconvenience as possible. The French government clearly hoped to indicate to the Islamic Republic of Iran that it was not about to make life easy for those who had sought refuge in France.

Hamid Finds a Job

Nayer flew from Houston to visit for a few days; one of my cousins had arrived from Tehran and we spent some time together. I was really upset at missing Hamid's graduation. He had never planned to stay in the U.S. and couldn't wait to return to Iran. The plan was for me to return with him. However, the events of 1980 (1359) forced him to try to find temporary work in the U.S. Now that his student visa was no longer valid, he asked me to send him documents that would enable him to stay in the U.S. and work there. I sent him whatever I had.

He was not the sort of person to stay illegally, nor did he want to postpone his plans and continue being a student. Everything we had was in Iran. He had graduated from

MIT with high honors and had received many excellent job offers, but with the change in our circumstances, the tables had turned. He called me one day and asked me to stay home and expect a parcel. I wondered what he was sending me. He joked and said, "Don't worry, it is not a bomb."

I told him we had a doorman and anything he sent would stay with the doorman if I happened to be out. It was Mother's Day in the U.S. and I received twenty-four dark red Baccara roses from him. They were magnificent and I managed to keep them fresh for two weeks by leaving them in the bathtub at night! This was the best present I have ever received.

One night I dreamt of Mohsen. We were at the airport, separated by metal barriers; it seemed as if we were boarding different flights. He seemed happy and we waved to each other. The following day, Hamid called to tell me that he had received a temporary residency. I came to the conclusion that the dead are always around and Mohsen's happiness had to do with Hamid's success. Hamid applied to tens of companies who had previously courted him. As soon as they saw his Iranian passport, in spite of his degrees from MIT and an MBA from Stanford, they would politely tell him, "Don't call us; we will call you!" And, of course, the calls never came.

He told me how he left his apartment in Menlo Park early each morning for San Francisco, returning home exhausted in the evening and empty-handed. He sent out eighty applications until, after six months, he finally landed a job at a small company run by one of his professors. I was able to visit Hamid a year and a half later. He was living in a small and attractive condo in Sausalito, tastefully furnished. At that time (May 1981), he was still working for McMahon and Associates.

He still had his Porsche—a reminder of the good old days—but took a bus to work as parking in the city was prohibitively expensive. One day I asked him why he worked so hard; others went to work at 9 a.m. and returned at 5 p.m. He laughed and replied, "Those people are content with living from paycheck to paycheck. I work sixteen hours a day and, because of the commitment I have shown, I have been given many projects abroad."

He was right. I thought of Iran and the disappointment of a generation of educated and talented young people who would no longer return there; this had been the greatest capital of our country and now it was lost.

Hamid's Passport

I tried to renew Hamid's passport in Paris in 1979. A few of the old-timers still worked at the consulate; a couple of high-ranking employees had been my students, and whenever I needed to renew a passport, would bring it over themselves with a bouquet of flowers. I was touched by their kindness, but their appointments soon ended and they were replaced by others. Hamid sent me his passport for renewal because the consulate in San Francisco was shut down. He didn't want to mail it to Washington DC to be forgotten among the piles of passports waiting at the embassy there. Years later, I had occasion to visit the Iranian embassy in DC and witnessed two strong young men dragging sacks of passports from one room to another. Iranian affairs were being handled by the Algerian embassy in Washington and it seemed to take for ever.

The Iranian embassy in Paris, which was situated next to the building where I lived, had undergone big changes. Officers now sat behind glass screens and the wait was long. When it was finally my turn, I handed over my file. The officer wanted to know why Hamid had not attended in person. I had no choice but to say he was in the U.S. and that, as there was no consulate nor an embassy there and because his passport had originally been issued in Paris, I had hoped it could be renewed here. The man was not about to return the passport to me, however, and insisted he would send it to Washington. No amount of pleading changed his mind and my son never received his passport after that. Whenever he contacted Washington to see why they would not renew his passport, he was told, "Whenever you decide to return to Iran, we will issue you a travel document." It was this kind of response that discouraged the young from ever returning.

Bad News

On the morning of 27 July 1980, we heard the news on the radio of the tragic death of the Shah in exile in Egypt. It was the end of an era; at least he died in a friendly Muslim country, surrounded by his family. The news was bad all round. Soon after this, Iraq attacked Iran. A few days later, I had occasion to visit the Iranian embassy and arrived a little late for my appointment. The officer asked me the reason for my tardiness. I told him I was watching the news on TV; Iraqis who had so far not even dreamt of attacking our country had just set fire to Abadan and the oil refineries.

Our weakness had emboldened the enemy. The young man stared at me with indifference. The war lasted for many years; millions of young men perished. In the same year, my friend and colleague Farrokhrou Parsa, the first woman to have been appointed a cabinet minister in Iran, was executed under horrific circumstances. She had four children and was completely innocent of all charges.

Short Trips

Two years had passed since I left Tehran and, during that time, I made several short trips to the south of France and to London. I also visited Berlin for a few days. It had been completely rebuilt after the devastations of the Second World War. The Kaiser Wilhelm Memorial church had been destroyed and a brand-new church built next to it. One day we were able to visit East Berlin and see the Berlin Wall.

How many had lost their lives trying to cross this wall! By contrast, East Germany seemed less damaged, and many historic buildings were left standing, though the city was soulless and deserted.

My House in Elahieh

News came from Tehran that my house had been rented out. The tenants were apparently disadvantaged people from the south of the city who were able to rent unoccupied homes at a very low cost. They sold off all the furniture in the house on the pretext that they had their own furniture. For the past two years, my two faithful members of staff, Fatemeh and Ghasem, had taken care of the house, before it was rented out but Hajieh Khanum wanted to retire and before she left I asked her to take whatever she wanted.

After the first tenants left, the house was rented to someone from Yazd who had sold his own home and was waiting for a residency permit from Canada. When his papers came through, he handed over the keys of my house to the local branch of the *Komiteh*![5] It turned out that there was some problem with his documentation, however, and he was turned back at the Canadian border.

---

5. Formed as one of the organizations of the Iranian Revolution in 1979, the Komiteh *(Committee) had branches in every district throughout the country. Responsible for enforcing so-called Islamic regulations and moral standards, and much else besides, it was eventually merged with the Gendarmerie.*

The *Komiteh* then handed the house over to a high-ranking official who was our houseguest for many years. I never met any of these people and don't want to judge them. Compared to the massive damage done to the country overall, these were minor issues. I just wished they had turned the house over to a charitable organization or made it into a library or art gallery. It is so much easier to destroy than to build, and the house itself would then have survived at least, but I'm getting ahead of myself.

The high-ranking official was thrown out of the government after some time and forced to vacate the house, which was then left to the mercy of the elements. In 1997 (1376), when I was finally able to visit the place, it was in ruins, with nothing left of the life we had lived there. Rain and snow had caused the roof to collapse and there were puddles in all the rooms. When I complained to the authorities, they shrugged their shoulders and said, "We have seen worse." Two days later, they stuck a notice on the door stating that no one was allowed in. In that house, we had done our *namaz* and fasted during Ramadan. We had held fundraisers for local charities. When people heard that our house had been confiscated, they asked, "Why you?" But compared to the fate of all those people who lost their lives, the loss of our home was unimportant.

The Trials and Tribulations of Ladan and Her Family

Back in Tehran, Ladan and her young daughters were trapped. They had returned home full of hope but Ladan then lost her job at the university and the children could no longer attend their schools. So she decided to come to Paris with her children and live with me. I managed to enroll the two girls in a school near my apartment. Unfortunately, Tehran airport was closed at that time and, after waiting for two weeks, Ladan decided to cross into Turkey by bus and then take a flight to Paris.

On the day they were due to travel, I decided to fast; I prayed that this young woman with her two small children would make it safely to Istanbul. I had asked a Turkish friend, Elchin, to meet them at the bus depot and let them stay with her that night so they could catch the Paris flight the next day. That day I received a couple of phone calls early in the morning. First, Ladan's sister-in-law called from Geneva for news. I told her I was also waiting. She asked me to let her know as soon as I had news. Next, a friend called from Nice and asked, "What has Ladan done to be stopped at the border?"

My heart sank. I asked her, "Has Ladan been detained?" My friend then realized that I didn't know. I collapsed. I called Istanbul; a young man answered the phone and in broken English told me that Elchin and her husband were on a flight to Paris. I asked about the passengers on the bus from Tehran. He told me that Elchin's driver had gone to the bus depot and was told that the young, blue-eyed woman and her two children had been left behind at the border.

Any mother will understand what I was feeling at that moment, with no news of my daughter or grandchildren. I called their house in Tehran, but the maid who answered knew nothing. The following day, I fasted again. Finally, after four days of silence, Mariam called from London to let me know that Ladan, the children, and my son-in-law were back home in Tehran and I could call them. Ladan's voice was unrecognizable on the phone; I just kept telling her I loved her and didn't ask any questions. I thanked God for the safety of this young family. Elchin had arrived in Paris and came to see me. Friends called me from everywhere, wondering why Ladan had been stopped. This is what actually happened.

Ladan had boarded a bus for Turkey with her two daughters, her husband Ali accompanying them as far as the border. They had a long wait at the border before they were finally asked to go through customs. At this point, an officer asked Ali why he was traveling without a passport. He replied that he was not leaving the country and had just accompanied his family to make sure they were safe. The officer said, "But you have just stepped over the border; I am sure you were planning to leave."

Ali replied, "I have a toothbrush and a small bag with me. I am planning to take the bus back in the morning." Overhearing the conversation, Ladan came immediately to Ali's aid and said, "This is my husband and he works in Tehran. I don't see a sign that marks the border here." The officer looked at Ladan and said, "Shut up, woman." When Ladan protested, the officer replied, "You think you have crossed into Turkey? Come back at once." My poor daughter came back with her children and all their suitcases. The four of them were then taken to the police station, where they spent the night.

The next day they were sent back to Tehran and straight to Evin Prison. Since the prison was full, they were kept in a room in the prison hospital where they spent a second night. Dr. Sheikholeslamzadeh, who was also incarcerated but was helping the sick prisoners, saw them and courageously approached the authorities, begging them to let the innocent family leave. His pleas were effective and they were released at midnight. God knows how they made their way home, only to find the house turned upside down. Ladan's car, Ali's hunting rifles, and many valuables had all been taken.

Needless to say, rumors abounded. People are really irresponsible and unaware of the damage idle gossip can cause in situations like this. Many years later, I met that wonderful doctor in Paris and thanked him profusely. He had risked his own safety by intervening in Ladan's case. We no longer knew anyone in Iran who could have come to our aid, and without his help, who knows what might have happened?

My depression deepened. I was desperately worried about Ladan and her family. She remained in Iran for the next three years and our only contact was by phone and the occasional letter. I was about to lose hope of ever seeing her again. My health wasn't too good either. I spent hours in churches praying for her family. At times, I would appeal to Jesus and then to Mohammad to protect her children. I had faith that wherever I prayed to Him, God would hear my pleas.

One day I was at a social gathering where a woman was gossiping about a young lady who had been caught trying to take out millions of dollars' worth of jewelry from Iran. I whispered to her, "Even if this rumor is true, she was taking out her own jewelry. You are wearing a considerable amount yourself right now. It is not as if either you or she had smuggled drugs or arms! Plus, if you ever needed to sell any of these, do you think you'd find a buyer easily? Please consider talking about other topics instead of gossiping about people's misfortunes." A few of those listening nodded in agreement and the woman in question appeared duly chastened.

End of the Hostage Crisis in Iran

On 20 January 1981 news came of the release of the American hostages from the U.S. embassy in Tehran after being held for 444 days, and everyone breathed a sigh of relief. None of the world leaders who had contributed to the ruin of Iran were re-elected. James Callaghan was replaced by Margaret Thatcher; Jimmy Carter lost to Ronald Reagan; and Valéry Giscard d'Estaing was defeated by François Mitterrand.

These three had been major players in the tragic destiny of Iran, even though it was eventually the Iranian people who had toppled the monarchy.

Helmut Schmidt was probably the least guilty of those involved but he, too, soon gave way to Helmut Kohl. Giscard d'Estaing sent an emissary to the Shah's funeral in Egypt and later expressed regret in a TV program for not personally attending as the Shah had been an old friend of France and de Gaulle. This is the way of the world. Nothing lasts forever, not wealth nor beauty nor youth. We should never rely too much on things that are transient.

Discovering Family and Friends in Paris

On 22 January 1981, a woman was elected to the Académie Française for the first time—the novelist Marguerite Yourcenar. I watched the ceremony on TV and felt sorry for the women of my country who were deprived of their basic rights. In later years, other women were elected to this honor; the road was opening for women everywhere.

One day when I was out walking, I ran into my cousin Dr. Ahmad Mostofi. I had been isolated from the rest of the family for so long that meeting a close relative in Paris delighted me. He was living in Paris with his young family and invited me to their apartment. In time, they would also visit me. This cousin was a Francophile and had studied in France; he had two young daughters who attended high school. Later, one of them became a physician and took good care of me.

I had been very close to the Japanese ambassador in Tehran, Mr. Ikawa, and his wife, who were now in Paris. One night they held a dinner party at their embassy—a modern building situated in a beautiful, old garden, near the Élysée Palace. The party included two former Iranian ministers and their wives, and reminded me of the magnificent parties they used to hold in Tehran. A little while later, I invited the ambassador and his wife to dinner and served *abgusht* and *gusht kubideh*[6] and a new invention of mine akin to *shirin polow* (a sweet rice dish, often served at weddings, made with slivered caramelized orange peel and carrots). The meal was such a success that the ambassador wanted to know why he had never tasted it in Iran. I replied that it was regarded as simple workman's food and inappropriate for a formal dinner party.

This couple showed me much kindness. That evening we talked about the Elahieh land and the half-finished building. Mr. Ikawa said I should have let it go for $2 million. I replied, "It was my husband's wish that it should not be sold; in any case, whether we had sold it or not, we will always be dispossessed." When he finally left after

---

6. Ab *means "water or broth" and* gusht *means "meat" in Persian, so* abgusht *means "meat broth." Meat, potato, and legumes are cooked in broth for a long time, then the broth is poured into a bowl while the solid ingredients are left in the pot and mashed into a paste or* gusht kubideh. *The paste is then eaten as a* loqmeh *(small wrap) by placing some of it on a piece of flatbread, adding your favorite trimmings (pickles and fresh basil or other herbs), folding it, and popping it into your mouth.*

several years in this post in Paris, he sent me a beautiful watercolor of Sheikh Lotfollah Mosque as well as several books on Persian art, saying, "I know you will have better use for these."

Among the books, I found copies of *Persia: Bridge of Turquoise*, the *Shahnameh*, and even the *Negar-e Zan* that I had once given him as a present. His wife came with the driver to say goodbye and explained that their house in Tokyo was very small and they didn't have room for these magnificent volumes. I was so grateful to them because I had lost all the books that I had collected in my library in Iran, among which were two priceless prayer books belonging to my father as well as his thesis "The History of Diplomacy in Iran," handwritten on parchment. Years later when I visited Tokyo, I called this lovely couple. They invited my sister Nayer and me to dinner at a beautiful restaurant. At that time, this former ambassador had been appointed CEO of Nippon Air. His driver, with immaculate while gloves, drove us to our hotel; I was always impressed by the cleanliness of their cars and how the driver would always wear gloves!

My American Visa

I had not seen Hamid for eighteen months; we communicated by phone and the occasional letter. This was about the time when the American hostages had been released and there was a new president in the White House. I decided to make a second attempt to apply for a visa to visit the U.S. Equipped with one of André Maurois's books to pass the time, I had a long wait at the consulate. Eventually my turn came. The young man at the window asked me about Hamid and I replied that he had fortunately managed to get a work permit and residency. He replied, "This is what always happens. First, they come in with a student visa and then they find a way to stay. Now you are going to join him and stay there."

When I explained that I wouldn't have a roof over my head in the U.S., he said that I should stay with Hamid. I asked him if he lived with his mother. Surprised at my question, he said no. I then said, "What makes you think I should live with my son?" He continued, "You could live anywhere—here, in London, or in the U.S." I assured him that I had no intention of leaving Paris except for short visits to see my children. He then returned my passport and, in excellent French, said he was sorry to refuse my application for a visa.

Furious and very frustrated, I returned home and wrote a long letter to the American consul in which I complained about the manner I had been treated and the three-hour wait I had had to endure for a three-minute interview. I pointed out that my son, at his own expense, and thanks to his intelligence and hard work, had obtained the highest academic qualifications in the U.S. If he planned to take American citizenship, it was America's gain. It would be better if they paid more attention to the smugglers and drug dealers entering the country instead of people like me! I lived in Paris; I was studying at the Sorbonne for my PhD thesis. If they truly did not want the likes of me to visit their country, I would never set foot there again—even if it meant not seeing my son.

It was a strongly worded letter; I called the consulate and asked to speak to the consul. I was told he was on leave. I informed the receptionist that I had an important letter for the consul which should not end up in the waste-paper basket; she advised me to address it to Linda Jackson. A few days later, I received a call asking me to visit the consulate on 4 May and bring along my passport and other documents. I turned up for the meeting at the appointed hour and was immediately ushered into an office where an attractive young woman received me at the door; it was Linda Jackson.

With great respect, she invited me to take a seat (in my letter I had remarked that I had been kept standing while the officer was seated—just like a criminal!). She started by saying, "Please accept my apology." I remained silent. She continued, "We have hundreds of applications each day for visas and sometimes our officers are overwhelmed." At this moment, the young man from my previous visit entered the room and left a folder on her desk before departing in a hurry. I replied, "I think it was this same gentleman." Ms. Jackson took my passport and went into the next room, returning after a few moments and giving me the passport. Without looking at it, I thanked her and said, "I am just going away for six weeks and I will call you on my return; I hope you will join me for dinner sometime."

I left the consulate and opened my passport outside; she had given me a four-year visa with multiple entries. In those days, Iranians had to spend thousands of dollars with immigration lawyers to get even a one-year visa! I never met this lady again, but I did call the consulate on my return as I had promised. After that, several friends tried the same approach, but they were unsuccessful—maybe their case wasn't as straightforward as mine.

Years later, I was a dinner guest at the home of an old Greek friend with guests from many nationalities. The person sitting next to me at dinner was a Greek lawyer who asked me about the situation of the Iranian diaspora. I replied that life was difficult for the Iranians living in exile, especially those who wished to travel to the U.S. A guest from the other end of the table then remarked, "Iranians are very generous and invite the embassy officers to dinner at expensive restaurants. The officers have no choice but to refuse these invitations for fear of losing their jobs. There is a quota for visas given to different nationalities each year and exceeding those numbers is not possible." Later I heard from my hostess that this man, who had worked in Greece for many years, was now the economic counselor at the U.S. embassy.

My Efforts to Free Ladan

Back in Tehran, Ladan was finding life intolerable on many different fronts; she had come to the conclusion that the only solution was to try to leave Iran and attempt once again to join me in Paris. My poor girl was neither involved in politics, nor had she ever held any government post. She was a mother, an educated young woman, but without being given any reason, she had been asked to leave her job at the university. When her children were also forced to change schools, she hired private tutors for them and home-schooled them. But she was still stuck in Iran and had no way of leaving even though she had been promised the return of her travel documents—nothing had come of it so far. As a backup, I enrolled her in the PhD program in economics at Dauphine University, even though I had no idea if she would ever reach Paris, and I registered my two granddaughters at the Assumption School for a second time.

I also paid a visit to the American Hospital in Paris, where they gave me a letter confirming that I had a heart condition. I then took this letter to the Iranian consulate, where I was given a hard time. By then, I was so upset and agitated that I felt my life depended upon the young officer approving the letter. After all my entreaties and explanations failed to persuade him to change his mind, I asked him, "Sir, do you have a mother?" When he said yes, I asked him if he wanted to see her again.

Then I explained that my daughter was in Tehran and wanted to visit her mother. What was wrong with that? By now, I was in tears. He was moved by my little speech and finally stamped the bottom of the doctor's letter. I breathed a sigh of relief. But this was only the first step in the long process that would enable Ladan to find her way to Paris.

I managed to send the letter to Tehran with a friend who was flying out; I also sent a parcel with a couple of modest, long-sleeved dresses for Ladan's thirty-third birthday.

Ladan Arrives in Paris and Hamid Pays a Visit

I traveled to London to be with Mariam and her family for Nowruz. My sister Mehri was still in Iran and could not leave; her sons would travel there to see her from time to time. There were many gatherings for the New Year but all I could think about was Ladan and her children. She seemed to be ready to leave but I had been disappointed too many times, getting my hopes up and then having them dashed. So I told her husband Ali, "Just call me when they are on the plane." On 5 April 1983, the phone rang in Paris; it was Ali letting me know that they were safely in the air. I could hardly contain my excitement. I rushed to get their room ready and started to make dinner. I didn't have the strength to go to the airport. It was Ladan's cousin Niloo and her husband who collected them instead and brought them home.

As the children walked into the apartment, I grabbed them both and hugged them, but they broke away and soon became absorbed in watching the TV, oblivious to me and everything around them! The phone rang constantly; friends and family from around the world wanted to know how they were. Three and a half years had passed since we had last been together, and we were beginning to lose hope of ever seeing each other again. We had a stream of visitors. Ladan did the cooking—she was a great cook—and I was the sous-chef. It was indeed a time for celebration.

Life gradually fell into a pattern. Within a few months, Ladan and her children had settled into Parisian life. The girls seemed to do well in school in spite of the fact that they had only been there for one semester. That summer, we all went to Nice together, my sister Nayer joining us from Houston. The round of parties started again; there wasn't much else to do except socialize. A short while later, Mariam and family also arrived, though my sister Mehri was still stuck in Iran and not free to leave.

We traveled to Nice to see the *Bataille de Fleurs* once again with its huge flower-filled floats and beautiful young girls riding in them. Ladan had watched the famous event years ago when she was seven—now it was the turn of her daughters to see it. We also visited San Remo in Italy; these trips were quite complicated as a visa was required—even for a day trip.

Hamid had left Iran in 1978 and had not been able to leave the U.S. after that. Finally, after five years, he was able to leave and arrived in Nice on his birthday. Ladan arranged a wonderful dinner party and invited thirty-five guests, managing to squeeze them all into our small apartment. After three years, in the U.S., Hamid and a colleague had decided to start their own company. I suggested we pay a visit to one of his father's old friends, a very successful businessman who was staying in Cannes and who advised Hamid to start small and build up his business gradually.

We returned to Paris with Hamid and the girls in early September (Shahrivar). After a few days, Hamid returned to San Francisco, leaving me sad and depressed. How long was I to be separated from my children? In Iran, we had all lived within a short distance of each other. Five years had passed since we had left our homeland and everyone seemed so far away.

Ladan and Mariam

Ladan seemed depressed, unable to see what the future held. Her husband was in Iran and the prospects of finding work in Paris were not great. It may have been Hamid's visit that caused her to focus on the future and her thoughts turned to the U.S. The first thing was to get a green card. Her immigration lawyer advised her to go to Rome and apply there. Ladan and the girls stayed in Rome for a month and finally managed to get their visas. In November 1983 (Aban 1362), Ladan left for the U.S. with her two daughters, the girls attending school until the very last day. Ladan had a long and difficult road ahead forging a new life for herself and her family, but she eventually bought a house, after staying with Hamid initially, and started looking for work in her own field of economics. Most importantly, she was waiting for her husband to join them.

Many educated young people fled our country after the revolution and carved out new lives for themselves all over the world. Mariam was working in London. In the past, she had lived in a magnificent, newly built house in Tehran. Now she was selling beautiful houses to other people. Her husband Fari had set up his practice in Harley Street and was doing very well, while their two daughters attended the famous St. Paul's School.

Defending My Thesis

I had surprised myself; after five years of diligent research and hard work, my thesis was finally ready for presentation to the examining committee. Insomnia had given me an opportunity to work on it every day in the quiet hours between 4 and 8 a.m. After studying close to eighty books, I had based my thesis on this extensive research. As each chapter was completed, I would show it to my professor, who would write comments that I would then incorporate into the text.

My problems started once I had finished writing and had handed over my completed thesis to the young women who would type them up. In those days, computers were not common and many grammatical and spelling errors would find their way onto the typed pages, which therefore had to be edited and corrected several times. I spent my evenings preparing the bibliography, glossary, and contents pages.

The defense of my thesis was scheduled for 10 a.m. on 16 December 1985 and I had invited a few of my friends to this event. I arrived a half hour beforehand and greeted my friends, who included Michelle Maurois, the daughter of the author. The judges sat at a long table at the end of the conference room. The date had been announced in *Le Monde* newspaper and there were a few others present whom I didn't know. One of my former students in Tehran had seen the announcement and had come.

Professor René Pomeau opened the meeting. I started by giving the title of my thesis, which was "*André Maurois—moraliste et humaniste.*" I explained that events outside of my control had resulted in my being in Paris and that I had met André Maurois in 1960 at Wilson College in the United States. I also noted similarities between André Maurois and my late father, who had passed away in 1950 (1329). I mentioned how the Second World War had brought about changes in my country that troubled people like my father, and how the occupation of Iran by the British, the Russians, and eventually the Americans was a big blow to our national pride. To avoid depression, my father had started to write an autobiography that was eventually entitled "The Administrative and Social History of the Qajar Period."

In a similar way, André Maurois had been disturbed by the invasion of France by Germany during the two world wars, which had upended his life. I felt that I, too, had suffered a similar fate. Maurois introduced the biographical style of writing in French. These days, everyone writes biographies but, at the time of Maurois, this was a novelty and very well received, just as my father's 2,000-page book had been.

After this short introduction, the questioning began. One of the committee members seemed to want to catch me out. I had written something about Balzac to which this lady objected. She asked me, "How well do you know Balzac?" I replied, "I have known him since I was twenty-one when I translated *Eugenie Grandet* into Persian." She said, "The title of your thesis sounds like a defense of the author." I replied in English, "What is in a name? In *Romeo and Juliet*, Shakespeare says that a 'rose by any other name would smell as sweet.'" Eventually she admitted that they were just testing me to see how I would react!

I told her that I had been attending presentations for the theses of other students and had seen how some had left the room in tears. As a precaution, I had brought some tissues with me to use if the same thing happened to me. I then pulled out a clean tissue from my pocket to prove it. The last judge to speak was complimentary and said, "Madame, we are happy that you didn't inflict modern psychology and the interpretations of Freud and Jung on us. The level of your written and spoken French is rarely seen outside of these walls today—and even sometimes inside of these four walls!" He then added, "You sound as if you were enchanted by Maurois—almost married to him." The meeting ended and the committee departed to make their decision; it was noon.

Two unforgettable hours had passed; I suddenly felt like that twenty-two-year-old university student I had once been who admired and was in awe of her teachers. The judges were out for just fifteen minutes. Everyone stood up when they returned; it felt like one was in court. After a short introduction, Professor Rameau announced the acceptance of my thesis with a "*très honorable*" mention. The meeting was over; I had passed.

I introduced Michelle Maurois to the judges who didn't know her. She was an excellent writer but clearly without the fame and reputation of her father. All my friends and acquaintances came forward to congratulate me. Two of them invited me to lunch; none of the members of my family were present. I never gave myself the title of "Dr." but I must admit the research and all the reading had expanded my horizons.

Having submitted my thesis and had it accepted, I felt a great burden lifted from my shoulders. Ladan arranged a dinner party for fifty guests in my honor and invited Novin Afrouz our friend the concert pianist. Despite working full time, Ladan had been really well organized and had prepared all the food in advance, which she kept in the freezer. Novin turned up very late, accompanied by several friends whom she had invited without telling us. One of her friends took someone else's fur coat as she was leaving and it required huge efforts to track down and switch the old coat with the new one with which the guest had flown to Los Angeles! Such is the way of artists, who tend to be impulsive and often careless about the effect of their actions on others.

Hamid and Tina

During his visit to Nice, Hamid took me out to dinner one night and, on the way back, asked for my blessing as he wished to marry Tina. I replied, "I am sure your dear father would agree with me that marriage with someone from another culture is not easy, and you are well aware of that. But if you have made up your mind, then I support your decision and wish you all good things in your life together."

I returned to Paris from Nice on the last day of July and flew to San Francisco a couple of days later. The wedding invitations had been sent out, Hamid having asked my permission to use his name and Tina's as the hosts, to which I had agreed; I have a feeling he didn't want to see his father's name missing from the card. He was also paying for the wedding himself, to which 230 guests had been invited at the Mark Hopkins Hotel. The Iranian *aqd* ceremony was to be held at Ladan's house.

Soon after I arrived, I invited Carol, Tina's mother, a lovely lady, to have lunch with me to discuss the arrangements for the Christian ceremony. Carol was worried that many of the Iranian guests had not yet responded. She gave me a list of names and I promised to follow up and let her know as soon as possible. They were planning to hold the ceremony in a beautiful period house in Franklin Street; the ceremony would be conducted by the priest who had baptized Tina.

After she left, I started to call the friends on her list, all of whom were planning to attend but had not bothered to confirm and send back the reply envelope. One gentleman gave as an excuse the fact that the dress code was dinner jackets. I told him, "You can wear a dark suit with a bow tie. The dress code is so people realize that it is a formal occasion." The Iranian officiant was Mr. Hasan Shahbaz, who was coming from Los Angeles. One of the young men offered to collect him from the airport.

I asked him how the young man would recognize him. He replied, "I will be arriving in the middle of the day dressed in a dinner jacket with a bow tie and carrying a burgundy-colored briefcase; I don't think there will be two of us looking like this." I knew Mr. Shahbaz from years ago and had heard him speak; his daughter Guity had been my student and I had written her a letter of recommendation when she came to the U.S. to study. Her father had written to thank me and I remembered his beautiful handwriting.

Persian Wedding Rice

The menu was similar to the one for Ladan's wedding but the hotel would not allow us to bring food from outside, for reasons of legal liability. In those days, there were few Iranian weddings and *shirin polow* as a wedding dish was unknown. I contacted a lady who had been an under-secretary at the Ministry of Education in Iran but was now doing catering for a living, asking her to provide a platter of this celebratory rice dish for the *aqd* ceremony. She was then supposed to go to the hotel kitchen the next day and make the same dish

Hamid and Tina's wedding, 1986

At Hamid and Tina's wedding: Houri and Hamid with Mariam and Ladan

under the supervision of the hotel chef for the big reception. I also visited the kitchen to find suitable platters for the rice. When the waiters entered the ballroom with the silver platters of *shirin polow*, everyone was impressed and kept asking for second helpings. Tina's officiant, who had traveled from Boston and was attending the dinner with his wife, asked to take some leftovers home in a takeaway container.

The Persian *Aqd* Ceremony

Ladan had set out a beautiful *aqd* spread with colored incense, *mobarak-bad* (congratulatory) coins, elegant crystalized-sugar sticks, a copy of the Qur'an, candelabras and a mirror—all according to tradition. Chairs were arranged behind the seats of the bride and groom. Only family, the witnesses, and a few of Hamid and Tina's American friends were invited. Ladan had prepared a dinner following the ceremony and made a big cake. This took place on Thursday 28 August 1986; the one person we all missed was Hamid's father.

I was overwhelmed with emotion and tears rolled down my cheeks the whole time—even as I was smiling broadly. Two days later, the American ceremony took place, followed by a dinner at the Mark Hopkins Hotel. The wedding cake was decorated with kiwi fruit and strawberries, the colors of the Iranian flag. The flower arrangements on the tables consisted of cream-colored roses and tuberoses. Everything was beautifully organized and dignified.

The following day, the newly married couple left for their honeymoon in Maui. Hamid gave his wife my wedding ring and I gave her a pair of emerald and diamond earrings. My sister Nayer, her husband, and granddaughter Noelle, who was one of the bridesmaids, had come from Houston. My nephew Abdi and niece Niloo came from Los Angeles, Reza and his wife Mariam from London. My daughter Mariam was there with her two girls. I stayed at Ladan's house, preferring to leave the coast clear for the new couple, who would be returning to the house in Sausalito, where I had been staying, after their honeymoon.

My Granddaughter Leila Gets Married

New Year's Day 1989 happened to fall on a Sunday. The French were not too happy that the holiday and Sunday coincided, but to me it made no difference! For years now, weekdays and weekends were all the same for me.

My next trip was in March, before the Persian New Year, when I left for San Francisco to see Ladan, Hamid, and their families. My granddaughter Leila also living in the U.S. now was about to get married and she had asked me to help her in choosing a wedding gown. Soon Mariam and Fari arrived from London. After ten years, our small family had all come together Leila's engagement party took place in Hamid and Tina's home.

Leila and Javad's wedding. Seated from left: Sanam, Marjan, Firouzeh. Standing: from left: Ali Lari, Ladan, Fari, Houri, Javad, Leila, Mariam, Tina, and Hamid

Hamid's company, AMB,[7] had grown, and they needed more office space. Apparently, they were initially rejected when they approached the neighboring office with an offer to take over their premises. Sometime later, however, the neighboring company whose partners were about to retire contacted Hamid, saying that they would now accept his previous offer. Hamid, who had not taken the earlier rejection well, responded that he would consider it only if the

7. *The letters AMB represent the initials of the last names of the company's three founders: Douglas D. Abbey, Hamid R. Moghadam, and T. Robert Burke.*

Marjan and Doug Fitzsimmons' wedding

directors would agree to shine his shoes first. One day, in the presence of press and photographers, those elderly gentlemen set up shoe-shine chairs in the fancy lobby of the building and got busy shining the shoes of the three young partners of AMB. The event made the news in the local papers! Later I remarked to Hamid, "You could have told me the story before I heard it from in the newspapers!" He simply shrugged his shoulders and said, "Not a big deal!"

Leila and Javad were married on 29 July 1989; the Persian ceremony took place in Ladan's house, followed by dinner at a San Francisco hotel. On 18 October, San Francisco was rocked by a major earthquake. Hamid called me before 6 a.m. in Paris to let me know that the family were all safe.

Defending Iranian Heritage

I knew Dr. N—— from Iran and considered him to be both scholarly and patriotic! Something had been troubling me for a while. A book had been published at the University of California, Berkeley, in which there was a reference to Molana Jalal al-Din, better known as Rumi, being born in Balkh, Afghanistan. As I read on, I realized there was no indication of this famous mystic philosopher being Iranian. In the introduction to the book, Dr. N—— was named as the editor of the work and responsible for its publication. I was truly upset by what I considered an obvious disregard for our rich Iranian heritage.

One evening at a function we were both attending, in Washington DC I found an opportunity to take Dr. N—— to one side and bring up the subject with him. He heard me out, then replied that surely it would have been mentioned somewhere else in the book that Rumi was Persian! As I reminded him, "Eight hundred years ago, Balkh was part of Iran; Afghanistan was only founded in 1709! How could you allow them to print this misinformation in the introduction to the book?" He became defensive as I went on: "What a pity that someone would be prepared to sell their country's heritage in exchange for a few thousand greenbacks." And I walked away, leaving him standing there, open-mouthed!

This was not the first time that I had defended Iran, its poets, and their outstanding contribution to world literature. I felt it had almost become my duty to speak up. The representatives of the Islamic Republic certainly did not have the education to notice such errors. And neither did those who lived abroad, claiming to be in opposition to the regime in Iran, appear to be bothered about such details. What can we expect of others when we Iranians ignore and devalue our own heritage?

Challenging Raymond Barre

In 1990 in Paris, I attended a conference given by Mr. Raymond Barre, who had served as prime minister under Valéry Giscard d'Estaing during the time of the Islamic Revolution. I had prepared several questions to ask him and was wearing a black dress with a bright red jacket so he would not be able to miss me! The event was moderated by a journalist from French TV and was attended by captains of industry and financial leaders. I was sitting at a table with several Egyptian politicians and their spouses. Saddam Hussein had just attacked Kuwait and the discussion centered around whether France should enter the war against Saddam or not.

I noticed that the moderator kept referring to "the Gulf" and not "the Persian Gulf." Raymond Barre is a moderate politician and always sits on the fence. I made a few notes about what he was saying and raised my hand as soon as an opportunity arose. I was handed a microphone; my hand shook a little as I hadn't held a microphone in many years. I made an effort to control myself.

After introducing myself, I started by saying, "My first question is addressed to the moderator of this meeting. Why do you avoid referring to 'the Persian Gulf' and keep saying 'the Gulf'? Don't you know that this gulf has a name and that name has been the Persian Gulf since the fifty century BCE and will continue being called that into the future? Please don't drop the proper name in favor of a few newly formed countries whose births I have witnessed." A few people applauded my comments.

I continued. "My second question is addressed to the prime minister. Don't you think, sir, that your support of Saddam Hussein at the time of the Iran–Iraq War was the cause of the present situation? Iraq compared to Iran is like Belgium compared to France. It was your encouragement and support that spurred Saddam to attack Kuwait." A few people clapped again.

Mr. Barre replied, "Madame, I never said 'the Arabian Gulf' . . . I look at the map and I read what is written there . . . but other countries have demands too." One of the journalists interrupted him and said, "Please answer the second question. Are you not sorry that you didn't support the Shah of Iran?"

The prime minister continued: "The Middle East is a land of contrasts and complexities that we can never quite understand." Realizing he was avoiding the question, I interrupted him and said, "Mr. Prime Minister, it is a fact that the Middle East is a complicated part of the world, but politics is even more complex than that. I was in Paris at the time of the Iranian Revolution and I saw how you helped and supported the revolutionaries."

He replied, "Khomeini was a political refugee!" I countered, "There are many political refugees in France. Does the French government install thirty-five phone lines and put three TV channels at their disposal so they can broadcast their message everywhere?" A few more clapped, and I sat down.

The last question was asked by a lady on the other side of the room; it was actually more of an agreement with my comments than a question. She asked whether I was an Iranian, to which I said yes. She introduced herself; she was Lebanese and confirmed what I had just said. She knew that gendarmes in plain clothes boarded Air France flights from Beirut to Tehran on a daily basis carrying hundreds of cassettes recorded by Khomeini to be distributed there. This was the final blow; the room went quiet—you could have heard a pin drop! The meeting came to an end; we all got up. That lady, whose name I don't know, came toward me and said, "I am so sorry that Iran ended up like, thanks to our money and support."

A few days later, a transcript of the conference, including my comments and the prime minister's feeble responses, was sent to my address. Everything had been recorded. The package also contained a photo of me standing up to speak.

I Wish . . .

In 1991 (1370), when my dear aunt Valieh Azam passed away in Tehran at the age of eighty-five, she donated her apartment to the Kahrizak Foundation. All the residents of Kahrizak followed her coffin and attended her burial. I wish what had been taken from us in Iran could have been used in the same way instead of being seized for the personal use of those in power.

In Houston, 1977, Valieh Azam and Houri seated, Abdi Mostofi and Nayer standing

Top: Houri entertaining her Zonta Club friends in her Paris apartment, 1995

I wish the houses and land confiscated from us could have been turned into schools, libraries, or art galleries for the benefit of a younger generation. Instead, property developers stepped in and built apartments that were then sold and converted into dollars, marks, and pounds and sent abroad. I wish factories could have restarted instead of all their equipment being dismantled and sold off. I wish our educated youth had remained in the country instead of fleeing abroad for a safer life. They were the hope for the future of Iran; the ones who stayed had to do three jobs just to put food on the table.

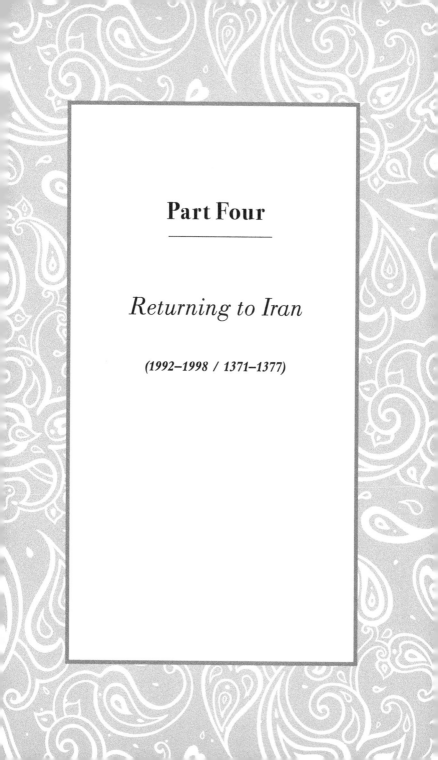

Part Four

Returning to Iran

(1992–1998 / 1371–1377)

Back in Tehran

On 14 November 1992 (23 Aban 1371), fourteen years after leaving Iran, I board an Air France flight bound for Tehran. The night before my departure, I did not sleep a wink. As we approach Tehran, the French magazines and newspapers are all collected from everyone who is due to disembark. Air France would be continuing the flight after dropping off the Tehran-bound passengers. None of the crew leave the plane.

The airport appears quite orderly. I present my passport to a young man at the booth; he is smiling—a good omen. He leafs through my passport, referring to his various lists, and having stamped it, he returns it to me. This is the first step in the process of arrival that I have been concerned about. Customs control is also uneventful. I have been away many years and have little with me except for some personal belongings and a few gifts.

Mr. and Mrs. K—— are waiting for me. I nod hello to them, remembering that I should not be shaking hands with any men in Iran. It is midnight and pitch dark outside. We drive to Shemiran, passing the monument previously known as Shahyad and now renamed Azadi (Freedom)! Somehow, Tehran is now more beautiful at night than during the day, the ugliness and mess less visible. Apart from Azadi Square, everything else seems unfamiliar. Many high-rise buildings completely at odds with their surroundings, garish neon lights, advertising billboards next to tall trees—beauty and disorder side by side.

The car enters through the garden gates. My suitcases are taken upstairs to the room I have been given. It is 2 a.m., and we all retire to bed. I wake up early as the call to prayer is sounding outside; hearing it is an unfamiliar yet pleasant experience. Images of all the years I'd been away pass through my mind like the scenes in a movie. It is Thursday and I spend the day with my wonderful hosts; a few friends come to visit and there are many phone calls too.

On Friday, the house is prepared for the visitors we are expecting. Friends and family start arriving around 11 a.m., bringing flowers, pastries, books, and, best of all, their warmth, their smiles, and their embraces. Apparently, I have not been forgotten. That evening, we go for a drive around Shemiran, passing by my father's and my brother's houses—now surrounded with ugly metal fences for security.

But this trip is not purely for seeing family and friends, as important as that is. There is much to be getting on with, and I have a to-do list:

- To give a power of attorney to a trustworthy individual.
- To clear out my house.
- To remove the restrictions placed on my right to buy or sell.
- To buy a few carpets and earrings.
- To collect thirty-nine years of retirement benefits.
- To get a new identity card.

Visiting Tehran

On Saturday, a working day, I accompany my host, who is on his way to his office in the city. New freeways have been built and many stories added to existing buildings. Tehran, which had never been a beautiful city, appears even more chaotic. Traffic, crowds, bicycles, and motorcycles weave in and out—a terrifying experience!

I then go to visit the family mausoleum at the Hazrat-e Abdol Azim shrine, where there is no sign of the carved marble headstones, the beautiful burial room, or its antique French windows with the colored glass. Two humble stones in the Bagh-e Touti with my parents' names inscribed on them are the only mementos left of our eminent family. Still, I am grateful for even that. As I wash the stones with rose water and say my prayers, I can't stop my tears.

Next, I visit Behesht-e Zahra. My late husband's private mausoleum was always kept locked, yet there is no sign of the chandelier, candelabras, or the copy of the Qur'an we had placed there. Fortunately, the beautiful Safavid tiles are still on the walls and the headstone is intact. I hire two men to clean the room, then lay a few flowers on my husband's grave and leave.

An Interrogation at the Revolutionary Court

On Sunday, I visit the prosecutor's office at the revolutionary court in Tehran.[1] After first being frisked by the black-veiled ladies at the entrance to the court, I climb the many flights of stairs to the prosecutor's office on the third floor. The interviewer is a youngish, bearded man, who makes an effort to be cordial. Another auspicious sign. I explain that I have come to get my house back from the authorities. After checking my name, age, and other details, he asks if I had any relationship with the imperial court or the royal family. Had I known the cabinet members of the time? Did I have any political connections? What was my father's job? He leafs through a thick file while he waits for my reply.

I give him the appropriate answers; but somehow, they don't satisfy him. He keeps looking through the file and shaking his head. Finally, he says, "Khanum, it is already late today. Please come back tomorrow and give us more comprehensive answers." I reply, "Please ask me your ques-

---

1 The Islamic Revolutionary Court is a special system of courts set up after the revolution of 1979 in the Islamic Republic of Iran designed to try all offenses against the internal and external security of the Country. The trials are not public, there is no jury, and a single judge decides the matter at hand. Information on the trial is disclosed at the discretion of the government. Iran also has a parallel conventional court penal system.

tions one by one and I will answer. I don't need time to think about my replies." With some concern, he repeats, "No, it is better if you come back tomorrow. It would be to your advantage." It is 4 p.m. I start making my way down those endless flights of stairs and return home.

I return to the court the next day, to be interviewed by a different official.

Q: You have been living abroad for many years.

A: Yes, for fourteen years.

Q: What were you doing during this time?

A: I left Iran for medical treatment; I had a tumor on my kidney and another on my breast. While abroad, I became seriously depressed. In order to help myself, I enrolled at the Sorbonne and obtained my PhD in 1985/1364.

Q: What was your job before that?

A: I was a high-school French teacher and an instructor in English at the Melli University.

Q: What else were you involved in?

A: I was twice elected as president of the International Women's Club

Q: Did you have any relationship with the imperial court?

A: No, sir.

Q: You are not telling the truth.

A: If you ask the right question, you will hear the right answer. Do I have a relationship with you?

Q: No.

A: I have come to you in order to resolve an issue. Having a relationship is quite a vague term in Persian. I had contact with the imperial court in order to secure a piece of land for the children's convalescence home.

Q: How many times did you visit Farah?

A: In each of my terms as president, two or three times. Farah Pahlavi [I avoid using the term "Shahbanu" since I don't want to trigger a negative response] made a huge effort on the club's behalf and managed to secure 5,000 square meters of land situated behind the Gendarmerie Hospital with the permission of the country's ruler [the Shah] for the convalescence home. That land had originally been earmarked for an officers' club; the floor plans had already been drawn up. I had to negotiate between four ministries and other organizations for eight months before the cabinet approved the gift. My relationships were of this order. Do you think those "relationships" served a useful purpose?

Q: Yes, it was a good idea. How could you afford to live abroad?

A: My son had a job and supported me.

Q: Do you own a house abroad?

A: I don't own so much as a square meter of land anywhere. But I do have the use of an apartment that does not belong to me.

Q: Do you have a job?

A: No . . . I run my house, I am my own lawyer and don't spend money on either of these services.

Q: Why have you stayed abroad?

A: Because my children live there. Also, you have confiscated my house in Tehran.

Q: Do you wear a headscarf?

A: No, I don't. If I did, it would draw unnecessary attention. The Qur'an says that women of my age don't have to wear the hijab.

The interviewer shakes his head and says, "That is true. Let us return to your file."

Q: Were you an adviser to Farrokhrou Parsa at the Ministry of Education?

A: May God rest her soul.

He interrupts me, shouting, "May God rest her soul?"

"Yes, sir," I reply. "She is dead and we have to ask for God's mercy for her. I taught for thirty-nine years since I don't like office work. What you see in my file was just a title; I never had an office nor a salary. I had never asked for this position and for this reason, after a couple of months, I called the minister and offered my resignation."

At this point, someone enters the room. The interviewer gets up and, in a loud voice, says, "See, we are dealing here with an adviser to Farrokhrou Parsa, the minister of education!"

I interrupt him, saying, "Please don't make such accusations; that is unfair. I was a teacher for thirty-nine years and an adviser for only two months—during which time I actually didn't have a proper function. If this is what you called justice, I will have nothing to do with you."

He falls silent and keeps leafing through the file before continuing:

Q: What other activities were you engaged in?

A: In my second term as president of the club, I took part in numerous important cultural activities.

He is now looking through photos of the historical fashion show in *Negar-e Zan.* "For example, research and producing women's dress in Iran from 3000 BCE to the present, all now exhibited in the museum . . ." he mutters. Totally absorbed in looking at the colorful pictures, he suddenly exclaims, "You have lost weight!"

"You mean I have aged!" I reply, thinking to myself, "How can he tell I've lost weight under this chador!"

Q: Where did this event take place?

A: At the Tehran Hilton ballroom.

Q: Who were the participants?

A: Members of the club and their families, government officials.

Q: For example?

A: Sir, I have no intention of naming other people here. You have full knowledge of everything and know answers to the questions you are asking. I am not about to involve other people and I hate gossip.

Q: Did you also invite Farah?

A: Yes, Farah Pahlavi was our guest.

Q: How about Ashraf?

A: You should know that two important personalities should never be invited to the same event.

Q: So, you also had statues present at this event.

I stand up and look over his shoulder at the picture he has in front of him. It is a photo of Shahbanu Farah together with Princess Fatemeh with myself in the background. I reply, "This is Princess Fatemeh, who was a guest of the queen, and I had forgotten that."

Q: Their heads are all uncovered!

A: We should not expect otherwise. As you can see, most of the models are wearing some sort of head covering, as was traditional at the time.

A few pages later, he comes upon the costumes from the Qajar period. One of the models is wearing a short skirt in green velvet and a veil decorated with a red rose. He takes one look at it and says, "This one has bare legs."

A: She is wearing tights.

Q: I can see her whole body.

A: It is your prerogative to think what you will. This is an *andarouni* outfit. The model is wearing skin-colored tights plus short white socks.

Q: And you were showing her off in public!

A: Forgive me, but just twenty years ago, young women wore miniskirts in public and it was not against the law.

I sense that, in spite of all his objections, there is an understanding between the interviewer and me. He has realized that I am not afraid to speak the truth; at the same time, I do not indulge in gossip. He is not unhappy at being put in charge of such a colorful case!

He glances at his watch and said, "I have to go now for *namaz* and lunch and I need to close the room. Are you willing to fill in a questionnaire in my absence? And please excuse me since I cannot invite you to lunch."

I ask where he wants me to fill in the questionnaire. He replies that he will put a chair out in the hall for me. Then he leaves.

These are some of the questions:

- What were your social, administrative, and political activities?
- Describe the assets of your family in detail.
- What was the nature of your connection with the Pahlavi family?

It takes quite a while to answer these questions in detail and relate the seventy years of my life on the form. I feel like a student writing an essay in an exam. I must stress that my interrogator, who has now left for his *namaz* and lunch, has been polite and cordial at all times. At 3 p.m., I have finished and I hand the paper to him when he gets back. He takes a look and asks me to add a few points, then he escorts me to the elevator and indicates to the young attendant, who previously barred me from entering the elevator, that I may use it and don't have to make my way down three flights of stairs! He looks pleased at having done me this favor.

The city outside the court looks dark and depressing. Yet, Persian good taste and hospitality shines in the house where I am staying, which is filled with gifts of flowers from our visitors. Some of them have tasted the bitter experience of prison and are now happy to resume their everyday lives. I find myself in two different worlds under the same sky. The revolutionary court with the depressing lines of people hoping for some sort of justice are in sharp contrast to the opulent homes and magnificent gatherings. Iran has always been a land of contrast and no form of government has yet been able to find a balance. People's lives nowadays are gloomy and tolerable only with the simple joys of family and friends coming together over a home-cooked meal. I can see the beauty and I can also see the ugliness around me.

The next day I am back with the judge:

Q: Is Abdollah Mostofi, the head of the Bureau of Registration of Real Estate, your father?

A: I have answered this question before and I repeat that my father was a high government official.

The interviewer leafs through the file; I can see he is looking at a photo of myself with my sister Mehri and brother Bagher in the company of the Japanese ambassador and his wife at their embassy. He asks about each person in the photo.

Q: Where was this picture taken?

A: At the Japanese embassy. I understand Iran now has friendly relations with Japan and people can travel there without a visa.

He then changes the subject.

Q: Do you read many books?

A: Yes, but I am quite choosy about what I read.

Q: Have you read the books by Ansari and Fardoust?[2]

A: No. I don't want to ruin my eyesight with this kind of rubbish.

Q: You should read these books to realize what the Pahlavi family did to this country.

A: Let me give you some advice. If I were you, I wouldn't trust people like these. Such individuals benefited from the system in the past and, as soon as the tables were turned, these ungrateful sycophants attacked their masters to save their own skin. I believe their words and their books are without value.

The interviewer smiles and remarks: "You may be right. It could even be that cousin Ansari who took off with all the money belonging to Reza Pahlavi."

I guess this is a good moment to speak my mind. "It would be better to think about the future instead of criticizing what happened in the past. Much better not to repeat the mistakes of the past and not to make trouble for individuals who served this country all their lives. Are you certain about your judgment? Do you believe what is happening now is fair?"

"What are you referring to?" he asks.

"Sir, I went to visit the graves of my ancestors, honest, God-fearing public servants in this land," I reply. "The graves had been desecrated and nothing was left of their

---

2. *Houshang Ansari (b. 1927) served as an Iranian diplomat and politician for eighteen years prior to the revolution of 1979.*
General Hossein Fardoust (1917–1987) was a childhood friend of the Shah and served for ten years as deputy head of SAVAK, the powerful Iranian intelligence agency.

resting places. Did you know that exhumation of a corpse is a sin?"

"At the beginning of the revolution, there were groups that cooperated with us and committed acts over which we had no control."

I realize that this young man doesn't know this evil act had happened only three years before. Not wanting to rub salt into the wound, I shake my head and say, "How old are you? Are you married? Do you have children?"

"I am thirty-five years old," he replies. "I am married and I have two children. I graduated from high school. At the time of the revolution, I was conscripted in the army and I am working here now."

"Is your conscience clear? Are you afraid of anything?"

He nods and says, "I am afraid for ourselves. We are not united." Then he leads me to the elevator once again.

The Caspian

Accompanied by my hosts, we set off for Sari at 7 a.m.; it is still semi-dark. I am heading for the revolutionary court in Sari to discuss the occupation ofVilla Hamid and to request it being vacated and returned to my son. My appointment is at 5 p.m. We sit in the car and wait for the arrival of the judge. A turbaned and well-rounded gentleman eventually pulls up in a dark-colored Mercedes and steps out—the driver bowing low. It is my turn. I enter the court wearing a chador. The holy man looks me up and down and permits me to take a seat. He addresses me: "You are?"

I reply, "I am Hamid's mother; he is working in the U.S. He lost his father at a young age."

He says, "We have business with him, not his mother!" I stand up. Before leaving the room, I say, "I sincerely hope that whatever belongs to my son will be returned to him since he was a minor at the time of the revolution."

We drove six hours to get here and the God-fearing holy man allowed me only five minutes to state my case. It is a dark and rainy evening; the return journey is more difficult and takes longer. We have wasted eighteen hours. In this great and magnificent land, hours, weeks, months, and years pass and nothing ever gets resolved.

The Prosecutor

I head back to the prosecutor's office at the Tehran revolutionary court. On the way, I reflect on the current situation in Iran. Many of those now in power rose from the underprivileged class. If only there were individuals among this group who were better educated, genuinely capable, and honest, the country could become heaven on earth. What a pity that prejudice has blinded them and the rift between the different classes of society appears to be unbridgeable.

I arrive at the court at 9 a.m. and pass through the body search before climbing three floors and reaching the office of the prosecutor. He had asked for several deeds and documents that I now present to another official, a different person from the previous occasion. Seeing an empty desk next to his, I ask, "Does someone else work in this room?" He replies, "This is the seat reserved for a highly educated colleague who speaks English as well!"

Here is an opportunity to get to know this new person; the interviewer from my previous visit is nowhere to be seen. This man is young and quite dignified; clearly a few years of university education have had an effect on him. They have my doctorate from Sorbonne in the file. He asks me about the education system in France. I ask him if he knows any French.

"No," he replies.

"Do you know any English?" I then ask.

"Some," he replies. "Enough to be able to look up references in books, but conversation is difficult."

I remind him that education abroad is expensive at the current exchange rates. However, if the government were to sponsor him, he could obtain foreign currency at a much-reduced rate and study abroad. I discover that, like my previous interviewer, he is married and has two children. I remind him that living abroad with a family is prohibitively expensive. But if accepted at a university, they can provide you with an apartment at a low rent and with many other benefits.

At this point, my interviewer from before returns and accompanies me to the floor below in the elevator. Each time, he tells the guard that this person is his "mother," "sister," or "wife" (my age being indeterminate beneath the chador) and that resolves the problem.

When I return home, my host tells me, "A miracle has happened. The prosecutor called just now, was really polite, asking how I was, and wanted me to remind you to be at his office first thing tomorrow morning. And he ended the conversation by saying, '*Qorban-e shoma*' [a polite Persian form of "goodbye"—literally, "May I be sacrificed for you"). We had not heard such niceties from these people in the last few years. What did you do to him?" I reply, "I didn't do anything. They don't want to return my house to me; instead they fall back on niceties. I just spoke to them truthfully, as I do with anyone."

The next day, I arrive at the prosecutor's office on the third floor. Sitting in this office, I see a blind-folded young man in a striped prison uniform—apparently on a visit with his mother. My interviewer from before leads me to a different, slightly better-furnished room with more comfortable chairs. The official from yesterday is sitting behind his desk. My interviewer is now seated at his desk; the phone rings and he answers it, taking a call from someone wanting to speak to a particular individual from the prosecutor's office. The young man in question, better presented than his colleagues and wearing a clean white shirt, backs out of the room, muttering, "Say I am not here."

My interviewer replies, "I am sorry, he is not here right now." Witnessing the little show put on by this cozy threesome, I realize my case is being handled by individuals with no intention of resolving it.

I give myself permission to say, "We call this a white lie, sir. You back out of the room and stand outside in the hallway so that it appears as if your colleagues are telling the truth, since you are not actually in the room at that moment." All three burst out laughing, and the official from yesterday asks, "Khanum, how did you find Iran after being away so many years?" I reply, "I am not very good at exaggerating or giving false compliments. Do you want to know what I really think?" They reply in the affirmative. I tell them that I found the airport clean and well organized; the escalator and the baggage carousel were also satisfactory.

"What was your impression of the city?" one of them asks. I reply, "The first day I came downtown and tried to cross Takhte Tavoos Avenue (forgive me—I haven't learned the new names yet!), I was terrified. Buses, taxis, motorcycles, bicycles, and people all milling around together in this broad avenue without a pedestrian crossing. It felt like a battlefield and not a city street. I was terrified that I would be run over by one of these vehicles. I waited until finally a young man helped me to cross to the other side. I have had nightmares about crossing streets. But now, after three weeks, I have also learned to stand in the middle of the road and yell, 'Moalem—100 tomans," to stop a taxi."

The gentlemen each try to keep a poker face, but without success. They burst out laughing. The official from yesterday then asks me, "Any other observations?" I reply,

"I fear you may feel offended by my response, though the truth should never be offensive. Since you ask, the population seems careless about cleanliness and personal hygiene; when you see the crowds in the street, they look like they just got out of bed and left the house without washing!"

He replies, "Are you referring to makeup and perfume?" Gently, I answer, "You know better than that—cleanliness has nothing to do with makeup or perfume. It has to do with soap and water. For example, this gentleman [indicating the man in the white shirt] is wearing a shirt that is clean and maybe even ironed." The young man thanks me and says, "I wash my shirt every night, though I don't always have time to iron it." The official from yesterday interrupts him saying, "Khanum, this young man is well-to-do. His father is . . ."

As if to confirm this, the white-shirted young man adds, "I live in the southern part of town and when I occasionally come uptown, I feel out of place."

I continue: "A city is not about south or north, affluent or not-so-affluent, honest or dishonest. Now you, who claim to be from the south, are in charge and have a huge responsibility. These are early days and history will make its own judgment. Good and bad exist north or south, east or west, among all people—regardless of race or religion—everywhere. To prove that you are better than those who live in other parts of the city, you should try not to make the same mistakes as they do."

It is an open discussion. The official from yesterday appears to be more educated than the other two and is listening carefully.

The conversation moves to other topics. The official asks, "I have no objection to the charitable works in your file. However, why did you choose the Hilton for your dress show?" I reply, "I understand that these days, in the same hotel, which has been renamed Esteghlal, you hold seminars and conferences as well as parties and social gatherings."

He retorts, "But we don't serve alcoholic drinks on these occasions." I reply, "I have personally never touched an alcoholic drink in my life and there is no mention of alcoholic drinks being served on our invitations. However, I cannot be responsible for other people. I believe, even these days, you have not managed to stop the consumption of alcohol!"

The official changes the subject and asks about Zonta. I explain that the word "Zonta" is a Native American word symbolizing friendship and service. He asks, "Any connection with Freemasons?" I reply, "None. You know that women were never allowed to be Freemasons, and it is only recently that some sort of relationship has been permitted. Zonta gatherings were held once a month in a restaurant and our members were all professional women. Their membership fees paid for scholarships for the education of needy girls."

The white-shirted young man, constantly on the move between this office and the one next door now turns to me and says, "These two gentlemen are just stalling, uncomfortable about letting you know what needs to happen before we can give you your house back. You need to pay *khoms*, then a second *khoms*, then the 'share of the Imam, and finally the cost of management of your property. After that it will be released to you."

I reply, "In that case, it appears that I will receive nothing; I would even need to give more than the value of the house to pay all this off!" He says, "It is the law and there are no exceptions." I smile at the three men and ask if I can relate a story told me by my father.

"A workman was having lunch. He was eating a bowl of yogurt in which he was dunking pieces of bread. A cat sat next to him and kept meowing as if to say, 'I am also hungry.' The workman offered the cat the piece of bread he was about to eat. This was repeated several times. The yogurt was almost finished and the workman had managed to enjoy only a couple of mouthfuls. So, the next time, he put the bread in his own mouth. The cat started to meow in protest . . . At this point, the laborer shouted, 'Now it is my turn to meow.'

"Gentlemen, you represent the law. This house was not gifted to me; therefore I cannot gift it to you. I bought the land with my savings after years of teaching. Right now, I am staying with a cousin and I should not have to take advantage of their hospitality. With your permission, I need my house back so I can have a roof over my head."

As I leave the room, I feel truly exhausted. The men appeared to be amenable and reasonable, but I don't have the slightest faith in them. I know that they take their orders from above and just carry out those orders.

I take a taxi to my hosts in Shemiran. The garden is peaceful . . . Another day comes to an end.

Retirement Benefits

I go to the Baharestan to try to sort out my retirement benefits. My pension was paid into my account for a couple of years after the revolution but nothing after 1981 (1360). They tell me that my file is in the Shemiran office. The trip from the city back to Shemiran is quite a journey! The people in that office are helpful and manage to extract my file from where it had been languishing after years of neglect. I am sent to the basement to collect it. Now I have to go to Mohseni Square with the file and present it to the official who decided to stop my pension.

The black-clad secretaries type up a sheet which requires that I visit the Mahmoudieh branch of Bank Melli to get it authenticated. Surprisingly, the bank has managed to hold on to some of its past glory! Someone tells me that, after so many years, it will take quite a while to extract my documents. I have been going from one office to another; it has been four weeks and I have made no progress. In this country, time seems to have no value . . . People have learned to become truly patient. Sometimes, only death brings resolution to these insoluble issues!

A New Interrogator

Back on the third floor of the revolutionary court, I meet a new interrogator. My file has been taken away from the three young men who had gradually become friendly and handed over to this gentleman, who doesn't even raise his head when I greet him. His replies are monosyllabic as if he has orders to treat me this way. I have a feeling the problem lies with a higher official. His secretary hands me a form to complete and asks, "*Madar, savad dari*?" ("Mother, can you read and write?")

Copying his tone of voice, I reply, "*jozvi*" ("a part of"), instead of "*jozii*" ("a little")! The questions are repetitive and purely intended to waste time as all the answers are already in my dossier. They want to see if there are discrepancies in my replies. One of the questions is "What is your level of education?" I start with elementary school all the way to law school, the University of Michigan, and my PhD from the Sorbonne. I must confess his question about whether I was literate or not has touched a nerve! Under the drab chador with its brown floral pattern, I have either been mistaken for one of the man's older relatives or he actually meant to be insulting!

I remind myself that these are puppets being controlled by higher-ups and he is probably not responsible for his behavior. At times, I actually feel sorry for them. I take the completed questionnaire and hand it to the new official. He signs my exit permit. I leave this depressing building and return home.

The Penalty for Having a Higher Education

I visit the Bureau of Registration of Real Estate in Shemiran; it is located in a mansion with a magnificent garden. Who knows where the deeds to my house, which should eventually pass to my children, are now and how they were lost! I am searching for the deeds to the land in Elahieh I bought from my cousin back in 1953 (1332)!

My next stop is the Conscription Organization, hoping to obtain Hamid's exemption from military service. Apparently the higher the level of education of the applicant, the higher the fine that needs to be paid. Hamid has a BA from MIT and an MBA from Stanford; hence we have to pay an additional 1.5 million tomans. I go up and down the endless flights of stairs in the building—no sign of an elevator. If it did exist, it would probably be out of order. If it was operational, they wouldn't admit women! Remember, it is 1992. We are in the first stages of this particular quest and payment of money will not resolve the problem. I need patience, persistence, and resilience. I feel like a football being kicked this way and that.

I return home in a taxi. The driver, a bearded young man, admits to belonging to Hezbollah (Party of God). He opens the conversation, quickly guessing that I come from abroad, and asks me about life outside Iran. When he hears that in the West even cats and dogs are cared for, have birth certificates and there are shelves of pet food in supermarkets, he is astonished. I avoid talking about politics and serious matters. On arrival home, when I want to pay, he starts with the usual "*ghabeli nadarad*" ("you are my guest"). I end up actually paying over the normal rate since I come from abroad!

Visiting the Children's Convalescence Home

I visit the convalescence home—almost my baby! I worked so hard to obtain the piece of land, then construct and equip the building. From the exterior, it looks like it has suffered the same fate as all the other places I have visited on this trip. A faded billboard announces that this is the Welfare Organization for Children. I can't imagine which part of the original name, Convalescence Home for Children, was deemed offensive to our religion, language, or tradition, necessitating a change of name and causing damage in the process to the façade of the building! Destruction of relics from the past and replacing them with inferior modern versions seems to be an incurable disease. The gate is locked and I call out until eventually a young man arrives but stands there blocking my entrance. I introduce myself saying, "I am the founder of this convalescence home; I was wondering if I could have a look." He relents and lets me in.

It is winter and one couldn't expect much to be happening in the garden, yet it doesn't seem as if springtime would make much difference to its neglected state. The lack of care is reflected inside the building too. The turquoise-colored tiles on the balcony are all broken, and part of the adjoining wall with the nursing school next door has been demolished in order to combine the two institutions; the neighbors always had an eye on our building. My sister Mehri ended up in prison trying to defend our children's home. If they had indeed demolished part of the wall years ago, why had they not cleared the rubble and repaired the damage? Destruction is always so much easier to achieve than construction. I leave the miserable garden and building.

Another Trip to the Prosecutor's Office

A family member suggests a visit to a holy man who has an important position in the Medical School. He receives us graciously and, after hearing my story, he writes a long letter for me to deliver to the second-in-command at the prosecutor's office.

I ask him, "Sir, does the word *mostazaf* [oppressed] apply to a particular class in society?" When he says no, I continue: "Therefore, anyone from any social class can find themselves at some point among the *mostazafin*?" He replies, "In my opinion, that is so."

"I am so happy you agree," I say. "At the present moment, I find myself among the oppressed since I don't even have a roof over my head." The holy man smiles and gently replies, "Soon, everything will sort itself out." I am aware that all this is *taarof* (politeness), but he seems like a good person and I am aware that any influence he has will be limited.

I visit the prosecutor's office one more time. The second-in-command will see me—a gentleman in a black turban. He reads the letter, makes some notes at the bottom, and sends me to another room. This other man is bad-tempered, reads the letter and just glances at the letter before putting it aside and saying, "Khanum, you are wasting your time here. Your case will take a very long time to be resolved."

Now I know what I must do. I go to the Air France office and book my return ticket. The flight to Paris leaves at 1:25 a.m. on 25 February. Despite having made little headway with my to-do list, I thank God for having arrived safely at home in Paris.

A Second Trip to Tehran

A year later, on 9 February 1994, I once again board an Air France flight for Tehran.

I start at the Ministry of Education, located in an old building in Ekbatan Street, to follow up the problem of my pension. I remember starting my working life here when I was twenty. Now, everything feels strange; most of all, I feel like an outsider. I take a cab back home. On the way, the cab driver starts to complain about the high cost of living, about his marriage, and about the absence of music. I ask him if he is interested in music. He replies that he plays the sitar and can sing. Then he starts singing. I must admit he has a great voice. He tells me, "Khanum, we are all dead here; there is no hope for any of us." Luckily, we soon arrive at my destination.

Today is 13 February and I have an appointment at the prosecutor's office. After the usual body search by two black-clad ladies, I enter the hallway and make my way to the third floor. I enter the room, where a shortish man in a white turban[3] is sitting behind an imposing desk. Two other bearded men sit at their desks on either side of him and are taking notes. I greet all three. The white turban responds and asks me to take a seat. The questions begin. My name, father's name, on and on . . . The man on the left writes down my replies. The questions that follow all concern my job and other activities.

Q: Were you an adviser to the minister of education?

A: Yes, on paper. And within two months, I offered my resignation on the phone. This was a mere title, with no office, no responsibility, no work and no pay."

Q: Were you a candidate for the Senate?

A: Yes, but obviously I didn't deserve the role since I wasn't elected!

Q: Were you the president of the International Women's Club of Iran?"

A: Yes; this was a cultural and educational charity. We built a fully equipped convalescence home for children in less than two years; it is still in use.

Q: You were president of the Zonta Club?

---

3. A white turban indicates that the wearer is not a descendant of the Prophet. Those who are descendants are called seyyeds *and can wear a black turban.*

A: Yes, this was also an organization made up of professional women formed to support society in general. Haj Agha, I am here to get my house back as I am presently staying in my cousin's house.

Q: Everything will happen in good time. You are neither condemned nor guilty of anything; neither is your son. We have been at war for many years with our Iraqi neighbors; many families lost their sons and they need our help.

Haj Agha appears polite and reasonable. The interrogation ends here and I leave the court. This is my second trip to Tehran and, so far, I have only managed to get a new identity card and find the deeds to my house!

I revisit the prosecutor's office. Haj Agha receives me again; I hand over the documents he requested. He sends me to the sixth floor for my dossier, which is nowhere to be found. I am told to come back in a couple of weeks. Yet again, I go to the prosecutor's office and climb the stairs all the way up to the third floor. My dossier has miraculously surfaced. I return to Haj Agha's office; his secretary grudgingly gives me an appointment to see him in two weeks.

On my next visit, things have changed and Haj Agha appears uncooperative. He starts asking the same questions and tells me: "You have been away from the country. If we had lost the war, your house would have now been occupied by the enemy and you would have no recourse at all. We lost a lot of young men in this war; many women were widowed, and many children orphaned. You need to help us take care of these victims of war."

I listen to him carefully and reply: "Haj Agha, you are right but I would like to give you an example before leaving. Recently in France, a right-wing party came to power while the president is a socialist. The new prime minister, Édouard Balladur, gave a speech that mirrored my situation. He said France was once a safe harbor for refugees who came there from all over the world. People from North Africa would arrive, find jobs, and start families. The government supported them. But now, France has a huge budget deficit and, with massive unemployment, it can no longer help new immigrants.

"I, too, used to offer regular financial assistance to educational and health charities in Iran. But now, sitting here in your presence, I am no longer able to finance the losses of the Iran–Iraq war." The judge and his secretary stare at me open-mouthed. I stand up and make a decision right then that I would return to France. On 28 April, after a stay of almost fifty days, I once again leave Tehran for Paris on Air France.

My Third Trip to Tehran

A year later, in 1995 (1374), I arrive at Mehrabad airport at 3:30 a.m.

Back at the prosecutor's office, I find my dossier. By now it is quite thick—the fruit of a lifetime's work, which should ordinarily make me proud, though in this case it reflects a pretext for justifying injustice. It is suggested by the man interviewing me that I write a letter and attach it to the file, which has been gathering dust for a year; this might attract the attention of a higher authority. The man permits me to use a desk in the room to write my letter. Others, waiting there, stare at me. The man leads me to the office of Haj Agha N——with my completed letter and leaves the file on his deputy's desk. The he turns to me and says, "*Khahar* [Sister], what we have just done [taking the file from one office to another] would have normally taken eight months, but I want to help you since I think you have been treated unjustly!"

After seventeen years, I pass by my house accompanied by Hassan Agha. The gates are half open; I enter to see if there is any mail. I am committing a big sin—visiting my own house. I look through the windows; the whole house is piled high with trash and filth. The furniture is all broken and thrown together on the veranda. The pool is empty and full of dead leaves. I look into the living and dining rooms; there is no sign of the chandeliers that once belonged to my parents. Seventeen years ago, this was a beautiful home that I left thinking I would be back after a month. Now the "oppressor" who used to live there is herself among the "oppressed." We pick up the overdue utility bills and leave.

Accompanied by a lawyer whom I don't really need, I visit the prosecutor's office once again. Today, I get to know a Dr. M. F—— who sits next to Haj Agha. He brags about having been present at the trial of Mrs. Farrokhrou Parsa, making accusations about her that are completely unfounded. He asks my lawyer to accept his daughter as a trainee in his law office. My naïve lawyer replies in the negative, and things start to go downhill from there. When I ask my lawyer why he was so careless, he replies that these people just want to spy on them and this is to their disadvantage. I remind him that we have not committed a crime to be fearful of spies. Anyway, it is too late now . . . Tired and disappointed, I leave and take a taxi to Shemiran.

My Fourth Trip to Tehran

It is now 1997 (1376) and I am back in Tehran. I visit my lawyer's office; he hands me the prosecutor's judgment. It makes no sense; every sentence is so vague it can be interpreted either way. Exhausted, I come back to the small, one-bedroom apartment that I had bought just before the revolution. It is just 83 square meters and is the only property I managed to salvage, from a tenant who never paid any rent! This person was the manager of the building, yet treated me dishonestly. My lawyer, who realizes that this property is not part of his brief, pays 840,000 tomans to the intermediary who managed to return the apartment to me. For now, I have an address in Tehran—something to be grateful for!

I am invited to dinner at a relative's home, situated on the hills of Shemiran. The house is newly built and immaculate. It is a large party and everyone is having fun. Suddenly, two strangers dressed in dark uniforms enter and everything comes to a stop. At first, I thought they must be workmen coming to fix something in the house. The women all leave and go to the room where they had left their manteaux and headscarves. I realize these are *pasdar*s (the nickname for Islamic Revolutionary Guard Corps) and are there to teach us a lesson in modesty! It is the first time I have experienced this. I stand up and follow the ladies to the dressing room and put on my manteau and headscarf. Our hosts lead us to another small room.

The men all remove their ties and put them in their pockets. Everyone is anxious. The party had just started and some of the guests have not yet arrived. We later find out that as soon as they saw the jeeps of the Pasdaran, they turned around and returned home. The two uniformed men begin their search. They wake up our hosts' two-year-old grandchild to search him too. The lady of the house patiently opens all the cupboards and shows them the *janamaz* (prayer mats) that are used by guests on solemn occasions. The *pasdar*s look suspiciously at everything, wondering whether to believe our hostess. Hours pass: the name of every guest is recorded. The *pasdar*s finally leave and dinner is served.

For some years now, men who used to occupy the higher ranks of Iranian society indulge in endless political discussion in social gatherings, coming up with ingenious solutions to the many problems facing our society—all to no avail. The ladies are all elegantly dressed—you would think they had been resting all day—yet it is mostly they who shoulder the family's responsibilities. The revolution has thrust women to the forefront of society. With only a few exceptions, the men have stood behind their wives, hoping to recover their positions and titles, while the women, who had been used to an easier life, now assume the management of the family, including finances and the education of the children.

I salute you men and women who chose to wake up from the dream of an easy life and who didn't succumb to depression. I have a message for you. And I have a message for all you brave ladies, echoing the words of Nancy Pelosi: "A woman is like a teabag. You can't tell how strong she is until you put her in hot water."

Cyrus is Two

25 September 1997 is Cyrus's second birthday. Hamid has taken the day off so we can visit the "jungle" to which his son's friends have been invited. The children, accompanied by their parents or babysitters, get to play in the different areas after removing their shoes. There are pictures of animals all round and little cars for them to drive, small houses for them to play in, and a replica of the Niagara Falls to slide down! Cyrus has a special high chair; today, he is king of the jungle and wears a crown to prove it. The children all gather around the table; lunch is pizza, followed by cake. Cyrus blows out his two candles and the cake is served. Hamid is the official photographer and I play the part of audience. Then gifts are opened and we all return home to Sausalito

where I'm staying with the family as part of a short trip to the U.S. Cyrus takes a bath and is put to bed.

The next evening there is a dinner for the family; and Tina is busy in the kitchen, refusing all help. Ladan, her daughters, Sanam and Firouzeh, and her husband arrive; we are fourteen in all. Cyrus is dressed in a white shirt and gray flannel shorts, dragging his navy jacket behind him. At the dinner table, I have the honor of sitting to his right. After dinner, there is another cake, which I get to serve. The first slice goes to the birthday boy. He has received so many presents that he doesn't know which to play with; among them is a golf cart! His bedtime is 8 p.m. and off he goes; the rest of us leave around 10 p.m. The following day, Hamid, Tina, Cyrus, and his nanny Lemoore fly to Portland to attend a friend's birthday and I leave for Ladan's house.

The Elahieh House after Twenty Years

The following year, 1998, Hamid calls me late at night. He has a proposal that he would like me to implement. He wants to donate all his assets and inheritance in Iran to a foundation at Stanford University to provide scholarships for deserving Iranian students. I pack my bags; this will be my fifth trip back to Iran.

I visit Bonyad-e Shahid (Foundation for the Martyred), waiting like a vulture for my house to be released. It looks like my problems are being resolved. On paper, the authorities have released my house to me. I have to sign the release without having inspected the house yet; no one knows where the keys are. There is back and forth conversation between my agent and the officials there.

Finally, they tell us we can go ahead and take over the house without the presence of a representative of Bonyad Shahid. They hand a big bunch of keys to my agent, and we make our way to Elahieh. It is cold and the front door of the house is blocked by snow and ice. None of the keys opens the big, ugly padlock; finally, a locksmith arrives and breaks the padlock. I enter the house. What a sight! It is the first time I have walked in after twenty years. I have been fighting to get it back for the last five years. A huge tree has fallen on the roof, creating an enormous rift through the bedroom area. Ice and snow have penetrated the house through the cracks and there are puddles everywhere.

The other half of the house looks fairly safe, but there is no sign of the wall paneling or the stone fireplace. No sign of the mirrors and chandeliers. The kitchen is a war zone; even the faucets have been taken. The veranda is covered in junk. The garden has not one flower in it, but the cypress trees are still there. The pool is empty, cracked and now the home of autumn leaves. It feels as if a beautiful young bride has been replaced by a soulless skeleton.

Hamid's project remains on my to-do list. The authorities talk of the 1.8 billion tomans taxes due, including management charges and *khoms*! Reema factory with its 50,000 square meters situated close to the airport is now no longer included in our assets but has been allocated to the "oppressed." Each organization claims its own share of the pie. The factory was one of the most valuable assets of our family, not just the land but all the equipment—now confiscated by the Bonyad-e Mostazafin (Foundation for the Oppressed). Bonyad-e Shahid also demands its share. *Khoms* belongs to yet another organization. It is beginning to feel as if there will be nothing left for us and we may even have to add something to the pot and hand it over. My three children who work twelve hours a day may have to donate some of their income earned abroad to the growing band of *mostazafin*! It seems that, after twenty years of revolution, the *mostazafin* have changed places with the *mostakbarin* (elite)!

I visit my house in Elahieh, which has ostensibly now been released to me. Another organization has their eye on this property and there is a new sign on the front door prohibiting entrance to the house! I go back to Mr. Roudsari, the deputy director of Bonyad-e Shahid,' who calmly informs me that I should first settle what I owe—1.8 billion tomans—after which he will resolve the problem. He reminds me that the share for his organization is only 818 million tomans and the balance belongs to *khoms*. He suggests that, if I don't have the money, they can easily take the Boustan Street property, Bagh-e Bala, instead. We talk about the management fees for the Elahieh house. I remind him that faucets have been ripped out and the bedrooms are under water. He replies, "We have seen properties in much worse shape than this." I ask him what services are included in the management fees of 818 million tomans he is claiming.

I visit Bonyad-e Shahid. They insist I should sign the documents needed to surrender 6,000 square meters of Bagh-e Bala to them. I find the director in his office; he looks calm and seems respectful. I explain my situation to him and add, "Sir, I can confirm that during my long life I have been a good daughter, a good student, a good wife, a good mother, and a good citizen. I have always put the needs of others before my own. Now after a lifetime of service, am I supposed to tolerate this kind of injustice and false accusations? My deceased husband had willed that we should keep Bagh-e Bala in Boustan Avenue and make use of it for the family. In return, we have 100,000 square meters of land on the periphery of the city that is more suitable for public housing. You say I have seven months to come up with this amount. This is too short a time, especially as the market is slow and no one is buying. In any case, why should I pay this exorbitant sum in exchange for management that was never done."

He listens patiently and promises that he will see if the time period can be extended and that he might explore the possibility of using the other piece of land in lieu of what we owe. As I am leaving, I give him a Persian translation of the book *The Alchemist* by Paulo Coelho and recommend that he reads it.

I manage to obtain a handwritten power of attorney from my three children which is faxed to me. I go straight to Bonyad Shahid. I am told that the director was impressed with my reasoning and has extended the deadline for settling what we owe from seven to twelve months. He is also trying to use the land in Yaftabad instead of the property in Elahieh. It is good news in principle; I have to wait and see whether it materializes in practice.

Hassan Agha calls and insists that I meet him in his office. It seems that Mr. Roudsari, who is now back in the office, is not happy with the new agreement and is not willing to forsake the 6,000-meter piece of land in Elahieh. In addition, he doesn't want to extend the deadline for payment. I ask him when he heard this news; today is Saturday. He replies that he was given the information on Thursday and went straight to Bonyad Shahid without any success.

I ask him, "What kind of an organization is this when the director agrees but his deputy doesn't? Why didn't you let me know so we could go to Bonyad together?" He replies that he didn't want to ruin my weekend! I remind him that I was not here to have fun at the weekends; I was here to get things done. I suggest we leave straight away for Bonyad to clarify things. He shakes his head and says that is not a good idea; it will make things worse. I retort, "How can it be any worse than this?" I leave his office, really upset.

The 6,000-meter property is a gem, with tree-lined avenues on two sides. It has three plots, each for 2,000 square meters; it even has a stream running through it. One of the parcels belongs to Hamid and the authorities value that at 100,000 tomans a meter to use against what they claim we owe. On the other hand, they value my house, which is bound on three sides, at 290,000 tomans a meter since they will base the *khoms* and thc share of the Imam on that valuation!

I visit the Pension Bureau and spend hours in the waiting room. I am granted a short meeting and then handed over to a deputy who promises he will look into my file. The fruit of thirty-nine years of teaching is in their hands.

All for Nothing!

Another year passes and I have an urgent call from my agent in Tehran. After the usual pleasantries, he tells me the same old story and reminds me that my house is ready to be handed over and all is in order. Etiquette stops me from reminding him that the authorities have taken all that belonged to my children and me; they even confiscated my house again after a few days of releasing it. Why should I believe these empty promises? But I know he is not to blame.

So I reply, "I have decided to donate my house to a dress museum or an art gallery where young people can promote their work. Hamid has also decided to donate his sizeable inheritance to a foundation to provide scholarships for deserving Iranian students applying to Stanford University. If I remember correctly, you rejected the idea and considered it impractical. Now I suggest you relax and don't waste any more of your time or ours, since nothing will be achieved anyway." In my heart, I know he is not listening and his involvement in our affairs is just a pastime for him and a boost to his ego!

The years pass. Life goes on. Tonight, there is a memorial service for our old doorman in my building in Paris. His wife speaks of his qualities and together with the homeowner association board, we decide to plant a tree in the name of Ernest Dawson in the inner courtyard of the building. Later, a bronze plaque engraved with his name, date of birth, and death will be placed by the tree. He was a truly dutiful and courteous gentleman.

I think of my own situation; thirty-nine years of service in the Ministry of Education and teaching thousands of students and no acknowledgment. To add insult to injury, after the revolution even my meager pension was denied. All those years of loyal service, and all for nothing!

Houri and Mehri visiting together for the last time in London—Mehri died soon after, 1999.

AFTERWORD

By
Mariam Safinia

The years went by. Mom's diary recorded every conversation, the news of each friend's passing, every time she had someone over for lunch. But the entries got shorter and shorter, the friends older and fewer. She continued to make her yearly visits from the U.S., where she was now based, to Paris and Nice; she used to say it made a nice change. I think she felt an obligation to check on the two properties she had used that actually belonged to Hamid and Ladan. We would see her from time to time when we also spent time in Nice. But she was alone for the most part. The interesting thing about Mom was that she had spent more than half of her life alone and yet she never complained. I don't think she was ever bored—or maybe she was too proud to admit it.

The apartments needed renovating. The kitchens and bathrooms were dated. But she belonged to a low-maintenance, make-do-with-what-you-have generation. For years, I had arranged her mail to be redirected to me and she had given me a signature over her accounts. One time I

Houri in London on Mariam's fiftieth birthday, London, 1994

found her in tears when she arrived in Paris after an absence of ten months. The concierge had given her a large plastic bag full of mail—99 percent of which was junk. She didn't have the heart or the confidence to throw away all the junk and she watched in horror as I ripped envelope after envelope and went back to London with a slim folder of the important letters.

In 2004, Fari and I moved to the U.S.—permanently. We wanted to be close to our daughters and grandchild—

Mariam, Marjan, Fari, and Leila at Marjan's wedding in Los Angeles, 2003

now grandchildren. By then, Mom was spending most of the year in a beautiful apartment in San Francisco with a stunning view over the Bay. Somehow, all her homes, and now all of ours, too, had outstanding views! We live in what she used to call the "village" of San Ramon. Still, we were in the same time zone and I would do her food shopping once a week and visit her in the city. We enjoyed family lunches on Sundays, and she continued to visit the Davies Symphony Hall and attend galas, where she was always treated with great affection and admiration. Gradually, I became aware that large, noisy, and glamorous events were becoming difficult for her. As each person would approach

Houri and Mariam entertaining, Paris, 1992

our table to greet her, I would whisper their name to her and she would smile graciously and thank them.

In 2011, at the age of ninety-two, she set off once again for France, flying alone albeit in business class. Now when I think of her arriving there, taking a cab to her apartment in Paris, letting herself into a dark flat with an empty refrigerator, unoccupied for the best part of a year, my heart sinks. Now I understand why she would wrap up a couple of hard-boiled eggs, any cheese left in her San Francisco kitchen, some bread, and a piece of fruit—so she would have something to eat before she hit the very chic *marché* down the street from her the next day.

Thanksgiving, 2008. Seated from left: Ladan, Kamran, Kian, Firouzeh, Sanam, Tina; standing: Robin, Carol Gwatkin, Houri, Cyrus; back row: Bill Gwatkin, Ali Lari, Hamid Moghadam, Mareza Larizadeh

After a week or so in Paris, she left for Nice. I believe a friend might have collected her from the airport and helped her with her heavy suitcases to the fifth floor. But after that, she was on her own again. She would take the bus to the city, do her food shopping, and return with several heavy bags. Her door was always open to friends and her table always full. She would never admit to being tired or incapable of keeping up her high standards.

One night while she was in Nice, the three of us—Ladan, Hamid, and myself, together with Fari, Ali, and Tina—went out to dinner at the Slanted Door restaurant

Houri with her beloved grandson Cyrus Moghadam on her ninetieth birthday, 2009

in San Francisco. For some reason, I announced that our neighbor in San Ramon was about to put his house on the market and wouldn't it be nice if we could move Mom there—next door to me! Ladan said, "She would never accept moving from the city to that village!" Then Hamid added, "If you can persuade her, we can buy the house for her." It was just an idea and I floated it by her at our next phone conversation, to which she replied, "Never. All my friends are in San Francisco. I know my way around and Hamid and Ladan are nearby."

As luck would have it, the very next day I received a phone call from her. Her voice was weak and exhausted; she told me she had tripped on the carpet the night before and had spent the entire night on the floor in the hall, unable to get up. I assured her that I would be on the next flight to Nice, even though Fari and I were booked to leave the following week for Delphi to attend a Plato-themed retreat. In the meantime, I arranged for a cousin to go over and see if he could help.

Mom was in no state to resist or argue; she was grateful at that point to surrender control. Once in Nice, I picked her up, together with some of her things and whatever she had in her fridge, to which she was very attached, took her back to our place and installed her in our bedroom. Leila was staying there with her family. We all squeezed in together to make her as comfortable as we could. After that, I sprang into action; my mind was made up and the plan was not up for discussion. I took advantage of her weak state to bully her into letting me make decisions for her.

My son-in-law Javad and I emptied her Nice apartment, giving away most of the stuff and sending into storage the things I knew she had collected lovingly over the years—beautiful pieces of furniture, paintings, and of course her beloved TV. Then, the two of us flew to Paris for two days and did the same to the Paris apartment. We became

Houri surrounded by family at Mariam's house in San Ramon. Top row from left: Robin Murray, Ali Lari, Javad Pourhashemi, Omid Pourhashemi, Hormuz Mostofi, and Cyrus Moghadam; middle row: Firouzeh Lari Murray, Lili Khosrowshahi, Lily Pourhashemi, Kian Murray, and Tina Moghadam; seated: Fari Safinia, Mariam Safinia, Nayer Glenn, Houri, Hamid Moghadam, and Ladan Lari

Back row from left: Doug Fitzsimmons, Nancy Glenn, and Jan Glenn; front row: Marjan Safinia, Kamran Murray, Leila Safinia, and Niloo Mostofi

more ruthless as the work went on—throwing away thirty years of *Paris Match* magazines she had kept, giving away furniture, kitchen equipment (she had porcelain-handled cutlery—all breakable!). I am glad she was not around to see us dismantle the life she had so carefully put together. We would have had to argue over every teaspoon. The moving people packed and sent what we wanted to keep into the same storage as the Nice stuff—awaiting our instructions to ship them to San Ramon.

Mom and I left Nice, flew back to California and to my house in San Ramon. In the meantime, the house next door was purchased by Hamid, and our contractor was busy installing an elevator and making a few small changes for her safety and comfort. The work took three months, during which she stayed in our guest bedroom and would only come downstairs once a day for dinner. She was a model of patience and tolerance. She realized that she could no longer live by herself and that this was the best solution going forward. I hope she forgave me for the bullying I had to do in the process.

One weekend when the house was finished and cleaned from top to toe, Ladan and I attacked the San Francisco apartment in the same way. We threw out and gave things away, packing what we wanted to keep. Then everything, including the stuff from Nice and Paris, arrived in San Ramon in a huge container. In her three apartments, she had a total of ten beds. Each bed had two sets of sheets and towels, some never used—all freshly laundered and ironed!

Let's have cake! Houri's ninety-seventh birthday celebration

There were numerous sets of dinner plates, trays, serving dishes.

By the time Ladan and I, with a team of helpers, had unpacked and placed everything in the new house, you would have thought she had lived there all her life. The only new piece of furniture we bought was a very fancy bed. Otherwise, every precious item—her paintings, forty years of diaries she'd kept, all her books, every delightful bureau and side table—fit perfectly in the large four-bedroom house.

She walked in like a new bride. For the first time, in as long as I remember, she had nothing to criticize. We were

At Houri's ninety-seventh birthday, 2016, from left to right: Niloo Mostofi, Fari Safinia, Cyrus Moghadam, Tina Moghadam, Hamid Moghadam, Kian Murray, Ladan Lari, Houri, Nayer Joon, Jan Glenn

Standing from left to right: Kamran Murray, Firouzeh Murray, Lily Pourhashemi, Mariam Safinia, Leila Pourhashemi, Javad Pourhashemi, Nancy Glenn, Ali Lari, Omid Pourhashemi, Robin Murray

home and dry. Her bedroom was the size of her Paris apartment. There was a swimming pool, which no one ever used in the seven years she lived there. Most importantly, I think she realized she was being cared for in a way and at a standard that would become the envy of all her friends!

The years passed. She would take a walk every afternoon in our quiet street, sometimes reciting aloud French poems she had memorized as a young girl. If any of the neighbors were out, they would always greet her, with her elegant walking stick and in her cool jogging outfit. Sometimes, she would come into our front yard and peer through the kitchen window to see if I was there. And every Friday night we would have dinner together.

In the afternoons I would visit her for a half hour; we watched old movies together and laughed when neither of us could remember the names of the actors. Caregivers came and went. She belonged to a generation when staff were staff and familiarity was not encouraged, even though she gradually needed their help to put on her stockings. After a while, she lost complete interest in what went on in the house and kitchen and her best caregiver, Emily, took charge. She would preside in the living room only when visitors came and then she would personally set a most elegant table for afternoon tea, her preferred time for entertaining.

I am really grateful for those years. Ours had not always been an easy relationship. I am sure we were all loved but it was not the warm, hugging kind of love we now have with our children. It was respectful, and she was always proud of our achievements, but it was never intimate. I had left home at fourteen and never really returned as I was married at eighteen and had my own life. Ours was not the kind of mother–daughter relationship where we went shopping together or missed each other. It was quite formal, cordial, and detached.

Those years when she was my neighbor went a long way to bring us closer. Our roles were reversed. She used to say, "When I am with you, I don't need money, ID, insurance, or even keys; you take care of me." She became more down to earth, more forgiving, quieter, and never complained.

Once when she was around ninety-six, she said, "Americans have it backwards. They celebrate someone's life after they are gone! Why not do it when they are alive?" I took the hint and again the three of us, Ladan, Hamid, and myself, put our heads together and organized a fabulous dinner at a very sophisticated location in San Francisco with around eighty-five guests. I had also organized for my friend Ziba Shirazi, singer, storyteller, and poet, to perform Mom's life story based on her memoirs. Ziba flew over for a week-long visit with us, when she would sit with Mom every day for a few hours asking her questions about her life.

I think Mom had forgotten about the interview and she was just as surprised as all the guests when Ziba walked toward the stage, dressed in a famous outfit my mother had worn at the gala fashion show in Tehran. She started her act by saying, "My name is Hourvash, my sister was

Houri at her ninety-seventh birthday

called Mehrvash. But since *vache* in French means 'cow,' I was always called Houri and she was called Mehri. Unlike all the other Houris, I spell my name with *hey-e havvaz* [Persian "H" with two eyes]." She insisted on always being different, never run-of-the-mill!

Ladan, Hamid, and I each sat at the head of the three front tables with the older guests. I kept looking right and left; my brother and sister were alternating between hilarious laughter and tears pouring down their faces. Afterward, Mom stood up to speak. She was ninety-seven, dressed in a gorgeous white dress, white boots, bejeweled as always. Without hesitation, she took the microphone and said, "One thing I have believed throughout my life: 'Always speak the truth!'" She announced this in Persian and when I asked her to repeat it in English for the benefit of our non-Persian speaking guests, she repeated it in French—then in English. I think she was very happy about that evening; it had met her own very high standards.

We also celebrated her ninety-eighth birthday on a beautiful summer day in 2017, at a more casual location, with balloons, flowers, Persian food, and lots of friends. Jeff, a friend who sings like Frank Sinatra, Mom's favorite crooner, performed and serenaded her with "My Way"! She loved those occasions, being the center of attention, surveying the life she had lived, and how people saw and admired her. She was proud of her capable, successful, and attentive children; all was well in the world.

Right until the end, she was herself—maybe less interested in the day-to-day events, maybe more detached from what was happening with the grandchildren, oblivious that her elegant Parisian shoes were gradually disappearing from her closet while the empty boxes remained stacked to the ceiling. It was only in the last two weeks of her life that she withdrew completely, becoming gradually more confused. She talked incoherently to people in the room who were invisible to us. She didn't have an appetite anymore. We ordered a hospital bed to be put in her bedroom to make it easier for her.

The night she died, I was there with Emily, her faithful caregiver, until midnight. She seemed comfortable and slipped in and out of sleep. I kissed her goodnight and went home. I had not gone to bed yet when Emily called. I went over. All was peaceful and Mom was gone. Fari came over. We covered her in her favorite Saint Laurent shawl, turned on the ceiling fan, opened the windows, kissed her forehead, and bid her farewell.

I called Ladan and Hamid; it was 1 a.m. on Saturday 16 June 2018. They wanted to come over. I said there was nothing to do and they should come over in the morning. I closed her bedroom door and went home. She left the world with dignity and grace; she had never been any trouble to anyone. It was an easy death.

We honored her life with a magnificent memorial in San Francisco City Hall—a happy occasion, a real celebration of a life well lived. We had 350 guests, a classical string trio; close family members spoke, there was an amazing dinner, and impromptu memories were shared by friends in the audience. As I said that night, with the memorial we were closing a chapter on the life of a remarkable woman, and acknowledging all we were grateful for in our lives—thanks to her.

Houri's grave high on a windy hill in Marin, California, tended lovingly and regularly by Ladan

Family Trees

Houri Mostofi Moghadam's Family

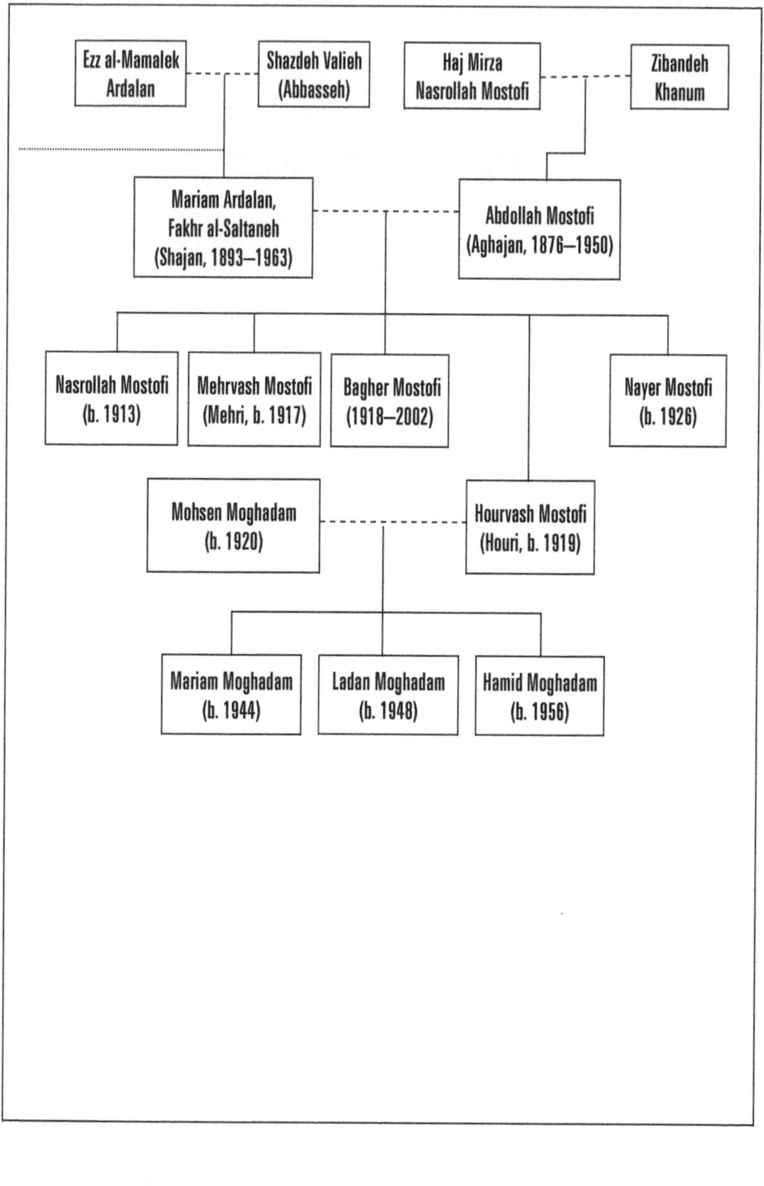

Houri's Children and Grandchildren

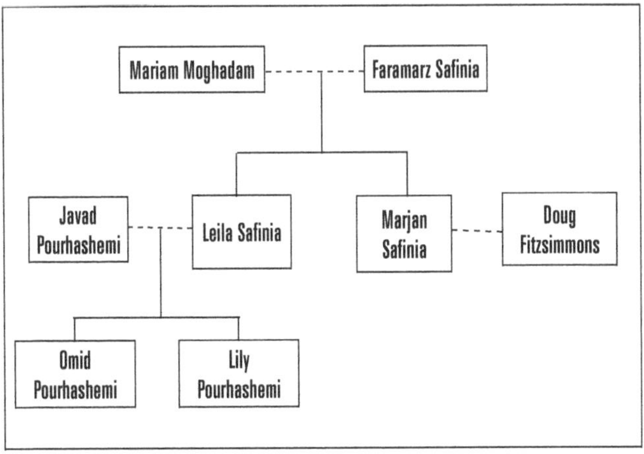

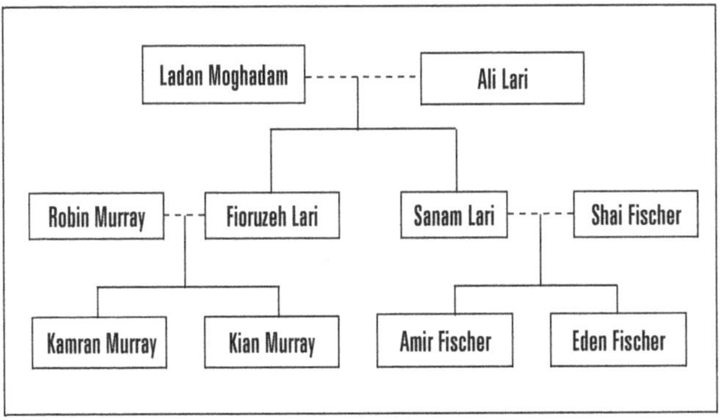

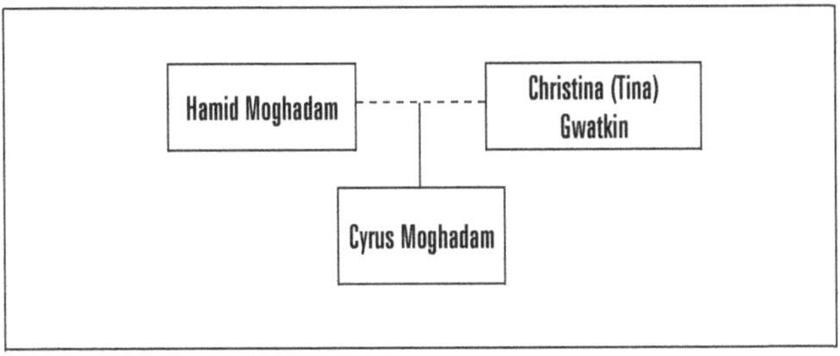

Mohsen Moghadam's Family

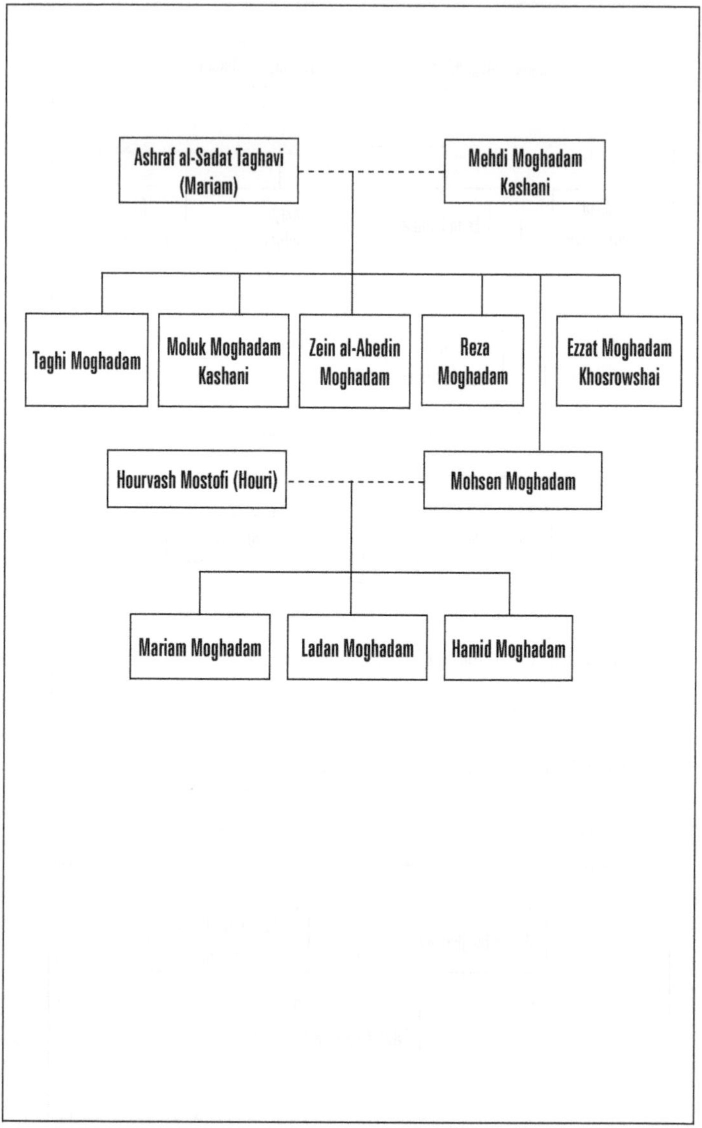

Houri's Brothers and Sisters and their Children

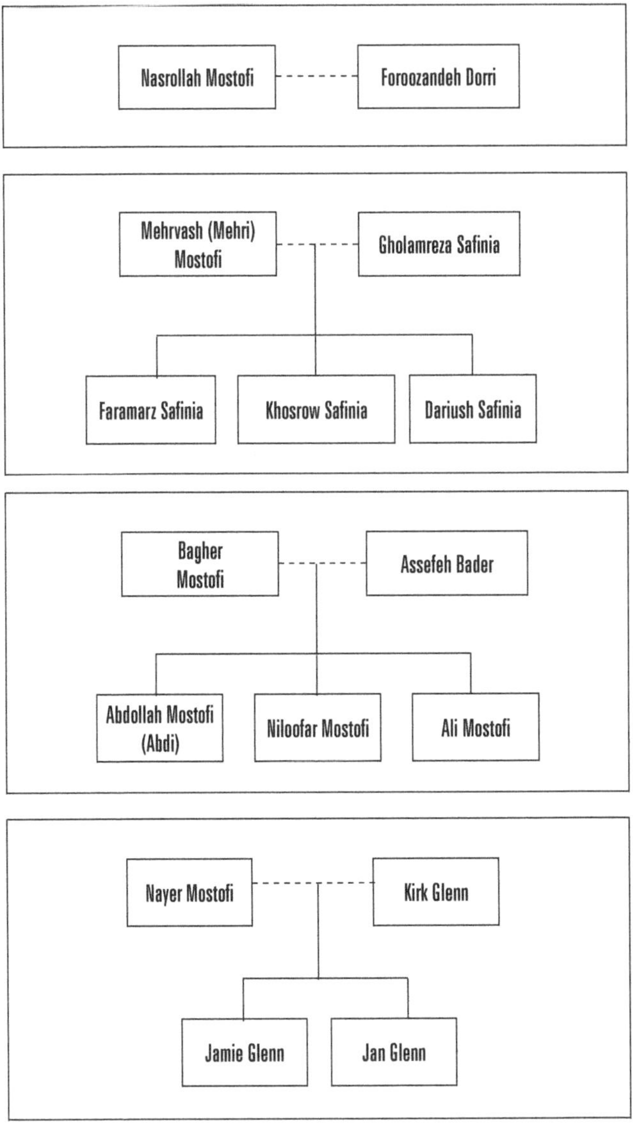

Contents
with Subheadings

PART TWO

Marriage, Children, Travels, and Work 103
(1942–1978 / 1321–1357)

Other Mage Titles by or about Iranian Women

Crowning Anguish: Taj al-Saltaneh
Memoirs of a Persian Princess
Introduction by Abbas Amanat / Translated by Anna Vanzan
(also available as an audio book)

Vis and Ramin
Fakhraddin Gorgani / Translated by Dick Davis
(also available as an audio book)

Savushun: A Novel about Modern Iran
Simin Daneshvar / Translated by M.R. Ghanoonparvar

Faces of Love: Hafez and the Poets of Shiraz
(Jahan Malek Khatun and Obeyd Zakani)
Translated by Dick Davis
(also available as an audio book)

The Mirror Of My Heart:
A Thousand Years of Persian Poetry by Women
Translated by Dick Davis
(also available as an audio book)

Layli and Majnun
Nezami Ganjavi / Translated by Dick Davis
(also available as an audio book)

Another Birth and Other Poems
Forugh Farrokhzad
translated by Hasan Javadi and Susan Sallée

When They Broke Down the Door: Poems
Fatemeh Shams / Introduction and translation by Dick Davis

Cooking in Iran: Regional Recipes and Kitchen Secrets
Najmieh Batmanglij